MACHIAVELLIAN RHETORIC

MACHIAVELLIAN RHETORIC

FROM THE COUNTER-REFORMATION
TO MILTON

Victoria Kahn

PRINCETON UNIVERSITY PRESS

PRINCETON, NEW JERSEY

COPYRIGHT © 1994 BY PRINCETON UNIVERSITY PRESS

PUBLISHED BY PRINCETON UNIVERSITY PRESS, 41 WILLIAM STREET,

PRINCETON, NEW JERSEY 08540

IN THE UNITED KINGDOM: PRINCETON UNIVERSITY PRESS,

CHICHESTER, WEST SUSSEX

ALL RIGHTS RESERVED

LIBRARY OF CONGRESS CATALOGING-IN-PUBLICATION DATA

KAHN, VICTORIA ANN.

MACHIAVELLIAN RHETORIC : FROM THE COUNTER-REFORMATION TO MILTON /

VICTORIA KAHN.

P. CM.

INCLUDES BIBLIOGRAPHICAL REFERENCES AND INDEX

ISBN: 0-691-03491-5 (ALK. PAPER)

1. RHETORIC—1500–1800. 2. MACHIAVELLI, NICCOLÒ,

1469–1527—POLITICAL AND SOCIAL VIEWS. 3. MACHIAVELLI, NICCOLÒ,

1469–1527—CRITICISM AND INTERPRETATION. 4. POLITICS

AND LITERATURE. I. TITLE.

PN173.K33   1994   93-45883   320.1'092—DC20   CIP

THIS BOOK HAS BEEN COMPOSED IN ADOBE SABON

PRINCETON UNIVERSITY PRESS BOOKS ARE PRINTED ON ACID-FREE PAPER
AND MEET THE GUIDELINES FOR PERMANENCE AND DURABILITY OF THE
COMMITTEE ON PRODUCTION GUIDELINES FOR BOOK LONGEVITY OF THE
COUNCIL ON LIBRARY RESOURCES

PRINTED IN THE UNITED STATES OF AMERICA

1   3   5   7   9   10   8   6   4   2

FOR

HELENE SILVERBERG

AND

NEIL SACCAMANO

CONTENTS

PREFACE

THIS BOOK is about how Machiavelli was read in the Renaissance, what Machiavelli came to symbolize in Renaissance culture, and why. I argue that Machiavelli offered Renaissance writers a rhetoric for thinking about politics, and that once we recover the ways Machiavelli was read, we gain a deeper understanding of how Renaissance thinkers conceptualized and responded to contemporary crises of political and religious authority. Machiavelli was reviled, approved, misrepresented, and appropriated precisely because his work spoke to many of the central concerns of the age: the legitimacy of de facto political power, the role of persuasion in acquiring and maintaining that power, the relationship of force to ethics, and of dispassionate political analysis to criticism of the status quo. In a justly famous book, J.G.A. Pocock defined "the Machiavellian moment" of early modern political thought as the moment when the secular political agent confronts the difficulties of acting in time and the republic confronts its own "temporal finitude" (*MM*, viii). I contend that the Machiavellian moment of Renaissance culture is a rhetorical moment rather than a moment of specifically secular self-consciousness, and that this insight has implications for the way we think about Renaissance political thought and culture in general. In particular, it requires us to revise many of the usual assumptions regarding the incompatibility of humanist rhetoric and serious political analysis, the secularism of Renaissance republicanism, and the irrelevance of the Machiavel to the history of Renaissance political and religious thought.

This book is the counterpart to my earlier work, *Rhetoric, Prudence, and Skepticism in the Renaissance*. In that book I was concerned with the humanists' reception of Aristotle's *Nicomachean Ethics* and with the ways in which the humanists' deliberative rhetoric (argument *in utramque partem*, or on both sides of a question) was designed to reflect and to educate the reader's prudential judgment or practical reason. Describing what I now understand as merely one strain of Renaissance humanism, I argued that dialogue and argument on both sides of a question were assumed to foster social and political consensus. Thus while Cicero recognized that such argument *in utramque partem* could take the form of irony if both sides or points of view were maintained at the same time, for many humanists the ambiguity of irony was held in check by rhetorical and social constraints. For example, Giovanni Pontano, an important humanist at the court of Naples in the fifteenth century, saw Socrates' ironic indirection not as an instance of rhetoric that threatens the possibility of community, of shared meaning and action, but rather as a rhetorical invitation to his audience to assume an attitude of ethical moderation. Even more significant, he turned irony into the chief social grace of decorum by identifying it with urbanity. In a move that is characteristic of this "consensual" strain of humanism, the epistemological threat of skepticism and the political threat of dissent are contained by the practice of social consensus. I then traced the development of such prudential rhetoric from its status as a positive theory of communication allied to Academic skepticism in the work of several early Italian humanists, through the threat to prudence by Pyrrhonist skepticism in the work of Erasmus and Montaigne, and finally to the apparent displacement of prudential rhetoric by logic in Hobbes's *Leviathan*. While I attempted to complicate this narrative by describing it as an allegory of the tensions inherent in humanist rhetoric from the outset, I now see that this rhetorical strategy was quite typical of the strain of humanism I was analyzing, which aimed to exclude whatever would threaten the possibility of consensus or unified interpretation. As I briefly acknowledged in the conclusion to the book, Machiavelli was one of the chief threats both to humanist rhetoric and to my argument.

As Pontano and his contemporaries recognized, the Renaissance counterpart to a consensual view of rhetoric and prudence is astuteness or craftiness—a faculty of judgment that is not simply allied with moral virtue and that is particularly associated in the later Renaissance with Machiavelli. That the Machiavel is regularly portrayed as a crafty rhetorician in the sixteenth and seventeenth centuries suggests both that Machiavelli was himself read rhetorically and that rhetoric gave rise to anxieties associated with Machiavelli's divorce of politics from ethics. Machiavelli, in short, comes to symbolize a series of tensions at the heart of Renaissance rhetorical culture. This book complements and revises my earlier work by focusing on the conflictual and critical potential of humanist rhetoric; it does so by analyzing Machiavelli's work and the rhetoric of Machiavellism in the Renaissance.

Several words of caution are in order. First, although this book offers a revised account of Renaissance Machiavellism, it does not pretend to offer a comprehensive history of the reception of Machiavelli's work. Many such histories already exist, and I have relied on them and cited them in the notes. Nor do I offer a detailed account of English and continental anxiety about the amoral or potentially immoral power of rhetoric. These arguments are familiar to Renaissance scholars and are available in any of a number of recent histories of Renaissance rhetoric. Rather, my aim has been to use the reception of Machiavelli to illumine those rhetorical habits of thought that were shared by those who read him and those who did not. To this end, I offer close rhetorical analyses of a number of works by representative readers of Machiavelli. I also focus more generally on the Machiavellism of contemporary thinking about a range of political and theological issues. In both cases, my aim has been to reconfigure the history of Machiavellism in order to highlight its intersection with the rhetorical culture of the Renaissance.

My selection of texts has been determined in part by existing histories of Machiavellism and in part by the logic of my argument. Thus, for example, I have left aside the Machiavel of Renaissance drama because he has been the subject of a generally well-informed, extensive scholarly literature. For similar reasons, I have not discussed Innocent Gentillet, Gabriel Harvey, Philip Sidney, Edmund Spenser, or Andrew Marvell, although each provides evidence for my argument that Machiavelli was read as offering a rhetoric of de facto political power. On the other hand, I have analyzed Giovanni Botero's *Ragion di stato*, which is frequently cited in histories of continental Machiavellism but insufficiently appreciated as an astute reading of Machiavelli's rhetorical politics. And I have devoted three chapters to Milton, because his work offers one of the most powerful Renaissance critiques of a simple thematic approach to thinking about politics and to the history of political thought. I have also focused on Milton because he is such an unlikely Machiavellian: if we can imagine the puritan Milton as one of Machiavelli's best readers, we will have gone a long way toward redrawing some of the traditional fault lines of Renaissance political thought and culture.

Two caveats deserve particular emphasis. First, and for the reasons mentioned above, this book is not primarily a study of Machiavelli's *influence* on later Renaissance writers. Though I do discuss particular cases of influence, my notion of reception is far broader than this and includes the language of Machiavellism that developed in the Renaissance independently of any direct familiarity with his texts. Second, this book is a study in the *continuity* of a tradition, especially in England. Thus, while I acknowledge the important differences between Counter-Reformation and Reformation readers, and between early sixteenth-century and mid-seventeenth-century England, I am chiefly concerned with the ways in which the tropes and topics of Machiavellism remained constant even as they were put to new uses, in new contexts.

Finally, I want to record my indebtedness to previous scholarship on Machiavelli and Milton. One of the pleasures of writing this book has been reading the exceptionally fine work on these authors in particular, and on Machiavellism and Renaissance political thought in general. I have tried to keep my quarrels with other scholars to a minimum, while acknowledging my many particular debts and influences in the notes. It is the nature of a book such as this one to be a work of synthesis and reconfiguration: some of the texts commented on have received extensive analysis by other critics and many of the historical details I include have been mentioned by others as well. Although the texts will be familiar to many of my readers, my hope is that they will appear here in a new light, as part of a revised history of Renaissance Machiavellism as a rhetoric.

ACKNOWLEDGMENTS

I BEGAN this book during a fellowship year at the Villa I Tatti and wrote much of it during a leave from Princeton University, with the assistance of a Guggenheim fellowship. I also received research assistance from the Princeton University Council on Research in the Humanities and the Social Sciences. I am grateful to my recommenders and to these institutions for their support.

In writing this book I have kept Neil Saccamano in mind as my ideal reader, and am particularly happy here to acknowledge his example, his friendship over the past fifteen years, and his advice about the manuscript. I owe many of my topic sentences to Helene Silverberg, whose ability to detect lapses of logic was positively frightening. Our conversations made writing this book both harder and easier than it would otherwise have been, and were a wonderful education in themselves. Throughout this project, David Quint has been an exacting critic and good friend. I am especially grateful for his detailed comments on the manuscript, and for his incisive suggestions for revision. For reading the manuscript in its entirety and for their encouraging responses, I would also like to thank Leonard Tennenhouse and Wayne Rebhorn. A timely last-minute reading by Carol Cook saved me from the slough of despond.

Chapters 4 and 5 in particular benefited from discussion with the members of my graduate seminar on Machiavelli, especially Elizabeth Kronzek, Christopher Hughes, Dietrich Tschanz, and Paul Wright. Thanks are due as well to Joel Altman, Joan S. Bennett, Rebecca Bushnell, Kathy Eden, Claire Fowler, Sally Freedman, Louise Clubb, Constance Jordan, Richard Kroll, Annabel Patterson, and Victoria Silver for reading chapters in draft. Midway through this project I was lucky to meet a kindred intellectual spirit in Lorna Hutson, who helped shape the middle chapters of the book through her energetic transatlantic correspondence. My thinking about Machiavelli was sharpened by reading the work of Nancy Struever and Eugene Garver, not to mention J.G.A. Pocock, Felix Raab, and Felix Gilbert. I am grateful to Robert Brown for his patience in shepherding this book through the Press, and to Rita Bernhard for her scrupulous copyediting. Last, but not least, Liz Huyck was a positively inspired research assistant.

Early versions of chapters 1 and 2 appeared as "*Virtù* and the Example of Agathocles in Machiavelli's *Prince*," *Representations* 13 (1986): 63–85, © by the Regents of the University of California; and as "Reduction and the Praise of Disunion in Machiavelli's *Discourses*," in *Journal of Medieval and Renaissance Studies* 18 (1988): 1–19. Parts of chapters 5 and 6 appeared in "Revising the History of Machiavellism: English Machiavellism and the Doctrine of Things Indifferent," in *Renaissance Quarterly* (Fall 1993): 526–61. Early versions of chapter 8 appeared as "Things Indifferent and the Justification of Dissent in *Paradise Lost*," in *Creative Imitation*, ed. David Quint et al., Medieval and Renaissance Texts & Studies, vol. 95 (Binghamton, 1992), 127–52; and as "Allegory and the Sublime in *Paradise Lost*," in *Milton*, ed. Annabel Patterson (London: Longmans, 1992), 185–201. I am grateful to the publishers for their kind permission to borrow from this material. Quotations from *The Prince* are reprinted from *The Prince* by Niccolò Machiavelli, translated and edited by Robert M. Adams. A Norton Critical Edition. With the permission of W. W. Norton & Company, Inc. Copyright © 1977 by W. W. Norton & Company, Inc.

For their moral support and much more, I also want to thank Deborah Gordon, Elisabeth Giansiracusa, Marsha Silverberg, Nancy Troy, Eleanor Anderson-Miles, Valerie Smith, Adrienne Donald, Sally Freedman, Peter Johnson (who suggested many alternative, eye-catching titles for the book), and especially my sisters, Madeleine Kahn and Lisa Davenport. I am particularly grateful to George Colnaghi, for his many conversations about life and art and for his yoga instruction. I regret that my mother did not live to see this book in print; I know she would have enjoyed casting the movie version. Finally, and for reasons they know best, this book is dedicated to Helene Silverberg and to Neil Saccamano.

V. K.

Princeton, July 1993

ABBREVIATIONS AND NOTE
ON SPELLING AND TRANSLATIONS

D   *Discorsi sopra la prima deca di Tito Livio*, in Niccolò Machiavelli, *Il Principe e Discorsi sopra la prima deca di Tito Livio*, ed. Sergio Bertelli (Milan: Feltrinelli, 1977); *The Discourses*, ed. Bernard Crick, trans. Leslie J. Walker, S. J. (Harmondsworth, England: Penguin, 1979). References are to book, chapter, and page in the Italian text and then to the English translation.

Hughes   John Milton, *Complete Poetry and Major Prose*, ed. Merritt Y. Hughes (Indianapolis: Bobbs-Merrill, 1957).

JH   *The Political Works of James Harrington*, ed. J.G.A. Pocock (Cambridge and London: Cambridge University Press, 1977).

Meinecke   Friedrich Meinecke, *Machiavellism: The Doctrine of Raison d'Etat and Its Place in Modern History*, trans. Douglas Scott, a Westview Encore Reprint of *Die Idee der Staatsräson* (1924) (Boulder and London: Routledge and Kegan Paul, 1984).

MM   J.G.A. Pocock, *The Machiavellian Moment: Florentine Political Thought and the Atlantic Republican Tradition* (Princeton, N.J.: Princeton University Press, 1975).

P   *Il Principe*, in Niccolò Machiavelli, *Il Principe e Discorsi sopra la prima deca di Tito Livio*, ed. Sergio Bertelli (Milan: Feltrinelli, 1977); Machiavelli, *The Prince*, ed. and trans. Robert M. Adams (New York: Norton, 1977). Page references are to the Italian text first, then to the English translation.

PL   John Milton, *Paradise Lost*, in Hughes.

Procacci   Giuliano Procacci, *Studi sulla fortuna del Machiavelli* (Rome: Istituto storico italiano, 1965).

Raab   Felix Raab, *The English Face of Machiavelli: A Changing Interpretation 1500–1700* (London: Routledge and Kegan Paul; Toronto: University of Toronto Press, 1964).

Note: In transcribing Renaissance texts, I have regularized *u*'s and *v*'s and expanded the macron. Unless otherwise indicated, translations are my own. Texts receiving extensive analysis are cited in the original and in translation. All other texts are cited in translation.

MACHIAVELLIAN RHETORIC

INTRODUCTION

Cromwell, and the few others with whom he con-sulted, first considered what was absolutely necessary to their main and determined end; and then, whether it were right or wrong, to make all other means subservient to it; to cozen and deceive men, as long as they could induce them to contribute to what they desired, upon motives how foreign soever; and when they would keep company with them no longer, or farther serve their purposes, to compel them by force to submit to what they should not be able to oppose; and so the one [the Presbyterians] resolved, only to do what they believed the people would like and approve; and the other [Cromwell and the Independents], that the people should like and approve what they had resolved. And this difference in the measures they took, was the true cause of so different success in all they undertook. Machiavel, in this, was in the right, though he got an ill name by it with those who take what he says from the report of other men, or do not enough consider what he says, and his method in speaking: (he was as great an enemy to tyranny and injustice in any government, as any man then was, or now is . . .).

A S THE EVENTS of the English civil war were unfolding, the royalist Edward Hyde, Earl of Clarendon, recorded his thoughts in his *History of the Rebellion*.[1] Reflecting on the struggle for power between Cromwell and the Presbyterians in 1647, after the imprisonment of Charles I in Carisbrooke Castle, Clarendon described Cromwell with a characteristic mixture of appreciation and biting irony. In Clarendon's judgment, Cromwell was a true Machiavellian: a brilliant tactician who was governed by considerations of necessity rather than morality, and who did not hesitate to use force and fraud to serve his purposes. Those who condemn Machiavelli for recommending such means, Clarendon added, have failed to understand Machiavelli's rhetoric, "his method in speaking": Machiavelli was "an enemy to tyranny," even as he analyzed the realities of de facto political power.

Although defending Machiavelli against the charge of crude Machiavellism, Clarendon went on to describe Cromwell as a stereotypical Machiavel, a hypocritical actor and dissembling rhetorician for whom necessity was as much a matter of design as of circumstance:

> Cromwell, though the greatest dissembler living, always made his hypocrisy of singular use and benefit to him; and never did any thing, how ungracious or imprudent soever it seemed to be, but what was necessary to the design; even his roughness and unpolishedness, which, in the beginning of the parliament, he affected . . . was necessary; and his first public declaration, in the beginning of the war, to his troop when it was first mustered, [was] "that he would not deceive or cozen them by the perplexed and involved expressions in his commission, to fight for king and parliament." (305–306)

Instead, Cromwell told his soldiers that he would charge upon the king "as any other private person," and "if their conscience would not permit them to do the like, he advised them not to list themselves in his troop, or under his command" (306). Machiavelli may have been "an enemy to tyranny"; whether Cromwell was, nevertheless, a casuistical Machiavel—fraudulently appealing to conscience in order to justify rebellion—is left to the reader to judge.

Clarendon's description of Cromwell as Machiavellian hypocrite and crafty rhetorician is part of a long Renaissance tradition which is the subject of this book. Taking the rhetorical Machiavel as a point of departure, I argue that this figure is not simply the result of a naive misreading of Machiavelli but is rather attuned to the rhetorical dimension of his political theory in a way that later thematic readings of Machiavelli are not. The aim of the book is to provide a revised history of Renaissance Machiavellism, particularly in England: one that sees the Machiavel and the republican as equally valid—and related—readings of Machiavelli's work. In this history, Machiavelli offered a rhetoric for dealing with the realm of de facto political power, rather than a political theory with a coherent thematic content; and Renaissance Machiavellism included a variety of rhetorically sophisticated appreciations and appropriations of Machiavelli's own rhetorical approach to politics. Once we recover the rhetorical dimension of Renaissance Machiavellism, we are able to understand how Machiavelli came to symbolize a series of tensions within both the humanist rhetorical tradition and contemporary politics—both for those who read him and for those who did not. Machiavellian rhetoric thus refers to Machiavelli's own rhetorical approach to politics, to the Renaissance association of rhetorical deception with the force and fraud of Machiavelli's prince, and to the rhetoric of Machiavellism that emerges in Renaissance debates about the nature and limits of political and religious authority.

It is important to clarify at the outset what I mean by the term *rhetoric*. I use the term generally as the humanists did, to refer to a repertoire of means of persuasion ranging from the figurative language and formal organization of a text to the ethos and pathos of the speaker. These means are ideally in the service of the good but are also available for evil purposes. Thus a tension exists within the humanist tradition between rhetoric conceived as an activity of ethical deliberation, which is a good in itself, and rhetoric conceived as an instrument or a neutral technique of argument. Of particular relevance to my argument in the latter case are the Ciceronian notions of the topic and the commonplace: the first is a way of structuring an argument according to the formal relationship between two terms (e.g., greater to lesser, cause to effect); the second a common opinion that can serve as the basis of an argument or practical syllogism, and that can be easily abstracted from a text and put to new uses. As we will see, Renaissance readers read Machiavelli both topically and as a storehouse of commonplaces or maxims; and in the course of the sixteenth century, Machiavellism developed into a rhetoric with its own specific topics and commonplaces—some of which Clarendon invokes in the passage above.

I also use the term *rhetoric* in opposition to thematic or positive argument. Here I am interested in how specific rhetorical techniques—topics, maxims, commonplaces, and, in particular, argument on both sides of a question—fragment, subvert, or otherwise qualify the literal sense of a text. Clarendon's remarks, for example, suggest that he perceived a certain doubleness—which we would call irony—in Machiavelli's "method of writing." Rhetoric in this sense can be usefully equated with dialectical thinking when it involves the internal critique and negation of positive claims to authority. While Renaissance writers do not describe their texts in these terms, such a description is often implicit in their own rhetorical analysis and in their anxieties about rhetoric's power to subvert the status quo.[2]

Here one needs also to remember that many Renaissance humanists saw a homology between politics, as the contingent realm of human affairs, and rhetoric as the study of arguments from probability, as a logic of persuasion rather than of apodeictic certainty. As Eugenio Garin has argued, humanist rhetoric entailed a theory of historical change and of the kinds of knowledge most appropriate to civic or political life. Renaissance treatises on imitation and on the education of a prince often imply a similar homology between literary imitation and politics. And they acknowledge that just as rhetoric and imitation can be used and abused in the case of poetry, so they are similarly helpful or harmful in the sphere of politics. For all these reasons, a consideration of Machiavellian rhetoric will of necessity be concerned with the uses of imitation—which writers such as Clarendon called "sembling" and "dissembling"—and with their political consequences.[3]

In proposing a rhetorical analysis of Machiavelli and of Renaissance Machiavellism, I take issue with the usual accounts by historians of political thought and by literary historians. Historians of Renaissance political thought have defined Machiavelli and the correct reception of his work in terms of secular political analysis or classical republicanism.[4] They have thus tended to dismiss the rhetorical Machiavel as the creation of an uninformed or unsympathetic public, particularly in the sixteenth century. According to this argument, as long as theology remained the dominant language of political discussion, Machiavelli was condemned as irreligious and immoral.[5] In contrast—so the argument runs—seventeenth-century Englishmen were well positioned to appreciate the author of *The Prince* and especially the *Discourses*. Thus in his important history of English Machiavellism Felix Raab stressed the continuities in the reception of Machiavelli as a secular thinker and analyst of the "politick" use of religion from the sixteenth to the seventeenth century, but he also charted a move away from the religious condemnation of Machiavelli to an appreciation of Machiavelli the republican thinker. According to Raab, the crisis of sovereignty leading up to the civil war signaled a crisis of theological justifications of political authority and allowed for the emergence of a more fully secular understanding of politics. Sympathetic readers now read Machiavelli as a dispassionate political observer or republican theorist, rather than as the diabolical Machiavel. In the end, while Raab admitted that the same individual was capable of reading Machiavelli in both ways in the sixteenth and seventeenth centuries, he tended to see the correct reading of Machiavelli as one that subordinates his rhetoric to his secular political analysis, and he argued that such a reading was most likely to appear in the seventeenth century.

This divorce of rhetoric and politics, religious condemnation and secular appreciation, governs J.G.A. Pocock's analysis of Renaissance Machiavellism as well. Like other historians of political thought, Pocock equates Machiavellism with the revival of secular, classical republicanism, which he defines as a set of ideas about a mixed constitution, a citizen militia, and individual *virtù*. Although Pocock allows that the rhetoric of civic humanism contributed to the emergence of Renaissance republicanism through its emphasis on dialogue and debate, he argues that Machiavelli, with his critique of the pieties of civic humanism and his insistence on the brutal realities of contemporary politics, most fully represents the secular republicanism of Renaissance political theory. In defining Machiavellism in this way, Pocock discounts the other reception of Machiavelli in the Renaissance: the reading of Machiavelli as the Machiavel, a figure of force and fraud, coercion and deceit, and—related to these—rhetorical skill. In Pocock's view, this reception of Machiavelli is simply incorrect—which is not to say it did not take place but that it was naive—a misreading dictated by the inability of Christian believers to see anything positive in Machiavelli's secular political theory. Like Raab, Pocock argues that it took the crisis of sovereignty during the English civil war, and the corresponding crisis of the usual theological modes of political explanation, for the real—secular, republican—Machiavelli to be discovered and appreciated by seventeenth-century Englishmen. In this account, James Harrington is the exemplary Machiavellian.

This bifurcation of the sixteenth-century Machiavel and seventeenth-century republican is endorsed by some literary historians as well. While devoting considerable attention to the Machiavel, literary historians also describe the recovery of a more sophisticated understanding of Machiavelli in the seventeenth century: the stage Machiavel, a figure of rhetoric, cunning, and hypocrisy, is increasingly accompanied by allusion or direct reference in the poetry and political tracts of the 1640s and 1650s to Machiavelli the republican analyst of *virtù* and author of the *Discourses*. As with the accounts of Raab and Pocock, here too the narrative tends to be one of progressive enlightenment regarding the republican content of Machiavelli's work by his readers—among whom we find Milton, Marvell, Robert Overton, George Wither, Algernon Sydney, Henry Neville, and Marchamont Nedham. Although some sixteenth-century readers appreciated Machiavelli's pragmatic political advice, and though many seventeenth-century authors still used *Machiavel* as a term of abuse, the general trend is away from moral and religious condemnation toward an appreciation of Machiavelli as a student of both de facto political power or "delegitimized politics," and secular republicanism.[6]

Note that what happens in these histories of Machiavellism is that theology and rhetoric appear on one side, the languages of republicanism and secular political analysis on the other. The reading of Machiavelli as rhetorician and Machiavel (dominant, according to Raab and Pocock, in the sixteenth century though still present in the seventeenth as well) is equated with the theologically rooted misunderstanding of Machiavelli, whereas the modern recuperation of Machiavellian discourse is defined in thematic terms as a set of ideas about sovereignty, agency, and the mixed constitution. And although civic humanist rhetoric is seen as contributing to the development of a republican sensibility, it is gradually superseded by the discourse of republicanism per se. Note also that writers such as John Milton, who was both a radical puritan and republican thinker, fall aslant this divide.[7]

This is now the dominant account of Machiavellism in the Renaissance but it is to my mind insufficiently flexible to make sense of the variety of languages—and of their rhetorical instantiation—in sixteenth- and seventeenth-century political debate. Attention to the lessons of humanist rhetoric suggests in contrast that a given language or idiom—such as Machiavellism—may serve competing interests at the same time, that languages may be used *in utramque partem*. This in turn means that the language of Machiavellism cannot simply be equated with secular, classical republicanism since it was available and used for sectarian religious purposes as well. The larger point I am making is not simply that historians of political thought have chosen to focus on one strain of Machiavellism rather than another, but that this choice is symptomatic of a methodology that locates ideological conflict between, rather than within, individual discourses. It analyzes competing discourses—such as secular republicanism versus the apocalyptic rhetoric of the Elect Nation—but pays insufficient attention to the fact that each of these discourses is itself an object of competition, capable of serving a variety of rhetorical interests.[8] In contrast, a serious consideration of the ties between humanist rhetoric and political theory requires that we analyze the rhetoric *of* political theory. When we do we emerge with a revised account of the relation of rhetoric and political thought in the Renaissance, one that has implications for both literary and political texts.

In taking up Machiavelli's relation to and revision of the humanist rhetorical tradition and the reception of Machiavelli's work, this book thus necessarily engages two important debates in Renaissance historiography, the first concerning the relationship of humanist rhetoric to republicanism in the Italian Renaissance, the second concerning the association of Machiavellism and republicanism with the increasing secularism of Renaissance culture. In contrast to many of the standard scholarly works, part 1 argues that Machiavelli does not supplant rhetoric with a more realistic view of politics but rather makes politics more deeply rhetorical than it had been in the earlier humanist tradition. One surprising consequence of this argument is that the Machiavel emerges as an intelligent representation of and response to Machiavelli's work. A second consequence is that an informed response to Machiavelli can no longer be simply equated with a secular, republican approach to politics, both because republicanism is espoused by religious as well as secular thinkers in this period, and because republicanism is not the only legitimate construction of Machiavelli's rhetorical politics.

As we will see, Machiavelli's rhetorical politics dramatized a tension between a technical and prudential conception of rhetoric that is at the heart of Renaissance humanist culture. On the one hand, rhetoric in this period was conceived of as an ethically and ideologically neutral technique of argument; on the other hand, rhetoric was seen as the embodiment of a faculty of practical reasoning or prudential deliberation that is tied to ethical norms. If the first technical conception of rhetoric gave rise to considerable anxiety concerning the immoral ends to which rhetoric might be put, the second prudential conception offered the response that the good orator is of necessity a good man. Though Renaissance humanists regularly acknowledged the possible abuse of rhetoric, they just as often attempted to define rhetoric in the prudential terms that would preclude such immorality. Machiavelli borrowed from the humanist notion of prudential rhetoric at the same time that he criticized such rhetoric for its subordination to ethics, that is, for not being practical enough. In making of *virtù* a faculty of practical reasoning and action that is not constrained by ethical norms, Machiavelli attempted to make rhetoric and prudential deliberation generate a new set of priorities in the domain of politics. Yet, in taking the generative possibilities of a practical conception of rhetoric more seriously than did the humanists themselves, Machiavelli paradoxically appeared to realize the humanists' worst fears about a technical or instrumental conception of rhetoric: its ethical indeterminacy, its concern with success, its use for the purpose of force and fraud, violence and misrepresentation.

Machiavelli's Renaissance readers understood his complicated relationship to the humanist tradition. Specifically, they saw that Machiavelli's rhetorical politics engaged a constellation of topics that epitomized the tensions within humanist rhetoric: the relation of imitation to misrepresentation, persuasion to coercion, means to ends, intention to effect, demonic flexibility to allegorical stability, and virtue or *virtù* to success. These topics amounted to a questioning of the Ciceronian ideal of harmony between the *honestum* and the *utile* (the good and the useful); they registered a tension between these terms, and an anxiety that the good might be sacrificed to the expedient or that rhetoric might become an instrument of force and fraud.[9] Interpreted in one way, such topics articulated the perception that rhetoric can be used for evil as well as good purposes; interpreted in another way, they implied that the rhetorician is inherently unreliable or unethical. In reading Machiavelli in terms of these topics, Renaissance readers registered their fears concerning the divorce of ethics from rhetoric and politics, and they ranged in their interpretations from the simple condemnation of Machiavelli as Machiavel to the recognition that the Machiavel is only one aspect—though a crucial one—of Machiavelli's rhetorical politics. Similarly, in articulating their fears about rhetoric in terms of Machiavelli, Renaissance readers offered a spectrum of interpretations from the simple identification of Machiavelli with the abuse of rhetoric, to the perception that rhetoric is Machiavellian because it presupposes a flexible faculty of judgment for dealing with contingent affairs, one that draws its arguments from the topics outlined above. In Machiavelli's own work and in Renaissance Machiavellism, these topics thus articulated a crisis in the assumptions of humanist rhetoric.[10]

This crisis was caused in part by a series of political crises, which brought home the role of force and fraud in the sphere of politics and the realities of de facto political power. For Machiavelli, the crises were the French invasion of the Italian peninsula in 1494 and the fall of the Florentine republic in 1512.[11] For Englishmen, the crises included Henry VIII's Act of Supremacy, the conflict between Anglicans and dissenters throughout the sixteenth and seventeenth centuries, the English civil war, and the Engagement Controversy. And for Counter-Reformation figures such as Botero, the crisis was the Reformation itself. Just as Machiavelli exposed the inadequacy of humanist assumptions for dealing with the political crisis of 1494 and after, so Machiavelli's rhetorical politics offered many writers of the later sixteenth and seventeenth centuries a more adequate mode of conceptualizing recent political events than had the assumptions of humanist rhetoric. Machiavelli's work was not the only or even the main channel of such rhetorical politics in the Renaissance; other sources—such as rhetorical handbooks, manuals of courtliness and casuistry, the "adiaphora" argument disseminated in political treatises, and the writings of Tacitus and Guicciardini—were important conduits of this conception of politics; and in many cases, as we shall see, they merged with the rhetoric of Machiavellism. But Machiavelli's work invested rhetorical resourcefulness and its ethical instability with clear conceptual lineaments, giving the double face of rhetorical politics a single name, so that its name came to signify two-facedness.[12]

It is this two-facedness of Machiavellian rhetoric that helps us rehabilitate the Machiavel. For if Machiavellism is a rhetoric for conceptualizing and responding to the realm of contingency, it includes not only republicanism but also tyranny; it involves the use of force and fraud not only to advance one's self interest but also to serve the commonwealth. In this light, the Machiavel should not be simply dismissed as the theologically determined misunderstanding of Machiavelli, for the problem of de facto political power to which Machiavellian republicanism responds in the seventeenth century is the problem the sixteenth century represented in the rhetorical Machiavel. The identification of the rhetorical Machiavel with force and fraud is thus not simply antithetical to the republican Machiavelli, just as *The Prince* is not simply antithetical to the *Discourses*. Rather, both are available and often compatible "arguments" in the political rhetoric Machiavelli was expounding.

In the following chapters I challenge the bifurcation of the rhetorical Machiavel and the republican first in Machiavelli's own work and then in the reception of that work on the continent and in Renaissance England. In part 1 I argue that Machiavelli's political thought is inseparable from his rhetorical or internal critique of humanism, and that we cannot understand his political thought without analyzing his rhetorical practice. In particular, once we see that *virtù* revises the humanist concepts of imitation and prudential rhetoric, we understand why Machiavelli should not be chiefly read as a theorist of republicanism but rather as a proponent of a rhetorical politics, one that proceeds topically and dialectically, and that can be used by tyrant and republican alike. In the final chapter of part 1 I briefly consider the Counter-Reformation reception of Machiavelli, and argue that Botero and his contemporaries were particularly attuned to the ways in which Machiavelli's rhetorical politics could be appropriated for the purposes of a Christian reason of state.

In part 2 of the book I explore the reception of Machiavelli by critics and admirers in sixteenth- and seventeenth-century England, and argue that both are informed by a rhetorical understanding of Machiavellism. For both, Machiavellism offered a new rhetorical approach to politics that was equally relevant to contemporary theological and political debate. Chapter 4 presents a series of case studies, focusing on the reading of Machiavelli by Stephen Gardiner, Sir Walter Ralegh, Francis Bacon, and Shakespeare. Chapter 5 takes up the topics of Machiavellism as they appear in the debate over Henrician policy and in subsequent debates concerning the relationship between church and state, sovereignty and de facto political power. Finally, in part 3, I analyze Milton's reception of Machiavelli and the tradition of Renaissance Machiavellism in *Areopagitica*, *Comus*, and *Paradise Lost*.

In all these cases, attention to the association of Machiavelli with rhetoric revises the usual polarized accounts of Renaissance Machiavellism in terms of the popular and learned reception, the Machiavel and the republican, the sixteenth and seventeenth centuries. In particular, it allows us to displace these distinctions from the plane of the temporal or developmental to the rhetorical: for there is a crucial ambivalence at the heart of all that was understood as Machiavellism from the 1530s through the

1660s. Machiavelli did not simply signify the threat of rhetorical manipulation in the sixteenth and early seventeenth centuries and classical republicanism in the mid- and late seventeenth century but also the unstable relationship between intention and effect, rhetorical persuasion and coercion, in the related spheres of religion and politics. My aim in proposing a topical account of Machiavellism is neither to deny that Machiavelli was often interpreted simplistically nor to deny that many seventeenth-century Englishmen were particularly drawn to Machiavelli the republican theorist; rather, my intent is to argue that the association of Machiavelli with rhetoric can tell us much about the anxieties and concerns, as well as the conventions of interpretation, that were characteristic of Tudor-Stuart political, literary, and religious culture. The recuperation of the Machiavel and of Machiavelli the theorist of force and fraud is not intended to replace the republican theorist, but rather to complement and complicate our sense of what Machiavelli's rhetorical politics offered his contemporaries.

Above all, once we see that the Machiavellian moment of Renaissance culture was a rhetorical moment, we see that Machiavellian rhetoric could be used not only pro and contra republicanism but pro and contra secular thought. The most insightful readers of Machiavelli in the Renaissance are those who, like Milton, do not simply reject the rhetorical Machiavel for Machiavelli the republican, or the diabolical Machiavel for the theorist of mixed government, but rather see the inseparability of these two aspects of Machiavelli's thought. In contrast to the usual histories of Machiavellism, theology proves to be a link between the rhetorical and republican Machiavelli, while rhetoric is the link between the Machiavelli who appears in theological debates and the republican Machiavelli of Renaissance political theory.

PART ONE
MACHIAVELLI

THE EARLY Italian reception of *The Prince* and the *Discourses* shows that, from the outset, Machiavelli's readers recognized and responded to his distinctive rhetorical flair. They were shocked (or pretended to be) by his brutal examples of practical politics; they resented his exposure of the inefficacy of the traditional virtues. They saw that the dramatic effect of Machiavelli's work depended on his subversion of the conventions of humanist treatises on politics.[1] And some, like Guicciardini, recognized that, precisely because of this, Machiavelli was more of a humanist than he would have his reader believe.

Writing to Benedetto Varchi in 1549, in what was probably a retrospective act of myth making, Giovan Battista Busini described the outrage which, he believed, many Florentines felt twenty years earlier when they discovered that the second chancellor of the republic had written *The Prince*. According to Busini, many of Machiavelli's contemporaries saw him as a Machiavel—a religious heretic and instructor in tyranny—whose fault did not lie in rhetorical indirection but in not being indirect enough:

> everyone hated him on account of *The Prince*; to the rich, it seemed that his *Prince* was a document for teaching the duke how to steal their possessions, to the poor their liberty. To the piagnoni [followers of Savanorola] he seemed a heretic, to the good dishonorable, to the wicked more wicked or more clever than they: so that everyone hated him.[2]

Francesco Guicciardini, in contrast, saw both the idealistic and the offensive sides of Machiavelli's work. He also saw how they were related. In a now famous passage in his *Considerazioni* on Machiavelli's *Discourses*, Guicciardini noted Machiavelli's frequent, shocking examples of force and fraud; yet he went on to imply that Machiavelli's inordinate fondness for such examples was motivated as much or more by a love of dramatic effect as by political concerns. In Guicciardini's view, Machiavelli's penchant for spectacular violence amounted paradoxically to political naiveté, even to an idealism of grand gestures. And he advised the prince not to take "for an absolute rule what Machiavelli says, who is always excessively pleased by unusual and violent remedies."[3] Elsewhere in his *Considerazioni*, he recast Machiavelli's naiveté as bookish idealism, remarking that some of the examples Machiavelli adduced of tyrants and monarchs giving up their power "are more easily portrayed in the books and the imaginations of men, than they are accomplished in reality" (21). And in the *Ricordi*, in maxims later readers have taken to refer to Machiavelli, he linked political naiveté with the humanist rhetoric of exemplarity when he complained, "How wrong it is to cite the Romans at every turn"; "To judge by examples is very misleading."[4] For Guicciardini, Machiavelli's shocking recommendations of force and fraud were perfectly compatible with bookish idealism and a humanist fondness for ancient Roman examples.

Guicciardini and Busini represent the two poles of the reception of Machiavelli in the Renaissance. While Busini recorded the views of those who failed to understand how the second chancellor of the Florentine republic could write a handbook for the Medicean "new prince," Guicciardini expressed the views of those who doubted that a commentary on Livy could revive the Florentine republic after its fall in 1512. On the one hand, Machiavelli was accused of being a Machiavel; on the other hand, he was represented as an idealistic humanist and republican thinker. In the following chapters I argue that we can make sense of both these responses—and of a wide range of intermediate positions—once we recognize, as Renaissance readers did, Machiavelli's debt to and criticism of the humanist rhetorical tradition.

Scholars of Machiavelli are now generally agreed about the humanist dimension of his education and of his cultural milieu. From his father Bernardo's diary and from his own works, we know that Machiavelli received an education in rhetoric, poetry, and the other "studia humanitatis." His prose style is often deliberately Latinate in syntax and lexicon, as though to declare his literary qualifications for public office.[5] And it is probably the case that his education did help him to gain his position in the second chancery.[6] We also know that Machiavelli was ambivalent about, even at times hostile to, the humanist culture of his day: in writing *The Prince*, Machiavelli broke with humanist treatises on princely conduct; just as in the *Discourses*, he took issue with the dominant humanist rhetoric of consensus in contemporary Florentine political discussion.[7] Yet, in both works Machiavelli adopts humanist rhetorical strategies in order to criticize the pieties of humanist political theories. In both works Machiavelli stages his innovation in political theory as a rhetorical innovation, as an immanent critique of humanist rhetorical theory.[8]

My aim in providing the following rhetorical analysis of *The Prince* and the *Discourses* is to highlight the conventions of interpretation shared by Machiavelli and his Renaissance readers, and to lay the groundwork for a recuperation of the reception of Machiavelli as Machiavel and rhetorician in the sixteenth and seventeenth centuries.[9] I focus on those passages and issues of key concern to the Renaissance reader conversant with the humanist rhetorical tradition, who encountered Machiavelli's works in the decades following their publication in the early 1530s. Like the modern reader of *The Prince*, the sixteenth-century reader was particularly struck by the example of Cesare Borgia in chapter 7 and the recommendation that the prince imitate the fox and the lion in chapter

18. Unlike many modern readers, however, the Renaissance reader also noted Machiavelli's ironic treatment of Moses in chapter 6 and the example of Agathocles the Sicilian tyrant in chapter 8. He was less interested in the depiction of Fortune as a woman—a holdover from medieval allegorizing after all—than in Machiavelli's habits as a reader of ancient history. He saw both *The Prince* and the *Discourses* as providing a storehouse of ancient and modern examples that could be put to new uses by the reader. He was made nervous by Machiavelli's use of the humanist vocabulary of imitation and exemplarity because he recognized that their traditional moral connotations were being subverted from within. He was disturbed by Machiavelli's preference for conflict over consensus, because he saw the challenge to the humanist ideal of social harmony through dialogue. Finally, he recognized in Machiavelli's work a set of topics or problems, such as the uses of imitation and the relation of force to popular consent, means to ends, and virtue to success.[10] This is the reader whose experience will guide the rhetorical analysis of Machiavelli's work in chapters 1 and 2, and whose own comments on and uses of Machiavellian rhetoric are the main subject of this book.

In chapter 1 I analyze Machiavelli's critique of the humanist notion of imitation and the humanist pedagogy of examples in *The Prince*, and show how the topics that figure in the Renaissance reception of Machiavelli emerge from this critique. In chapter 2 I argue for the similarity between *The Prince* and the *Discourses*, while focusing in particular on Machiavelli's attack on the humanist rhetoric of consensus. Both chapters demonstrate that the problems of political innovation in the realm of contingency that the new prince encounters are rhetorical problems: problems that cannot be resolved by applying fixed moral principles on the one hand or mere force on the other, problems whose solutions are inextricable from the use of imitation, representation, and persuasion. Thus rhetoric is not simply an instrument of *virtù* but is also analogous to *virtù* in the sense that both are faculties for responding to the realm of contingency or fortune; and *virtù* is rhetorical because what counts as *virtù* is produced from within a rhetorical analysis of the circumstances at hand and varies accordingly. Political innovation proves to be inseparable from rhetorical invention.[11]

ONE

THE PRINCE

MACHIAVELLI scandalized his Renaissance reader not because he advised the prince to use force and fraud but because he refused to cloak his advice in the rhetoric of scholastic or Christian humanist idealism. Instead, he insisted that the prince acts in a world in which there are "no prefigured meanings, no implicit teleology,"[1] in which order and legibility are the products of human action rather than the a priori objects of human cognition. To recognize this, he argued, is to acknowledge the truth of power, as opposed to an idealistic notion of truth conceived in terms of representation, as correspondence to some a priori standard of judgment or moral ideal. Machiavelli accordingly declared his divergence from the idealistic tradition of reflection on political affairs in the famous opening to chapter 15:

> Ma, sendo l'intento mio scrivere cosa utile a chi la intende, mi è parso piú conveniente andare drieto alla verità effettuale della cosa, che alla immaginazione di essa. E molti si sono immaginati repubbliche e principati che non si sono mai visti ne conosciuti essere in vero; perche elle è tanto discosto da come si vive a come si doverrebbe vivere, che colui che lascia quello che si fa per quello che si doverrebbe fare, impara piú tosto la ruina che la preservazione sua. (65)

> Since I intend to write something useful to an understanding reader, it seemed better to go after the real truth of the matter than to repeat what people have imagined. A great many men have imagined states and princedoms such as nobody ever saw or knew in the real world, for there's such a difference between the way we really live and the way we ought to live that the man who neglects the real to study the ideal will learn how to accomplish his ruin, not his preservation. (44)

We should note, however, that while Machiavelli criticized the idealistic moral philosophy of some humanists, he borrowed from the more flexible pragmatism of others, according to which truth is governed by the rhetorical and ethical standards of prudence, decorum, and consensus. Only when we recognize Machiavelli's imitation of and final divergence from this humanist rhetorical tradition will we be able to understand and appreciate the way Machiavelli was read and what he came to signify in the later Renaissance.

In the following pages I argue that Machiavelli offers an immanent critique of humanist imitation and the humanist pedagogy of examples in *The Prince*: he does not so much abandon the resources of humanist rhetoric as use them against humanism itself. Faced with the dilemmas of contingent action, Machiavellian *virtù* responds not only with a rhetorical analysis of options—through argument on both sides of a question—but also with a rhetorical critique of the usual humanist approach to, or the dominant ideology of, politics. Specifically, the humanist technique of argument on both sides of a question becomes a mode of dialectical thinking, in which positive terms are logically implicated in and give rise to their opposites. Machiavelli thus insists on what humanists had always known and feared: faithful imitation inevitably involves the possibility of feigning; what appears to be virtue may in practice turn out to be vice. Machiavelli's rhetorical view of politics is thus inseparable from his use of rhetoric as a critique of ideology: for in showing the reader how to think rhetorically—on both sides of a question—about notions such as imitation, virtue, and the good, Machiavelli exposes the ideological nature of all such positive terms. In so doing, he presents the humanists' prudential rhetoric as insufficiently rhetorical and flexible, as itself a version of instrumental thinking or idealism.[2]

The logic of such dialectical analysis leads Machiavelli to try to incorporate as resources within imitation and rhetoric that which the humanists would ordinarily exclude: physical force, misrepresentation, and conflicting interests.[3] It also leads him to suggest in chapters 8 and 9 of *The Prince* that the superiority of republics emerges out of a rhetorical and dialectical analysis of principalities. The rhetorical considerations that make the prince a theatrical Machiavel, a hypocrite and fraud, may also lead in Machiavelli's analysis to republicanism. Yet, precisely because there is a rhetorical and dialectical link between the new prince and the republican, there is no necessary connection between the two. Machiavelli's critique of humanist imitation and rhetoric thus gives rise to a series of topics concerning the vexed relation of *virtù* and success, force and persuasion, means and ends, tyranny and republicanism.

Finally, I argue that Machiavelli's rhetorical, dehypostatized *virtù* is a source of both analytical strength and weakness. On the one hand, it exposes as ideological the humanist's claim to link virtue and rhetoric, ethics and effectiveness, while excluding force and fraud; on the other hand, in taking the realm of contingency and the practical conception of rhetoric more seriously than humanism itself, it runs the risk of merely reproducing the problem it set out to solve. Here, as Pocock has remarked, *virtù* "is not merely that by which men control their fortunes in a legitimized world; it may also be that by which men innovate and so delegitimize their worlds" (*MM*, 166). The final section of this chapter examines Machiavelli's response to this dilemma in chapters 25 and 26 of *The Prince*. As we will see, although Machiavelli's rhetorical analysis of the realm of politics avoids the ethical domestication of *virtù* on the one hand, it threatens to allegorize, reify, or demonize *virtù* on the other, thus finally undermining the flexible political skill that the rhetoric of *The Prince* was designed to encourage. In the end, *The Prince* dramatizes both the dangerous instability and demonic aspect of rhetorical politics that later readers of Machiavelli would personify in the Machiavel.

Imitation and Misrepresentation

From the very beginning of *The Prince* it is clear that Machiavelli is drawing on the humanist notions of imitation and exemplarity.[4] Like the humanists, he wants to educate his reader's practical judgment, the faculty of deliberation that allows for effective action within the contingent realm of fortune; like them he recognizes that such education must therefore offer particular examples for imitation rather than the general precepts appropriate to theoretical reason. Furthermore, Machiavelli is concerned, as the humanists were, to criticize an unreflective relation to past examples, one that would take the form of slavish imitation or of a one-to-one correspondence. In fact, it is precisely in not perfectly imitating the exemplar that the humanist prince or poet finds both the room to exercise his own will and the measure of his own achievement. Correct imitation accordingly involves a flexible principle of prudential judgment or rhetorical decorum. This in turn gives rise to texts designed to dramatize and inculcate such judgment, texts whose rhetoric is therefore not ornamental but strategic.

Thus, in the prefatory letter to *The Prince*, Machiavelli justifies his gift to Lorenzo de' Medici by suggesting that the latter will be a more effective ruler if he learns to imitate the double perspective, the reflective distance, offered in *The Prince*: "To know the people well one must be a prince, and to know princes well one must be, oneself, of the people" (14, 3). And in chapter 14, "Military Duties of the Prince," Machiavelli makes the humanist claim for textual imitation even more forcefully by comparing skill in government to skill in reading, by making the ruler's landscape into a text and the text into a realm of forces. The prince is advised to learn to read the terrain ("imparare la natura de' siti") and to "read history and reflect on the actions of great men." Here, to imitate great men means to imitate imitation, that is, to "take as a model of conduct some great historical figure who achieved the highest praise and glory by constantly holding before himself the deeds and achievements of a predecessor" (64, 43).

Notoriously, however, imitation is not an ethical practice for Machiavelli; the orator is not necessarily a good man. This point is brought home with particular irony in those passages where Machiavelli invites the prince to *pretend* to imitate. For example, in chapter 6 he notes:

> camminando li uomini quasi sempre per le vie battute da altri, e procedendo nelle azioni loro con le imitazioni, né si potendo le vie d'altri al tutto tenere, né alla virtù di quelli che tu imiti aggiugnere, debbe uno uomo prudente intrare sempre per vie battute da uomini grandi, e quelli che sono stati eccellentissimi imitare, acciò che, se la sua virtù non vi arriva, almeno ne renda qualche odore: e fare come li arcieri prudenti, a' quali, parendo el loco dove disegnono ferire troppo lontano, e conoscendo fino a quanto va la virtù del loro arco, pongono la mira assai piú alta che il loco destinato, non per aggiugnere con la loro freccia a tanta altezza, ma per potere, con lo aiuto di sí alta mira pervenire al disegno loro. (30)

> Men almost always prefer to walk in paths marked out by others and pattern their action through imitation. Even if he cannot follow other people's paths in every respect, or attain to the *virtù* of his originals, a prudent man should always follow the footsteps of the great and imitate those who have been supreme. His own *virtù* may not come up to theirs, but at least it will have a sniff of it. Thus he will resemble prudent archers who, seeing how far away the target lies, and knowing the *virtù* of their bow, aim much higher than the real target, not because they expect the arrow to fly that far, but to accomplish their real end by aiming beyond it. (16; translation modified)

The goal here is not so much imitation as it is the prudent pretense of imitation, as though the deferential practice of following in the footsteps of the great will serve to camouflage one's "real end by aiming beyond it." In making the agent an actor who is capable of (mis)representation and in arguing that such fraudulent representation is a means to power, Machiavelli exposes the hypocrisy, force, and fraud, that are the demonic underside of the humanist notion of imitation. At the same time he alters the meaning of prudence from the humanists' practical reason, informed by moral considerations, to the calculating, potentially amoral faculty of judgment appropriate to the man of *virtù*. In typical Machiavellian fashion, he also dramatizes such prudent misrepresentation in his own treatment of Moses in the following paragraph.[5]

Renaissance readers of this chapter were particularly disturbed by the inclusion of Moses among those who became princes "by their own *virtù.*" They could not help noticing Machiavelli's ironic deference to Moses's "teacher" and his sly imputation that Moses had feigned divine favor:

> Ma, per venire a quelli che per propria virtù e non per fortuna sono diventati principi, dico che li piú eccellenti sono Moisè, Ciro, Romulo, Teseo, e simili. E, benché di Moisè non si debba ragionare, sendo suto uno mero esecutore delle cose che li erano ordinate da Dio, *tamen* debbe essere ammirato *solum* per quella grazia che lo faceva degno di parlare con Dio. Ma consideriamo Ciro e li altri che hanno acquistato o fondato regni: li troverete tutti mirabili; e, se si consideranno le azioni e ordini loro particulari, parranno non discrepanti da quelli di Moisè, che ebbe sí gran precettore. (30–31)

> Turning to those who have become princes by their own *virtù* and not by accident, I would say that the most notable were Moses, Cyrus, Romulus, Theseus, and a few others. And though we should not consider Moses, because he was simply an agent sent by God to do certain things, he still should be admired, if only for that grace which made him worthy of talking with God. But let us turn to Cyrus and the others who acquired or founded kingdoms. You will find them all deserving of admiration; and if you consider their individual actions and decrees, they will be found not much different from those of Moses who had such a great teacher. (16)

In these remarks Machiavelli conflates the language of divine providence with that of princely *virtù*, and so negates the distinction between Moses and Cyrus even as he insists on it: Moses may have been taught by God, but God is an "ordinatore" like Cyrus and others who established new "ordini"; conversely, Cyrus and the others are described as "mirabili"—not only admirable but wondrous, as though they too had been favored by grace. Machiavelli's claim that we should admire Moses "if only for that grace which made him worthy of talking with God" clearly suggests that Moses had the wit—or grace—to feign grace. In case we should miss the point, in the next paragraph Machiavelli explicitly calls attention to the similarity of Moses and Cyrus: "It was necessary for Moses to find the children of Israel in Egypt, enslaved and oppressed by the Egyptians, so that they should be disposed to follow him. . . . It was necessary that Cyrus should find the Persians unhappy with the rule of the Medes, and the Medes soft and effeminate from years of peace" (32, 17). Like Cyrus, Moses knew how to make the most of the occasion by means of his own *virtù.*

Chapter 6's redefinition of imitation as ruse and thus as power is an aim of *The Prince* as a whole, but it finds a particularly forceful articulation in chapter 18, in which Machiavelli criticizes the humanist equation of *honestas* and *utilitas*, the faith that rhetoric and prudence are inseparable from moral virtue.[6] Machiavelli begins this chapter by distinguishing between human law and bestial force, but he then abandons the first pole of his binary opposition and proceeds to locate the range of political invention and imitation within the second term of force. In doing so, however, he redefines force to include craft or fraud as well:

> Sendo adunque uno principe necessitato sapere bene usare la bestia, debbe di quelle pigliare la golpe et il lione; perché il lione non si defende da' lacci, la golpe non si defende da' lupi. Bisogna adunque essere golpe a conoscere e' lacci, e lione a sbigottire e' lupi. Coloro che stanno semplicemente in sul lione, non se ne intendano. Non può per tanto uno signore prudente, né debbe, osservare la fede, quando tale osservanzia li torni contro, e che sono spente le cagioni che la feciono promettere. (72–73)

> Since a prince must know how to use the character of beasts, he should pick for imitation the fox and the lion. As the lion cannot protect himself from traps, and the fox cannot defend himself from wolves, you have to be a fox to be wary of traps, and a lion to overawe the wolves. Those who try to live by the lion alone are badly mistaken. Thus a prudent prince cannot and should not keep his word when to do so would go against his interest, or when the reasons that made him pledge it no longer apply. (50)

In making force, in the inclusive sense of force and fraud, the object of imitation, Machiavelli implicates force in the narrow sense of brute strength in questions of discretion and representation. A rhetoric of force is different from the simple application of force—"Those who try to live by the lion alone are badly mistaken"—since at times such rhetoric will involve the representation of and appeal to what is conventionally accepted as virtue.[7]

> A uno principe, adunque, non è necessario avere tutte le soprascritte qualità, ma è bene necessario parere di averle. Anzi, ardirò di dire questo, che avendole et osservandole sempre, sono dannose, e parendo di averle, sono utile; come parere pietoso, fedele, umano, intero, relligioso, et essere; ma stare in modo edificato con l'animo, che, bisognando non essere, tu possa e sappi mutare el contrario. Et hassi ad intendere questo, che uno principe, e massime uno principe nuovo, non può osservare tutte quelle cose per le quali li uomini sono tenuti buoni, sendo spesso necessitato, per mantenere lo stato, operare contro alla fede, contro alla carità, contro alla umanità, contro alla relligione. E però bisogna che elli abbi uno animo disposto a volgersi secondo ch'e' venti e le variazioni della fortuna li comandono. (73–74)

> In actual fact, a prince may not have all the admirable qualities we listed, but it is very necessary that he should seem to have them. Indeed, I will venture to say that when you have them and exercise them all the time, they are

harmful to you; when you seem to have them, they are useful. It is useful to appear merciful, truthful, humane, sincere, and religious; it is useful to be so in reality. But you must keep your mind so disposed that, in case of need, you can turn to the exact contrary. This has to be understood: a prince, and especially a new prince, cannot possibly exercise all those virtues for which men are called "good." To preserve the state, he often has to do things against his word, against charity, against humanity, against religion. Thus he has to have a mind ready to shift as the winds of fortune and the varying circumstances of life may dictate. (50–51; translation modified)

Here representation becomes ruse in order to present an illusion to the people that will at the same time be effective for the prince. In response to the humanist ideal of a rhetoric that is grounded in morality and also effective, Machiavelli demonstrates that even those practical "virtues for which men are called 'good'" are insufficiently attuned to the rhetorical concerns of effective political action. This immanent critique leads Machiavelli to redefine the antithesis of representation and force. Correct or successful imitation is no longer constrained by the humanist exercise of self-knowledge and moral discretion[8] but has itself become a rhetorical topic of invention to be manipulated in the interests of power. Conversely, however, power becomes in part, if not entirely, a rhetorical effect of imitation: for the prince must appear to be good, virtuous, and so on, not only in order to deceive his enemies but also to satisfy his people and to maintain his power.

As the preceding remarks suggest, Machiavelli's immanent critique of humanist imitation follows from his recognition of the intrinsic irony of politics, or of action within the contingent realm of human affairs: "If you look at matters carefully, you will see that something resembling virtue, if you follow it, may be your ruin, while something resembling vice will lead, if you follow it, to your security and well-being" (66, 45).[9] But this formulation also allows us to see that Machiavelli wants to control this irony, or rather that he conceives of the man of *virtù* as someone who can use the ironies of political action to achieve political stability.[10] This recognition of the irony of politics leads in turn to a revision of humanist argument *in utramque partem*. The humanists, following Aristotle, believed that one needs to be able to argue on both sides of a question, not so that one might actually defend a false position but so that one might anticipate and thereby more effectively rebut one's opponent. Machiavelli, however, argues that the prince will actually have to oppose what may appear to be good at a given moment. In fact, in Machiavelli's view, it is the humanists who are guilty of trying to accommodate in a single moment contrary qualities or arguments when they claim that the good and the useful are always compatible (see chaps. 16 and 17). Knowledge *in utramque partem* is necessary according to Machiavelli because "the conditions of human life simply do not allow" one "to have and exercise" only morally good qualities (65, 45). Rather, the conditions of human life require the ruses of imitation and persuasion—and the amoral, flexible faculty of judgment—that Machiavelli calls *virtù*.

Examples of *Virtù*

> For hyperbole is a virtue [virtus], when the magnitude
> of the facts passes all words, and in such circumstances our
> language will be more effective if it goes beyond the
> truth than if it falls short of it.
> —*Quintilian*

It is precisely the intrinsic irony of politics—the gap or lack of a correspondence between intention and result—that both allows for and requires solutions that seem extreme from the perspective of the humanist ideal of *mediocritas*.[11] Hence the place of hyperbole and exaggeration in Machiavelli's examples of *virtù*. On the one hand, the examples of great men will always seem hyperbolic or excessive to—beyond the reach of—the imitator. On the other hand, Machiavelli argues, this hyperbole has a rhetorical and pedagogical function. If we return to the example from chapter 6 of the archer shooting beyond his target, we see that Machiavellian examples do not correspond to things as they are but to what they might be; they are figures of action rather than perception, of desire rather than cognition or representation. Hyperbole as a mode of speech or behavior is thus the proper response to the irony of politics: it is predicated on a recognition of one's distance from the situation one would like to create, but it also involves the recognition that such distance is itself a precondition of considered action. Finally, hyperbolic action is often ironic according to the classical definition of irony because it involves saying or doing one thing in order to arrive at its opposite.[12] In short, the world of Machiavellian politics is intrinsically ironic, and often the most effective mode of acting—and of teaching—in such a world is theatrical and hyperbolic.

Given Machiavelli's dramatic and rhetorical view of the world of politics, it is not surprising that he offers us no substantive or thematic definition of *virtù*. This is not simply a failing of analytical skill but a sophisticated rhetorical strategy, the aim of which is to destabilize or dehypostatize our conception of political virtue, for only a destabilized *virtù* can be effective in the destabilized world of political reality.[13] In this context the most effective critique of humanist assumptions will be one that stages or dramatizes this lack of conceptual stability, rather than simply stating it as a fact. An analysis of the examples of Cesare Borgia and Agathocles in chapters 7 and 8 will serve to illustrate this point. Together, these chapters exemplify the most prominent features of Machiavelli's strategic rhetoric—his dichotomizing mode of argument, hyperbolic and theatrical style, apparent contradictions and deliberately failed examples. At the same time, they should also help us to see how Machiavelli's own rhetorical virtuosity dramatizes the *virtù* of his ideal prince. Chapters 7 and 8 stage a characteristically Machiavellian coup de théâtre, in which Machiavelli's rhetorical force and fraud are central to his innovation in political thought.

Chapter 7 on Cesare Borgia has long been recognized as Machiavelli's most notorious example of the "new prince." Sandwiched between chapter 6, in which Machiavelli discusses those who founded states or introduced "nuovi ordini" by *virtù*—that is, by their own energy and force of arms (32, 18)—and chapter 8 on those who acquired power by crime, Borgia seems designed above all to illustrate the ordinary case of *virtù* in the realm of politics. In contrast to Moses, Cyrus, Romulus, and Theseus in chapter 6, Borgia rose to power by fortune and the arms of others. Nevertheless, he had "so much natural *virtù* that [he] quickly prepared himself to preserve what fortune had showered on [him]" (34, 19). For this reason, Machiavelli tells us, there is no "better advice to give a new prince than the example of his actions" (34–35, 20). Precisely because Borgia is the Machiavellian prince par excellence and because he is explicitly contrasted to the criminals Agathocles and Oliverotto da Fermo in the next chapter—a contrast most readers have taken at face value—this example needs to be analyzed closely.

Unlike the mythical founders of new orders in chapter 6, who had only to impose form on unformed matter, Borgia confronted an already formed matter. His effectiveness in dealing with this situation seems to have been due to his uncommon ability to use fraud as a means to power. Having put down the "disorders" caused by the Orsini in the Romagna,

> né si fidando di Francia né di altre forze esterne, per non le avere a cimentare, si volse alli inganni; e seppe tanto dissimulare l'animo suo che li Orsini, mediante el signor Paulo, si riconciliorono seco; con il quale el duca non mancò d'ogni ragione di offizio per assicurarlo, dandoli danaro, veste e cavalli; tanto che la simplicità loro li condusse a Sinigallia nelle sua mani. Spenti adunque questi capi, e ridotti li partigiani loro amici sua, aveva il duca gittati assai buoni fondamenti alla potenzia sua. (36)

> he put no further trust in the French [who had assisted him], nor in any other outside forces, since he found them too risky; so he turned to trickery. And he was so skillful in disguising his intentions that the Orsini themselves sought to be reconciled with him through the mediation of Signor Paolo

[Orsini], whom the duke tried to placate in every way conceivable, giving him money, fine clothes, and horses. Thus the simple-mindedness of the Orsini brought them to Sinigaglia, and into the duke's hands. And when he had killed all the leaders, and won over their followers to be his friends, the duke had laid excellent foundations for his power. (21)

Yet, if Borgia is an example of the necessity of relying on one's own power, including the ruses of representation, he is also, as Machiavelli recognized and as later Renaissance readers were quick to point out, a powerful illustration of the intrinsic irony of fortune. For while Borgia "acquired authority through his father's fortune," he also "lost it in the same way" (34, 19). The chapter thus enacts the dilemma that Pocock ascribes to *The Prince* as a whole: *virtù* is not only an attempt to control fortune but a source of the fortuitous and uncontrollable consequences of action as well (*MM*, 166).

In contrast to Borgia, Agathocles is presented in chapter 8 as a man who rose to power not by fortune but by crime. Yet few modern readers have noticed that Agathocles is presented as a counterexample to Borgia in another way as well. For while Borgia ruled over the Romagna for a month, Agathocles had a long and successful reign. Thus, ironically, Borgia is an example of failure to maintain control over the innovations he set in motion, while Agathocles is an example of success. If chapter 7 shows Borgia's use of representation as ruse and thus the mutual implication of representation and force, chapter 8 stages its own forceful misrepresentation in pretending to distinguish between *virtù* and crime. And it does so in order to suggest a possible response to the ironies of innovation dramatized in the example of Borgia. As we will see, the longevity of Agathocles's reign is related to a different sort of ruse of representation, according to which the exigencies of representing oneself to one's subjects prove to be a forceful constraint on tyrannical power.

Modern readers of *The Prince* have tended to interpret the example of Agathocles in one of two ways. In this narrative, some argue, Machiavelli registers his own discomfort with the notion of *virtù* he has been elaborating: it does violence to his sense of morality, as well as to his reader's. While some critics speak of Machiavelli's condemnation of Agathocles[14] others see the story as an illustration of a cruel but effective use of violence. The interpreters who fall into this camp then differ as to whether this use of violence is immoral or amoral.[15] But in neither case is Machiavelli's own interpretation of Agathocles as one who rose to power by crime subject to scrutiny.[16] Thus, although the proponents of the first interpretation note Machiavelli's qualification of Agathocles's actions ("non si può ancora chiamare virtù ammazzare li sua cittadini" [42]), they read this qualification as a simple pun ("It certainly cannot be called 'virtue' to murder his fellow citizens" [26]) and so save Machiavelli from the charge of failing to make moral distinctions. The second group of interpreters, in accepting the story of Agathocles as an illustration of the uses of crime rather than of *virtù*, make an analogous moral distinction between the excessive cruelty of Agathocles and the politic restraint of the man of *virtù*. Following from the story of Cesare Borgia in chapter 7, the next chapter serves, in these readings, to correct the reader who had begun to think *virtù* identical with crime: in chapter 8 Machiavelli reassures the reader by acknowledging a difference between the two.

Yet, there is hardly a less reassuring experience of reading in *The Prince* than that of chapter 8. And it is a chapter whose disturbing effect increases as we read on: although in chapter 6 Machiavelli describes the relation of *virtù* and *fortuna* as a dialectical one, he goes further in chapter 25 when he claims that *fortuna* and *virtù* divide the world of events between them. How, then, we wonder, could crime be a third term in Machiavelli's analysis of the way princes rise to power?

In spite of the title and the first paragraph of chapter 8, Machiavelli's introductory remarks about Agathocles seem to confirm the polar opposition of chapter 25. He tells us that Agathocles "joined to his villainies such *virtù* of mind and body that after enlisting in the army he rose through the ranks to become military governor of Syracuse" (41, 25). And a little further on he reiterates that Agathocles's success was due to *virtù*: "Considering the deeds and *virtù* of this man, one finds little or nothing that can be attributed to fortune" (41, 26). But then, anticipating his reader's objections, he quickly adds:

> Non si può ancora chiamare virtù ammazzare li sua cittadini, tradire li amici, essere sanza fede, sanza pietà, sanza relligione; li quali modi possono fare acquistare imperio, ma non gloria. Perché, se si considerassi la virtù di Agatocle nello intrare e nello uscire de' periculi, e la grandezza dello animo suo nel sopportare e superare le cose avverse, non si vede perché elli abbia ad essere iudicato inferiore a qualunque eccellentissimo capitano. Non di manco, la sua efferata crudeltà et inumanità, con infinite scelleratezze, non consentono che sia infra li eccellentissimi uomini celebrato. Non si può adunque attribuire alla fortuna o alla virtù quello che sanza l'una e l'altra fu da lui conseguito. (42)

> Yet it certainly cannot be called *virtù* to murder his fellow citizens, betray his friends, to be devoid of truth, pity, or religion; a man may get power by means like these, but not glory. If we consider simply the *virtù* of Agathocles in facing and escaping from dangers, and the greatness of his soul in sustaining and overcoming adversity, it is hard to see why he should be considered inferior to the greatest of captains. Nonetheless, his fearful cruelty and inhumanity, along with his innumerable crimes, prevent us from placing him among the really excellent men. For we can scarcely attribute to either fortune or *virtù* a conquest [quello] which he owed to neither. (26)

How are we to make sense of the vertiginous distinctions in this paragraph? Russell Price has suggested that Machiavelli is differentiating in this passage between the *virtù* and glory won by military leaders and the political *virtù* and glory that are attributes of "the really excellent men."[17] Of the former he writes:

> It seems that [Agathocles] . . . deserves credit for his martial spirit and deeds (that is, as a *capitano*) after he became ruler; what blackens his reputation is how he became ruler, because he treacherously slaughtered his friends and fellow citizens. Trickery and violence are to be condemned in a ruler or an aspiring ruler. . . . The stain he incurred by the way he seized power is indelible like original sin. (611)

As we will see, however, Agathocles is a shifty rhetorician and although the stain might be "like" original sin in ways that will be discussed more fully in part 2 of this book, no stain in this world of shifting shapes and meanings is indelible. Price's analysis fails to take account of the fact that Borgia also used trickery and violence to secure his power but is nevertheless not offered as an example of one who rose to power by crime. Furthermore, although Borgia is not condemned by Machiavelli, neither is he described as one of the really excellent men, a phrase, as Pocock reminds us, that refers to legislators rather than new princes (*MM*, 168).

A more sophisticated version of Price's analysis is presented by Claude Lefort, who argues that the introduction of the theme of glory in chapter 8 signals a turning point in the argument of *The Prince*. Whereas the earlier chapters were concerned with the necessary exercise of violence in the acquisition of power, chapter 8 introduces the necessity of favorably representing oneself to the people in order to hold on to one's power. And, whereas Machiavelli had previously emphasized the self-sufficiency of the prince, he now places the actions of the prince in the social context in which they acquire their real significance (380–81). In Lefort's reading, *virtù* is neither identical with nor exclusive of crime, but it does require glory, which eventually induces the prince to moderate his behavior and take a greater interest in the welfare of his people. Because Machiavelli refuses to ascribe glory to Agathocles, he cannot really be considered a man of *virtù*.

In the end, if Lefort is not as reassuring as those readers who claim that Machiavelli is asserting a clear-cut distinction between crime and *virtù*, he nevertheless claims that there is a distinction between Borgia and Agathocles, one that does not lie in the nature of their deeds, since both were guilty of criminal behavior, but rather in the fact that the deeds of the latter "were committed without justification, or without pretext, by a man whom nothing, except his ambition, destined to reign . . . a man— Machiavelli took the trouble to point out—*di infima e abjetta fortuna*, the simple son of a potter" (380). It is not so much the crimes of Agathocles that constitute his original sin, according to Lefort, as his lowly birth. But this interpretation trivializes both the notion of representation and that of fortune in *The Prince*, neither of which, as Lefort elsewhere recognizes, is a static concept according to which the bad fortune of lowly birth would forever restrict Agathocles's possibilities for acquiring glory or representing himself in a favorable light.[18] In fact, by the end of the chapter, Agathocles is offered as an example of someone who used cruelty well rather than badly, and who consequently was "able to reassure people, and win them over to his side with benefits" (44, 28). It would seem, then, that far from excluding Agathocles from the category of representative men of *virtù*, Machiavelli goes out of his way to stress his inclusion. That he refuses to ascribe glory to Agathocles may then suggest that Machiavelli is playing on *gloria* in much the same way that he plays on *virtù*: unlike Moses in chapter 6, Agathocles was not favored with heavenly glory but he was successful nonetheless.

As we have seen, most readings of chapter 8 respond to the pressure to make distinctions that is implicit in the apparently contradictory reiteration of *virtù*. But it is important to see that clear-cut or permanent distinctions finally cannot be made. Throughout *The Prince* Machiavelli sets up concepts in polar opposition to each other and then shows how the opposition is contained within each term so that the whole notion of opposition must be redefined.[19] Thus in chapter 25 he begins by telling the reader that "fortune governs one half of our actions, but that even so she leaves the other half more or less in our power to control." Fortune is then presented as a natural force, a torrential stream against which men can take countermeasures "while the weather is still fine." But this opposition is a generalization that undergoes startling revision when we come to "the particulars." For a man's ability to take countermeasures—his *virtù*—turns out to be a fact of (his) nature and thus a potential disaster over which he has no control:

> se uno che si governa con respetti e pazienzia, e' tempi e le cose girono in modo che il governo suo sia buono, e' viene felicitando; ma se li tempi e le cose si mutano, rovina, perché non muta modo di procedere. Né si truova uomo sí prudente, che si sappi accomodare a questo; sí perché non si può deviare da quello a che la natura l'inclina, sí etiam perché, avendo sempre uno prosperato camminando per una via, non si può persuadere partirsi da quella. (100)

> If a prince conducts himself with patience and caution, and the times and circumstances are favorable to those qualities, he will flourish; but if times and circumstances change, he will come to his ruin unless he changes his method of proceeding. No man, however prudent, can adjust to such radical

changes, not only because we cannot go against the inclination of nature, but also because when one has always prospered by following a particular course, he cannot be persuaded to leave it. (71)

In this more particular view, human nature is itself a torrential stream that cannot redirect its course with dikes and restraining dams: the favorable constraints are instead introduced by fortune. The purely formal *virtù* that is the ability to "adjust one's behavior to the temper of the times"—and that is precisely *not* constancy of character—is not a quality that can be attributed once and for all: it is rather a generalization that designates only the fortunate coincidence of "nature's livery and fortune's star." Or, as Machiavelli writes of men of *virtù* in chapter 6, "Without the opportunity their *virtù* of mind would have been in vain, and without that *virtù* the opportunity would have been lost" (31, 17).

If we now return to chapter 8, we can begin to see why Machiavelli cannot call Agathocles's crimes virtuous. In the light of chapter 25 it seems we should place an even stronger emphasis on *called*: neither in the case of Borgia nor in the case of Agathocles can crime be called *virtù*, because *virtù* cannot be *called* any one thing. In short, once the temporal dimension of circumstance is introduced, the fact that crime cannot necessarily be called *virtù* means also that it can be called *virtù*. The danger of the preceding chapter 7 is not only that we might identify Borgia's murder and treachery with *virtù* but also that we would identify *virtù* with any particular act—criminal or not. The aim of the passage in chapter 8 is to dehypostatize *virtù*, to empty it of any specific meaning. For *virtù* is not a general rule of behavior that could be applied to a specific situation but rather, like prudence, a faculty of deliberation about particulars.

This reading is borne out by the end of chapter 8, where Machiavelli makes a distinction between two sorts of cruelty—between cruelty used well or badly—thereby placing the distinction between crime and *virtù* within cruelty itself:

Bene usate si possono chiamare quelle (se del male è licito dire bene) che si fanno ad un tratto, per necessità dello assicurarsi, e di poi non vi si insiste dentro, ma si convertiscono in piú utilità de' sudditi che si può. (44)

Cruelty can be called well used (if it's permissible to speak well about something that is evil in itself) when it is performed all at once, for reasons of self-preservation; and when the acts are not repeated after that, but rather are turned as much as possible to the advantage of the subjects. (27–28; translation modified)

Once again the emphasis is on *chiamare* ("Bene usate si possono chiamare"), but here the temporal dimension is explicit, as is the consequent and necessary making of distinctions within cruelty. And once again, in the parenthetical remark Machiavelli speaks to the reader's moral sensibility—but he has answered the implied question even before it has been posed. Cruelty *can* be called "well used" because Machiavelli has just done so in the preceding clause. The adverbial *bene* then takes on some of the paronomastic color of the earlier paragraph on *virtù*. The reader wonders if it is permissible to speak good words (*bene*) about evil, while Machiavelli replies by speaking well (*bene*).[20]

These lines are important because they contain in miniature Machiavelli's critique of humanism. The humanist's assumption that *honestas* is compatible with *utilitas*, reflected in the maxim that the good orator is necessarily a good man, is politically useless to Machiavelli, however it is interpreted. When the goodness of the orator is interpreted to mean in conformity with ethical goodness (*honestas*), then the maxim is a stoic tautology and the question of the orator's effectiveness (*utilitas*) need not enter in. When the orator's goodness is interpreted to mean persuasiveness, as well as moral rectitude, then the claim that the orator is a good man is a synthetic judgment that is also idealistic and unfounded. One has only to look to experience to see that many morally good men have been politically ineffective. Here the criterion of correct action is not moral goodness or the intrinsically moral judgment of prudence but the functional excellence or effectiveness of *virtù*: a *virtù* we might say, parodying Aristotle, that demonstrates its own excellence in being effective.[21] In speaking well rather than speaking good words, Machiavelli both dramatizes and thematizes this functional virtuosity. He shows that *virtù* is not a substance but a mode of action (not a noun, but an adverb) by speaking well about acting well.

The linguistic play of this paragraph and the earlier one on *virtù* are thus part of a rhetorical strategy to engage the reader in a critical activity that will allow him to discover not the content of "what should be" but the formality of what in any particular situation "can be."[22] If the reader's "natural" disposition to make moral distinctions ("everyone agrees") may be compared to the natural force of the river which serves as a metaphor for fortune in chapter 25, Machiavelli's prose is the countermeasure that attempts to channel or redirect this course by introducing the element of reflection. Because his goal is to make the reader deliberate more effectively about the realm of practical political action, he duplicates on the rhetorical level the practical problem of judgment that the prince will have to face—that of applying the rule of *virtù* to the particular situation at hand. Or, as Roland Barthes has written of Machiavelli's work, "The structure of the discourse attempts to reproduce the structure of the dilemmas actually faced by the protagonists. In this case reasoned argument predominates and the history [or discourse] is of a reflexive—one might say strategic—style."[23]

Theatricality

That Machiavelli's style is strategic means not only that the prince may learn something about strategy by reflecting on Machiavelli's prose (the syntax, structure, and vocabulary of his examples) but also that the actual strategies he recounts may tell us something about Machiavelli's strategy as a writer. This reciprocity in turn allows us to read the example of Agathocles in the light of Machiavelli's earlier remarks on Borgia. As a number of critics have remarked, Machiavelli's position as a counselor is in some ways analogous to that of the new prince. Both are "student[s] of delegitimized politics" (*MM*, 163), and for both the problem is how to impose a new form not only on matter but on an already informed matter. But Machiavelli's *virtù* as a writer is not simply, as some readers have suggested, to dramatize in *The Prince* the resourcefulness and inventiveness of the effective ruler but also to manipulate his audience in much the same way that the prince must manipulate his subjects.[24] In the first case, imitation involves the cultivation of a purely formal flexibility of judgment or *disponibilità*; in the second, that judgment is tested by the appearances of the text itself. Thus in chapter 7 Machiavelli proposes Borgia's behavior in the Romagna as an example worthy of imitation, and in chapter 8 he imitates it in order to test whether the reader has learned the lesson of chapter 7. In short, there are striking analogies not only between the careers of Borgia and Agathocles but also between the effect of Borgia's behavior on his subjects in the Romagna and Machiavelli's effect on the reader in chapter 8.

When Borgia took over the Romagna he discovered that "the whole province was full of robbers, feuds, and lawlessness of every description" (37, 22). His way of "establish[ing] peace and reduc[ing] the land to obedience" was to counter lawlessness with lawlessness: "He named Messer Remirro De Orco, a cruel and vigorous man, to whom he gave absolute powers. In short order this man pacified and unified the whole district, winning great renown" (37, 22). But like Agathocles, Borgia knew that excessive authority can become odious:

> e proposevi uno iudicio civile nel mezzo della provincia, con uno presidente eccellentissimo, dove ogni città vi aveva lo avvocato suo. E, perché conosceva le rigorosità passate averli generato qualche odio, per purgare li animi

di quelli populi e gaudagnarseli in tutto, volle monstrare che, se crudeltà alcuna era seguíta, non era nata da lui, ma dalla acerba natura del ministro. E, presa sopr'a questo occasione, lo fece mettere una mattina a Cesena in dua pezzi in sulla piazza, con uno pezzo di legno et uno coltello sanguinoso a canto. La ferocità del quale spettaculo fece quelli populi in uno tempo rimanere satisfatti e stupidi. (37)

so he set up a civic court in the middle of the province, with an excellent judge and a representative from each city. And because he knew that the recent harshness had generated some hatred, in order to clear the minds of the people and gain them over to his cause completely, he determined to make plain that whatever cruelty had occurred had come, not from him, but from the brutal character of the minister. Taking a proper occasion, therefore, he had him placed on the public square of Cesena one morning, in two pieces, with a piece of wood beside him and a bloody knife. The ferocity of this scene left the people at once stunned and satisfied. (22)

This story provides us with two examples of cruelty well used. The first is De Orco's, the second Borgia's. The function of the first is primarily destructive and repressive: to pacify his subjects; the function of the second is theatrical and cathartic: this, too, pacifies the subjects but by the theatrical display of violence rather than its direct application to the audience. The first example reestablishes justice from the perspective of the ruler; the second stages this reestablishment from the perspective of and for the ruled. As this theatrical display suggests, the story also provides us with two examples of representation well used. In the first case, there is an element of representation insofar as Borgia delegates his power, but this delegation is ultimately a way of concealing the fact of representation (that is, representation has become ruse) so that he can deny responsibility for De Orco's cruelty—as he does so effectively by means of (and this is the second example) his theatrical representation in the square of Cesena.

The example of Agathocles in chapter 8 is just such a theatrical display on the part of Machiavelli. Like Borgia, Machiavelli is concerned to make distinctions between *virtù* and crime—not because they are mutually exclusive but because they are not identical. And like Borgia, he sets up a court with the reader as judge. "He determined to make plain that whatever cruelty had occurred [in the example of Agathocles] had come, not from him, but from the brutal character of his minister" (that is, of his example). The reader is morally satisfied or reassured by Machiavelli's supposed condemnation of Agathocles, just as the people of the Romagna were by the dramatic and brutal disavowal of Remirro's brutality. But the reader who is taken in by this excuse is in the position of a subject rather than a prince—for Machiavelli has not presented the example of Agathocles in order to pacify his readers but rather to try them. In short, Agathocles is proposed as an example for the prince who might need to follow him, and the ability to determine that necessity is also the *virtuous* ability to make discriminations about what constitutes *virtù* with respect to any given situation. The example of Agathocles is a test of *virtù*.

Force and Persuasion: Agathocles as Machiavel and Proto-Republican

As the preceding analysis has demonstrated, if Agathocles is the archetypal Machiavel, using force and fraud, so is Borgia: in this regard there is no difference between them. The difference lies rather in the longevity of their reigns, for while Borgia ruled over the Romagna for a month, Agathocles the Sicilian ruled over Syracuse until the end of his life. And he did so in part because of his greater rhetorical flexibility, his ability to respond to circumstances and to change with the times. Agathocles knows what the reader comes to learn through Machiavelli's dehypostatizing rhetoric: *virtù* cannot be simply equated, once and for all, with violence or deception or what we would call crime. For if the goal of the prince or tyrant is to "mantenere lo stato" (maintain his power), he will eventually have to moderate his use of force and fraud and take into account the interests of his subjects.

We can now see that Machiavelli stages the distinction between *virtù* and crime not only to test the reader's acceptance of his demoralized politics but also to highlight the difference between cruelty used well or badly, for it is this difference that explains "how it happened that Agathocles and others of his ilk, after they had committed so many acts of treachery and cruelty, could live long, secure lives in their native cities," while "other princes were unable, because of their cruelty, to maintain their power" (44, 27). The rhetorical strategy that undermines the simple distinction between *virtù* and crime by stressing the rhetorical criterion of good usage ("bene usate") also shows the link between tyranny and republicanism. The exercise of force must be governed by rhetorical circumstances of occasion and the exigencies of persuasion; like glory, these considerations will lead the prince to modify his behavior:

> Onde è da notare che, nel pigliare uno stato, debbe l'occupatore di esso discorrere tutte quelle offese che li è necessario fare, e tutte farle a uno tratto, per non le avere a rinnovare ogni dí, e potere, non le innovando, assicurare

li uomini e guadagnarseli con benificargli. Chi fa altrimenti, o per timidità o per mal consiglio, è sempre necessitato tenere el cotello in mano; né mai può fondarsi sopra li sua sudditi, non si potendo quelli per le fresche e continue iniurie, assicurare di lui. . . . E debbe sopr'a tutto uno principe vivere con li sua sudditi in modo, che veruno accidente o di male o di bene lo abbia a far variare: perché, venendo per li tempi avversi, le necessità, tu non se' a tempo al male, et il bene che tu fai non ti giova, perché è iudicato forzato, e non te n'è saputo grado alcuno. (44)

We may add this note that when a prince takes a new state, he should calculate the sum of all the injuries he will have to do, and do them all at once, so as not to have to do new ones every day; simply by not repeating them, he will thus be able to reassure the people, and win them over to his side with benefits. Whoever believes otherwise, either through fearfulness or bad advice, must always keep his knife in hand, and he can never count on his subjects, because their fresh and recurring injuries keep them suspicious of him. . . . Above all, a prince should live with his subjects on such terms that no accident, whether favorable or unfavorable, can force him to change his conduct. When misfortune strikes, harsh measures are too late, and the good things you do are not counted to your credit because you seem to have acted under compulsion, and no one will thank you for that. (28)

The prince who is forced to use force or forced to do good things has lost the rhetorical control that allows him to choose force as a means of persuasion. He has become a creature of necessity rather than master of it. Conversely, it is precisely the concern with maintaining power that persuades the prince to change his conduct, to substitute persuasion—reassuring the people and winning them over to your side—for brute force. Once force is seen as one weapon among many in the prince's rhetorical arsenal, it is no longer simply opposed to persuasion and consent but logically—that is, dialectically—related to them. The concern with persuasion thus becomes a check upon the exercise of force at the same time that it holds out the promise of controlling the process of innovation ("non le innovando") that the prince has set in motion. If chapters 7 and 8 (among others in *The Prince*) provide an immanent critique of the humanist ideals of imitation and persuasion by showing that a truly flexible political rhetoric includes the previously excluded resources of crime, chapter 8 also provides an immanent critique of tyranny by showing how the same flexible rhetoric may lead the tyrant to alter the foundations of his power. If the tyrant's concern is to maintain his power and keep his subjects obedient, he will in the long run have to take into account—represent and respond to—the interests of his subjects. Chapter 8 thus looks forward to the discussion of civil principalities in chapter 9, in which Machiavelli insists that "the prince must have people well disposed toward him" (47, 30). It also anticipates the argument for republicanism in the *Discourses*.

Virtù and Success, Ends and Means

The paired examples of Borgia and Agathocles are illustrative in another way as well. While chapter 8 shows the rhetorical considerations that lead from tyranny to republicanism, the example of Borgia's failure in chapter 7 serves to remind us that success—including the successful transition from tyranny to a republic—is not a necessary consequence of *virtù*. It is because success is not guaranteed that *virtù* can be attributed both to Cesare Borgia, who failed to achieve his ultimate goal, and to Agathocles, who succeeded.

This uncertainty concerning the relation of *virtù* to success is reflected in Machiavelli's claim to be guided by the "verità effettuale della cosa." On the one hand, he means that he will approach politics realistically, rather than idealistically, by beginning with things as they are. On the other hand, implicit in the claim to be guided by the "verità effettuale" is the assumption that such an approach will prove to be effective: that one does not simply imitate necessity but that one can manipulate it—effect it—to one's own advantage. Yet, while Machiavelli argues in chapter 15 that *virtù* involves knowledge that is useful or effective, he does not want to claim that *virtù* guarantees success. To make this claim would be to fall into a version of the equation of *honestas* and *utilitas* that he condemns in the same chapter. If *virtù* always yielded success, then there would be no fortune or contingency; but contingency is precisely what makes room for *virtù*—indeed, what makes *virtù* necessary in Machiavelli's eyes. Still, a *virtù* that never resulted in success would be patently absurd. Thus Machiavelli claims early in *The Prince* that if we follow the examples of *virtù* that he presents, success will usually or most often result (12, 11).

Once we understand the contingent relation between *virtù* and success, we are in a better position to understand Machiavelli's revision of the humanists' prudential rhetoric, as well as his critics' reduction of such rhetoric to the justification of the means by the end. Machiavellian *virtù* is structurally like the classical and humanist notion of prudence or practical reason, as opposed to technical or instrumental reason. Whereas the former involves an activity of deliberation which is an end in itself, the latter involves deliberation about the best means to a given end. Those many critics who argue that *virtù* is a technical skill are right if they mean by this that the prince is concerned with results, but wrong if they equate *virtù* with the result rather than with deliberative skill and energy in action. *Virtù* is not completely technical because technical skill must result in a product (however much that product may reflect a compromise with one's original conception of the object), while *virtù* does not have to produce something else in order to be *virtù*. Or, as Martin Ostwald observes, "Practical wisdom is itself a complete virtue or excellence while the excellence of an art depends on the goodness or badness of the product" (*NE*, 154 n. 20). Like prudence, *virtù* implies practical success but does not guarantee it. Unlike prudence, however, it implies nothing whatsoever about the compatibility of the practical wisdom of *virtù* with ethical norms.

In his demoralization of prudence, Machiavelli implies that the humanist view of politics is not rhetorical enough. For all the humanist emphasis on prudence as a faculty of deliberation about particulars, the insistence that prudence also be ethical amounts to a refusal to admit that to be ethical in every case is harmful and impractical. A truly rhetorical view of politics does not simply consider rhetoric as a means to realizing some extrinsic ethical norm; rather, as Felix Gilbert remarked in a different context, "the measure of worth of a political figure [is] . . . formed by his capacity to use the possibilities inherent in the political situations; politics [has] its own criteria to be derived from existing political opportunities."[25] Thus Machiavelli's rhetorical politics confounds the usual distinctions between means and ends because it involves a mode of action that both is an end in itself and aims at success.[26] *Virtù* is the rhetorical and prudential faculty that allows one to maintain power but is not identical with success in doing so.

From the perspective of his critics, however, *virtù* seems to involve the simple justification of the means by the end. Like the critics of rhetoric, critics of *virtù* charge it with substituting expediency for morality, the goal of success for that of virtue, and thus sanctioning the use of immoral means for the end of maintaining the state. It is a striking feature of *The Prince* that Machiavelli takes into account this interpretation of his work. In fact, he ascribes this interpretation to the moralizing masses who would appear to condemn it. Thus in chapter 18, "The Way Princes Should Keep Their Word," Machiavelli seems first to invite the reading of *virtù* in terms of means and ends when he advises the prince to feign the virtues in order to preserve his state. Yet in the next paragraph he characterizes the masses as follows:

E li uomini in universali iudicano piú alli occhi che alle mani; perché tocca a vedere a ognuno, a sentire a pochi. Ognuno vede quello che tu pari, pochi sentono quello che tu se'; e quelli pochi non ardiscano opporsi alla opinione di molti, che abbino la maestà dello stato che li difenda: e nelle azioni di tutti li uomini, e massime de' principi, dove non è iudizio da reclamare, si guarda al fine. Facci dunque uno principe di vincere e mantenere lo stato: e' mezzi saranno sempre iudicati onorevoli, e da ciascuno laudati; perché el vulgo ne va preso con quello che pare e con lo evento della cosa; e nel mondo non è se non vulgo. (74)

Men in general judge more by the sense of sight than by the sense of touch, because everyone can see but only a few can test by feeling. Everyone sees what you seem to be, few know what you really are; and those few dare not take a stand against the general opinion, supported by the majesty of government. In the actions of all men, and especially of princes who are not subject to a court of appeal, we must always look to the end. Let a prince, therefore, win victories and uphold his state; his methods will always be considered worthy, and everyone will praise them, because the masses are always impressed by the superficial appearance of things, and by the outcome of an enterprise. And the world consists of nothing but the masses. (51)

In this passage Machiavelli anticipates one prominent interpretation of his work in the sixteenth and seventeenth centuries and, at the same time, makes this interpretation a topic of invention for the successful prince. It is the people who justify the means by the end, who are incapable of appreciating examples such as that of Borgia, a man of *virtù* who failed to maintain his power. So the prince should incorporate this common opinion into his repertoire of political argument but he should not confuse it with *virtù*.

Irony and Allegory

> Irony descends from the low mimetic: it begins in realism and
> dispassionate observation. But as it does so, it moves steadily
> towards myth, and dim outlines of sacrificial rituals and dying
> gods begin to reappear in it.
> —*Northrop Frye*

As I have argued in the preceding pages, Machiavelli's reflection on the political uses of imitation is tied to his revision of the humanist concept of prudential action. The prince is powerful to the extent that he diverges from a naive or moral concept of prudence, but he also maintains his power by "naively" imitating—or representing himself as faithfully reproducing—the conventional virtues. As in chapter 18, power is in part, if not entirely, the effect of the rhetorical illusion of truth. But, as the case of Agathocles demonstrates, the exigencies of persuasion, conceived of now as the means or the ability to generate the consensus and support of the people, also finally prove to be a forceful constraint on the abuse of power (see chap. 18:74, 51; *D*, 2.23, 3.19–23). Cruelty will be well used if "it is performed all at once, for reasons of self-preservation; and when the acts are not repeated after that, but rather turned as much as possible to the advantage of the subjects" (chap. 8:44, 27–28). The prince must in the long run please his audience if he is to maintain his rule. In the end, the use of the rhetorical topic of virtue proves to involve an ironic version of the ethical constraint that the humanists located in custom and consensus. More than this, it proves to generate consensus itself. This constraint also helps us to see how the analysis of power in *The Prince* logically gives way to that of the *Discourses*: if the prince is to be a man of *virtù* in the long run, he must found a republic, because republics are capable of greater longevity and greater *virtù* than principalities. The understanding reader will see that when representation and force are mutually implicated, when representation becomes a means of power, and thus when power is mitigated by the exigencies of persuasion, the short-lived individual self-aggrandizement of the prince gives way to communal glory, and the prince becomes a fellow citizen.[27]

This is the optimistic way to read the self-destructing rhetoric of *The Prince*, and I will pursue such a reading in the following chapter on the *Discourses*. But, as most readers have noted, there is a way in which the analysis of *virtù* undermines itself and Machiavelli's pedagogy in *The Prince*: for a perfectly dehypostatized *virtù* threatens to turn into its opposite, a *virtù* of demonic or allegorical stability. Here, as we will see, Machiavelli's text anticipates Milton's linking of the Machiavel's rhetorical flexibility with the "fixed mind" of Satan (*PL*, 1.97).

As Machiavelli tells us again and again, there are no general rules for virtuous behavior, and there is no guarantee that the skill one practices in the interpretation of particular examples will enable one to respond appropriately in the next situation (e.g., chap. 20:85, 59). This is, of course, as it should be. As Machiavelli writes in chapter 21, "No leader should ever suppose he can invariably take the safe course, since all choice involves risks. In the nature of things [*nell'ordine delle cose*] you can never try to escape one danger without encountering another; but prudence consists in knowing how to recognize the nature of the different dangers and in accepting the least bad as good" (92, 65). But the essential emptiness of the concept of *virtù* receives a rather different and potentially devastating articulation in chapter 25, where the role of fortune in the individual's ability to act virtuously seems to deprive the individual of any initiative whatsoever. As we saw, Machiavelli begins this chapter by discussing the relation of fortune and *virtù* in general terms. On this level he gives fortune a certain stability, as though fortune were something external to *virtù* that the latter had only to resist. When he descends to particulars, however, fortune has no stability whatsoever. The irony of politics becomes so great—the possibility of action so compromised—that the distance constitutive of reflection finally collapses altogether. To recognize which situations require which kinds of imitation finally necessitates that the prince imitate the absolute flexibility of fortune itself. But one's ability to learn is itself a function of the *fortune* of one's natural disposition and is necessarily limited by it. In thus conflating the agent of *virtù* with the realm of nature, Machiavelli runs the risk of reducing *virtù* to the mere repetition—that is, the willed acceptance—of necessity.[28] In so doing, he also risks substituting for the equation of *honestas* and *utilitas* that of *virtù* and success. It is not surprising, then, that Machiavelli should at this moment invoke the personified figure of Fortune as a woman in a desperate, inconsequential attempt to redeem the possibility of action by relocating it in an interpersonal context.[29] Thus he writes in the famous conclusion to chapter 25, "But I do feel this: that it is better to be rash than timid, for Fortune is a woman, and the man who wants to hold her down must beat and bully her" (101, 72).

A few remarks about the allegorical tendency of *The Prince* may help to clarify this point. According to Angus Fletcher, the allegorical hero confronts a world of contingency, a world in which the individual has little control over the consequences of his actions, and in which there often seems to be little causal connection between events.[30] Narrative sequence is threatened by parataxis but restored on the level of cosmic, often magical necessity.[31] As a result, the hero also seems not simply at the mercy of external events but in the control of some external power. In fact, the allegorical hero could be said to operate in a world of demonic powers, a world in which functions have been compartmentalized and personified. The hero, too, becomes depersonalized, no longer a person but a mere personification of a function. In a world of Fortuna, in short, the hero becomes, of necessity, the embodiment of *Virtù*.

In such a world, the virtues no longer seem to be attributes of individual agents; rather, they recover their original sense of powers or forces, of *virtù*. As Fletcher remarks, "Like a Machiavellian prince, the allegorical hero can act free of the usual moral restraints, even when he is acting morally, since he is moral only in the interests of his power over men" (68). To redefine virtue as *virtù* is thus "to rediscover a sense of the morally ambivalent power in action" (an advance one might say in the direction of realism) but it is also, ironically, to run the risk of doing away with free will. Although the intention behind Machiavelli's various examples of *virtù* is to help the reader understand the formal, innovative character of this faculty, and the role of the will in determining what constitutes *virtù* in any particular situation, the quasi-allegorical status of the man of *virtù*, or of the prince as a personification of *Virtù*, suggests that the individual is not at all in control of his behavior—a suggestion that, as we have seen, becomes explicit in chapter 25. The way Machiavelli chooses to combat this demonization or personification of the person is to repersonalize what was becoming an increasingly abstract and unmanageable concept of fortune by introducing the figure of Fortune as a woman. In a kind of parody of humanist rhetoric *in utramque partem*, allegory is used to fight the allegorization or reification of the prince's *virtù*.

In light of these remarks, one can also see how the allegorical tendency of *The Prince* is manifest in the sublime rhetoric of the concluding chapter. Fletcher calls our attention to the structural similarity between allegory and the sublime. Simply stated, the experience of the sublime begins with the failure of the imagination to comprehend sensuous experience. This failure leads to the demand for comprehension on the part of reason and thus to an awareness of reason as a higher faculty and as proof of a destiny that transcends mere nature. This discrepancy between sensuous experience and the higher claims of reason is analogous to the separation between the sign and signified in the allegorical text. Furthermore, as Longinus reminds us, allegory is not only analogous to the sublime but can itself have a sublime effect, an ideological or epideictic force, when it "incites to action." But, as the epigraph to this section suggests, allegory and the sublime can also have an ironic effect, by suggesting that the principle of authority or meaning or *virtù* (e.g., reason, God) is infinitely removed from the world of sensuous immediacy.[32] Chapter 26 supports both optimistic and pessimistic or ironic readings of its sublime rhetoric.

Machiavelli obviously intends the rhetoric of his concluding chapter to function as the best of all hyperboles: to incite the Medici to action. Thus he argues that the opportunities facing the Medici in Italy are analogous to the occasions that allowed the exemplary figures of Moses, Cyrus, and Theseus to exercise their *virtù*. And he presents the Medici as the providentially destined saviors of Italy:

> Né ci si vede al presente in quale lei possa piú sperare che nella illustre casa vostra, quale con la sua fortuna e virtù, favorita da Dio e dalla Chiesia della quale è ora principe, possa farsi capo di questa redenzione. (102)

> There is no figure presently in sight in whom she [Italy] can better trust than your illustrious house, which, with its fortune and its *virtù*, favored by God and the Church of which it is now the head, can take the lead in this process of redemption. (73)

In these lines Machiavelli wittily conflates the fortune of the Medici with divine providence and the Church, and thus simultaneously debases religion and confers a certain grandeur on the rulers of Florence.[33] As this formulation should suggest, here and in the following paragraph Machiavelli also flatters the Medici by ironically exposing such providential rhetoric as a ruse of political necessity. Commenting on the exemplary figures of *virtù*—Moses, Cyrus, and Theseus—he writes:

> E benché quelli uomini sieno rari e maravigliosi, non di manco furono uomini, et ebbe ciascuno di loro minore occasione che la presente: perché l'impresa loro non fu piú iusta di questa, né piú facile, né fu a loro Dio piú amico che a voi. Qui è iustizia grande: *iustum enim est bellum quibus necessarium, et pia arma ubi nulla nisi in armis spes est.* (102–103)

> Men of this sort are rare and wonderful, indeed, but they were nothing more than men, and each of them faced circumstances less promising than those of the present. Their cause was no more just than the present one, nor any easier, and God was no more favorable to them than to you. Your cause is just: "for war is justified when it is necessary, and arms are pious when without them there would be no hope at all." (73)

Here Machiavelli suggests that the Medici have the opportunity to be like Moses, who should be "admired, if only for that grace which made him worthy of talking with God" (30, 16), especially if—like Moses and Machiavelli—they know how to dress up necessity as providence. He also intimates that "providential justification" will follow upon political necessity—approval upon success. As Machiavelli writes in chapter 18, a prince's "methods will always be considered worthy, and everyone will praise them . . . because the masses are always impressed . . . by the outcome of an enterprise" (74, 51).

In its divine justification of the Medici as the redeemers of Italy, chapter 26 is the final, brilliant example of Machiavelli's theatrical overshooting of the mark, of a rhetoric that is neither constrained by logic to represent the truth nor guided by practical reason in its achievement of ethical decorum but that aims rather to produce the effect of truth—and to achieve success. Yet the obvious alternative reading of the lines quoted above is that the rhetoric of providential justification is mere hyperbole—a desperate gesture to respond to the dilemmas of chapter 25 that paradoxically amounts to a sublime exposure of the inefficacy of human reason and *virtù*.[34] In this way, the collapse of the distance and difference necessary for action in chapter 25 turns out to anticipate the providential rhetoric of chapter 26, a rhetoric that appears to have been designed precisely to recoup the losses of the preceding chapter. In this concluding chapter it seems that exaggeration may not free itself "from the weight of the factual, so that instead of merely reproducing being it can, at once rigorous and free, determine it."[35] In a final ironic twist, Machiavelli's providential rhetoric then seems to suggest that only God can save us from such ironies. In some situations, however, republicanism also proves to be an inspired response to the ironies of political action.

TWO

THE DISCOURSES

WHILE *The Prince* illustrates the role of rhetorical politics in principalities, the *Discourses* argues that this rhetorical flexibility is a structural feature of the life of republics and the reason for their superiority to other forms of government:

> una republica ha maggiore vita ed ha piú lungamente buona fortuna che uno principato, perché la può meglio accomodarsi alla diversità de' temporali, per la diversità de' cittadini che sono in quella, che non può uno principe. Perché un uomo che sia consueto a procedere in uno modo, non si muta mai, come è detto; e conviene di necessità che quando e' si mutano i tempi disformi a quel suo modo che rovini. (3.9.417–18)

> a republic has a fuller life and enjoys good fortune for a longer time than a principality, since it is better able to adapt itself to diverse circumstances owing to the diversity found among its citizens than a prince can do. For a man who is accustomed to act in one particular way never changes, as we have said. Hence when times change and no longer suit his ways, he is inevitably ruined. (431)

In proposing that republics are better able to respond to change and contingency, the *Discourses* responds to what Pocock has described as the "original sin" of Machiavellian politics: precisely because the prince's *virtù* is a source of innovation, it also sets in motion patterns of action whose consequences are beyond the prince's control.[1] If *The Prince* reveals a politicized version of original sin, of the unforeseen results of individual action and the inability of the prince to change with changing circumstances, the *Discourses* offers a politicized version of paradise regained, a this-worldly republic whose greater *virtù* is generated from among its citizens. Yet, while the *Discourses* responds to the problems of innovation and stability dramatized in *The Prince* by showing that the flexibility demanded by a rhetorical politics leads logically to republicanism, like *The Prince* it rejects the identification of *virtù* with success. Machiavelli's rhetorical politics makes republicanism a more plausible argument for political longevity, but it cannot guarantee the republic as the necessary result of tyranny in practice.

Despite the overt argument in favor of republicanism, Renaissance readers recognized that the *Discourses* and *The Prince* were similar in topic and method. They saw that in both texts Machiavelli recommends the use of force and fraud, the theatrical display of violence, the politic feigning of religion; in both he argues that political legitimacy is a consequence of de facto power combined with the arts of persuasion; and in both he attacks the assumptions of humanist rhetoric and imitation, while borrowing from them in practice. Judging from the (usually unattributed) quotation of Machiavelli's works by Renaissance readers, often no distinction was made between *The Prince* and the *Discourses*, while those readers who did comment on the republicanism of the *Discourses* tended to see it as the logical outcome of Machiavelli's description of tyranny in *The Prince*.

My aim in this chapter is to propose an interpretation of the *Discourses* in conformity with these observations and thus to further my reader's appreciation of the Renaissance reception of Machiavelli's rhetorical politics. While in chapter 1 I was particularly concerned with the vexed topics that later Renaissance readers came to associate with the Machiavel, in this chapter I want to elucidate the dual reception of Machiavelli as dispassionate political analyst purveying a storehouse of political arguments and as idealistic republican offering a critique of the status quo. First, I demonstrate that the *Discourses*, like *The Prince*, offers a critique of the humanist doctrine of imitation and its moralizing rhetoric of exemplarity; and I argue that, like *The Prince*, the *Discourses* dramatizes a tension between a practical and an instrumental conception of rhetoric—between rhetoric as a critique of the status quo and rhetoric as the neutral codification of argument. Second, I illustrate the critical use of rhetoric by analyzing Machiavelli's attack on the humanists' rhetoric of consensus and his related argument for the superiority of the Roman republic to other forms of government. Finally, I show how Machiavelli's own examples undermine the republican thrust of his text by offering political strategies that are equally relevant to the prince.

Ridutte in ordine: Reading Livy

We can begin our exploration of the rhetorical politics of the *Discourses* by turning to Machiavelli's remarks on his method in the proem to book 1. As in *The Prince*, Machiavelli uses the humanist vocabulary of imitation to stage his own innovation in politics. In particular, he attacks the aestheticizing tendency of humanist imitation, offering in its place a systematic reduction of ancient history to a compendium of useful examples, whose intended effect is to revive Florentine *virtù*. While generations of readers have remarked on Machiavelli's reductive and fragmentary style, viewing it as a sign of Machiavelli's break with his predecessors or of his fatal love of dramatic effect, it has not generally been recognized that Machiavelli explicitly redefines humanist imitation in terms of reduction. *Reducere* (to reduce to smaller compass and to lead back) describes not only Machiavelli's method in collecting examples but also his exemplary *return* to the first principles of the Roman republic. Consider the following passage:

> Considerando adunque quanto onore si attribuisca all'antiquità, e come molte volte, lasciando andare infiniti altri esempli, un frammento d'una antiqua statua sia suto comperato gran prezzo, per averlo appresso di sé, onorarne la sua casa e poterlo fare imitare a coloro che di quella arte si dilettono, e come quegli dipoi con ogni industria si sforzono in tutte le loro opere rappresentarlo; e veggiendo da l'altro canto le virtuosissime operazioni che le istorie ci mostrono, che sono state operate da regni e da republiche antique, dai re, capitani, cittadini, latori di leggi ed altri che si sono per la loro patria affaticati, essere piú presto ammirate che imitate, anzi, in tanto da ciascuno in ogni minima cosa fuggite, che di quella antiqua virtù non ci è rimasto alcun segno: non posso fare che insieme non me ne maravigli e dolga. (123–24)

> When, therefore, I consider in what honour antiquity is held, and how—to cite but one example—a bit of old statue has fetched a high price that someone may have it by him to give honour to his house and that it may be possible for it to be imitated by those who are keen on this art; and how the latter then with great industry take pains to reproduce it in all their works; and when, on the other hand, I notice that what history has to say about the highly virtuous actions performed by ancient kingdoms and republics, by their kings, their generals, their citizens, their legislators, and by others who have gone to the trouble of serving their country, is rather admired than imitated; nay, is so shunned by everybody in each little thing they do, that of the virtue of bygone days there remains no trace, it cannot but fill me at once with astonishment and grief. (97–98; translation modified)

This passage is usually, and correctly, read as an argument for systematic as opposed to dilettantish or eclectic study of the ancients. But the place of aesthetic admiration in this opposition also needs to be noted. While Machiavelli seems at first to be contrasting the active appropriation of antiquity on the part of artists and craftsmen to the neglect of such imitation by statesmen and citizens, there is clearly another way in which the merely aesthetic imitation of ancient fragments is an activity of limited worth in his eyes. Hence the implied contrast between the modern collector of old statues, who purchases his honor on the market, and the ancient king, general, citizen, or legislator, who achieves it through great deeds. The virtuous modern collector, we may extrapolate, is not the art

connoisseur but rather the political counselor whose advice makes it possible for his prince to reproduce in action the achievement of the ancients.

Accordingly, after allying the aesthetic imitation of antiquities to the
merely passive admiration of ancient *virtù*, Machiavelli argues that the
way to undo the mesmerizing aesthetic effect of ancient authority is to
reduce Rome's political achievement to the collection of decisions it originally was—to reduce the history of Rome, that is, to a collection of examples. This reduction is the essential prelude to correct imitation of
antiquity:

> perché le leggi civili non sono altro che sentenze date dagli antiqui iurecon-
> sulti, le quali, ridutte in ordine, a' presenti nostri iureconsulti iudicare inse-
> gnano. Né ancora la medicina è altro che esperienze fatte dagli antiqui
> medici, sopra la quale fondano e' medici presenti e' loro iudizii. Non-
> dimanco, nello ordinare le republiche, nel mantenere li stati, nel governare
> e' regni, nello ordinare la milizia ed amministrare la guerra, nel iudicare e'
> sudditi, nello accrescere l'imperio, non si truova principe né republica che
> agli esempli delli antiqui ricorra. (124)

> For the civil law is nothing but a collection of decisions, made by the jurists
> of old, which the jurists of today have tabulated in orderly fashion for our
> instruction. Nor, again, is medicine anything but a record of experiments,
> performed by doctors of old, upon which the doctors of our day base their
> prescriptions. In spite of which in constituting republics, in maintaining
> states, in governing kingdoms, in forming an army or conducting a war, in
> dealing with subjects, in extending the empire, one finds neither prince nor
> republic who repairs to antiquity for examples. (98)[2]

This is an astonishing statement when one considers the humanist love
of ancient examples; but, as we read on, we discover that collecting examples is only the first step. For, as Machiavelli complains in the passage
that follows, his humanist contemporaries do read the ancients but have
"fail[ed] to appreciate the significance of what they have read" (124, 98).
Along with the corruption of contemporary Florence and related to it,
reading has itself undergone a process of degeneration: it has become an
aesthetic practice that gives rise to pleasure rather than an experience that
leads to *virtù* in the realm of politics. Just as corrupt cities need periodically to be returned or "reduced" to their first principles, so Machiavelli
proposes to return the reader to the practice of imitation by reducing or
collecting examples from the history of Rome in such a fashion that the
reader will be led to understand their significance. In fact, he suggests that
the examples he has chosen are already informed by an act of interpretation, a judgment of their relevance to contemporary affairs: his commentary on Livy "will comprise what I have arrived at by comparing ancient

with modern events" (125, 99). On the one hand, then, Machiavelli proposes that politics emulate law and medicine, which have recourse to systematic records of the decisions and experiments of the past. On the other, Machiavelli appears as the exemplary humanist reader, who recalls his contemporaries to the critical activity of imitation.

Here we begin to see the analogy Machiavelli develops throughout the *Discourses* between Rome's ability periodically to return to its first principles and his own ability as an author to return the reader to the first principles of political *virtù*. But we also see that Machiavelli's pragmatic reduction of Livy's history to a collection of maxims and examples, which are by definition open to interpretation, may run counter to his desire to convince his Florentine readers to imitate the *virtù* of the Roman republic. As later readers were quick to recognize, Machiavelli's "commentary" on Livy does not slavishly follow the Livian narrative but rather exemplifies a pragmatic approach to the text, one that is more concerned to "draw practical lessons" than to admire—and preserve—Livy's work as an aesthetic whole. To read Machiavelli as he read Livy might be to reduce Machiavelli's own texts to a series of fragments, which could then be put to new, not necessarily republican, uses. In commenting on the problems of reading—of "reducing" and "leading back to"—the ancients, Machiavelli thus stages the conflict between the indeterminacy of examples, their availability for use *in utramque partem*, and his own rhetorical argument for the superiority of Rome. His remarks on method register the tension between rhetoric as the neutral codification of arguments and as a critique of the status quo, and help to explain how Machiavelli can be read as both a dispassionate political analyst and a committed republican theorist. This tension informs the *Discourses* as a whole.[3]

A Rhetoric of Conflict

Machiavelli's encomium of the Roman republic is the most important instance in the *Discourses* of a rhetorical politics in which conflict is not equated with humanist argument *in utramque partem* but with a dialectical critique of the status quo. Beginning in book 1, chapter 2, Machiavelli argues that the excellence of the Roman republic—its liberty and power—was the result of the class conflict between the nobles and the plebs. This is at once Machiavelli's most striking departure from Livy and his most obvious break with the dominant humanist rhetoric of social and political consensus.[4] Yet, Machiavelli declares his allegiance to rhetorical thinking here as well. For, just as he uses the humanist language of imitation to propose an activist imitation of the ancients, so he uses the language of rhetoric—specifically, rhetorical debate—in order to argue that Rome's superiority emerges from within a rhetorical and dialectical analysis of politics.

> Ma vegnamo a Roma; la quale non ostante che non avesse uno Licurgo che la ordinasse in modo nel principio che la potesse vivere lungo tempo libera, nondimeno furo tanti gli accidenti che in quella nacquero, per la disunione che era intra la Plebe ed il Senato, che quello che non aveva fatto uno ordinatore lo fece il caso. Perché se Roma non sortí la prima fortuna, sortí la seconda: . . . onde sendo diventata la Nobilità romana insolente . . . si levò il Popolo contro di quella; talché, per non perdere il tutto, fu costretta concedere al Popolo la sua parte; e dall'altra parte il Senato e i Consoli restassono con tanta autorità che potessono tenere in quella republica il grado loro. (1.2.134)

> In spite of the fact that Rome had no Lycurgus to give it at the outset such a constitution as would ensure to it a long life of freedom, yet owing to the disunion between the plebs and the senate, so many things happened that chance effected what had not been provided by a lawgiver. So that, if Rome did not get fortune's first gift, it got its second. . . . This came about when the Roman nobility became so overbearing . . . that the populace rose against them, and they were constrained by the fear that they might lose all, to grant the populace a share in the government; the senate and the consuls retaining, however, sufficient authority for them to be able to maintain their position in the republic. (110–11; translation modified)

Livy had attributed Rome's success to *fortuna*, and Machiavelli appears to follow Livy's account in attributing Rome's success to *caso* or chance. But this gloss on Livy's *fortuna* also subtly changes the meaning of that term from fate to contingency—a shift of meaning that is apparent as well in the passage above in the use of terms such as *accidenti* (accidents) and *sortire* (to fall out; literally, to obtain or choose by lot).[5] At the same time, Machiavelli identifies such accidents with the contingent, yet productive conflict between the nobles and the plebs. In this way, he redefines Rome's fortune as disunion.[6]

Machiavelli's point about the beneficial effects of conflict was controversial for his contemporaries, not least of all because under the Medici they had themselves experienced how easily class conflict could degenerate into faction. Furthermore, the concern with the destructive consequences of faction had been a commonplace in Florentine chronicles, histories, and political treatises—whether of scholastic or humanist persuasion—from the thirteenth century on. Giovanni Villani began his discussion of Florence by remarking, "[The] Florentines are always at war and in dissension among themselves; and this is no surprise since they are derived from two peoples so contrary and with such inimical and diverse customs—that is, the noble and virtuous Romans and the rude and aggressive Fiesolani."[7] In his *Florentine Histories* Machiavelli announced his intention to describe these conflicts in detail by noting "From such divisions came as many dead, as many exiles, and as many families destroyed as ever occurred in any city in memory."[8] Yet, while authors of the period seemed to agree that faction and discord could be avoided by equating the individual and the common good, both the rhetorical and scholastic tradition begged the question of how to identify the two in practice.[9] Machiavelli's aim in the *Discourses* was to show how class struggle in Rome provides a model of a nonfactional polity that nevertheless acknowledges the existence of different and conflicting interests; his name for this effective identification of the individual and the common good in the passage quoted above and elsewhere is "disunion." In his revision of the humanist rhetoric and politics of consensus, conflict is seen to be a source of strength rather than weakness and is inseparable from increased political representation for the people (1.4.136–38, 113–15).

While readers of the *Discourses* have agreed on Machiavelli's equation of Rome's good fortune with class conflict, the emphasis on conflict has itself given rise to conflicting interpretations. To some, beginning with Guicciardini, it looks like yet another example of Machiavelli's dualistic world view, his theatrical preference for conflict over consensus.[10] Such readers have seen the dualistic tendency of Machiavelli's arguments as a symptom of his extremism—his rejection of humanist *mediocritas* or the middle way. Others have construed this dualism as evidence of Machiavelli's pragmatic concern to secure the state through the almost mechanistic counterpointing of conflicting interests. While neither of these interpretations does justice to the complexity of the *Discourses*, it is particularly the second alternative that Machiavelli's reflections on Roman conflict in the next chapters are designed to avoid.

In book 1, chapters 5 and 6, Machiavelli stages the comparison of Rome to ancient Sparta and modern Venice in order to show that his rhetorical politics does not simply involve a disinterested analysis of the facts on both sides of the question, but rather a dialectical argument in which the Roman republic emerges as the better form of government, the better argument. I use the term *argument* advisedly, since throughout these chapters Machiavelli uses the language of debate, discourse, argument on both sides of a question, to describe not only the choice between Rome and Venice or Sparta, but also the dispassionate weighing of ends that is superseded by Rome's properly dialectical mode of political reasoning. He thus establishes an analogy between his own rhetoric and the rhetorical approach to politics that he sees embodied in ancient Rome.

Machiavelli begins chapter 5 by self-consciously debating "into whose hands it is best to place the guardianship of liberty" (1.5.139, 115)—the people's (as in Rome) or the nobles' (as in Sparta and Venice): "If we appeal to reason arguments may be adduced in support of either thesis; but if we ask what the result was, the answer will favour the nobility, for the freedom of Sparta and of Venice lasted longer than did that of Rome" (139, 116). Although such a statement might suggest that political decisions between contrary courses of action and contrasting forms of government should be made on the basis of results, Machiavelli insists that the choice between the criteria of reason and results is itself debatable. As in *The Prince*, Machiavelli's rhetorical politics is not pragmatic in the sense of being simply success- or result-oriented. For the value of success—here equated with stability and longevity—is not a given but must itself be an object of deliberation.

> E veramente chi discorressi bene l'una cosa e l'altra, potrebbe stare dubbio, quale da lui fusse eletto per guardia di tale libertà. . . .
> Ed in fine chi sottilmente esaminerà tutto, ne farà questa conclusione: o tu ragioni d'una republica che voglia fare uno imperio, come Roma, o d'una che le basti mantenersi. Nel primo caso gli è necessario fare ogni cosa come Roma; nel secondo può imitare Vinegia e Sparta. (1.5.140)

> And, truly, he who reasons well on both sides may be in doubt which he would select as the guardians of liberty. . . .
> All things carefully considered, however, we shall arrive in the end at this conclusion. Either you have in mind a republic that looks to founding an empire, as Rome did; or one that is content to maintain the *status quo*. In the first case it is necessary to do in all things as Rome did. In the second it is possible to imitate Venice and Sparta. (117; translation modified)

As though to parody argument on both sides of a question, Machiavelli announces that the "conclusion" to such argument is itself debatable: "either . . . or." Although this conclusion suggests that the choice between empire and stability is a matter of weighing alternative ends, in the next chapter Machiavelli pulls the rug out from under such dispassionate deliberation by claiming that, though Sparta and Venice lasted longer, Rome demonstrated greater *virtù* or "grandezza" (1.6.143, 121):

> Considerando adunque tutte queste cose, si vede come a' legislatori di Roma era necessario fare una delle due cose a volere che Roma stesse quiete come le sopradette republiche: o non adoperare la plebe in guerra, come i Viniziani, o non aprire la via a' forestieri, come gli Spartani. E loro feciono l'una e l'altra: il che dette alla plebe forze ed augumento, ed infinite occasioni di tumultuare. Ma venendo lo stato romano a essere piú quieto, ne seguiva

questo inconveniente, ch'egli era anche piú debile, perché e' gli si troncava la via di potere venire a quella grandezza dove ei pervenne: in modo che volendo Roma levare le cagioni de' tumulti, levava ancora le cagioni dello ampliare. (1.6.143–44)

All things considered, therefore, it is clear that it was necessary for Rome's legislators to do one of two things if Rome was to remain tranquil like the aforesaid states: either to emulate the Venetians and not employ its plebs in wars, or, like the Spartans, not to admit foreigners. Rome did both these things, and, by doing so, gave to its plebs alike strength, increase and endless opportunities for commotion. On the other hand, had the government of Rome been such as to bring greater tranquillity, there would have ensued this inconvenience, that it would have been weaker, owing to its having cut off the source of supply which enabled it to acquire the greatness at which it arrived, so that, in seeking to remove the cause of tumults, Rome would have removed also the causes of expansion. (121)

With one gesture, Machiavelli dismisses the "either/or" model of political reasoning—debate on both sides of the question—and the consensus model of politics that is represented by Sparta and Venice. Politics is not a matter of choosing between Rome and Sparta or Venice, or of deliberating about what Rome would have had to do to become Sparta or Venice. Nor is it a matter of producing "unione" or consensus within the state. For conflict rather than consensus is the source of strength and greatness. While the political union or consensus ("vivere uniti" [1.6.143]) that results from excluding plebs and foreigners was the cause of Spartan and Venetian stability, Roman *virtù* was produced dialectically from the disunion—what Machiavelli calls the "controversie" (1.6.141, 118)—of the plebs and the senate. Disunion or class conflict is thus preferable to consensus and stability because it provides a structure or institution that constrains private interest to take the form of public good, that is, a structure that preserves civic liberty and generates greatness and *virtù* (1.4.137, 114).[11]

Of particular interest in this argument for Roman superiority is Machiavelli's own rhetoric. For, by using the vocabulary of rhetorical controversy, he suggests that Rome's greatness was a consequence of its ability to conduct its politics rhetorically and dialectically.[12] Like the rhetoric of Machiavelli's ideal prince, Rome's polity includes resources previously excluded from humanist rhetoric: here, the resources of class conflict. In the controversy between Rome and Sparta, Rome emerges as the superior republic because it is the superior "controversialist." Such incorporation of controversy explains the *virtù* of Rome's external, as well as internal, political affairs: for just as Rome's *virtù* is both manifest in and a consequence of its ability to give representation to conflicting interests within the republic, so *virtù* is both the cause and effect of an expansionist foreign policy, which aims not only to conquer but also to integrate and give representation to the conquered within the Roman state. In each case Roman strength is predicated in part on Rome's decision to represent and to arm those who had been previously excluded—whether the plebs or the conquered people. In this light, Roman imperialism is the best historical example of a rhetorical and dialectical approach to politics.

If Rome is superior to Sparta and Venice because of its greater *virtù*, a *virtù* that emerges dialectically from class conflict, it is also greater because, in the end, it includes both the Spartan and the Venetian alternatives. Machiavelli tells us that Rome "did both [of the] things" that Sparta and Venice each separately refused to do: it armed its plebs and admitted foreigners as citizens. Then, with typical irony or—one might say—a dialectical twist, Machiavelli adds that the choice between expansion and stability is illusory because *all* states eventually will be forced either to expand or to confront internal factions (1.6.145, 123; 2.19.334–35, 335–36), and those, like Rome, that are prepared to, will do so with greater *virtù* (cf. 1.6.145, 123–24). In Machiavelli's account of the alternative, Sparta already implies and must yield to Rome.[13]

Yet, while Machiavelli presents a dialectical argument that reduces rhetoric on both sides of a question to a rhetorical critique in which the Roman republic emerges as superior to Venice and Sparta, a rhetorical politics makes even such dialectical argument contingent. Just as the purpose of the initial contrast between Rome and Sparta or Venice was to show that *virtù* could not be simply identified with the successful maintenance of the status quo, so in developing the contrast between Rome and Sparta Machiavelli is careful to note that the dialectical "controversie" that were the cause of Rome's *virtù* were eventually the cause of its downfall:

> Noi abbiamo discorsi di sopra gli effetti che facevano le controversie intra il Popolo ed il Senato. Ora sendo quelle seguitate infino al tempo de' Gracchi, . . . furono cagione della rovina del vivero libero. (1.6.141)

> We have just been discussing the effects produced by the controversies between the populace and the senate. Now, . . . these controversies went on until the time of the Gracchi when they became the causes which led to the destruction of liberty. (118)

As in the case of Venice and Sparta, Rome's strength is a source of weakness. In ascribing the cause of Rome's rise and fall to these "controversie," Machiavelli suggests that *virtù* is the result of a rhetorical politics that cannot be simply equated with a humanist rhetoric of consensus or with a merely expedient emphasis on success.

Examples *in utramque partem*

While Machiavelli offers a dialectical defense of the Roman republic, he also has recourse throughout the *Discourses* to examples of individuals of extraordinary *virtù*. In so doing, he shows that *virtù* is not simply the practical effect of conflict or disunion but also a possible cause. By returning to the individualism of *The Prince*, Machiavelli highlights further the contingency of his own dialectical defense, at the same time that he calls attention to the stereotypical Machiavellism of his exemplary republicans. He thus not only illustrates the compatibility of Machiavellism with republicanism, but also shows that every example of republicanism can be interpreted in the interests of the prince as well. In this way, Machiavelli's examples of Roman *virtù* offer commentaries on Machiavelli's own rhetoric. In the following pages, I discuss two such examples, Numa Pompilius and Junius Brutus, which were of particular interest to later readers.

Numa, Romulus's successor, is Machiavelli's example of the lawgiver who uses the appeal to divine authority strategically in order to introduce new institutions and extraordinary laws (1.11). The chapter functions both as an exposure of the ideological function of religion, and as an illustration of the link between the Machiavel's force and fraud, and republicanism:

> [Numa] trovando un popolo ferocissimo, e volendolo ridurre nelle obedienze civili con le arti della pace, si volse alla religione come cosa al tutto necessaria a volere mantenere una civiltà, e la constituí in modo che per piú secoli non fu mai tanto timore di Dio quanto in quella republica. (160)

> Numa, finding the people ferocious and desiring to reduce them to civic obedience by means of the arts of peace, turned to religion as an instrument necessary above all others for the maintenance of a civilized state, and so constituted it that there was never for so many centuries so great a fear of God as there was in this republic. (139)

In this example Machiavelli uses the language of "reduction" to describe not the return to republican first principles but rather the pacification of the Roman people. Here religion is a fraud perpetrated on the citizens, and an instrument of compulsion: the citizens were "forced to swear that they would not abandon their country" (161, 140), and this oath was

binding because of their fear of God. Not only the defense, but also the
good laws of the republic are a consequence of its religion, for religion
serves to persuade—or to stupefy—the populace into accepting new laws.
When Numa pretended "private conference with a nymph" (161, 140),

> il Popolo romano . . . cedeva ad ogni sua diliberazione. Ben è vero che l'es-
> sere quelli tempi pieni di religione, e quegli uomini con i quali egli aveva a
> travagliare grossi, gli dettono facilità grande a conseguire i disegni suoi, po-
> tendo imprimere in loro facilmente qualunque nuova forma. (162)

> the Roman people accepted all his decisions. True, the times were so impreg-
> nated with a religious spirit and the men with whom he had to deal so stupid
> that they contributed very much to facilitate his designs and made it easy for
> him to impress on them any new form. (141)

Yet, if the Machiavellian manipulation of "divine worship is the cause of
greatness in republics," it is equally useful to princes: "the security of *a
republic or a kingdom*, therefore, does not depend upon its ruler governing it prudently during his lifetime, but upon so ordering it that, after his
death, it may maintain itself in being" (1.12.162, 141–42; my emphasis).
Thus, the lesson of Numa is stereotypically Machiavellian but not necessarily republican.

In book 3 of the *Discourses*, the example of Junius Brutus recapitulates
the ambiguous lesson of Numa. Brutus, Machiavelli tells us, executed his
sons for conspiring against the republic; in doing so, he performed an
exemplary act of violence that recalls Cesare Borgia's execution of Remirro De Orco, though to different ends. For in the *Discourses* Machiavelli argues that a leader of extraordinary *virtù* must intervene to restore
the republic to its first principles when a state is corrupt and incapable
of regenerating itself. Such leaders perform services not unlike those of
founders and legislators: "Horatius Cocles, Scaevola, Fabricius [and oth-
ers] . . . wrought the same effects in Rome as laws and institutions would
have done" (3.1.382, 388). In the example of Brutus, Machiavelli shows
the compatibility of force and fraud with republicanism, and comments
on his own rhetoric as well:

> gli ordini che ritirarono la Republica romana verso il suo principio, furono
> i Tribuni della plebe, i Censori e tutte l'altre leggi che venivano contro
> all'ambizione ed alla insolenzia degli uomini. I quali ordini hanno bisogno
> di essere fatti vivi dalla virtù d'uno cittadino, il quale animosamente con-
> corra ad esequirli contro alla potenza di quegli che gli trapassano. Delle
> quali esecuzioni . . . furono notabili la morte de' figliuoli di Bruto, la morte
> de' dieci cittadini [etc.]. . . . Le quali cose perché erano eccessive e notabili,
> qualunque volta ne nasceva una, facevano gli uomini ritirare verso il segno:
> e quando le cominciarono ad essere piú rare cominciarono anche a dare piú

spazio agli uomini di corrompersi e farsi con maggiore pericolo e piú tu-
multo. Perché dall'una all'altra di simili esecuzioni non vorrebbe passare il
piú dieci anni: perché passato questo tempo, gli uomini cominciano a variare
con i costumi e trapassare le leggi; e se non nasce cosa per la quale si riduca
loro a memoria la pena, e rinnuovisi negli animi loro la paura, concorrono
tosto tanti delinquenti che non si possono piú punire sanza pericolo.
(3.1.381)

the institutions which caused the Roman republic to return to its start were
the introduction of plebeian tribunes, of the censorship, and of all the other
laws which put a check on human ambition and arrogance; to which institutions life must needs be given by some virtuous citizen who cooperates stren-
uously in giving them effect despite the power of those who contravene
them. Notable among such drastic actions . . . were the death of Brutus' sons
[for conspiring against the republic], the death of the ten citizens [etc.]. . . .
Such events, because of their unwonted severity and their notoriety, brought
men back to the mark every time one of them happened; and when they
began to occur less frequently, they also began to provide occasion for men
to practise corruption, and were attended with more danger and more commotion. For between one case of disciplinary action of this type and the next
there ought to elapse at most ten years, because by this time men begin to
change their habits and to break the laws; and unless something happens
["nasce"] which recalls to their minds the penalty involved and reawakens
fear in them, there will soon be so many delinquents that it will be impossible
to punish them without danger. (387–88)

In this passage Machiavelli suggests an analogy between Rome and the
Discourses: just as Rome needs to be returned to its first principles by the
drastic actions of a man of *virtù*, so the reader of the *Discourses* needs to
be brought back to the mark by shocking examples. Like Brutus, Machiavelli aims to remind the reader ("reducersi a mente") of the experience of
necessity—the reduced circumstances—that he has forgotten. He aims, in
other words, to reproduce in reading the experience that led the Romans
to form true opinions, the experience that taught them what to praise and
blame, what to imitate and avoid. While urging in humanist fashion the
voluntary imitation of antiquity, Machiavelli also proves to be a most
coercive proponent of Renaissance republicanism. Accordingly, in the
passage just quoted, the metaphor of birth ("unless something happens
['nasce']") serves to emphasize not only that the renaissance of classical
antiquity and of republican principles is a violent process but also that
this violence is not an unfortunate by-product of rebirth but instrumental
to it. Both civic allegiance and the correct imitation of antiquity require
the forced remembrance of drastic actions. As we will see, although both
Brutus and Machiavelli place such drastic actions in the service of the

republic, both demonstrate that such Machiavellism may be put to other uses as well.

Brutus is from the outset an exemplary Machiavellian, using both fraud and force in theatrical ways to restore and maintain the republic. Not only did Brutus feign madness in order to appear harmless to the king whom he then overthrew (3.2.384, 391), he also used the rape of Lucretia to coerce his fellow conspirators into swearing an oath of allegiance to the new state:

> sopra la morta Lucrezia, intra 'l padre ed il marito ed altri parenti di lei, ei fu il primo a trarle il coltello della ferita, e fare giurare ai circunstanti che mai sopporterebbono che per lo avvenire alcuno regnasse in Roma. (3.2.384)

> on the death of Lucretia he was the first to pull the dagger out of the wound in the presence of her father, her husband and other of her relatives, and to make the bystanders swear that they would never tolerate for the future any king reigning in Rome. (391)

Here Brutus's actions recall those of Numa, who was able to compel an oath of allegiance by using the threat of divine retribution. In both cases, violence is used theatrically in the service of the state.

Particularly impressive to Machiavelli was Brutus's presence at the murder of his sons for conspiring against the republic. In this instance, Brutus used violence theatrically not only to compel obedience to the state but also to teach a lesson about imitation and political representation. In thematic terms what occurs in this example is the sacrifice of the part (his sons), and of partisanship, for the whole.[14] Brutus's presence thus testifies to what is important in formal terms—that the realm of representation can be used to distance oneself from, and thereby in some sense control, the realm of necessity or of fortune—in the case of Brutus, the misfortune of his sons' conspiracy. In staging the death of his sons, Brutus the victim also dramatizes the violence to which he has been subjected, and thus becomes both author and spectator of his own fortune. Violence turns out to be a synecdoche for necessity, and the theatrical staging of it a means (by turning effect into cause) of controlling fortune. Thus in 2.29 (367, 372), Machiavelli writes that "men may second [secondare] their fortune but not oppose it"; but this seconding of nature or willing of necessity—which here takes the double form of the theatrical staging of a violent punishment and seconding it with one's presence—is itself *virtù*. Finally, both in the case of the individual and of the republic, what is important for Machiavelli is the *secondariness* of imitation. For by imitating nature, we willfully take our distance from it, and in this distance resides the possibility of determining rather than being determined by nature, of criticizing rather than reproducing the status quo.

And yet the example of Brutus—like *virtù* itself—creates as many problems as it solves; for, as Machiavelli reminds us, Brutus's republican severity can be interpreted pro and contra the republic:

> la severità . . . è di uno esempio raro in tutte le memorie delle cose: vedere il padre sedere pro tribunali, e non solamente condennare i suoi figliuoli a morte, ma essere presente alla morte loro. E sempre si conoscerà questo per coloro che le cose antiche leggeranno, come dopo una mutazione di Stato, *o da republica in tirannide o da tirannide in republica*, è necessaria una esecuzione memorabile contro a' nimici delle condizioni presenti. E chi piglia una tirannide e non ammazza Bruto, e chi fa uno stato libero e non ammazza i figliuoli di Bruto, si mantiene poco tempo. (3.3.386; my emphasis)

> Of such severity one rarely comes across a case in history in which a father not only sits on a tribunal and condemns his own sons to death, but is present at their death. Those, however, who are familiar with ancient history are well aware that, when the form of government has been changed, *whether from a republic to a tyranny or a tyranny to a republic*, it is in all cases essential that exemplary action be taken against those who are hostile to the new state of affairs. He who establishes a tyranny and does not kill "Brutus," and he who establishes a free state and does not kill "the Sons of Brutus," will not last long. (392–93; my emphasis)

Like the example of Numa, the example of Brutus comments on Machiavelli's own rhetoric. It illustrates not only the stereotypical Machiavellism of Machiavelli's exemplary republicans but also the way Machiavelli's rhetorical politics turns even Brutus into an example *in utramque partem*.[15] It is precisely because a rhetorical politics is available for use by a prince or republic that Machiavelli has been read as both a dispassionate political scientist, arguing on both sides of the question, and as a republican theorist and critic of the status quo. As we will see in the following chapters, Machiavelli's rhetorical politics also helps to explain his Renaissance reception as a cynic, ironist, and above all, rhetorician.

In conclusion, I want to emphasize Machiavelli's debt to, as well as his criticism of, the humanist rhetorical tradition. For, even more than the humanists, Machiavelli wanted to devise a political ethic that was capable of responding to the particular without losing its critical force. To the pseudo-objectivity of a certain kind of scientific disinterestedness, Machiavelli opposed the objectivity that is available only to the interested. Thus he did not simply reject the humanist equation of the *honestum* and the *utile*, substituting the criterion of efficacy or technical efficiency for that of morality. Instead, Machiavelli criticized both the technical and humanist prudential views of rhetoric—the first, one might say, for lacking idealism and the second for having it in excess. Recognizing that humanist argument *in utramque partem* was a form of dialectical thinking that had the power to undermine the prudential conception of rhetoric, he attempted to forge a new rhetoric of politics that was simultaneously descriptive and prescriptive—a rhetoric that could generate compelling political arguments for republicanism from within a critical analysis of the status quo. At the same time, he made the indeterminacy of rhetorical argument, its availability for evil as well as good, central to his rhetorical politics. Thus in both *The Prince* and the *Discourses* Machiavelli used humanist imitation and rhetoric, particularly the humanist pedagogy of examples, in order to educate the reader to a view of politics that is more deeply rhetorical than that of civic humanism. Machiavelli was disturbing to his Renaissance readers not because he revealed that "politics [is] more than rhetoric" (*MM*, 63) but because a Machiavellian politics is rhetorical through and through.

THREE

RHETORIC AND REASON OF STATE:

BOTERO'S READING OF MACHIAVELLI

IN 1531 and 1532 the *Discourses* and *The Prince* were published by Blado in Rome with the papal imprimatur. By 1559 Machiavelli's works appeared—along with those of Erasmus, Boccaccio, and Savonarola—on the papal index of prohibited books.[1] The Counter-Reformation was in full force and Machiavelli was censured as an enemy to religion in treatise after treatise in Spain and Italy. In particular, Machiavelli was condemned as the proponent of reason of state—the use of any and all available means, however immoral, to preserve the state and to increase the power of its ruler. For many Counter-Reformation theorists, Machiavellian reason of state was simply the term the tyrannical prince used to rationalize his own immoderate desires and interests.[2] To combat Machiavelli's malignant influence and to rebut his charge that Christianity was detrimental to the state (*D*, 11–15), Counter-Reformation critics proposed a Christian reason of state, which claimed to reconcile religious belief and behavior with the exigencies of practical politics. In the case of Giovanni Botero, such a Christian reason of state amounted to a Christianizing of Machiavelli's rhetorical politics.

Historians of political thought—particularly those who see Machiavelli as a secular and republican thinker—have tended to condescend to the literature of reason of state, relegating it to an obscure corner of the history of Machiavellism, a history of misreading, error, and naiveté. This is particularly the case with Botero, who attempted to reconcile Machiavelli's analysis of politics with his own religious convictions in the first full-length treatise on reason of state, *Ragion di stato* (1589). Together with anti-Machiavellians such as Ammirato, Ribadeneyra, and many others, Botero is judged to have been incapable of appreciating the "true" Machiavelli—the secular analyst of de facto political power or the republican theorist.[3] In this chapter I argue that a reexamination of Counter-Reformation treatises shows that Catholicism was not an impediment to an appreciation of Machiavelli, precisely because Counter-Reformation thinkers understood that Machiavelli's rhetorical politics could be appropriated for their own purposes as well. As such, their works provide an important analogue to the Protestant reception of Machiavelli in sixteenth- and seventeenth-century England, and an important corrective to the identification of the Machiavellian moment with republican or secular thought. By closely analyzing these works, we begin to see that the rhetoric of Machiavellism in the Renaissance is first and foremost the product of a religiously motivated critique of Machiavelli.[4] But rather than rejecting such anti-Machiavellians, I suggest that these writers correctly perceived both what was threatening in Machiavelli's rhetorical politics and what was open to appropriation or reinterpretation.

Specifically, I argue that Botero and his contemporaries were intelligent readers of Machiavelli not simply because they understood his "discourse of necessity," as Meinecke and others have claimed,[5] but because they understood his rhetoric: unlike many modern interpreters, Counter-Reformation readers were sensitive to the rhetorical form of Machiavelli's work, and to the rhetorical dimension of his conception of politics. They read Machiavelli as Machiavelli had read Livy—as a storehouse of historical examples that could be appropriated for a variety of uses, analyzed in terms of a range of thematic and formal topics. Precisely because they had been schooled in the assumptions of humanist rhetoric and poetics, and the rhetorical dimension of princely conduct, they were able to understand how Machiavelli's rhetorical conception of politics was applicable to the needs of Christian princes. They recognized the role that rhetoric and imitation can play in the *construction* of necessity and of political power; and they were particularly sensitive to the moral ambiguity—the potential immorality—of Machiavelli's recommendations regarding the uses of representation—of reputation, simulation, and dissimulation. What was disturbing to Counter-Reformation critics of Machiavelli was less his discourse of necessity, and the possible conflict between the politic world of necessity and the city of God,[6] than the realization that necessity can be feigned. But rather than ruling these recommendations out of hand, they attempted both to respond to them on Machiavelli's own terms and to adapt them (in Machiavellian fashion) to their own religious and political purposes.

In particular, Counter-Reformation critics recognized the tension within Machiavelli's rhetorical politics between a neutral, or instrumental, and a normative conception of rhetoric.[7] But, unlike him, they attempted to forge a unity between the two that was compatible with the dictates of Christianity. They strove to find new ways of differentiating between true and false uses of representation, true and false prudence, while at the same time preserving the Machiavellian emphasis on practical results. While condemning certain uses of dissimulation, critics of Machiavelli argued for a legitimate feigning or imitation, whether in the form of well-intentioned deception or in the sublime spectacle of the prince's power. Yet, their reflections on reason of state—what Botero would call reasoning from interest—also exposed the fiction of a sovereign reason, uncontaminated by interest; they thus dramatized the necessity of responding to Machiavelli by distinguishing not between Christian truth and Machiavellian falsehood but between more or less persuasive interests, more or less powerful results. It is not surprising that some of those who attempted to rebut Machiavelli on his own terms were themselves condemned as Machiavellian.

In the following pages I briefly discuss the intersection of rhetoric, poetics, and politics in cinquecento discussions of imitation, as a way of introducing the assumptions that governed the Counter-Reformation reception of Machiavelli. I then illustrate this reception through a close analysis of Botero's *Ragion di stato*. I have chosen to focus on Botero not only because his treatise was one of the all-time best-sellers of political theory (contemporaries compared its popularity to that of Tasso's *Gerusalemme liberata*) but also because, in its topical approach and in its reflection on the uses of rhetoric and imitation, *Ragion di stato* is representative of other treatises on reason of state in the late sixteenth and seventeenth centuries. Some of Botero's contemporaries complained that his definition of reason of state was unconscionably wide, and argued for stricter moral and religious criteria for reason of state; others noted with approval what was implicit in Botero—that reason of state is only loosely or contingently related to moral considerations. But all of the authors who took up the challenge of Machiavelli and of reason of state reflected as Botero did on the relationship of virtue to success, means to ends, imitation to misrepresentation. *Ragion di stato* thus helps us to see that reason of state involved a rhetorical approach to politics that allowed the insights of the Machiavel to be wedded to those of the Counter-Reformation religious thinkers of the sixteenth century.[8]

Rhetoric, Poetics, and Politics

By the time Botero published *Ragion di stato* in 1589, there was a well-developed humanist discourse concerning the intersection of rhetoric, poetics, and politics. Many of the basic assumptions of this discourse were shared by Counter-Reformation writers, especially those who turned to Aristotle's *Rhetoric* and *Poetics* in an effort to rearticulate the relationship of rhetoric and Catholic theology in the wake of the Council of Trent.[9] A brief discussion of the available arguments will help us see that sixteenth-century treatises on poetics and rhetoric shared with Machiavelli a language of imitation and persuasion, as well as a concern with the political uses of these faculties. A related concern with issues of persuasion and representation is apparent in sixteenth-century manuals of casuistry. Once we have surveyed these treatises, we will be in a better position to see that Botero read Machiavelli through these available discourses, while attempting to assimilate Machiavelli's critique.

Most sixteenth-century treatises on poetics are governed by the axiom that poetry is like politics in dealing with practical matters and that poetry has political consequences. Alessandro Piccolomini discussed the close relationship of poetry and civic prudence in his *Annotationi nel libro della Poetica d'Aristotile* (1575), arguing that poetry, like politics, "is a habit of the practical intellect."[10] Giacopo Mazzoni made the same point in his *Della difesa della Comedia di Dante* (1587), claiming that poetry considered as instruction in moral philosophy is governed by the "civil faculty," and that Aristotle's *Poetics* is the ninth book of his *Politics*.[11] Scipione Ammirato, who later wrote a commentary on Tacitus in which he condemned Machiavellian reason of state, also subsumed poetry under civil philosophy: "The poet bears the same relationship to the physician as the legislator does to the surgeon, and the 'end of poetry is to induce virtue into the soul by driving vice out of it.'"[12] For these and other critics, imitation does not simply have political effects but is like politics in being governed by the practical intellect or civil faculty.

Cinquecento Italian commentaries on Aristotle's *Poetics* manifest an acute anxiety about mimesis as an instrument of deception and misrepresentation, and a corresponding awareness of the uses to which mimesis may be put to preserve the social and political status quo. In these treatises, acknowledging the political effects of imitation and rhetoric is only the first step to controlling them. Mazzoni, for example, argued that, although some kinds of poetry "disorder . . . the appetite with immoderate delight, producing complete rebellion against reason and bring on damage and loss to a virtuous life" (97), appropriate imitation will subordinate delight to civic instruction. In a discussion of the political effects of comedy and tragedy he remarked that these "two kinds of poems are directed by the civil faculty to the extinguishing of sedition and the preservation of peace" (105–106). In Mazzoni's account, drama is a creation of the civil faculty, and the lessons of comedy and tragedy function as the rhetorical counterweight to the potentially destabilizing recognition of social inequality, whether on the part of humble citizens or proud rulers.[13]

Much of the Renaissance debate concerning the meaning of catharsis reflects similar considerations of its civil utility, that is, its usefulness in preserving the status quo.[14] While critics sometimes argued that the effect of tragedy is to make us abhor and thus, potentially, resist tyranny,[15] the usual discussions of catharsis stressed that purgation of the passions makes us more obedient citizens, whether of a monarchy or a republic. In *De la purgazione de la tragedia* (1586), Lorenzo Giacomini argued that the purpose of purgation is to render the audience "obedient to exhortation" (*Trattati*, 3:368–69). Sperone Speroni, a defender of the Venetian republic, claimed that "republics need a purging of pity more than monarchies do, since the overly compassionate citizen is likely to be unjust in a republic, but in a monarchy a king is responsible for justice. The too-fearful citizen will not offer up his life for his country. Monarchies need pity and fear in the citizenry so the people will be obedient."[16] Although admitting that a poem can be directed to many ends, Giason Denores insisted that the correct end will be determined by the governor of the state (*Trattati*, 3:351; see Castelvetro, 2:227).

Cinquecento treatises on rhetoric are even more concerned with the civic dimension of persuasion. In his *Dialogo della retorica* (1542), Speroni argued that rhetoric is essential to a republic because "the orator's art, governance, practices, and words are eminently civil matters" (cose propriamente cittadinesche).[17] Similar assertions concerning the civil and practical function of rhetoric may be found in Francesco Sansovino's *Della rhetorica* (1543), Daniele Barbaro's *Della eloquenza* (1557), Antonio Maria Conti's *De eloquentia dialogus* (1582), and Giason Denores's *Breve trattato dell'oratore* (1574). And, as in treatises on poetics, here too we find a concern with the power of imitation or representation to move (and possibly to deceive) the reader or hearer, a concern that is equally evident in Counter-Reformation treatises on sacred eloquence.[18]

Cinquecento assumptions regarding the political uses and abuses of imitation and rhetoric are also apparent in commentaries on Aristotle's *Politics*, and it is here we begin to see the explicit mention of Machiavelli. Bernardo Segni published an Italian translation of the *Politics* in 1549, the same year he published the first Italian translations of the *Poetics* and *Rhetoric*. Commenting on book 1, chapter 10, where Aristotle discusses the art of acquisition, Segni noted that the same precepts were in "buona parte" recommended by "Machiavello nel suo libro del Principe." And, in his commentary on Aristotle's *Ethics* the following year, Segni also referred Aristotle's discussion of parsimony and liberality to Machiavelli's analysis of public relations in *The Prince*. That Segni read Aristotle in part through Machiavelli is also apparent in his dedication of the translation to Duke Cosimo: echoing chapter 15 of *The Prince*, he contrasted Plato, who discussed forms of government "which are beautiful to hear about but hard to see in the world," to Aristotle, who pragmatically analyzed forms of government that were "less good," even "transgressive or sinful," in order to aid or improve them.[19]

Other commentators noted the similarities between the prince's use of fraud and his manipulation of the passions in chapters 15 through 21 of *The Prince*, and the tyrant's use of imitation and his appeal to the passions in book 5 of the *Politics*. As Rebecca Bushnell has recently reminded us, in his discussion of the tyrant in book 5 Aristotle "vindicates mimesis," both pragmatically and morally. In the first case he teaches that "if the tyrant wishes to remain wicked and to maintain his illegitimate and absolute rule, he should at least practice public relations—or political theater" by appearing to be virtuous and kinglike. In the second case he argues that the best way to seem virtuous is to become virtuous, and that the tyrant may become a good king by pretending to be so.[20] It was particularly the first, pragmatic lesson that Renaissance writers associated with Machiavelli. In his 1568 commentary on the *Politics*, Louis Le Roy commented on Aristotle's advice to feign kingly behavior: "Machiavelli, writing his *Prince*, drew from this passage the principal foundations of his teaching." And Botero followed suit, declaring in the preface to his *Dell'officio del Cardinale* (1599), "Niccolò Machiavelli has created a prince who is no different from the tyrant Aristotle describes in his *Politics*."[21] At times, this comparison had the effect of mitigating the charges against Machiavelli; at other times, as we will see, Machiavelli was read as recommending what Aristotle only described. But, in either case, the role of imitation in the creation and maintenance of political power was taken for granted.

In addition to treatises on poetics and politics, manuals of casuistry provided a source of reflection on the political uses of imitation in the sixteenth century.[22] Both Catholic and Protestant writers on casuistry debated whether it was appropriate to misrepresent the truth in words or behavior; both argued that misrepresentation was justified in certain contexts, if governed by good intentions. Of particular importance to Counter-Reformation writers was the work of the Spanish Catholic, Martín de Azpilcueta—or Dr. Navarrus. In 1549 Navarrus published a casuistical handbook for confessors and penitents, in which he argued for the "licitness of mental reservation and dissimulation," based on a distinction between the speaker's intention, which God knows, and the spoken words heard by human ears.[23] Navarrus linked such licit dissimulation to reason of state, and quoted with approval the Latin tag, *Qui nescit dissimulare nescit regnare* (He who does not know how to dissimulate does not know how to rule); at the same time, he rejected the use of mental reservation to dissimulate one's faith. As these equivocal remarks suggest, manuals of casuistry were not only important as a context in which Machiavelli could be read and rebutted; they also offered a way of thinking that was compatible, to some extent, with Machiavelli's remarks on dissimulation. Thus in his *Trattati nove della prudenza*, Bartolomeo Carli

Piccolomini applied Pontano's and Machiavelli's analyses of the prudent use of dissimulation for the purpose of self-preservation to cases of religious dissimulation.[24]

It is not surprising, given the widespread discussion of the uses of imitation in the sixteenth century, that Machiavelli's own disturbing reflections on imitation were foremost in the minds of Counter-Reformation readers. Critics were particularly concerned to rebut chapters 15–21 of *The Prince*. As we have seen, these chapters parody the traditional humanist catalogue of princely virtues by exposing the inherent instability of the humanist doctrine of imitation. Imitation here is a means of misrepresentation or deception; and necessity is a function of rhetorical argument rather than of any external coercion. But Counter-Reformation critics also noted Machiavelli's reflections on the use and abuse of imitation, and the feigning of necessity, in the *Discourses*. In book 1, chapter 11, Machiavelli had discussed Rome's theatrical use of religious ceremony to instill fear and obedience in soldiers; and he had repeatedly emphasized the rhetorical effectiveness of violent and brutal examples throughout the *Discourses*. These passages from *The Prince* and the *Discourses* were regularly cited by Machiavelli's detractors. In *De libris a Christiano detestandis et a Christianesimo penitus eliminandi* (1552), the Dominican priest Ambrogio Caterino Politi attacked Machiavelli as a heretic for seeing religion only as a "persuasive instrument of human credulity."[25] He went on to quote from and rebut in detail chapter 18 of *The Prince*. The Portuguese bishop Jeronimo Osorio also attacked Machiavelli for his remarks on religion in the third book of his *De nobilitate christiana*, which was published in Florence in 1552 and translated into English in 1576. He noted at the outset Machiavelli's disingenuous claim in the *Discourses* that he was not attacking Christianity, only the misinterpretation of it; he particularly objected to Machiavelli's arguments for the rhetorical force of Rome's bloody sacrifice and omens, and for the political usefulness of "the counterfaite and deceiptfull resemblaunce of humaine vertue."[26]

In contrast, the Flemish scholar Justus Lipsius articulated an important defense of Machiavellian dissimulation in the service of reason of state in the fourth book of his *Politics* (1589). In this book Lipsius took up the topic of "mixed prudence," or prudence tempered with considerations of political expedience. In his discussion of the difference between prudence and art, Lipsius stressed the rhetorical dimension of prudence to an even greater extent than did classical rhetoricians such as Cicero and Aristotle:

> Now, if the things themselves are uncertaine, *Prudence* itselfe likewise must of necessitie be so, and so much the rather, because it is not onely tied to the things themselves, but to their dependents, having regard unto the times, the places, and to men and for their least change, she changeth her selfe, which

is the reason why she is not in all places alike, no nor the same in one and the selfe same thing. But the nature of *Art* is farre different, *We give best credit to that which we know of his owne nature is not subject to change.* And surely it is impossible for any man to reduce that which is uncertaine to certaine and strict limits of precepts.[27]

Here prudence is no longer simply the faculty of responding to contingency but has itself become contingent. It is this contingency which critics of Machiavelli feared would "of necessitie" lead to force and fraud. Lipsius confronted the charge, distinguishing between licit and illicit kinds of "mixed prudence," just as his Italian and Spanish contemporaries distinguished between true and false prudence and dissimulation. Precisely because we are embarked on a "tempestuous sea of the affayres *of the world,*" he argued, it is "sometimes lawfull, and reasonable *to trace out indirect courses*" (114):

> Who will blame mee so farre herein, or demaund the cause why I forsake vertue? Wine, although it be somewhat tempered with water, continueth to be wine: so doth prudence not change her name, albeit a fewe drops of deceipt bee mingled therewith: For I always meane but a small deale, and to a good end; Mothers, and Phisitions, doe they not often deceive little children, *to the end they might beguile their improvident age by a deceiptfull taste: and the deceipt may not be perceaved?* And why should not a Prince do the like towards the simple people, or towards some other Prince his neighbor? Surely *when one is not strong enough to debate the matter, it is not amisse secretly to intrappe.* And as the King of Sparta teacheth us; *Where we cannot prevaile by the Lions skinne, we must put on the Foxes.* I will always with *Pindarus* prayse him, who *in matters of variance [sic] doth make showe to have the courage of a Lion, but in Consultation is as craftie as a Foxe.* Be thou the like in time, and place, *and carelesse of that* these young men do say at schoole, or within doores: whome I knowe, *not to be capable hearers of civill doctrine,* and much lesse iudges: and surely this tribunall seate requireth a man, *who is not ignorant of those things which happen in this life.* Of such a person we shall easily obtain this, neither will we so strictly condemne the Italian *faulte-writer,* (who poore soule is layde at of all hands) and as a holy person sayth, that *there is a certaine honest and laudable deceipt.* (114)

And in the margin, Lipsius noted "Some kinde of persons rage too much against Machiavell."

In this passage, Lipsius touched on many of the important topics of Machiavellian rhetoric, while at the same time dramatizing their instability. In his justification of deceit, Lipsius used the topic of means and ends, asserting that "a small deale" of deceit is allowed to "a good end." Thus, although he implied that success in this world is contingent upon one's willingness to "forsake vertue," at least as far as means are concerned, he required that such prudence be governed by a virtuous intention. And, while fracturing virtue into means and ends, and means into lawful and unlawful deceit, he insisted that prudence retains its identity. Yet, precisely because prudence is a faculty that is always shifting, its identity amounts to a nonidentity. This principle of nonidentity begins to inflect other terms of Lipsius's rhetorical politics. For example, in his allusive gloss on chapter 18 of *The Prince*, Lipsius made it clear that force is not extrinsic to the rhetorical politics Machiavelli and he are expounding but is rather an argument among others, a part to be assumed: the courage of a lion is not simply something one possesses but that one "make[s] showe to have." In the rhetoric of reason of state, force is, at least in part, a matter of representation. Similarly, what counts as prudence or reason will depend on the rhetorical criteria of person, time, and place.

Such criteria appear to make politics rhetorical for Lipsius in two ways. First, the ruler must "purchase the favor" of his subjects, he must "gaine the affections of men, and . . . appropriate them to [his] own use" (118). Echoing sixteenth-century discussions of rhetoric and poetics, Lipsius noted that such favor may be purchased by means of "a false tale," and that the use of such indirect means gives "pleasure" to princes (who are the only ones to recognize such indirection and who are therefore their own audience). Second, the good ruler is one who is able to persuade his subjects of the necessity of reason of state: the uses of deceit

> are referred to the profit of the common wealth, which easilie draweth and draineth to itselfe all the venime of vice that is therein. And as in the application of medicines, they do with approbation, mingle venimous drugs for the good of the patient, so *these things* do seeme *profitable as it were a medicine*. (119)

For Lipsius, a rhetorical politics does not simply use false tales to purge subjects of dangerous affections, but effects the simultaneous justification and purgation of its own Machiavellian means.[28] In response to such arguments (and to the shifting religious and political allegiances that appeared to be one consequence of his belief in mixed prudence), critics condemned Lipsius as a figure of Protean inconstancy. One rival even accused Lipsius of "supporting the procedures of the Inquisition and, furthermore, of being a Machiavellian" himself.[29]

If Lipsius provided a justification of Machiavellian means that seemed to verge dangerously at times on stereotypically Machiavellian ends, Lodovico Zuccolo offered an analysis of reason of state that made ends a matter of deliberation as well. In his short treatise, *Della ragione di stato* (1621), Zuccolo argued that reason of state has no intrinsic or ideal moral content, nor is it tied to any particular form of government. It is simply a way of reasoning about the best means for realizing the interests of particular states:

> because the immediate end of the ruler is to introduce and preserve that form of government which he has in mind, it emerges that reason of state is concerned with the knowledge and use of those means which are appropriate for ordering and preserving any form of government, whatever it may be.[30]

Such an instrumental definition of reason of state means that reason of state is not incompatible with the rule of law, though it is also not identical with it. It also implies that it is impossible to distinguish between a good and bad reason of state in terms of the ethical nature of the state to which such reasoning is applied:

> in good republics reason of state is nothing other than prudence regarding the means and ways which we have discussed; and in bad governments, it is a certain shrewdness. . . . But, since that little bit of justice between corsairs and thieves is usually also called justice, perhaps it is not inappropriate to call the reason of state of tyrants and the powerful few prudence, on account of its resemblance to that other prudence. (30)

In fact, reason of state has no single identity, and no normative content, but is simply a way of reasoning about particulars. Yet, like most of his contemporaries, Zuccolo drew back from such a radical conclusion at the end of his treatise. Here he differentiated between those who describe the reason of state employed by tyrants in order to teach us how to avoid tyranny, and those who teach "the ways and means of using reason of state in bad governments," such as "Machiavelli and his followers" (38).

Caterino, who condemned Machiavelli outright as a dissembling heretic, and Zuccolo, who condemned Machiavelli in an afterthought, represent the two poles of the Counter-Reformation reception of Machiavelli: the outraged rejection of Machiavellian dissimulation versus the assimilation of this problem to an analysis of reason of state as a formal capacity for reasoning about means and interests. In the first case, Christian ethics are applied, as it were, from without in order to pass judgment on Machiavelli's own use of religion as an instrument of persuasion; in the second case, reason of state is analyzed as a morally neutral faculty of reason, one that is chiefly concerned with reasoning about the means to a given end. Whereas Caterino assumed Christianity as the framework within which he reasoned, the logical conclusion of Zuccolo's analysis is that the "end" of the state is itself subject to deliberation. As we will see, Botero's *Ragion di stato* lies somewhere between these two extremes: for Botero is more receptive to the challenge of Machiavelli's rhetorical politics than Caterino and more intent on preserving a normative content for reason of state than Zuccolo. In attempting to derive the superiority of Christian reason of state from a rhetorical and pragmatic analysis of political interests, Botero is closer in method to Machiavelli than either of his fellow critics.

Botero's *Ragion di stato*

Something of the context of *Ragion di stato* can be reconstructed from Botero's own biography and from the dedication of the treatise. Botero was educated as a Jesuit and although he eventually left the order, he remained closely tied to its vision of a resurgent Catholicism throughout his life. While still in the order, he taught philosophy and rhetoric in Jesuit schools in Italy and France. After leaving the order, he was briefly secretary to Carlo Borromeo, Archbishop of Milan, which was then a center of Counter-Reformation intellectual activity. Under the tutelage of Borromeo, he published a treatise on ecclesiastical rhetoric, entitled *De praedicatore verbi dei* (1585), in which he discussed the sublime style appropriate to the Counter-Reformation preacher (and, as we will see, to the Counter-Reformation prince). He traveled to France as part of a diplomatic mission of Duke Charles Emmanuel of Savoy, and it was here that he observed the French religious wars and became acquainted with the work of Bodin and perhaps Gentillet. He later became tutor to Borromeo's cousin, living in Rome and fraternizing with humanists such as Piero Maffei and Francesco Patrizi da Cherso.[31]

Like many of his Catholic contemporaries, Botero associated the burgeoning interest in reason of state not only with Machiavelli and Tacitus but also with reformers such as Luther and Calvin. And he saw his treatise as part of the Counter-Reformation effort to reestablish the political as well as spiritual hegemony of the Catholic church. In the dedication of *Ragion di stato*, he writes:

> chi sottrae alla conscienza la sua giuridizione universale di tutto ciò che passa tra gli umonini, sì nelle cose publiche come nelle private, mostra che non have anima, nè Dio. Sino alle bestie hanno uno istinto naturale, che le spinge alle cose utili e le ritira dalle nocevoli: ed il lume della ragione e 'l dettame della conscienza, dato all'uomo per saper discernere il bene e 'l male, sarà cieco negli affari publici, diffetoso ne' casi d'importanza? Spintô io non so se da sdegno o da zelo, ho più volte avuto animo di scrivere delle corruzioni introdotte da costoro [Machiavelli and Tacitus] ne' governi e ne' consigli de' prencipi, onde hanno avuto origine tutti gli scandali nati nella Chiesa di Dio e tutti i disturbi della Cristianità. (52)

> he who would deprive conscience of its universal jurisdiction over all that concerns man in his public as well as in his private life shows thereby that he has no soul and no God. The very beasts possess a natural instinct which

turns them towards useful things and away from harmful ones: shall then the light of reason and dictates of conscience, bestowed upon man to enable him to distinguish between good and evil, be obscured in affairs of state, mute in matters of importance? Provoked by indignation or zeal, I have often been emboldened to write of the corruption fostered by these two men [Machiavelli and Tacitus] in the policy and counsel of princes, from which have arisen all of the scandals within the Church of God and strife among Christians. (xiv)

To combat Machiavelli and Tacitus was also to combat those who "have strayed from the truth of the Gospels, sowing everywhere the seeds of heresy, revolution and the overthrow of kingdoms" (2.16.138, 67).[32] One way to do so was to insist on the unity of reason of state and conscience, the interest of the prince and of Christianity. Yet, despite the dedication's language of natural law, Botero does not simply counter the Reformers' emphasis on conscience with an appeal to Aristotle's *Ethics*. Nor does he simply assert that there are two reasons of state—a good Christian one and a bad Machiavellian one. His goal is rather to show that there is only one truly effective reason of state, only one truly effective rhetorical politics—one that both justifies and transforms Machiavellian means by suffusing them with Christian ends.

From the very beginning of *Ragion di stato*, it is clear that Botero shares Machiavelli's rhetorical approach to politics, and that he has designed the treatise as a rhetoric for producing political effects. Botero defines reason of state as "knowledge of the means appropriate to founding, preserving, and extending the state" (notizia di mezzi atti a fondare, conservare ed ampliare un dominio). In this definition, reason of state is like rhetoric in that it involves deliberating about the means appropriate to the realization of one's ends in particular circumstances. It also includes rhetoric in the sense that among those means are imitation and techniques of persuasion—the resources of the actor and orator. In fact, the prince is described as a political rhetorician who must learn the topics of particular disciplines, not in order to become an expert but "to make judicious use of those" who are; like the orator, the prince must to be able to "calm a nation, win round the multitude, or soothe their passions" (see especially 2.1.104–106, 34–36). The prince must also stage theatrical spectacles and religious ceremonies to instill obedience in his subjects; he must encourage ecclesiastical preaching (3.1.48–51, 74–75); and he must strive to create the impression of virtue and power (2.11.120–26, 54–58).

That *Ragion di stato* offers a rhetoric of practical politics is apparent not only from the definition of reason of state but also from the form of the treatise. Like *The Prince*, Botero's work is organized topically around such subjects as the acquisition, maintenance, and increase of reputation; the uses of the virtues; the control of magistrates. Like Machiavelli, Botero insists on the impossibility of exact rules in the realm of practical politics; in a chapter entitled "capi di prudenza" (maxims of prudence), which reads as a compendium of advice drawn from *The Prince* and the *Discourses*, Botero urges: "Deliberate carefully the enterprise you are about to undertake, but do not plan the details of its execution, for this must depend largely upon circumstances and opportunities, which are continually changing" (2.6.111, 46). The formal corollary of such an injunction is that each chapter individually, and the treatise as a whole, appears as a storehouse of commonplaces, maxims, and examples, which can be used or abused by the reader.

If *Ragion di stato* is like *The Prince* and the *Discourses* in offering the reader a compendium of political commonplaces, it is also like Machiavelli's work in registering a tension between a neutral and a normative conception of rhetorical politics. Botero does not simply want to present the reader with a storehouse of examples that may or may not be put to good uses (however the good is defined). Rather, his aim is to present the reader with a rhetorical politics that is at once descriptive and prescriptive. He does not want simply to demonstrate that the resources of rhetoric may be used *in utramque partem* but also that a truly pragmatic analysis of political affairs will prove the superiority of a rhetorical politics informed by Christianity. This tension is particularly apparent in Botero's discussion of imitation, which he describes both as a morally neutral faculty and one that reveals the ultimate pragmatism of Christian virtue.

In *Ragion di stato*, as in cinquecento treatises on poetics, imitation is not chiefly a source of disinterested pleasure but a means or instrument for preserving the social and political status quo. Imitation, correctly used, is tied to the faculty of civic prudence. And, as in such treatises, the awareness that a prince can feign virtue as well as faithfully represent it, that he can stir up the passions as well as purge or channel them, leads to significant tensions. Botero wants to acknowledge the utility of imitation for the prince, and to preserve the prince from the charge of mere expedience or feigning. Similarly, he wants to acknowledge the effect of imitation on the passions and interests of the audience, and to ward off the threat of Machiavellian manipulation. At times Botero tries to control the wayward rhetorical effects of imitation by specifying the content, means, or intention of imitation and by insisting that the prince be what he seems. At other times he accepts Machiavelli's displacement of the criterion of imitation from truthful representation to rhetorical effect; and he attempts to respond to Machiavelli's advice about sembling and dissembling on its own pragmatic terms.

Botero's remarks about the prince's reputation can serve as an example of the rhetorical effects of imitation, unconstrained by moral considerations. In book 2, chapter 11, Botero treats "De' modi di conservare la riputazione" (how to preserve reputation) in a manner reminiscent of chapter 21 of *The Prince*, as well as of Castiglione's discussion of *sprezzatura* in *The Courtier*. He observes that "many weak rulers have succeeded in maintaining a reputation for strength not by making themselves stronger, but simply by hiding their weakness" (2.11.120, 54) and urges that the prince ration his appearances in public so he will be respected more (2.11.124, 57). In this and other maxims, Botero suggests that the reputation of prudence and valor is not simply maintained—but also created—by strategic understatement or display. As Hobbes would write in his own account of reason of state in *Leviathan*, "Reputation of power, is Power," and "Eloquence is power; because it is seeming Prudence."[33] The same is true, according to Botero, of the reputation of religion. In his discussion of the uses of religion Botero notes, as Machiavelli did in the *Discourses*, that the Romans never embarked on any military campaign without first staging the necessary religious spectacles, since they "regarded religion as one of the chief bases of government." And he mentions Aristotle's advice in the *Politics* that "the tyrant should do his utmost to be thought pious" (2.15.133, 63). Christianity is particularly recommended for its practical effects; in a passage that takes up his prefatory remarks concerning the blasphemous separation of reason of state from conscience, Botero argues that it is far more practical to join them both by appearing to be religious and by encouraging religion in one's subjects:

> tra tutte le leggi, non ve n'è alcuna più favorevole a prencipi che la cristiana, perchè questa sottomette loro non solamente i corpi e le facoltà de' sudditi, dove conviene, ma gli animi ancora e le conscienze, e lega non solamente le mani, ma gli affetti ancora ed i pensieri, e vuole che si obedisca a' prencipi discoli nonchè a' moderati e che si patisca ogni cosa per non perturbar la pace. (2.16.137)

> of all religions none is more favorable to a ruler than the Christian law, according to which not merely the bodies and possessions but even the souls and consciences of his people are subject to him: their affections and thoughts are bound, as well as their hands, and they are enjoined to obey wicked rulers as well as moderate ones, and to suffer rather than disturb the peace. (66)

In this description, which glosses Machiavelli, Romans 13, and contemporary arguments about the right of resistance, Christianity proves to be the best way of maintaining power, whether of a tyrant or a good ruler.

Yet, at other moments, Botero draws back from such amoral advice, and insists that imitation and persuasion be morally serious in intention and content. Thus in book 3 he recommends the use of spectacles, especially tragedy and "the spectacles [trattenimenti] provided by the church," to "please, delight, and divert" the people; and he warns by way of contrast that the too frequent viewing of violent tournaments will make the populace itself violent and rebellious (3.1.148–50, 74–75). Similarly, in book 5 he cautions against the enervating effects of theater with the example of Caesar Augustus, "who set out to break the pride of the Romans and to convert them from devotion to arms to a preference for the delights of leisure by encouraging spectacles and the theatre" (5.4.184, 102). And in the conclusion to the chapter on reputation, Botero urges that the prince "Tenga per risoluto finalmente, che la riputazione dipende dall'essere, non dal parere" (finally be convinced that reputation depends upon what is, rather than what seems [2.11.126, 58])—an injunction that attempts to respond, by fiat, to the fear provoked by Machiavellian dissembling and the staging of political power.

Although Botero vacillates between amoral examples and moral prescription in much of *Ragion di stato*, he also proposes a dialectical argument that attempts to reconcile the two: rather than asserting a priori that the prince should follow the dictates of Christianity, Botero argues that the necessity of morality and Christian faith emerges from within a rhetorical and practical analysis of the interests of state.[34] Specifically, he uses the concept of interest to bridge the gap between a rhetoric based on the useful and one informed by the Christian criterion of the good: he insists that it is in the prince's interest to imitate the conventional virtues, because the prince's staging of these virtues is interesting both to his subjects and to God. As Botero writes: "Religion is the foundation of kingship, for all power proceeds from God, and since the grace and favour of God can only be won by piety, any other foundation will be disastrous" (2.15.135–36, 65). Just as the virtues are part of the rhetoric the prince uses to secure power over the people (2.14), so religion is the rhetoric he uses to address God as well as the people: since all power comes from God, it is a good political wager to be religious. As with Botero's earlier discussion of the uses of imitation, God is revered for his power, and religion is valued first and foremost in terms of its effects. But, Botero goes on to argue, in the long run it is in the prince's interest to *be* religious—because, in the end, being religious is more effective than seeming so. Thus he claims that the prince should avoid simulation, not only because it is morally wrong but also because "it cannot last, and when it is discovered entirely discredits the dissimulator" (2.16.138, 67). And, referring to the passage in the *Politics* where Aristotle advises the tyrant to feign religion, Botero comments: "It is, however, extremely difficult for one who is not truly religious to be thought so, for nothing lasts so short a time as pretence" (2.15.133, 63).[35] The criterion of political behavior is not in the first instance faithfulness to an a priori standard of the good but rather efficacy; it is precisely such calculations of effects that transform a rhetoric of seeming into one of being. In an ironic revision of Machiavelli's reflections in chapter 18 of *The Prince* and chapters 11–15 in book 1 of the *Discourses*, it turns out that being religious is the most efficacious way of seeming religious (though we should also note that such a subordination of being to seeming makes being religious indistinguishable from perfect dissimulation).[36]

As these examples illustrate, Botero vacillates in his attitude toward the rhetorical dimension of princely power. On the one hand, while propounding a rhetoric of seeming—even to the point of suggesting with Machiavelli that reputation creates, as well as represents, the virtues of the prince—Botero also insists that the prince be what he seems. On the other hand, while defining reason of state as reasoning from interest, Botero argues in Aristotelian fashion that it is in the prince's interest to conform to the dictates of the Church—and that the most effective way of seeming religious is actually to be so. If, in the first case, Botero presents reason of state simply as a means subordinate to Christian ends, in the second case he claims that Christian ends are generated from within a rhetorical and pragmatic analysis of interest. Undoubtedly, it was this second argument that led Botero's contemporaries to object that Botero was uncomfortably close to Machiavelli's pragmatic approach to politics. The view that all positions are interested, but not all interests are equal, is a consequence of the rhetorical politics that Machiavelli himself espoused—though to different ends. It is this argument, according to which imitation does not simply reflect the truth but is inextricably intertwined with the interest of actor and audience, that Botero pursues in the 1598 appendix to *Ragion di stato*, and that provides the most intriguing, and unsettling, reflection on reason of state.

Sublime Politics in the *Aggiunta* on Reputation

While *Ragion di stato* analyzes the rhetorical and political uses of imitation, Botero's 1598 addition, "On Reputation," both reasserts the centrality of rhetoric to reason of state and explores some of the more subversive implications of locating the prince's power in reputation and interest.[37] As we have seen, Botero had already discussed reputation in book 2 of his treatise; his prefatory letter to the *Aggiunta* makes clear that this "supplement" is central to the entire work precisely because reputation is the crucial supplement to political power, seeming the crucial supplement to being:

Uno de i principali fondamenti di Stato, e di governo, à giudicio di più intendenti, si è un certo concetto alto, e fermo, che si ha della saviezza, e del potere di un Prencipe. Il qual concetto viene ordinariamente chiamato Riputatione.

Conciosia cosa che, si come à un mercatante non è meno necessario il credito, che i contanti; cosi a un Potentato non importa meno l'essere stimato possente, che la possanza istessa. Perche questa è soggetta à molti pericoli, & incontri, dai quali la tien lontana, e la fa quasi riparo, e scudo la fama, e la opinione, che si ha della stabilità, e grandezza. Quinci è avvenuto che alcuni personaggi di molta qualità, si come si son dilettati particolarmente di quel capo della mia Ragion di Stato, nel qual io discorro della Riputatione, come di cosa nuova, e non trattata ordinatamente da altri: cosi hanno desiderato, che io alquanto più diffusamente ne trattassi. (33)

One of the principal foundations of state and government, in the judgment of the prudent, is a certain high and fixed conception that is held of the wisdom and power of the Prince, which conception comes ordinarily to be called reputation. For just as credit is not less necessary than cash to a merchant, so to a potentate it is no less important to be deemed powerful than to have the power itself, because the latter is subject to many perils and accidents, from which the fame and opinion, which result from stability and greatness, protect it and serve almost as a rampart and shield. Hence has it come about that some personages of great quality, as they are delighted particularly with that chapter of my *Ragion di stato* in which I discourse on Reputation as of something new and not ordinarily treated by others, have thought that I should treat it here at more length. (231)

As his parenthetical "as of something new" suggests, Botero was well aware that Machiavelli had discussed the uses of reputation in chapters 15–21 of *The Prince*. In particular, in chapter 17, he had notoriously recommended the manipulation of the passions ("it is much safer to be feared than loved"), and in chapter 18 he had linked the use of deception to reputation and power:

Alcuno principe de' presenti tempi, quale non è bene nominare, non predica mai altro che pace e fede, e dell'una e dell'altra è inimicissimo; e l'una e l'altra, quando e' l'avessi osservata, li arebbe piú volte tolto o la reputazione o lo stato. (*P*, 74)

A certain prince of our own time [Ferdinand of Spain], whom it's just as well not to name, preaches nothing but peace and mutual trust, yet he is the determined enemy of both; and if on several different occasions he had observed either, he would have lost both his reputation and his throne. (51)

In the *Aggiunta*, Botero pursues the implications of Machiavelli's remarks on reputation, even to the point of identifying reputation and power. In the passage quoted above, Botero makes reputation more powerful than force itself, less vulnerable to "perils and accidents." And, in book 2 of the *Aggiunta*, he effectively identifies reputation and the throne when he uses the language of acquisition and conservation (Italian: acquistare, conservare) that Machiavelli reserves for "lo stato" (39, 237). Insisting that the ability to confer reputation rests with the prince's subjects, Botero then proceeds to analyze the ways in which the prince can manipulate the passions and interests of his subjects in order to ensure his reputation and maintain his throne. Specifically, he recommends that the prince engage his subjects' interest by staging what I would like to call— borrowing from Botero's own treatise on sacred rhetoric—a politics of the sublime.[38] If *Ragion di stato* is a rhetoric of princely behavior in general, the *Aggiunta* is itself a rhetoric for producing the subject's experience of sublimity and its corresponding political effects. The goal of such political rhetoric is both to manipulate and to mask the prince's dependence on his subjects. Yet, in analyzing the operations of such rhetoric, Botero also reveals the instability of the prince's power, its availability for conflicting interests. The *Aggiunta* plays the *Discourses* to *Ragion di stato*'s *Prince*.

Although, in his discussion of reputation in the *Aggiunta*, Botero touches on what Aristotle termed *ethos* (the character of the speaker) and *logos* (the material for constructing arguments about reputation), he is chiefly concerned with reputation as the effect of the subject's *interests* and *passions*. Concerning interest, he writes,

> perche la riputatione di un Prencipe è posta nell'opinione, e nel concetto, che il popolo ha di lui, la materia, nella quale egli si deve, per far acquisto di un tanto bene, occupare, deve esser tale, a che il popolo vi habbia interesse, e tali sono la pace, e la guerra. (36)

> because the reputation of a Prince consists in the opinion and in the conception that the people have of him, the material with which he ought to occupy himself, to acquire so great a good, should be such as the people would have an interest in. Such are peace and war. (233)

Interest is maintained by awesome deeds and a "loftiness of virtue and perfection . . . almost . . . beyond the ordinary limits of human nature" (36, 233). It is maintained, in short, by staging a sublime spectacle of the prince's greatness or his power. In book 1 of the *Aggiunta*, Botero defines the man of reputation as "that man whose virtue (*virtù*), by its not being possible to be penetrated and comprehended at a stroke, would be worthy of being more and more often considered and estimated" (35, 232); and he goes on to describe the subject's experience of reputation as one of sublime greatness:

> Non è cosa, che habbia maggior somiglianza con la riputatione che la meraviglia, ma non è l'istesso. Perche la meraviglia si stende più alle cose speculative, e naturali, che alle humane, e prattiche; ma la riputatione non si allarga fuor delle cose prattiche. Quella nasce perche non s'intende la ragione dell'effetto. Onde l'ecclisse della Luna, e del Sole, la cometa, e le altre cose

cosi fatte, paiono meravigliose à chi non ne sa il perche. Ma la riputatione procede non perche non si sappia la ragione dell'effetto; ma perche non si comprende facilmente la sua grandezza. (35)

There is nothing that has more resemblance to reputation than wonder; but it is not the same. For wonder extends more to the speculative and natural than the human and practical; but reputation does not extend beyond practical matters. The former occurs because the reason for the effect is not understood. Therefore the eclipse of the moon, and the sun, and the comet, and other such phenomena appear wondrous to him who does not know the reasons for them. But reputation is not the consequence of our not knowing the reason for the effect, but of our not easily understanding its greatness. (232–33; translation modified)

Such lack of easy comprehension provokes an activity of reflecting, of considering and estimating, which itself confers value on its object.[39]

Whereas book 1 stresses the sublime difficulty of comprehending the prince's greatness, in book 2 of the *Aggiunta* Botero emphasizes the sublime effect of the prince's imitation of divine power:

Prudente sarà colui, che con poche asprezze, & esecutioni, terrà i suditi in officio, e si sarà tener per terribile, imitando in ciò Dio, il quale con tuonare spesse volte cagionna ne gli animi de gli huomini paura, e terrore senza danno; ma accioche i tuoni non perdano il credito, per non far mai colpo, tra mile tuoni saetta qualche volta, e per lo più qualche cima d'albero ò giogo di monte. (42)

That man is prudent who, with little harshness and few executions, holds his subjects to their duties, imitating in this God, Who by thundering frequently causes in the minds of men fear and terror without hurt; but so that his thunderbolts will not lose their credit by never reaching their mark, amid a thousand such bolts, one occasionally strikes, and most of the time the top of a tree or the peak of a mountain. (241; translation modified)

In this spectacular demonstration of power, which causes "fear and terror without hurt," the prince places his subjects in the position of the Lucretian spectator who looks on shipwrecks without fear. In staging his power, the prince masks its coerciveness as persuasion—as an appeal to the independent judgment of the spectator. The prince's interest in maintaining his power is aestheticized as the spectator's interest in a sublime scene, one that includes a few executions.

In book 2 of the *Aggiunta*, Botero develops his rhetoric of political sublimity, by discussing how "to make without ostentation a showing of one's own powers" (39, 237). In particular, he discusses how the illusion of greatness may be achieved by understatement in word and action. As in his earlier remarks in *Ragion di stato*, he recommends secrecy, which keeps the prince's subjects "in a state of suspense and eager[ly] awaiting his intentions"; in addition, he devotes some attention to the rhetorical ideal of *brevitas*, which he associates with Tacitus. Botero had also discussed brevity as a rhetorical ideal in his treatise *De praedicatore verbi dei*. Like other Counter-Reformation writers on sacred eloquence, Botero saw brevity as a sign of divine inspiration and of sublimity—rather than of rhetorical artifice. Yet, Tacitean brevity was also regularly perceived as a difficult style, at odds with "easy comprehension." Thus, although the recommendation that the prince "avoid . . . amplifications and . . . hyperbole" might seem to conflict with the emphasis on grandeur in book 1 of the *Aggiunta*, the two share a structure of incommensurability that provokes reflection and admiration in the viewer. As in *Ragion di stato*, Botero pursues this insight by translating the stylistic ideal of brevity into one of scarcity, arguing, like Shakespeare's Henry IV, that the prince "should not show himself daily and in all places, but rarely and on occasion. *Continuus aspectus verendos magnos homines, ipsa satietate facit*" (Continuous sight causes great men, by the very satiety, to be less respected [42, 241]). Just as in *Ragion di stato*, so here Botero articulates what will become the Hobbesian logic according to which reputation of power is power.

Yet, precisely because the people are "by nature insatiable and hard to please" (37, 234; translation modified)—one might say hard to keep interested—the response of admiration needs to be mixed with that of fear. Describing the passions that subject the people to the prince, Botero insists that "every principate be supported by one of three foundations, that is on love, or fear, or reputation; of which the first two are simple, the third composed of both" (37, 234). He goes on to argue for the superior stability of a rule based on reputation, which is brought about chiefly through "spetie di timore" (images of fear):

> perche l'amore è in podestà del suddito: ma il timore dipende da chi si fà temere: e le maniere di rendersi amabile non sono cosi sicure, & universali come quelle di farsi formidabile. D'amore e di timore, si compone la Riputatione, che è migliore dell'uno, e dell'altro: perche contiene quel ch'è di buono, e di utile in ambidue. Conciosia che ella prende dall'amore l'unione dei sudditi col Prencipe, e dal timore la soggettione: perche quello unisce, e questo sottomette. Ma mi domandarà alcuno, quale ha più parte nella riputatione, l'amore o il timore? il timore senza dubio; perche si come il rispetto, e la riverenza, cosi anche la riputatione, sono per la eminenza della virtù, onde procedono, spetie di timore, anzi che d'amore. (38)

For love is in the power of the subjects, but fear depends on him that causes the fear; and the means of keeping himself lovable are not so sure and universal as those of making oneself formidable. From love and fear is composed reputation, which is the better of both; since it contains what is good and useful in each. For it takes from love the union of the subjects with the prince, and from fear, the subjection; because the former unites, and the latter subjects. But someone asks me, "Which has more influence in reputation, love, or fear?" Fear, without doubt. For just as respect and reverence, through the eminence of virtue whence they proceed, are images of fear, rather than love, so also is reputation. (235)

If reputation lies in the one granting reputation rather than in the reputed, the prince can nevertheless minimize his dependence on the people and assure his control by creating images of fear.

Like Machiavelli's *Prince*, Botero's *Aggiunta* teaches the prince how to consolidate his power by manipulating the realm of appearances; yet, like *The Prince*, Botero's rhetorical analysis of the political sublime also exposes the resources of princely power, even as it counsels brevity and concealment. Two examples dramatize this instability of rhetorical politics, its availability to subjects as well as to sovereigns. In book 1, as we have seen, Botero recommends that the prince rely on fear rather than love, and he cautions that princes "chosen with the greatest acclaim" who ignore this teaching will be found "abandoned or dead" (37, 235). He then proceeds to illustrate the power of images of fear with the example of Cid Ruidias:

> Hor di quanta importanza sia la riputatione si può conoscere da questo, che anche huomini morti hanno con essa fatto cose, da huomini vivi. Conciosia che si legge di Zid Ruidias, personaggio di altissimo valore nell'arme, che havendolo doppò morte i suoi acconcio sopra un cavallo, con la sola presentia di lui vinsero un grosso essercito di Mori, venuti sopra la Città di Valenza: e Baldrino Panicaglia fù di tanta riputatione presso à Soldati, che anco dopò morte si reggevano quasi per lui; imperoche portavano il suo corpo imbalsamato attorno, e li piantavano il padiglione, come quando era vivo, e con certe sorti esploravano il suo parere, e con esse si governavano. . . . Tacito scrive, che Tiberio già vecchio, conosceva che le cose sue si mantenevano più per beneficio di riputatione, che per fondamento di forze: e Nerva, veggendo che, per esser troppo vecchio, haveva perduta la riputatione, depose l'Imperio. (38)

Now of how great importance is reputation can be known from the fact that even dead men have by this accomplished things with living men. For it is read of Cid Ruidias, a personage of the highest valor in arms, that his men placed him after his death upon a horse, and by his presence alone they beat a great army of the Moors who had come against the city of Valencia. Also Baldrino Panicaglia had such a great reputation with his soldiers that even after his death they were ruled, as it were, by him; since they carried around his embalmed body and erected his pavilion as when he was alive; also by

certain lots they sought his wish from him, by which they were governed. . . .
[And] Tacitus writes that Tiberius, when aged, realized that his affairs were
maintained more by his reputation's efficacy than on the basis of force. Also
Nerva, seeing that by reason of growing old he had lost his reputation, re-
signed the Empire. (236; translation modified)

This passage demonstrates the subversive implications of the rhetorical
and figurative analysis of sovereign power. In the story of Cid Ruidias the
distinction between history and poetry collapses, since the dead body of
the historical Cid turns into something like the poetic figment of a hero;
and, as with the poets Botero discusses in *Ragion di stato*, so with Cid
Ruidias's men: "Even if what [they] tell us is false, they tell it in such a
manner as to rouse a man's spirits." Interestingly, once representation is
defined in terms of its effects rather than its faithfulness to the truth, a
dead prince turns out to be as effective as a live one, the fiction of "presence" as powerful as its reality. Whereas in his earlier discussion of
princely power, Botero showed how such a figurative logic worked to
consolidate the prince's power, here he shows the converse—that the fiction of sovereignty can be manipulated by the people as well: the corpse
of Cid Ruidias becomes the representative and instrument of his men.
Furthermore, fear is no longer the emotion that the subjects experience in
the presence of their prince but rather the effect that is created in others by
their own rhetorical adroitness.

This reversal of cause and effect, ruler and subject, is reminiscent of
Hobbes's *Leviathan*, where fear—the effect of the sovereign threat of
force—is also the cause of the sovereign's absolute power. So for Botero
fear is both the effect and the cause of reputation. As the example of Cid
Ruidias suggests, one implication of this sublime rhetoric of political effects is that sovereignty as well as reputation is a figure of the subject's
passions. Another, related implication is that the ruler who does not represent the interests of his subjects will either resign (as Nerva did) or be
found "abandoned or dead"; for a justification of regicide is one logical
consequence of rooting the prince's rule in the approval of his audience,
that is, the consent of his subjects.

The second example of the instability of rhetorical politics is the comparison of the prince's sublime rhetoric with God's display of thunder
and lightning, quoted above. The comparison works both ways: just as
the prince needs to be "credited" with reputation by his subjects (33,
231), so "in order that the thunders do not destroy his credit by not ever
causing damage, among a thousand thunders, sometimes [God sends] a
flash of lightning" (42, 241). We can now see that a further implication
of Botero's analysis of the force of representation is that God himself uses
reason of state—or what Botero defines in the *Aggiunta* on neutrality as

"reasoning from interest" (223)—to stage his representation of himself to men. In a world where the exigencies of imitation make even God a rhetorician and Machiavel, the rhetoric of reason of state seems as much a cause of divine sovereignty as an effect. This is the implication of the myth that Botero reports to confirm his remarks on the importance of fear to the creation of reputation:

> Hor chiara cose è, che nella riputatione compariscono molto più le proprietà, e gli effetti del timore, che dell'amore: perch'ella hà più forza di ritirare, e di separare, e di dispareggiare, che di conciliare, ò di unire, ò di uguagliare. Di questo parere fù anche Ovidio là, dove havendo vagamente detto, che doppò l'antico Chaos, le cose restarono un gran tempo confuse, senza distintione di maggioranza, or di minoranza: si che li Dei di bassa lega si ponevano spesse volte à sedere presso à Saturno, & à Giove; soggiunge che finalmente l'honore, e la riverenza diedero à ciascuno il grado, & il seggio conveniente. Onde nacque la maestà; presso à cui si assisero il rispetto, e la paura. (38)

> Now it is clear that in reputation the properties and effects of fear are more in evidence than love; for reputation has more force to make shrink back, to separate and make unequal, than to conciliate, or to unite, or to equalize. Of this opinion also was Ovid, there where, having charmingly said that after the ancient chaos things remained for a long time confused, without distinction between the majority or the minority, so that the Gods of low degree set themselves many times to be seated near Saturn and near Jove, he adds that finally honor and reverence gave to each his place and suitable seat. Thence is born majesty, near to which respect and fear are seated. (235–36; translation modified)

In this myth, hierarchy and sovereignty, decorum and the "suitable seat," are the effects rather than the causes of respect and fear. Even divine majesty is begotten from a *rhetoric* of majesty and reputation.

Not surprisingly, Botero draws back from the subversive consequences of his argument, insisting in the conclusion to book 2 of the *Aggiunta* that princes should be what they seem: "Reputation in the long run depends on being, not appearing" (45, 245); "majesty without forces is little secure" (45, 246). As in the conclusion to book 1, so here the example of Tiberius appears again, this time to opposite effect:

> Onde scrive Tacito, che Artabano disprezzava la vecchiaia di Tiberio, come imbelle, & inetta all'arme: & il medesimo Tiberio nun [sic] hebbe ardire di risentirsi contra le minacie di Getulico, perche considerava, *Publicum sibi odio, extremam aetatem, magisque fama, quam vi stare res suas.* (45)

> Therefore Tacitus writes that Artabanus deprecated the old age of Tiberius as unwarlike and unsuited to arms; and Tiberius himself had not the bold-

ness to resent the threats of Gaetulicus, because he was considering "the public hate of himself and his extreme age, and that his fortunes stood more on fame than strength." (246)

The effect of these contrary uses of the example of Tiberius is not, however, to secure the prince from the contaminations of rhetoric, but to illustrate that any example is open to a variety of interpretations and uses. As in *Ragion di stato* proper, the criterion of use (including the use of quotations) is not in the first instance moral virtue but rather interest. But, like Machiavellian *virtù*, interest is a flexible criterion that may be used not only pro and contra morality, but also pro and contra princely rule.[40]

As these examples illustrate, and as Botero's contemporaries recognized, reason of state—reasoning from interest—is threatening because it is not a faithful imitation of reason but—like all imitation—a necessary supplement to it. As Botero writes in book 1, chapter 1, of *Ragion di stato*:

> Stato è un dominio fermo sopra popoli e Ragione di Stato è notizia di mezzi atti a fondare, conservare ed ampliare un dominio così fatto. . . . E sebbene tutto ciò che si fa per le suddette cagioni si dice farsi per Ragione di Stato, nondimeno ciò si dice più di quelle cose che non si possono ridurre a ragione ordinaria e commune. (55)

> State is a stable rule over a people and Reason of State is the knowledge of the means by which such a dominion may be founded, preserved, and extended. . . . And although all that is done to these purposes is said to be done for Reasons of State, yet this is said rather of such actions as cannot be considered in the light of ordinary reason. (3)

The ambiguity of these remarks is exemplary: whereas, on the one hand, reason of state seems to involve ordinary reasoning about the means of founding, preserving, and extending a state, on the other it refers specifically to actions that "cannot be considered in the light of ordinary reason." *Ragion di stato* shows that ordinary reason must always be supplemented by a rhetoric of the passions and interests—both the prince's and the people's. Once reason of state is defined as a supplement to reason, once rhetoric is recognized as a supplement to the prince's power, it becomes impossible to distinguish between prudence and astuteness in terms of either means or ends. What distinguishes Botero's prince from Machiavelli's is not a truer representation of the virtues or even truer interests but—so Botero claims—a more powerful use of them.

As the preceding pages have illustrated, Counter-Reformation readers of Machiavelli were particularly sensitive to the moral ambiguity of Machiavelli's recommendations regarding the uses of rhetoric and representation. Yet, in attempting to respond to Machiavelli on his own terms, they dramatized the very ambiguity or equivocation they attempted to preclude. As the German Caspar Klockius was to write a hundred years later, in his *Rationis status monstrosa aequivocatio* (1685): "Ratio status manet aenigma saeculi, materia subtilitatum; cum Proteo, Thetis; cum Paride, Helena; cum Ulysse, Penelope" (Reason of state remains the enigma of the age, the material of subtleties; with Proteus, it is also Thetis; with Paris, Helen; with Ulysses, Penelope).[41] In arguing that the Christian prince is more successful in practice than the Machiavel, Botero and his contemporaries ran the risk of idealistically equating virtue with success; while in admitting that tyrants such as Tiberius were effective in maintaining their power, they seemed to suggest that reason of state might on occasion take the form of a Machiavellian abuse of power. Ironically, the concept of interest—invoked as a way of mediating between intention and effect, morality and politics—involved the same dilemmas. At the same time, it exposed the fiction of a reasoning about politics uncontaminated by rhetoric.

Finally, Counter-Reformation treatises on reason of state illustrate the ways in which rhetoric, as a means of responding to the contingency of "practical matters," may also aggravate that contingency. They show the difficulty of using rhetoric as an instrument of ideological closure, since rhetoric provides argument on both sides of a question and thus contains its own immanent critique of ideology. To answer Machiavelli on his own terms is to run the risk of making ends as debatable as means. For this reason, many sixteenth- and seventeenth-century writers preferred to demonize Machiavelli, even as—or precisely because—they took to heart his rhetorical politics.

PART TWO

ENGLISH MACHIAVELLISM

DECADES before the condemnation of Machiavellian reason of state in Counter-Reformation treatises of the 1590s and early 1600s, Cardinal Pole provided a quick sketch of the Machiavel in his *Apologia ad Carolum Quintum* (1539). He tells us that Machiavelli's works "stink of the malice of Satan" (malitiam Satanae redolent) and that *The Prince* was written "by Satan's hand" (Satanae digito). He also offers a synopsis of Machiavelli's rhetorical politics, noting that the prince must learn to simulate and dissimulate according to the age-old rhetorical criteria of time, place, and audience. And he condemns Machiavelli's divorce of ethics from politics and his merely instrumental use of the virtues as immoral cunning.[1] Pole's letter was probably designed as a preface to his *De unitate ecclesiastica*, the treatise in which he argued against Henry VIII's divorce and royal supremacy. Machiavelli is a figure for Henrician policy, for in the same letter Pole recounts a conversation ten years earlier with Thomas Cromwell, the architect of the policy, whom he describes as "Satan's ambassador" and a reader of Machiavelli.[2] He might also have referred to Stephen Gardiner, Cromwell's successor and defender of royal supremacy in a treatise entitled *De vera obedientia*, for in his *Actes and Monuments* John Foxe described Gardiner in similarly satanic and Machiavellian terms.[3] Gardiner himself would go on to write a treatise of advice to Philip II, the "new prince" of England, in which he assimilated Machiavelli's rhetorical politics and included long, unacknowledged quotations from *The Prince* and the *Discourses*.

The conjunction of Pole and Gardiner is emblematic of the complicated reception of Machiavelli's work in the English Renaissance. On the one hand, critics of Machiavelli such as Pole describe him as a Machiavel and they regularly establish simple equivalences between politics, religion, and literary modes of representation: the Machiavel's tyranny, idolatry, and atheism are seen as inseparable from his rhetorical force, fraud, and manipulation of his audience. On the other hand, readers such as Gardiner see Machiavelli's rhetoric and political machinations as neutral or indeterminate means that can be used well or badly, by princes or usurpers. They are sensitive to the dangers of appearing Machiavellian and so usually do not cite Machiavelli by name; but they are equally aware of the wealth of political insight to be drawn from *The Prince* and the *Discourses*.

As in the Counter-Reformation culture of Italy, this dual reception of Machiavelli reflects not only ambivalence about the de facto political power of newly emergent nation states but also a widespread ambivalence about the potentially immoral techniques of persuasion. For, even more than continental writers, Renaissance Englishmen were nervous about the divorce of rhetoric from ethical considerations; and they represented this anxiety about rhetoric, and about Machiavelli's rhetorical politics, in the Machiavel.[4] Authors of treatises on rhetoric, courtiership, casuistry, and government regularly distinguished between moral art and immoral technique, often associating the latter with Machiavellian force and fraud. In *The Arte of English Poesie* (1589) George Puttenham invoked the stereotype of the Machiavellian courtier when he tied rhetorical dissimulation to the denizens of "the Princes Courts of Italie," who "seeme idle when they be earnestly occupied and entend to nothing but mischievous practizes, and do busily negotiat by coulor of otiation."[5] And in *The Scholemaster* (1570), Roger Ascham made the link explicit between Italianate courtiers and Machiavelli:

> And though for their private matters they can follow, fawn, and flatter noble personages, contrary to them in all respects; yet commonly they ally themselves with the worst papists, to whom they be wedded, and do well agree together in three proper opinions; in open contempt of God's word, in a secret security of sin, and in a bloody desire to have all taken away by the sword or burning, that be not of their faction. They that do read with indifferent judgment Pighius [a Catholic propagandist] and Machiavel, two indifferent patriarchs of these two religions, do know full well that I say true.[6]

Similar equations of rhetorical dissembling and Machiavellism can be found in Renaissance English treatises on casuistry. In his *Dissertatio contra aequivocationem* (1625), John Barnes argued that "like the Florentine, proponents of mental reservation allowed evil to be done in order that good might result." Mental reservation was also condemned as Machiavellian by Thomas Morton in *A Full Satisfaction concerning a double romish Iniquitie; hainous Rebellion, and more then heathenish Aequivocation* (1606) and Henry Mason in *The New Art of Lying, covered by the Iesuites under the Vaile of Equivocation* (1624).[7] Finally, just as the abuse of rhetoric was linked to the Machiavel's atheism and political subversiveness in handbooks of rhetoric, courtesy, and casuistry, so political subversion was associated with the abuse of rhetoric in contemporary political treatises. The anonymous *Treatise of Treasons* (1572) typically described the "Machiavellian state" not only as one in which "Religion is framed to serve the time and policy" and "the ruled are taught with every change of Prince to change the face of their faith and Religion" but also as one infected by the "impudencie of lying without limite or measure both in writing and woorde, [and the] forging and faining of frindship by fairest woordes, when woorst was meant."[8]

As the association of the Machiavel with hypocrisy and dissembling suggests, the anxiety about the political and religious abuse of rhetoric was equally an anxiety about theatrical representation. Hence the particular appropriateness of the Machiavel as a stage villain. On the stage, the Machiavel is not simply a figure of force and fraud, rhetorical coercion and deception—he is also a meta-theatrical embodiment of the fear of theater. Although the preceding remarks have indicated that the Machiavel was well known in England before his appearance in Elizabethan drama, the theatrical Machiavel provides further evidence that contemporaries recognized the contribution of rhetoric and theatrical representation to the subversion—or maintenance—of the political and religious status quo. Richard III's boast in Shakespeare's *Henry VI, Part 3* is exemplary:

> I'll play the orator as well as Nestor;
> Deceive more slily than Ulysses could;
> And, like a Sinon, take another Troy;
> I can add colours to the chameleon;
> Change shapes with Proteus for advantages;
> And set the murdrous Machiavel to school.
> Can I do this and cannot get a crown?
>
> (3.2.188–94)

Just as Richard III assumes the connection between rhetoric, protean flexibility, and the crown, so in the prologue to Marlowe's *Jew of Malta* "Machevill" [*sic*] demystifies the sanctimonious rhetoric and pretended ignorance of his contemporaries to the same effect: here, too, rhetoric creates the effect of legitimacy—the "title" of pope or sovereign—but only if laws are written first in blood:

> Admir'd I am of those that hate me most.
> Though some speak openly against my books,
> Yet they will read me, and thereby attain
> To Peter's chair. . . .
> Many will talk of title to the crown:
> What right had Caesar to the empery?
> Might first made kings, and laws were then most sure
> When, like the Draco's, they were writ in blood.
> (Prologue to *The Jew of Malta*, 9–12; 18–21)

As these and other passages suggest, sixteenth-century Englishmen from Pole to Marlowe saw Machiavelli as the convenient symbol of a range of cultural anxieties about threats to the social, political, religious, and linguistic status quo.

Yet, at the same time that Englishmen condemned the Machiavel for his dissembling rhetoric of appearances and his protean indeterminacy, they recognized the relevance of Machiavelli's rhetorical approach to politics to contemporary crises of political and religious authority. Here, too, I believe, they were influenced by the rhetorical culture of the English Renaissance. For the same treatises of rhetoric, courtliness, and casuistry that condemn the immoral abuse of language also offer their readers a storehouse of arguments that are neither intrinsically good nor evil, and are thus available for a variety of purposes. For example, Puttenham defined poetry as a technique rather than as an intrinsically moral art when he noted that in poetry, as opposed to grammar, there are no fixed rules concerning the "vertues" and "vices" of speech:

> In which respect it may come to passe that what the Grammarian setteth downe for a viciositee in speach may become a vertue and no vice, contrariwise his commended figure may fall into a reprochfull fault; [thus, with] a speciall regard to all circumstances of the person, place, time, cause and purpose he hath in hand . . . [the poet] maketh now and then very vice goe for a formall vertue in the exercise of this arte. (167)

Similarly, while treatises of casuistry condemned lying as immoral, the distinction between lying and equivocation or mental reservation could be said to amount to the view that lying is a neutral means that can be used with a godly or sinful intention. The same focus on morally neutral means emerges from the theological and casuistical distinction between actions that are prohibited by Scripture and "morally neutral or indifferent" actions. The latter, according to William Perkins and others, "in themselves beeing neither good nor evill, may be done or not done without sinne; In themselves I say, for in their circumstances they are, & may be made either evill or good."[9] It is finally both context and intention rather than the action itself that indicates whether a given action is morally reprehensible.[10]

As in Counter-Reformation Italy, this emphasis on intention had a number of paradoxical consequences. First, the emphasis on the religious ends of politics eventually allowed for the assimilation of Machiavellian reason of state by Christianity. For, although Machiavelli was initially attacked for his secular and immoral means and ends, in time the two were separated and some Machiavellian means were sanctioned by Christian ends. As George Mosse has argued, reason of state was acceptable to both Catholics and Protestants if it was pursued for reasons of faith, that is, governed by a godly intention. Second, not only were some Machiavellian means sanctioned by Christian ends, but Christian intentions sanctified Machiavellian ends as well—such as the preservation of the state. As we have seen, Giovanni Botero implied as much in *Ragion di stato* when he defined the *state* as "a stable rule over a people," and *reason of state* as "the knowledge of the means by which such dominion may be founded, preserved and extended."[11] Like Botero, Protestant casuists claimed to reject Machiavelli's politics, but ended up articulating something like his recommendations in their own theological vocabulary. The remarks of the puritan divine, William Ames, are exemplary:

> God can use the same instrument to produce divers and contrary effects, and these effects depend not upon the human instrument but upon God Himself. This may serve to direct us in time of danger not to look so much upon the means which God uses, as to depend upon God Himself who can turn any means unto the good of those that are His.

As Mosse has observed, this makes God into the consummate politician.[12]

Just as treatises on casuistry discuss the relationship of means to ends, intention to effect, in ways suggestive of Machiavellian policy, so some English commentators on Machiavelli considered his examples as cases of policy that had been falsely separated from cases of conscience. Thus in *The First Part of a Treatise concerning Policy and Religion* Thomas Fitzherbert argued not only that God sometimes uses evil to good ends but also that "true Religion [is necessary] for the perfection of policy."[13] Borgia is an example of failure precisely because true reason of state requires "the consideration of God's justice," which in turn legitimates Machiavellian means, now referred to as Christian prudence rather than policy. Yet, Fitzherbert's discussion of prudence also makes it clear that, as in Machiavelli's work, so in casuistry, the distinction between intention and effect need not amount to the simple justification of the means by the end. For even with God on our side, there is no guarantee of success: like Machiavellian *virtù*, Christian prudence articulates without equating intention and results. However, to the extent that Christian prudence is presented as a technical skill of deliberation informed by Christian ends, political strategy becomes—like Puttenham's rhetorical figures—"a formall vertue" that can be used well or badly and that is governed by rhetorical considerations of circumstance, place, and audience.

This investigation into the formal and rhetorical foundations of political power occurred in the theater as well. That the stage Machiavel is typically a powerful rhetorician not only registers the anxiety about the power of rhetoric or illusion to persuade to evil; it also hints at Machiavelli's deeply rhetorical view of sovereignty as something that must be staged.[14] In the first case, theater is seen to be manipulative or coercive and must therefore be banned; in the second, it exemplifies the faculty of imitation that can be used well or badly and, in any case, is unavoidable in human life.[15]

For all these reasons, readers of Machiavelli who were schooled in contemporary rhetorical and theological treatises did not simply condemn the Machiavel; they also saw that Machiavelli provided a storehouse of morally neutral argument that could be used to support or undermine the status quo. And they associated him with the formal topics which have been analyzed in the previous chapters. In chapter 4 I explore the favorable reception of Machiavelli in the work of Gardiner, Ralegh, Bacon, Shakespeare, and in the prefaces to English editions and translations of Machiavelli's work. In chapter 5 I discuss the rhetoric of Machiavellism as it emerges in a series of political and religious crises of the sixteenth and seventeenth centuries. In both chapters we will encounter English Renaissance writers who read Machiavelli and appreciated the relevance of his analysis of the dilemmas of *fortuna* and *virtù* to their own political and theological concerns. And we will meet others who did not know Machiavelli firsthand, but who used the rhetoric of Machiavellism to describe the tensions between the demands of conscience and royal supremacy, and between the indeterminacy of human affairs and the belief in the real truth of divine providence.

FOUR

READING MACHIAVELLI,

1550–1640

IN THIS chapter I propose a typology of sixteenth-century English interpretations of Machiavelli, ranging from the "domesticated" Machiavelli—the assimilation of his more obviously shocking recommendations to the mainstream of political thought and the appropriation of Machiavellian topics for English political debate—to the "methodical" Machiavelli, whose rhetorical method of arguing by example is seen to be particularly appropriate to the exigencies of political life, to the "dialectical" Machiavelli, who is read both as a Machiavel and as a critic of tyranny. At one end of the temporal spectrum, Stephen Gardiner understands the Machiavellian dimension of arguments for the divine right of monarchs and, like Counter-Reformation writers, he recommends a rhetoric of religion to shore up the authority of the new prince. At the other end of the spectrum, we find Shakespeare's *Coriolanus*, which demonstrates the relevance of Machiavelli's rhetorical politics and the Machiavel's force and fraud for the maintenance of a republic. While Gardiner and Shakespeare recuperate the Machiavel's dissembling rhetoric of appearances, Ralegh and Bacon dramatize the relevance of Machiavelli's protean examples for the complicated negotiations of de facto political power. Specifically, they see a homology between Machiavelli's rhetorical method of arguing by maxim and example, and his flexible response to the contingencies of political life.

In the conclusion to this chapter, I show that these principles of interpretation are codified in prefaces to and comments on *The Prince* and the *Discourses* in the late sixteenth and early seventeenth centuries. Strikingly, in defending Machiavelli, editors and translators draw on precisely those rhetorical features that are condemned in the Machiavel—his deceptiveness and indeterminacy. In their view, *The Prince* is deceptive because it is only apparently a manual for tyrants, while actually serving as a dialectical critique of tyranny; and Machiavelli's rhetoric is protean and indeterminate, and for this reason available for a variety of uses. The response to the charge of dissembling is to recast it as irony, while the response to the charge of indeterminacy is to argue that Machiavelli's work is not an ideological program but a rhetoric. With this second response, we come full circle to the domesticated, topical, and methodical readings of Machiavelli in the sixteenth century.

I have chosen to discuss this range of responses to Machiavelli's work as a typology rather than as a historical progression, because the continuity of available approaches to Machiavelli is what is most striking about his reception in the sixteenth and early seventeenth centuries. Although there is some evidence of an increasing receptiveness to Machiavelli's republicanism from the 1580s on, a republican Machiavelli does not simply replace Machiavelli the analyst of de facto political power, nor does the image of Machiavelli as rhetorical Machiavel fall by the wayside. Rather, readers of Machiavelli continue to see Machiavelli as both a rhetorician and a discriminating political thinker, and they see the two as related.

Before turning to specific readings, we need briefly to consider how Machiavelli would have been encountered by English readers in the sixteenth century. As the preceding pages have already suggested, Englishmen did not need to wait for the seventeenth-century translations of the *Discourses* (1636) and *The Prince* (1640) to have access to Machiavelli's works.[1] Men such as Cardinal Pole, Richard Morison, and Roger Ascham could read Machiavelli in the Italian editions of the 1530s and 1540s. In 1556 Sir William More of Surrey's inventory of books included "two books of Machevale's works, in Italion"; Sir Thomas Smith, author of *De republica anglorum*, owned Italian texts of *The Prince*, the *Discourses*, and *Florentine Histories*; Sir Christopher Hatton, an important privy counselor during the reign of Elizabeth and the dedicatee of Bedingfield's translation of the *Histories*, owned a copy of *The Prince*. Gabriel Harvey remarked in 1579 that his Cambridge friends were "pretty well acquainted . . . with a certain parlous book called . . . *Il Principe di Niccolò Machiavelli*," and that others were "as cunning in his *Discorsi*."[2] Then, in the 1580s the English printer John Wolfe brought out Italian texts of *The Art of War*, the *Discourses*, *The Prince*, the *Florentine Histories*, and *L'Asino d'oro* with the false publication information "In Palermo [or Rome, or Piacenza] appresso Antoniello degli Antonielli." In addition to all this, several English translations of *The Prince* and the *Discourses* circulated in manuscript during the Elizabethan period.[3]

By the second half of the century, the English reader of Machiavelli would also have had access to continental editions and works of criticism, whether in their original languages or in translation. In 1560 Sylvester Telius's Latin translation of *The Prince* was published, along with Telius's sympathetic preface, by the Protestant printer Pietro Perna in Basle. This translation was reprinted many times throughout the century, in ever more interesting editions: in 1580, it was bound with the Huguenot treatise, *Vindiciae contra tyrannos*, Beza's *De jura magistratum*, as well as orations pro and contra monarchy from Dion Cassius; in 1600 Possevino and Osorio were added.[4] The first two of these works were by Protestant theorists of resistance, while Possevino and Osorio, as we have seen, were Catholics who criticized Machiavelli as a Protestant subversive avant la lettre. Although each of these texts might be thought of—and in some cases was explicitly announced as—an antidote to *The Prince*, their inclusion in the 1580 Perna edition seems to have been intended somewhat differently. In one of the dedicatory letters to the edition, Nicolaus Stupanus describes the compilation of this edition as a rhetorical exercise in deliberation: texts with opinions contrary to Machiavelli's have been added "so that the clever reader, by weighing arguments on either side, might more easily judge this controversy concerning the absolute power of princes and magistrates over their subjects." Perna himself prefaced a different issue of this edition with a defense of Machiavelli's *Prince* against the charge of inculcating tyranny.[5]

By the 1570s most of Machiavelli's work had been translated into French, with a series of important prefaces defending the author. Sir Walter Ralegh probably read Machiavelli's *Prince* and *Discourses* in the French translation by Gaspard d'Auvergne.[6] In the prefatory epistle to the 1577 Latin translation of Innocent Gentillet's *Discours contre Machiavel* (1576), which was dedicated to the Englishmen Francis Hastings and Edward Bacon, the anonymous author remarked sourly on these French translations of Machiavelli: "Sathan useth strangers of France, as his fittest instruments, to infect us stil with this deadly poyson sent out of Italie, who have so highly promoted their Machiavellian bookes, that he is of no reputation in the Court of France, which hath not *Machiavels* writings at the fingers ends, and that both in the Italian and French tongues."[7] And while he went on to rejoice that "the infectious Machiavellian doctrine [had] not breathed nor penetrated the intrails of most happy England," the very fact that he translated Gentillet's book argued to the contrary. Hence the necessity of "an Antidote and present remedie, to expell the force of so deadly poyson, if at any time it chance to infect you." By 1602 Gentillet was available in English; although he is now best remembered for his attack on Machiavelli, both the preface and the work as a whole offered a serious, if critical, evaluation of Machiavelli's method of arguing by maxims and examples.[8]

Particularly during the second half of the century, the reader interested in Machiavelli would likely have read him alongside or in the context of his defenders and critics—whether in a single volume, as in the Perna edition, or not.[9] He would thus have construed Machiavelli in terms of classical, medieval, and Renaissance discussions of the tyrant. He would probably have been familiar with Louis Le Roy's commentary on Aristotle's *Politics* (1568), including the claim that Machiavelli drew "most of his instructions" from Aristotle's discussion of the tyrant in book 5, chapter 11.[10] He may have known Bodin's criticism in the preface to *Six livres de la république* (1576). He may even have read Botero's *Ragion di stato* in the original Italian, in the French translations of 1599 and 1601, or the Latin translation of 1602; and he may have known Lipsius's approving remarks about and use of Machiavelli in his *Politics*.[11] In all these cases it is important to remember that even those authors who condemned Machiavelli in their prefatory material regularly demonstrated a more complicated appreciation of Machiavelli in practice, that is, in their use and appropriation of Machiavelli in the body of their texts.

Stephen Gardiner: Machiavellian Providence

Stephen Gardiner's *Ragionamento dell'advenimento delli inglesi et normanni in Britanni* (Discourse on the coming of the English and Normans to Britain) provides a good example of the relevance of Machiavelli to debates about providentially sanctioned authority and de facto political power in sixteenth-century England.[12] Gardiner was Bishop of Winchester during the reign of Henry VIII and Lord Chancellor under Mary and Philip II. At a time when his contemporaries Thomas More and Reginald Pole defended papal supremacy in England, Gardiner bowed to royal pressure and wrote *De vera obedientia* in support of royal supremacy. (I will return to his role in this controversy in chapter 5.) During the reign of Philip and Mary he was once again a spokesman for the Catholic faith and in 1555, shortly before he died, composed a treatise of Machiavellian advice and counsel to the Hapsburg ruler. The "Discourse," a dialogue between "Stephano" and the foreigner "Alphonso," included long, unacknowledged quotations from Machiavelli's *Prince* and *Discourses*, as well as from works derivative of *The Prince*, such as Agostino Nifo's *De regnandi peritia* (1523) and Paolo Rosello's *Ritratto del vero governo* (1552). The work was translated into Italian and presented in manuscript to Philip II; it was not published or publicly circulated.

The ostensible subject of the dialogue is "the more memorable alterations that have occurred in the realm of England, and their causes up to the present time" (46, 104); the actual purpose is to instruct Philip II in his role as "new prince" of England. As Peter Donaldson has noted, by alteration Gardiner intends first and foremost the invasion of the Anglo-Saxons and Normans; "but the coming of Brutus, the Roman conquest and the Danish rule are also discussed, so that the treatise includes all the great dynastic changes. The coming of Philip is placed in this context."[13] Just as Machiavelli draws on ancient history and contemporary examples to advise the Medici in *The Prince*, so Stephano domesticates Machiavelli's method by recounting the dynastic upheavals and invasions in the course of English history to show Philip how to hold on to his power ("mantenere lo stato"). And he does so by borrowing Machiavelli's maxims and examples; by adopting his rhetoric of *fortuna*, *virtù*, prudence, necessity, and occasion; by mimicking his syntax, wordplay, and ironic concessions to ethical common sense; and, most of all, by making all rule a function of de facto power and *virtù*.

Gardiner reads Machiavelli both as a storehouse of maxims regarding political conduct, and as a storehouse of topics regarding the relation of prudence to fortune, *virtù* to necessity, means to ends, reputation to power. In the first case, for example, he includes Machiavelli's maxim against using mercenaries and his recommendation that the new prince should live in his newly acquired territory (112, 146). He also advises the prince to attend to the concerns of the people and to avoid changing their laws and customs; that is, he urges the efficacy of the rule of law. In the second case, he remarks on the topic of *fortuna* and prudence, "The stars have not such power over our human affairs that prudence is not able to affect them: the stars only prompt men; they do not force them" (52, 110). And Alphonso illustrates the prince's ability to create, as well as respond to, necessity in a sentence that recalls Machiavelli's playing with necessity in chapter 25 of *The Prince*:

> Mi pare che li houmini quando piglianno l'armi per il commandamento del principe o sforsati della peste, o d'una guerra, che tutto venne di necessità, perche è di necessità che il voler del principe in questo caso sia obedito. (57)

> It seems to me that whether men take up arms because of a prince's command, or because compelled by famine, or war, they do so in all cases because of necessity: it is a necessity that the prince's will be obeyed in such cases. (114)

Necessity here is manufactured by the prince who desires to extend his power, as it is in the case of the prince who is compelled to use cruelty:

> il principe dee esser pietoso et clemente, et non crudele, si non sforzato per la malvagità delli huomini, et alhora anche monstrare de farla contra la sua voglia sforzatemente, per causa di giusticia, o per esser nuovo principe, il qual havra molte occasioni desser piu crudele che li altri. (88)

> the prince ought to be compassionate and merciful and not cruel, unless compelled by the wickedness of men; and when he is cruel he should show that he is constrained to be so against his will, because justice requires cruelty, or because he is a new prince faced with many situations in which he must be crueler than other princes. (141)

The language of necessity, in other words, is part of the rhetoric that the prince uses to respond to necessity itself. As in Machiavelli's *Discourses*, the imitation of necessity proves to be a forceful response to the constraints of fortune; and justice proves to be a useful rhetorical topic for justifying one's acts.

Although in the conclusion of the treatise Stephano tactfully distinguishes between princes who have come to power "by force of arms" and those who have done so "through favor of friends, hereditary laws or [as in Philip's case] by matrimony" (93, 145), the overall effect of Stephano's discussion of "alteration" is to break down distinctions between legitimate and illegitimate power, hereditary sovereignty and de facto possession of the throne. Stephano repeatedly shows that maintaining one's power does not depend on legitimate succession but on the Machiavellian virtues of force, fraud, and prudence (including the prudent management of one's reputation and the prudent feigning of the conventional virtues). Thus, while urging Philip to respect English law and custom, Stephano does not shy away from recommending that he use cruelty well and that he forcefully do away with rivals to the throne (84–85, 138).[14] Not the least striking in Gardiner's Machiavellian treatise is the fact that he simultaneously exploits and exposes the appeal to providence as a rhetorical argument in defense of de facto political power.[15]

The first part of the treatise is organized around the contrast between Vortigerius, the elected but ineffectual king of the Britons, and Hengest, the Saxon mercenary who usurped power from Vortigerius and effectively ruled in his place. Stephano shows in some detail how Vortigerius lost his power through bad judgment and insufficient *virtù*, whereas Hengest became de facto ruler of England through the shrewd exercise of force, fraud, and cruelty. In Stephano's description, Hengest emerges as the Saxon Agathocles, who used cunning brutally to slaughter his Briton allies and "who from a private man made himself a prince" (61, 117).[16] The comparison with Agathocles—and the implications of such a comparison—become explicit a little further on. In criticizing the Briton Vortigerius's lack of military knowledge, Stephano remarks:

L'era l'opinione de i savii, che non è cosa si debole et infermo come il principato fondato sopra l'armi d'altrui. Percio un principe debbe haver principal cura d'instituire i suoi popoli piu atti et disposti nelli ordini della militia, la qual è una scientia sola, che fa lo principle amato et honorato di suoi, et lo rende temuto dall'inimici. Questa scientia non solamente fa quelli che sono nati principi nelli stati lor sicuri, ma molte volte gli houmini [*sic*] di basissima fortuna fa venire à tal grado come Agatocle et Hengisto et infiniti altri. Et il contrario si vede, quando i principi si danno buon tempo, et studiano piu al vivere dedicato, che alli armi: diventino dispregiati dall'nimici et odiati

di suoi proprii soggetti. Come Edouardo secondo, et Giovanne re d'Inghilterra, iquali tutti duoi, per lor ignavia venerò (come indegni di tal honore) di
lor baronni privati del stato et poi delle vite anchora. (61–62)

The opinion of wise men has been that there is nothing so weak and infirm
as a principality founded on the arms of another. Therefore a prince must
have particular care to train the more apt and inclined of his subjects in
military discipline, which is a peerless science for making a prince loved and
honored by his own people and feared by his enemies. This science not only
makes those who are born princes secure in their rule, but often elevates men
of lowest fortune to such a station as Agathocles and Hengest and many
others. And the reverse is seen when princes have a good time and concern
themselves with luxurious living rather than with military matters: they become despised by their enemies and hated by their own subjects, like Edward
II and John of England, who were both deprived of their state (as unworthy
of such honor) and later of their lives because of their laziness. (118)

As this passage illustrates, in discussing the means of maintaining one's
state, Stephano does not distinguish between legitimate and illegitimate
power. Edward II was deprived of the throne because of his luxurious
living and his laziness; King John (who came to the throne as a usurper)
met a similar end for similar reasons. In contrast, the usurpers Hengest
and Agathocles were successful rulers, and Brutus, who came to power by
the use of force, ruled for 1,040 years (49, 107).

In his note to this passage Donaldson remarks that Machiavelli's description of Agathocles "approaches a tone of moral condemnation,"
whereas Gardiner "ignores the moral question" (158). But, if my interpretation of the example of Agathocles in chapter 1 is convincing, Gardiner's reading of Agathocles is more attentive to Machiavelli's rhetoric
than is Donaldson's. For Gardiner, as for Machiavelli, Agathocles is an
example of someone of lowly station who rose to power by the use of
force. Equally instructive, however, is the context in which this example
of Agathocles is inserted. For Gardiner's reading calls attention to an aspect of Agathocles' career that has not been noted by modern commentators: his reliance on his soldiers not only to butcher the senators of
Syracuse and secure power but also to defend against the Carthaginian
siege and to invade Africa. To read Agathocles as an example of someone
who relied on a citizen "militia" may be to note Machiavelli's insistence,
at the end of chapter 8 of The Prince, on Agathocles' marshaling of popular support to secure his long and successful reign; at the very least, it
suggests the perceived compatibility of The Prince and the Discourses.[17]

This reading does not stress the republican Machiavelli but rather Machiavelli the pragmatic political counselor who presents an arsenal of
means that can be used well or badly and who recognizes the role of

reputation and opinion in the securing of power. Thus when Alphonso objects that arming the people leads to sedition and rebellion, Stephano replies that it is not the arming of the people but the ruler's lack of prudence that leads to civil unrest:

> Mi pare che voi siate di natura di quelli, che non leggono le rose per esser offeso delli spine: ma bisogna che gli houmini [sic] hanno tanta prudentia di pigliare la dolcezza del una, et scifare l'asperità del altra. L'ape tira d'un fiore mele, et la ranea del medesima veleno. L'houmo che ha la febre non gusto altro che amarezza, et l'houmo sano del medesimo cibo prendo saporito notrimento. La colpa non è nel fiore che rende al uno mele, et al' altro veneno, ne nel cibo, che ad uno pare amaro, et al altro saporito, ma in la diversa natura del ape et della ranea; et delli diversi humori del houmo sano et del houmo amalado. Dico per tanto, che la disciplina et cognitione della scientia militare non recca seco mai male; quantunque ella sia piu volte delli ignoranti et tristi male usata, non si dee pero imputare tal male à la scientia (qual per se è buona) ma a i tristi che malamenta la usano, perche non e cosa al mondo che non puole esser malae usata. Pero le ragioni da voi preallegate non provino, che la cognitione di questa arte non conviene à i popoli generalmente, quantunque egli la usano qualche volte male. La colpa di questo procede dalli principi et che debbono insignarli il retto uso di quella. (64–65)

> You seem to be like those who will not pick roses for the thorns; but men must have enough prudence to take the sweetness of the rose and shun the sharpness of the thorns. The bee takes honey from a flower and the frog poison. The feverish man tastes nothing but bitterness, and the healthy man takes savory nourishment from the same food. The fault is not in the flower that yields honey to the one and poison to another, but in the different natures of the bee and the frog and in the different humors of the healthy man and the sick. I say, therefore, that the discipline and knowledge of military science never of itself entails evil. Though it be often used ill by ignorant and wicked men the evil ought not to be therefore imputed to the science (which is in itself good) but to the wicked who misuse it, for there is nothing in the world that cannot be misused. Therefore the arguments you adduce do not prove that acquaintance with this art is unsuitable for the general populace even though they may sometimes use it wrongly. The blame for this belongs to the princes, who ought to teach the people the right use of the science. (120)

As in traditional Renaissance defenses of rhetoric, imitation, and the reading of pagan literature, Stephano argues that military science can be used well or badly. (The same images of the honey and poison appear in the 1532 Giunta edition of *The Prince* and in the prefaces to English editions and translations.) He then uses this argument to recommend that the citizenry be armed, since the effect of such militarization will in any case depend on the discretion of the prince. He thus combines something like Machiavelli's argument for a citizen militia with his insistence in *The Prince* that the prince control his subjects' arms. While Stephano claims in this passage that military science is in itself "good," he later argues that it is irrelevant whether or not such means are good as long as they are effective. In all his actions, William the Conqueror (who takes over Hengest's function as exemplary man of *virtù* in the second half of the treatise)

> monstrò grand prudentia, et piglio sempre la via sicura senza cura d'esser tenuto ò avaro ò crudele, perche si messe le mani adosso di coloro, che per ragione ò titolo potorno aspirare a la corona, et li spense tutti, insieme con li altri, i quali co'l favore del popolo, o per lor authorita giudicò, poter per adietro offenderlo. (85)

> showed great prudence, and always took the safe way, without concern for being thought avaricious and cruel, for he laid hands on those who by reason or title could aspire to the crown and extinguished them all, as well as others whom, by reason of their influence or favor of the people, he judged capable of attacking him. (138)

When Alphonso objects, "This is a more common practice among princes than divine law permits" (85, 138), Stephano responds:

> Il nostro proposito al presente, non e da monstrare la cosa licitae ò illicito d'un principe a fare, ma solo per monstrare per quale via e mezi un principe puol mantenere o perdere suo stato. (85)

> Our purpose at present is not to show what a prince is permitted to do and what he is not permitted to do, but only to show by what ways and means a prince can maintain or lose his state. (138)

And a little further on, in response to Alphonso's objection to Stephano's examples of Turkish cruelty, Stephano remarks:

> Io non li lodo, anzi dico che sarebbe meglior per i christiani vivere privati, che con tanta crudeltà di regnare. Ma questo e un giogo di sicuro che puol farlo. (87)

> I do not praise them, on the contrary I say that it would be better for Christians to live privately than to reign with such cruelty. But such a trick is sure to work. (140)

The criteria of the right use of such "via e mezi" (ways and means) are not moral but rhetorical: cruelty should be used if it is dictated by "the place, the time and the people" (90, 143). Such rhetorical criteria explain how Stephano could speak with typical Machiavellian irony of Hannibal's "cruelty . . . together with his other virtues" (90, 143). In this and other examples, the ethos of the prince is not determined by ethical norms but by rhetorical considerations of the sort Machiavelli puts forward in chapter 18 of *The Prince*. Stephano remarks accordingly that

> un principe nuovo non puole (quando volesse) osservare tutte le cose, per le quale i huomini sono tenute buoni, essendo piu volte necessitato per mantener lo stato, d'operare contra la clementia, contra la religione, et contra la fede, per tanto bisogna che habia un animo disposto à volgersi come il vento, secondo la varieta di fortuna nelle sue fatte, ma nele sue parole di parere pieno di fede, di clementia, et di charità, perche questi parere l'acquistono apresso la moltitudine grand riputatione et un popolo nota piu l'effetti delli occhi et dela lingua, che quelli delle mani. (97)

> A new prince especially cannot observe all the things by which men are held good, even if he wants to, since it is often necessary, to maintain his state, to act contrary to mercy, religion and faith. Therefore his character must be such that he can change what he does like the wind according to the variety of fortune while what he says seems full of faith, mercy and charity, for these semblances gain him great reputation with the multitude, and a people marks more the effects of the eyes and of the tongue than those of the hand. (149)

As in chapter 18 of *The Prince*, the prince must learn a rhetoric of the virtues in order to maintain a dissembling image of constancy; at the same time, he must be capable of changing his actions to suit the circumstances and to do whatever is necessary behind the scenes.

As Stephano is well aware, it is hard to reconcile such a rhetorical politics with Christian ethics. When Alphonso objects that such advice is un-Christian, and offers counterexamples of princes who have "gained entry in provinces and kingdoms" through mercy, Stephano quibbles in exemplary fashion:

> Questi essempi da voi legate sono rare, et fuora d'uso in questi nostri giorni . . . pero dico al proposito dela clementia et crudelta, che giove ad un principe talhora monstrarsi crudele, pure che non habi l'animo pregno di crudelta, accioche facendo poi mistero di monstrarsi benigno, lo possa fare agevolmente. Perche ad ogni modo la clementia debbe vincere la crudeltà, altremente il principe non rassimigliarà à Dio, di cui è il vivo imagine. . . .
>
> *Alph*: Talche voi conchiuderete, che il principe dee esser piu tosto clemente, che feroce.
>
> *Steph*: Si, che habi l'animo semper pietoso et benigno, ma non tanto benigno, che non puole quando havra occasione monstrarsi anche crudele. (92)

> These examples you adduce are rare and quite out of date for our times . . . for I say, as regards mercy and cruelty, that it helps a prince to seem sometimes cruel, provided that his mind is not dominated by cruelty, so that

afterwards, when he shows himself kind in secret, he can do so comfortably. For mercy ought in any case to vanquish cruelty, otherwise the prince will not resemble God, of whom he is the living image. . . .

Alph: So you would conclude that the prince ought to be rather merciful than fierce?

Steph: Yes, he should always be compassionate and kind in spirit but not so kind that he be unable to practice cruelty as well, when the occasion arises. (145)

In playing with "seeming" and "resembling" in this passage, Stephano dramatizes in his lexicon the Protean flexibility that he recommends to the new prince, at the same time that he exposes the rhetorical resources of princely power, including the claim to divine favor: the prince must seem cruel, but he must also seem (rassimigliarà) like God, of whom he is the living image (di cui è il vivo imagine). The deliberate staging of cruelty then seems to contaminate the prince's resemblance to God, suggesting that such resemblance involves a theatrical performance as well.[18] By this, I do not mean to suggest that Gardiner did not believe in God; rather, the Christian prince resembles God precisely because God himself sanctions Machiavellian principles. This is one implication of the discussion of mercy and cruelty: the prince who uses cruelty may still be in the image and likeness of God because, just as one of the traditional attributes of God is severity, so one of God's divine attributes in this treatise is Machiavellian cruelty.[19]

The rhetorical dimension of the argument from providence can be illustrated more forcefully by attending to those passages where Stephano and Alphonso discuss the violent acquisition of power. As we have seen, Stephano's dispassionate discussion of the means of securing political power runs the risk of justifying resistance to the legitimate sovereign. In a typically Machiavellian exchange with Alphonso, Stephano both acknowledges and brackets the orthodox line on disobedience to divinely sanctioned political power. On the one hand, we learn that it is impermissible to rebel against the ruler, even if he is a tyrant:

> perciochè egli e il ministro di Dio ordinato à tal ministerio per governar' gli popoli alla cura suo commessi: non fatto à caso come altri affirmano, ma per la providentia di Dio ordinato . . . quantunque i principi si lascino se stessi esser menati di cattivo consiglio, o di lor appetiti dal vero; nondimeno i popoli debbino sempre manere nella debita obedientia, et non cercare da pigliare la spada fuora del mano di colui, alqual Dio ne hà dato. (69–70)

> for he is the minister of God ordained to such office to govern the people committed to his charge not by chance, as others affirm, but by the providence of God. . . . however princes stray from a true course, led either by evil

advice or by their appetites, nonetheless the people are always obliged to obey them and not seek to take the sword from the hand of him to whom God has given it. (125–26)

On the other hand, Gardiner assumes that conquest or usurpation is an unremarkable way of acquiring power: both Hengest and William the Conqueror are examples of rulers who seized power through force and *virtù*, and maintained it through prudence and the exemplary use of cruelty; providence is not invoked to justify their success (133–34, 141).[20] Even more striking, Moses's conquest of foreign territory is described in purely secular terms.[21] Finally, Stephano tells us that King John, though a usurper, would have held on to his power if he had been more prudent and had respected the laws (79, 130). Here are four examples of conquest by force, and of maintenance of power by attention to the rhetorical principle of decorum, prudence, or discretion.

Gardiner's alternation of the language of providential favor with that of conquest works to expose the appeal to providence as a rhetorical argument about de facto political power. Thus it is not surprising that, in the passage warning against rebellion, Stephano admits that divinely sanctioned authority is an argument, one that will need to be bolstered by the prudent management of one's reputation:

> non sia licito in caso alcuno *quantunque egli fusse tiranno, pigliar l'armi in contra.* Ma perche gli houmini spesse volte cascono, per debolezza di nostra natura, et fanno molte cose illicite et prohibite, instinti et mossi della occasione, egli è buono anche che i principi, volendo assicurarsi di lor popoli, hanno l'ochio et la mente al ufficio, per non darli occagione di ribellare, ma monstrarne virtuosi essempi di se stesso. (70)

> It is never permissible in any circumstances to take arms against a prince, even if he is a tyrant. But because men often stumble, through the weakness of our nature, and do many illicit and prohibited things on the impulse of the occasion, it is good also that princes who wish to take precautions against their people attend carefully to their office, so as not to give them occasion to rebel, but rather set a virtuous example themselves. (126)

The syntax here is reminiscent of Machiavelli's in *The Prince*: first, one announces the ethical rule; then the exception that ends up making the ethical principle an argument to be invoked only when—or because—it is useful. Note also how "men [who] . . . do many illicit and prohibited things"—which could describe the tyrants of the previous sentence as well as the would-be usurpers—confuses the distinction between legitimate and illegitimate rule which the preceding clause asserts. And, as in Machiavelli, one conclusion of seeing all power as de facto political power is the necessity of prudently cultivating one's reputation for virtue. The orthodox language of the passage invites us to recast this insight in theological terms: while in principle the king is one of God's elect and, by definition, cannot do anything to earn his election, in the fallen world of potential rebellion the king is invited to merit the obedience of his subjects. And he is invited to do so, not because such behavior is moral but because it is politically effective.[22]

This point can be further illustrated by the conclusion of the treatise, in which both the Machiavellian rhetoric of *virtù* and the Christian rhetoric of providence are in full force. Philip II is praised as the Christian prince who is providentially destined to restore true religion to England. At the same time, Gardiner, in Machiavellian fashion, plays on the word *virtù*, asking us to identify military success with Christian virtue: speaking of Philip's ancestor Maximilian, Stephano asks, "Who knows not how much piety, goodness and valor [*virtù*] was in him, and what honorable exploits he made in Brabant, Flanders and Italy, and what zeal he always had for religion, and towards all virtuous men [*virtuosi*]?" (97–98, 150). Given that, on the previous page, Stephano had offered Pope Alexander VI as an example of the new prince, who hid "an ambitious endeavor with a veil of piety" (97, 149), one might be inclined to reduce the Christian rhetoric of piety and virtue that appears at this point to an irreligious Machiavellian *virtù*, and to read the peroration as an imitation of chapter 26 of *The Prince*. I would like to suggest, instead, that what Gardiner does is to sanctify *virtù* by identifying it with divine purpose: *virtù* may not be identical with the traditional virtues, but it is equivalent to the sword of divinely sanctioned temporal power.

Thus the conclusion of this treatise, which praises Philip for his Christian virtues of "religion, piety, and mercy" (97, 150), is particularly instructive for the relevance of Machiavelli to sixteenth- and seventeenth-century English discussions of providentially sanctioned political power. As for Counter-Reformation writers on the continent, religious belief was not incompatible with a sophisticated appreciation of what Machiavelli had to offer the "new prince." To the contrary, religion served to justify the means employed by the secular ruler.[23] And for some, religion seemed to promise success in ways that a purely secular world view could not. Thus Stephano concludes:

> ha piaciuto per tanto all'immenso Iddio, che el sia preposto a le signorie di tante provintie et regni, non a caso o per sceleratessa come molti altri principi sono preposti, ma per giustitia et per la somma providentia divina, produtto in questo tempo accioche la christianita dopo tanta scurita di nevole habia la chiara luce del sole, et i popoli christiani dopo si lungi et crudeli guerre goderebberò lo precioso et inestimabile gioio della pace. (98)

> it has pleased God that he [Philip] be given sovereignty over so many provinces and kingdoms; not advanced by chance, or crime, like many other princes, but brought forth in this age of justice by the highest divine

providence so that Christianity after such dark clouds would have the bright light of the sun, and the Christian people, after such long and cruel wars, would enjoy the precious and inestimable jewel of peace. (150; translation modified)

The description of Philip's succession as divinely ordained is particularly striking in contrast to the example of Pope Alexander VI's purely pragmatic use of religion to forward his political objectives. Here, in his peroration, Stephano seems to suggest that "maintaining the state" will prove all the more successful if God really is on your side. (As we have seen, this argument is echoed by critics of Machiavelli who claim that Borgia lost power not so much because he was immoral but because he failed to take into account the workings of divine providence.) It is not "crime," "chance," or fortune that has advanced Philip to the English throne but providence; however, such providential favor, Stephano has argued in the preceding pages, is not at all incompatible with Machiavellian *virtù* and the more spectacular and violent means associated with it. Rather, once Philip has ascended to the throne, providential favor turns what might have been called chance or crime into the divinely sanctioned—albeit immoral—means of securing true religion in the Christian state.

Ralegh and Bacon: Rhetorical Method and De Facto Power

If Gardiner saw in Machiavelli a way of strengthening the Catholic rule of Philip and Mary, Machiavelli was equally of interest throughout the sixteenth century to English Protestants. Blair Worden has discussed the influence of Machiavelli on Ralegh and Bacon—men who, along with Sidney and Spenser, favored a strong Protestant foreign and domestic policy in the 1580s and after. He has demonstrated that the Essex circle was a conduit of Machiavelli's ideas, as well as of Tacitism and Neostoicism, in the late sixteenth century. In particular, Machiavelli offered support to arguments for a "commonwealth of expansion," as well as for a mixed constitution.[24] He was thus an important source of imperialist and republican ideas, which members of the Essex circle espoused to a greater or lesser degree. Just as Tacitism and Neostoicism were vehicles of political dissent for the members of the Essex circle, so Machiavelli seems to have been read as a republican critic of the status quo—in conjunction with theorists of political resistance, rather than as the poison to which they were the antidote. Sidney, who had contacts with theorists of resistance, such as Buchanan in Scotland and DuPlessis Mornay on the continent, recommended Machiavelli to his brother Robert, and may have drawn on Machiavelli's ideas about the mixed constitution in the *Arcadia*.[25] Ralegh, whose Machiavellian commonplace books I will examine below, wrote a defense of *The Prerogative of Parliaments*, which may have been influenced by his reading of Machiavelli. Equally important, however, and neglected by Worden, is Machiavelli the Tacitean rhetorician and pragmatic analyst of second causes.[26] Like Gardiner, Ralegh and Bacon realized that Machiavelli offered a rhetoric of political power, one that can be used pro and contra absolute rule, religious belief, or republicanism. Unlike Gardiner, their readings of Machiavelli were colored by late sixteenth-century debates about rhetorical, dialectical, and pedagogical "method."

Scholars such as Walter Ong, Neal Gilbert, and Cesare Vasoli have demonstrated that sixteenth-century humanism differs from Italian humanism of the fifteenth century in part by its preoccupation with method. Although the term remained vague throughout the sixteenth century, in general *method* referred to—or indicated the desire for—a more systematic pedagogy than that offered by the Italian schools of Guarino and others. To contemporary readers *method* in the title of a work promised speed, efficiency, even a shortcut, that would make humanist instruction both more practical and more widely available.[27] In northern Europe this methodical tendency was particularly associated with the widely disseminated textbooks of the Dutch humanists Rudolph Agricola and Erasmus. It is significant for our purposes that Agricola's conception of dialectic— and the method he purveyed—was topical. As Anthony Grafton and Lisa Jardine note, the marketing of Agricola's topical logic by his editors Alardus and Erasmus "produced a commitment on the part of generations of humanist teachers to an ingenious set of readily transmitted routines for classifying the accumulation of matter for debating or declaiming (or composing poetry or fiction) by 'commonplaces.' "[28] Such topical organization of subject matter (*res*) was also manifest in Erasmus's enormously popular *Adagia* and *De copia*; and in Melancthon's *Erotema dialectices* (1547) and *Loci theologici*, the latter a collection of theological commonplaces that amounted to a Protestant "methodizing [of] the doctrines of Christian theology."[29] The interest in topics for persuasion was also encouraged by humanist pedagogues who urged students to keep their own commonplace books, where they could store up matter for future debate and argument.[30]

There is some evidence that the interest in method—with its connotations of speed, efficiency, and practical success—was in tension with the traditional moral claims of Renaissance humanism.[31] To put it another way, method revealed the fissures that plagued the Ciceronian and humanist effort to link the *honestum* and the *utile* from the very outset. By the later sixteenth century in England, method seems to have been perceived by some students and teachers as divorced from ethical considerations altogether and thus especially compatible with a Machiavellian approach to politics. It is not surprising, given the charged climate of methodological debate, that Protestant writers of the 1570s and 1580s both praised and blamed Machiavelli for his method. It is also not surprising, given the debate over the precise meaning of method, that Machiavelli's maxims and examples were sometimes proposed as a counter to other excessively rigid or instrumental concepts of method.[32] Thus, although the puritan John Stubbes objected to Machiavelli's inductive logic ("thys absurd manner of reasoning is very Macchiavelian logick by particular examples then to govern kingdoms and to set down general rules for his prince whereas particulars should be warranted by generals"), Gabriel Harvey defended it in a marginal note in his text of Livy:

> One who wants political axioms should here read Daneau's political axioms from Polybius, or rather should himself collect more prudent ones, and more appropriate to civil and military discipline, from political principles. . . . There is no specialist in political, or economic, or ethical axioms drawn from histories and poems to match Aristotle in his Politics, Oeconomics, Ethics. But how much greater would he have been had he known histories that were so much greater—especially Roman history? Machiavelli certainly outdid Aristotle in observation of this above all, though he had a weaker foundation in technical rules and philosophical principles. Hence I generally prefer Aristotle's rules, Machiavelli's examples.[33]

Just as Livy was a treasure house of ancient examples to be applied to and imitated in the present, so Machiavelli offered a similar storehouse of examples and inductive method of argument that were of use to the soldier, courtier, and nobleman of the 1580s and 1590s.[34] And this flexibility of method, with its corollary that political virtue and legitimacy are contingent on circumstances, seems to have been associated, in particular, with the Machiavellian world of force and fraud, construed as neutral or deleterious means of political behavior, rather than exclusively with republican ideas.

Although Ralegh's authorship of *Maxims of State* and *The Cabinet-Council* is now contested, Milton believed that the latter, at least, was by Ralegh and published it under his name in 1658. Given Ralegh's references and allusions to Machiavelli in his *History of the World*, *The Prerogative of Parliaments*, and other works, the attribution is not surprising. Yet, for the purposes of my argument, it is less important to determine the exact authorship than to see that these works provide an exemplary illustration of the ways of reading Machiavelli in the period.[35]

Although it is difficult to tell whether *The Cabinet-Council* is a later revision and elaboration of *Maxims of State*, or the latter a condensed and better organized version of the former, both are essentially rhetorics for the founding and preserving of states: commonplace books or compendia of arguments drawn from Machiavelli, Guicciardini, Bodin, Lipsius, Botero, Aristotle, Tacitus, and others.[36] Passages drawn from *The Prince* and the *Discourses* appear throughout both works, but particularly often in the last two chapters of *The Cabinet-Council*, which announce themselves as a collection of commonplaces (the title of chapter 26 reads in part: "Maximes of State, or Prudential Grounds and Polemical Precepts, concerning all Estates, and forms of Policie . . ."). The term *maxims* here, like the words *policy* and *cabinet-council*, may itself have suggested Machiavellism and reason of state to contemporaries.[37] Yet, the pejorative connotation of these terms is countered by the author's discrete refusal to quote Machiavelli by name, and by his apparently disinterested account of the political sphere. The commonplaces are organized topically ("Of Government," "Of Policy," etc.) and each topic is then subdivided (into, for example, "Monarchy," "Aristocracy," "Popular State," "Tyranny"). Although no preference is expressed for any particular form of government, Ralegh is careful to distinguish between hereditary absolute monarchies, such as England and France (2, 40), and tyrannies. Yet, while tyrannical behavior is condemned as both immoral and impractical, even this condemnation emerges as an argument that may be suspended under certain conditions.

Although there is some attempt at completeness in *Maxims of State* and *The Cabinet-Council* (each surveys different kinds of government, and a wide range of topics having to do with government under a variety of conditions), neither work is governed by the criteria of theoretical consistency or aesthetic wholeness, but of usefulness. It is hard to imagine anyone reading either of these works from cover to cover; the reader, one imagines, would simply skip to the section relevant to his immediate needs. Even by these practical standards, passages in *Maxims of State* and *The Cabinet-Council* are often strikingly abbreviated. If Machiavelli's style is famously terse and epigrammatic, reading these works is sometimes like reading Machiavelli in Morse code: where Machiavelli will dilate upon a given historical example, the author simply gives a name and expects the reader to fill in the details. Thus the paragraph-long chapter 5, "Of monarchies tyrannical," advises the prince to commit his cruelties quickly, concluding: "Example, Dionysius and Agathocles" (42).

Consistent with their nature as commonplace books, these texts employ Machiavelli to diverse ends. Just as Ralegh presents a range of approaches to political issues, so he presents us with various ways of reading Machiavelli. In this sense, the works do not simply provide the reader with a storehouse of political arguments but also call attention to homologies between rhetorical and political method: like the example, the maxim is a rhetorical form that encapsulates a particularly flexible approach to politics. This is particularly the case with *The Cabinet-Council*. Whereas in *Maxims of State* Ralegh makes some attempt to rationalize his use of Machiavelli, in *The Cabinet-Council* he more often lets the contradictions stand, forcing the reader to confront his—and Machiavelli's own—rhetorical politics, in which political realities are constructed, as well as negotiated, by means of argument. Thus, in contrast to readers such as Raab and Strathmann who simply point to the inconsistencies, remarking at most that the author is characteristically Elizabethan in simultaneously condemning Machiavelli while appropriating some of his observations (Strathmann, 168), I suggest that the use of Machiavelli here is exemplary in its topical *method*. As I have argued in preceding chapters, although we do not now read *The Prince* and the *Discourses* as storehouses of arguments for a variety of political contingencies, such a reading is no less sophisticated—nor any less in tune with Machiavelli's "intention," so far as we can construct it—than is our modern effort to construct Machiavelli as an aesthetic unity.[38]

In *Maxims of State*, Ralegh explicitly rejects "the false doctrine of Machiavellian policy" (15); although he goes on to describe it in detail, he says that he aims to inform rather than persuade to action (a line of argument that, as we will see, was also used in defenses of Machiavelli): "These rules of hypocritical tyrants are to be known, that they be avoided . . . and not drawn into imitation" (26–27).[39] In this way, the various Machiavellian recommendations regarding the feigning of religion, the opportune invocation of necessity to justify unpopular actions (24), and "extinguishing the royal blood" of the country you have conquered by force all appear in quotation marks. At the same time, he adopts some of Machiavelli's recommendations with a different sort of qualification. Thus he remarks that it is not just for a Christian prince to invade a foreign country to which he has "no right" (18); but he then proceeds to advise the prince how to invade: "The safest way is, (supposing a right) that some good part of the natives be transplanted into some other place, and our colonies . . . be planted there in some part of the province" (19).

Whereas, for Machiavelli, right is a consequence of de facto political power, here it is assumed that it must exist prior to invasion. Yet, because the method of conquest will in either case be the same, the question of right can be bracketed, both literally and figuratively. Not surprisingly, the nearness, even the indistinguishability of the two Machiavellis is registered a few pages later when the prince is advised

> not to put much trust, nor practice too often the sophisms of policy, especially those that appertain to a tyrannical state, which are soon to be detected by men of judgment, and so bring discredit to the prince and his policy among the wiser and better sort of his subjects, whereof must needs follow very ill effects.
>
> The sophisms of tyrants are rather to be known than practised . . . by wise and good princes. (21)[40]

Not all sophisms of policy are relevant to the tyrannical state; yet those that are should not be used too often by wise princes, not so much because they are unethical but because, in the long run, they are ineffective.[41]

As in *Maxims of State*, so in *The Cabinet-Council* the Machiavel is condemned, while Machiavelli the analyst of "policy" is cited with approval. And, although the division of monarchies into "signioril" such as Turkey, "royal" such as England and France, and "tyrannical" such as Agathocles's, is systematic and ideologically loaded in favor of England, the Machiavellian recommendations regarding political policy are applicable to all states. In discussing the difficulty of annexing "a monarchy newly conquered" to a royal monarchy, for example, "Ireland annexed to the crown of England," Ralegh remarks that one must first "extinguish the race of him that was anciently prince." He goes on, as Machiavelli does in chapter 3 of *The Prince*, to recommend, in addition to maintaining the laws and customs of the conquered country, other more violent means:

> As for the people inhabitant . . . they cannot have the power to offend; for in that case this rule or maxim shall be found true, that men must be either kindly entreated, or with all extremity oppressed; because of light injuries they may be revenged, but of utter oppression they cannot. (40)[42]

When in the next chapter, entitled "Of monarchies tyrannical," he remarks that "a prince by such impious means aspired, and desiring to hold that he hath gained, will take order that the cruelties he committeth may be done roundly, suddenly, and, as it were, at an instant," we see that the means employed by tyrants do not differ very much from those of royal monarchs. As in *The Prince*, the effect of such juxtapositions is less to distinguish between legitimate and illegitimate rule than it is to point out the similarities between them.

At the same time, we are offered a pragmatic and rhetorical defense of popular representation. Discussing "Of new-found monarchies and principalities" in the very next chapter (the equivalent of chapter 7 of *The Prince*), Ralegh remarks that not only "force and violence" are useful but also the "mere good-will and favour of men" (43). Echoing book 1, chapter 58, of the *Discourses*, he writes:

> So it appeareth that a prince made by the multitude is much more secure than he whom the nobility preferreth; for common people do not desire to enjoy more than their own, and to be defended from oppression; but great men do study, not only to hold their own, but also to command and insult upon inferiors. (44)

The recognition that these remarks do not square with the earlier definition of the monarch as an absolute sovereign who rules "without consent of any other person" (38) is recorded in his coda to this chapter:

"Note: That all monarchies are principalities, but all principalities are not monarchies."

That the defense of "a prince made by the multitude" is pragmatic and Machiavellian rather than moral helps to explain the apparent inconsistencies in the recommendations regarding the means of maintaining political power. Precisely because the first issue to be looked to "in matter of state" is "occasion" (115), little or no attempt is made to justify or rationalize apparent inconsistencies or conflicting views regarding such means: for example, the author tells us both that money is crucial to military success (60) and that money is not the "sinews" of war (173). He urges the prince to inspire love in his subjects (58), but also admiration and fear (59). He tells us that divine favor is necessary for success (96), and that one should not judge by the success of an action (86). We learn that the remedy for tyranny is either "persecution" (that is, tyrannicide) or "patience"; and, although patience is recommended to Christians because all kings are sent by God, tyranny is also defined as "a certain violent government, exceeding the Laws of God and nature" (85). While the conflicting passages are in most cases drawn from different sources, the effect on the reader is to suggest that politics is a matter of prudential choice among a selection of maxims, rather than the application of fixed rules. It is also to suggest that politics is a matter of determining the best means to achieve the end at hand, rather than of implementing the moral law. Not surprisingly, then, while Ralegh cannot "commend . . . great subtlety and frauds contrary to virtue and piety" (68), he also notes with Machiavelli in chapter 18 of *The Prince*: "He that doth not as other men do, but endeavoureth that which ought to be done, shall thereby rather incur peril than preservation; for whoso laboureth to be sincerely perfect and good shall necessarily perish, living among men that are generally evil" (103; see 122). As in *The Prince* and the *Discourses*, context determines what is effective; political decorum is based on rhetorical and practical considerations of maintaining power, rather than ethical considerations of goodness and justice.[43]

Finally, compared to *Maxims of State*, *The Cabinet-Council* devotes more attention to the rhetorical aspect of politics that Machiavelli discussed in chapters 15–21 of *The Prince*: reputation, or the managing of the prince's public image (e.g., chaps. 6, 13, 17, 23). The use of eloquence as a substitute for force is discussed on a number of occasions (84, 126), as is the swift or exemplary use of violence: Agathocles (42) and Junius Brutus are mentioned, and in the latter case Ralegh goes out of his way to record the details that made the scene memorable according to Machiavelli: "Brutus . . . caused his own son not only to be condemned to death, but was himself present at the execution" (141). The theme of imitation is also prominent: the author remarks that "all people do naturally imitate the manners of the prince, and observing his proceedings resolve to hate or love him" (89); he recommends the imitation of the ancients in warfare (87); and he provides the Machiavellian defense of such imitation from the prefaces to books 1 and 2 of the *Discourses*:

> The most part of men are delighted with histories, for the variety of accidents therein contained; yet are there few that will imitate what they read, and find done by others; being persuaded that imitation is not only hard, but impossible; as though the heavens and men were changed in their motion or order, and power, which they anciently had. (94)

There is also more explicit attention to the Machiavellian topics of *fortuna* and *virtù*, virtue and success, means and ends, intention and effect (esp. 60–80). Finally, the language of necessity is frequently invoked, making clear that necessity in the political arena is as much an argument as a fact (67, 100, 122).

The point here is not that what Machiavelli had to say was new, nor that Machiavelli is singled out for special notice (though he occasionally is). To the contrary: *The Cabinet-Council* suggests that what Machiavelli has to teach is, for the most part, compatible with the teachings of Aristotle, Lipsius, Tacitus, Bodin, Guicciardini, and others. This is the case not because these authors agree on all points but because the author reads topically and opportunistically; his work invites his readers to do the same. In contrast to the mirror of princes or the systematic treatment of government in some medieval texts, which ground effective government on the virtues and natural law, this rhetorical approach to politics simultaneously exposes and exploits the contingent, de facto nature of political power. Quoting from both *The Prince* and the *Discourses*, among other texts, the author shows us that authority is created by rhetorical argument, which includes all the resources of reputation, spectacle, force, and fraud. And, although at times he gives good reasons for preferring a monarchy grounded in popular consent, he makes it clear that the form of government will itself be determined by contingent political circumstances.[44]

Bacon makes explicit the connection between rhetorical method and politics that is only implicit in the form of *Maxims of State* and *The Cabinet-Council*. In fact, Bacon's reading of Machiavelli provides some of the best evidence for the argument I have been making in this book: his appreciation of Machiavelli's pragmatism is inseparable from an appreciation of his rhetorical method. This reading of Machiavelli also helps us to see that Bacon's much vaunted empiricism, his interest in inductive method, does not involve a rejection of rhetoric but rather an extension of rhetorical method into new areas of investigation. Like Machiavelli, Bacon reads the sphere of politics rhetorically; unlike Machiavelli, he extends this reading to the natural world as well.[45]

Bacon's pronouncements on rhetoric and his use of rhetorical terminology are not always consistent; yet the inconsistency is itself instructive for a study of his Machiavellism. Like Machiavelli, Bacon is interested in questions of method; also like Machiavelli, he uses rhetoric as both an emblem of the failures of humanist investigation and a paradigm that needs to be developed rather than abandoned. Thus, on the one hand, Bacon contrasts the sterility of rhetorical invention of already existing arguments to the fruitful invention of new knowledge by means of induction. On the other hand, he does so by applying the old terminology of rhetoric to the investigation of the natural world. Thus, in *The Advancement of Learning*, he writes:

> The *Arts intellectual* are four in number; divided according to the ends whereunto they are referred: for man's labour is to *invent* that which is sought or propounded; or to *judge* that which is invented; or to *retain* that which is judged; or to *deliver over* that which is retained. So as the arts must be four: *Art* of *Inquiry* or *Invention*: *Art* of *Examination* or *Judgment*: *Art* of *Custody* or *Memory*: and *Art* of *Elocution* or *Tradition*.[46]

Borrowing from Cicero's division of rhetoric into inventio, dispositio, elocutio, memoria, and actio, Bacon applies these modes not only to "speech and arguments" but also to "arts and sciences" (122).

Although Bacon uses rhetorical terminology to describe the invention and transmission of scientific knowledge, he also uses rhetoric in the restricted sense to describe the persuasive communication of knowledge. Thus Bacon defines rhetoric in *The Advancement* as the application "of Reason to Imagination for the better moving of the Will" (146); less well known is his description of rhetoric as "Imaginative or Insinuative Reason" (121). These definitions draw near to the Ramist view of rhetoric as mere ornament or elocution, subordinate to logical invention; but here, too, Bacon's differences with Ramus are instructive for an understanding of his Machiavellism.[47] Whereas Ramus tends to focus on logic as the "single method" of presenting arguments, Bacon sees rhetoric as the necessary supplement to logic, if individuals are to be moved to action or to further investigation. Such a conception of rhetoric might be allied with Machiavellism not simply because it divorces the study of style from the ethical preoccupations of the humanists but also because it implies that "all presentation is misrepresentation to some specified end."[48] Rhetoric in this view is both an aid to and distortion of reason, in the service of particular interests. The very attempt to subordinate rhetoric to logic thus paradoxically reveals the threat of Machiavellian fraud that it is intended to control: rhetoric is necessary precisely because logical invention is not always sufficiently convincing on its own; and this persuasive function of rhetoric introduces manipulation and distortion as well as communication. Indeed, at times it may be difficult to distinguish these three.

Bacon's conception of rhetoric is also non-Ramist because it is more capacious than the Ramist equation of rhetoric with elocution. Although Bacon distinguishes between the logical invention of new knowledge and the rhetorical presentation of existing knowledge, he both rejects Ramus's view of a "single method" of presenting arguments in favor of a plurality of methods, and describes rhetoric in ways that suggest that it, too, can be a means of encouraging further investigation. For example, when we turn to his discussion of the methods of tradition (the communication of knowledge), we see them described in a way that confounds Ramus's distinction between logical invention and rhetorical presentation. While approving the inclusion of "method" in logic, Bacon goes on to make a distinction between the "Magistral" and "Probative" methods of transmitting knowledge (140). The first presents knowledge "in such a form as may be best believed, and not as may be best examined" (141); the second method is preferable because it not only transmits knowledge but also increases it:

> But knowledge that is delivered as a thread to be spun on, ought to be delivered and intimated, if it were possible, in the same method wherein it was invented: and so is it possible of knowledge induced. . . . For it is in knowledge as it is in plants: if you mean to use the plant, it is no matter for the roots; but if you mean to remove it to grow, then it is more assured to rest upon roots than slips. (141)

In this passage, induction is not a logical process separate from persuasion, as it is in Ramus. Rather, induction is a function of rhetoric, and the best form of persuasion is one that induces the reader or listener to investigate further.[49]

We are now in a better position to see why Bacon appreciates Machiavelli. Bacon reads Machiavelli not simply or even primarily as a secular analyst of politics but rather as a writer who extended rhetorical methods of investigation to the sphere of politics.[50] Machiavelli is praised as a rhetorician because he does not simply rehearse commonplaces (as the author of *Maxims of State* and *The Cabinet-Council* sometimes seems to do) but engages the reader in a process of deliberation that advances both his understanding and his political position. Two frequently quoted passages are relevant here and deserve close analysis. In the first, Bacon approves Machiavelli's use of examples as a method of political instruction:

> And therefore the form of writing which of all others is fittest for this variable argument of negotiation and occasions is that which Machiavel chose wisely and aptly for government; namely, discourses upon histories or examples. For knowledge drawn freshly, and in our view, out of particulars,

knoweth the way best to particulars again; and it hath much greater life for practice when the discourse attendeth upon the example, than when the example attendeth upon the discourse. For this is no point of order, as it seemeth at first, but of substance: for when the example is the ground, being set down in a history at large, it is set down with all circumstances, which may sometimes control the discourse thereupon made, and sometimes supply it as a very pattern for action; whereas the examples alleged for the discourse' sake are cited succinctly, and without particularity, and carry a servile aspect towards the discourse which they are brought in to make good. (*Advancement*, 186)

The inductive method Bacon is describing here is closer to Erasmus's method in his collections of parables and similitudes than it is to any modern conception of scientific method. The best use of examples is not to illustrate abstract principles but rather to complicate and ultimately to invalidate a purely theoretical approach to politics.[51] In Bacon's rhetorical view of politics, "circumstances," rather than precepts, control discourse and provide patterns of action.

This passage also suggests that the use of examples as mere "servile" illustrations creates a "servile" attitude on the part of the reader and imitator.[52] Bacon thus implies that the opposite rhetorical method has the power to induce a politic insubordination or at least a questioning of accepted authorities. This observation may be supported by the passage in *De Augmentis* where Bacon advises those pursuing "Knowledge of Advancement in Life" "to take especial heed how they guide themselves by examples, and not vainly to endeavor to frame themselves upon other men's models; as if what is open to others must needs be open to them, not at all reflecting how far the nature and character of their models may differ from their own."[53] Although at first glance this passage seems to recommend the cautious evaluation of one's abilities, the "circumstances" or context in which it appears suggest a different interpretation. In the very next paragraph, Bacon advises the politic man how "to set himself forth to advantage," and "to turn and shape himself according to occasion" (66). These recommendations of Machiavellian flexibility imply that political success is partly the result of choosing one's examples rather than servilely following the example of others. Or, to put it another way, examples might be chosen after the fact, to authorize or justify a particularly advantageous mode of behavior:

It is therefore no unimportant attribute of prudence in a man to be able to set forth to advantage before others, with grace and skill, his virtues, fortunes, and merits . . . and again, to cover artificially his weaknesses, defects, misfortunes, and disgraces; dwelling upon the former and turning them to the light, sliding from the latter or explaining them away by apt interpretation and the like. Tacitus says of Mucianus, the wisest and most active politician of his time, "That he had a certain art of setting forth to advantage everything he said or did." (66)

That this advice, which resembles Castiglione's discussion of courtly *sprezzatura*, has potentially a Machiavellian and casuistical dimension is apparent in Bacon's comment that "some persons of weaker judgment and perhaps too scrupulous morality may disapprove of it" (67). And, although he later distinguishes between good arts and evil, Machiavellian arts, the latter are described in terms that suggest Bacon's own recommendations for the "politic man, I mean politic for his own fortune" (75):

> if any one, I say, takes pleasure in such kind of corrupt wisdom, I will certainly not deny (with these dispensations from all the laws of charity and virtue, and an entire devotion to the pressing of his fortune,) he may advance it quicker and more compendiously. But it is in life as it is in ways, the shortest way is commonly the foulest and muddiest, and surely the fairer way is not much about. (76)

The conclusion would appear to be that if one is really concerned with the politic "Advancement in Life," Machiavellian arts are the most efficient, though not the moral, way to proceed. As Bacon remarks earlier: "For the things necessary for the acquisition of fortune are neither fewer nor less difficult nor lighter than those to obtain virtue; and it is as hard and severe a thing to be a true politician, as to be truly moral" (58–59). In this passage, Bacon plays in Machiavellian fashion with "necessity" and "virtue" in order to aggravate the distinction between virtue and politics; so that, by the end of the paragraph, when Bacon writes that "fortune as an instrument of virtue and merit deserves its own speculation and doctrine," "virtue" is at the very least equivocal and may be construed as *virtù* (59).

In the second passage relevant to an understanding of Bacon's Machiavellism, Bacon praises Machiavelli as a teacher of the "verità effettuale," at the same time that he passes moral judgment on such knowledge:

> We are much beholden to Machiavel and others, that write what men do, and not what they ought to do. For it is not possible to join serpentine wisdom with columbine innocency, except men know exactly all the conditions of the serpent: his baseness and going upon his belly, his volubility and lubricity, his envy and sting, and the rest; that is, all forms and natures of evil: for without this, virtue lieth open and unfenced. Nay, an honest man can do no good upon those that are wicked to reclaim them, without the help of the knowledge of evil. For men of corrupted minds presuppose that honesty groweth out of simplicity of manners, and believing of preachers, schoolmasters and men's exterior language: so as, ex-

cept you can make them perceive that you know the utmost reaches of their own corrupt opinions, they despise all morality; *Non recipit stultus verba prudentiae, nisi ea dixeris quae versantur in corde eius* [A fool receiveth not the words of prudence, unless you say what is already in his heart]. (*Advancement*, 165–66)

The first part of this passage sounds like Milton in *Areopagitica*: the virtuous man needs to know evil in order to combat it. And, as with the passage in Milton, the more one reads these lines, the more difficult they are to unravel. According to Bacon, the corrupt man believes that the virtuous are unskilled in recognizing words as signs ("exterior language"), and thus in distinguishing behavior from intention. In order to meet the corrupt man on his own terms, the virtuous man thus needs to prove that he has the ability to read signs. The logic of the passage resembles those Counter-Reformation responses to Machiavelli which argue that Machiavelli must be refuted on his own terms: not by appealing to the ethical superiority of Christian virtue but by claiming that virtue is closer to *virtù* than has previously been thought. The best way for wisdom to deal with the serpent and preserve "columbine innocency" is, paradoxically, to become serpentine. To recognize the inevitable mediation of signs is to acknowledge both the necessity of staging one's virtue, and the possibility of feigning it.

Two of Bacon's essays are especially pertinent to this last observation. The first, "Of Simulation and Dissimulation," uses the terminology we are familiar with from Counter-Reformation treatises and works of casuistry. "Dissimulation," Bacon begins, "is but a faint kind of policy or wisdom" (17).[54] From the outset, policy and wisdom are joined, as they are in the passage cited above on serpentine wisdom. The difference between policy and dissimulation is that the former involves a finer ability to discriminate: for the politic individual, dissimulation is only one of several options. Yet, it is also representative of the way in which virtue necessarily enters the realm of feigning once "negotiation" or social interaction is seen to be constituted by signs:

> Certainly the ablest men that ever were have had all an openness and frankness of dealing, and a name for certainty and veracity; but then they were like horses well managed; for they could tell passing well when to stop or turn; and at such times when they thought the case indeed required dissimulation, if then they used it, it came to pass that the former opinion spread abroad of their good faith and clearness of dealing made them almost invisible. (17)

This passage is reminiscent of chapter 18 of *The Prince*, where Machiavelli advises that it is good to seem virtuous, good even to be virtuous, but that one should know how to respond differently when appropriate. Such a view of politic flexibility makes veracity "a name," a reputation for "good faith" that it is good—that is, expedient—to have. As Bacon writes in the essay "Of Goodness and the Goodness of Nature":

> The Italians have an ungracious proverb, *Tanto buon che val niente: So good, that he is good for nothing.* And one of the doctors of Italy, Nicholas Machiavel, had the confidence to put in writing, almost in plain terms, *That the Christian faith had given up good men in prey to those that are tyrannical and unjust.* Which he spake, because indeed there was never law, or sect, or opinion, did so much magnify goodness as the Christian religion doth. Therefore, to avoid the scandal and the danger of both, it is good to take knowledge of the errors of an habit so excellent. (37–38)

Here, too, Bacon seems deliberately to mimic Machiavelli's syntax and wit. He signals his awareness of Machiavelli's irony with the phrase "almost in plain terms"; he also imitates Machiavelli's characteristic play with good or "buon" in his translation of the Italian proverb and his final sentence. As we saw in chapter 1, Machiavelli plays on the word "bene" in discussing Agathocles's politic use of violence: "Bene usate si possono chiamare quelle (se del male è licito dire bene)" (Cruelty can be described as well used [if it's permissible to speak well about something that is evil in itself]). Bacon achieves a similarly witty discrimination between the ethical and political meanings of "good" when he remarks that "it is good to take knowledge of the errors" of ethical goodness. Just as Machiavelli scandalizes his reader's ethical sensibilities precisely by acknowledging the claims of ethics in the private sphere, so Bacon uses the stereotypical figure of the Machiavel (the teacher of "evil arts") to set off Machiavelli the rhetorician and pragmatist.

Shakespeare's *Coriolanus*: The Machiavel and the Republican

The last reader and interpreter of Machiavelli I wish to consider here is Shakespeare in *Coriolanus*. My placement of this dramatic treatment of the Machiavel last is both strategic and historically accurate. Both because the theatrical Machiavel has been the object of so much discussion, and because the reception of Machiavelli in the drama is not the decisive turning point in the history of Machiavellism it was once taken to be, I have chosen to focus on other, nondramatic works in this book. Nevertheless, Shakespeare's *Coriolanus* is particularly instructive for my argument concerning the intersection of the stereotypical Machiavel and Machiavelli the theorist of republicanism. For this reason, a brief discussion of this play is in order.

While *Coriolanus* has not figured significantly in histories of Machiavellism, in recent years critics have discussed Machiavelli's possible influence on this play. In particular, Anne Barton has argued that, in his depiction of the struggle between the Roman patricians and plebs, Shakespeare was drawing not only on Livy but also on Machiavelli's *Discourses*.[55] For Barton, *Coriolanus* offers further evidence that Shakespeare and his contemporaries "were clearly familiar not only with the devilish practices and opinions popularly attributed to Machiavelli, but with what he had actually written" (122). Because Barton equated the real Machiavelli with the sympathetic analyst of the Roman republic, she failed to see that the force and fraud of the Machiavel—here represented in particular by Volumnia—are also a part of the play's political order. Significantly, although Shakespeare could have found the description of the productive disunion between the nobles and the plebs in Livy or in Plutarch's "Life of Coriolanus," he invented all the scenes in which Volumnia appears (with the exception of 5.3). These invented scenes suggest that the Machiavel is as much a part of the contemporary political thinking Shakespeare incorporated in his drama as is Machiavelli the author of the *Discourses*.

Even before Volumnia gives Coriolanus her Machiavellian advice, Cominius's speech in praise of Coriolanus reveals the uncertain place of Roman or stoic *virtù* in the complex world of political realities depicted by the play:

> It is held
> That valor is the chiefest virtue and
> Most dignifies the haver. If it be,
> The man I speak of cannot in the world
> Be singly counterpoised. At sixteen years,
> When Tarquin made a head for Rome, he fought
> Beyond the mark of others. Our then dictator,
> Whom with all praise I point at, saw him fight,
> When with his Amazonian chin he drove
> The bristled lips before him. He bestrid
> An o'erpressed Roman, and i' th' consul's view
> Slew three opposers; Tarquin's self he met,
> And struck him on his knee. In that day's feats,
> When he might act the woman in the scene,
> He proved best man i' th' field, and for his meed
> Was brow-bound with the oak.
>
> (2.2.83–98)

As Cominius's conditional "If it be" suggests, "valor" (one common English translation of *virtù*) is no longer obviously the "chiefest virtue" in the world of the play. Something more is required: those skills of rhetoric and self-representation which inflect Roman virtue in the direction of Machiavellian *virtù*. These theatrical skills are alluded to in the description of the young—and beardless—Coriolanus's ability to "act the woman in the scene," in contrast to Coriolanus's actual manly valor.

Although Cominius opposes theatrical effeminacy to military *virtù*, he himself undercuts this opposition in calling attention to Coriolanus's "Amazonian chin." Cominius's description of Coriolanus is at once praise and parody: in juxtaposing such effeminate features with a proof of manhood, Cominius suggests that Coriolanus's rejection of theater and its protean transformations is tied to an uncertainty about his own identity, a desire to fix his self in action once and for all. Yet, the nature of Coriolanus's action is itself ambiguous: although "struck him on his knee" is usually glossed as "to his knees," it may also be read literally as a blow to the knees—as though to suggest that Coriolanus managed to touch Tarquin but not seriously wound him.

If Coriolanus's manly, military *virtù* is represented as a response to the threat of the feminine or of theater (*fortuna* as a woman who requires chameleonlike, theatrical adaptation), Volumnia represents the Machiavellian *virtù* that emerges from the critique of Roman or stoic virtue. In contrast to her son, who equates flattery with harm, and who flees "from words" (2.2.72), Volumnia the Machiavel understands the staging and voicing of reputation as the necessary supplement to political power. In Act 3, scene 2, she tells Coriolanus:

> If it be honor in your wars to seem
> The same you are not, which for your best ends
> You adopt your policy, how is it less or worse
> That it shall hold companionship in peace
> With honor as in war; since that to both
> It stands in like request?
> *Coriolanus*:   Why force you this?
> *Volumnia*: Because that now it lies you on to speak
> To th' people, not by your own instruction,
> Nor by th' matter which your heart prompts you,
> But with such words that are but roted in
> Your tongue, though but bastards and syllables
> Of no allowance to your bosom's truth.
> Now, this no more dishonors you at all
> Than to take in a town with gentle words,
> Which else would put you to your fortune and
> The hazard of much blood.
> I would dissemble with my nature, where
> My fortunes and my friends at stake required
> I should do so in honor.

> (3.2.46–64)

In Volumnia's view, Coriolanus's own military *virtù* already includes deception; force and fraud, honor and policy, are thus not opposites but rather dialectically related aspects of a single, rhetorical conception of virtue. It is noteworthy that Coriolanus perceives his mother's equation of war and peacetime as rhetorical coercion ("Why force you this?"); he thus admits in spite of himself that rhetoric is a force to be reckoned with in the struggle for political power. In response, Volumnia elaborates a view of rhetoric reminiscent of Thomas Wilson's well-known preface to the *Arte of Rhetorique*.[56] Just as persuasion may allow one to "take in a town with gentle words" instead of military force, so rhetorical dissembling may allow one to achieve one's goals in peacetime. Honor receives redefinition in the process: no longer adherence to a fixed code of moral precepts, honor refers to those actions or means that allow one to achieve the desired ends. As with Machiavelli's play on good and well in *The Prince*, honor here becomes an adjective rather than a noun, the quality attributed to means that may not be good in themselves but are nevertheless "well used" (*bene usate*). Like Machiavelli, Shakespeare suggests that the theatrical and rhetorical nature of political power is better acknowledged than rejected: only by including the resources of rhetoric and acting in one's arsenal of political behavior can one respond fully to fortune, the threatening underside of rhetoric that "returns to plague the inventor."

In contrast, then, to Coriolanus's "absolute" sense of a self that speaks for itself (3.2.39), Volumnia urges her son to stage his person, even his own reluctance to speak:

> I prithee now, my son,
> Go to them with this bonnet in thy hand;
> And thus far having stretched it (here be with them),
> Thy knee bussing the stones (for in such business
> Action is eloquence, and the eyes of th' ignorant
> More learnèd than the ears) . . .
>   or say to them,
> Thou art their soldier, and being bred in broils
> Hast not the soft way which, thou dost confess,
> Were fit for thee to use, as they to claim,
> In asking their good loves; but thou wilt frame
> Thyself, forsooth, hereafter theirs, so far
> As thou hast power and person.
>
>   (3.2.75–89)

In Volumnia's view, action is eloquence both because actions speak like words, and because the sphere of politics is governed by rhetorical considerations. Her own rhetoric reflects this inflection of the realm of action by rhetoric: "stretched" refers both to Coriolanus's taking off his hat to the people, and to his "stretching" his own inflexible conception of self; "frame" means both represent and distort; "power and person" are less prerequisites of effective action in the political realm than they are a rhetorical construction or the result of such action. Finally, although editors have speculated that lines 74–80 may be corrupt, the remark that "the eyes of th' ignorant [are] more learnèd than the ears" suggests Machiavelli's comment in chapter 18 of *The Prince* that "men in general judge more by the sense of sight than by the sense of touch. . . . Everyone sees what you seem to be, few know what you really are" (51).[57]

Once we recognize the theatrical dimension of political power, we are better prepared to understand the position of the people in Shakespeare's play. As in *The Prince*, the recognition that power needs to be staged leads to the rhetorical consideration of one's audience. Volumnia is no idealistic republican; nevertheless, she sees that Coriolanus must seek approval from the people if he is to secure his power. And, just as Volumnia sees that military *virtù* must be supplemented by a rhetorical appeal to the people, the play shows that the necessity of such an appeal gives the people a voice—and greater representation in the state. As Barton remarks, here Shakespeare borrows from Livy, who "teases out the intimate connection . . . between Rome's need to cultivate the arts of peace as well as war, and the internal struggle between her patricians and plebeians" (120). If Rome is to succeed in its military ventures abroad, it must give its citizens representation at home: "Moreover, Shakespeare altered the order of events as they occur in both Plutarch and Livy. It is plain in *Coriolanus* that only after tribunes have been granted them do the citizens stop stirring up strife in the city and agree to provide soldiers for the Volscian campaign" (120). Although one can quarrel about the extent to which Shakespeare's sympathies lie with the people, the tie between rhetoric and popular representation in the play is clear. Coriolanus may be insincere in his rhetorical address to the people, the tribunes themselves may cynically manipulate the people with their rhetoric; still, a rhetorical conception of political power requires that the people be addressed and represented. Thus Cominius's qualification and Volumnia's critique of stoic virtue are matched by the play's political critique of Coriolanus's desire to be "author of himself" (5.3.36): the division of authority within the state is represented as necessary, as the new order.

Barton is right to note the sympathetic representation of the Roman republic in *Coriolanus* but, as I have argued, a full appreciation of Shakespeare's Machiavellism requires that we attend to the Machiavel as well. In *Coriolanus*, as in *The Prince* and the *Discourses*, these two aspects of Machiavellism are intricately intertwined. In his essay on the play, Kenneth Burke hints at this when he writes,

> The Renaissance was particularly exercised by Machiavelli because he so accurately represented the transvaluation of values involved in the rise of nationalism. A transvaluation was called for, because *religion* aimed at *uni-*

versal virtues, whereas the virtues of *nationalism* would necessarily be *factional*, insofar as they pitted nation against nation. Conduct viewed as vice from the standpoint of universal religious values might readily be viewed as admirable if it helped some interests prevail over others.[58]

The play depicts a new order predicated on the acceptance of faction, and dramatizes the role of rhetoric, acting, and dissembling, in the construction of political power.[59] The resources of the Machiavel are not separate from (although they are also not identical with) those of the republican.

Editors and Translators

The principles of interpretation governing the readings of Gardiner, Ralegh, Bacon, and Shakespeare are codified by editors and translators of Machiavelli's work. While Machiavelli's amoral virtue is itself an object of fear and loathing to his critics, to his defenders Machiavelli's representation of the indeterminate connection between virtue and *virtù* amounts to both an objective portrayal of political affairs and a lever for political change. Unlike those sixteenth-century readers who silently appropriate Machiavelli's insights, editors and translators must explicitly respond to the image of the stereotypical Machiavel; they do so not only by pointing to the availability of Machiavelli's work for a variety of uses but also by arguing for Machiavelli's ironic depiction of the tyrant. The republican Machiavelli is one form of this ironic defense; his appearance in the rhetoric of English Machiavellism seems to have been as much or more a defense against the stereotypical Machiavel as it was a result of radically changed political circumstances.[60]

Translators of Machiavelli often shift the responsibility for the meaning of Machiavelli's work from the author to the reader, arguing that Machiavelli only provides the material for the reader's exercise of discretion. In an Elizabethan translation of the *Discourses* that circulated in manuscript, John Levett answers those critics of Machiavelli who condemn him for not distinguishing between true and false religion, "as though he would hold, religion to bee but a meere civill intention to hold the world in reverence & feare." He responds with pragmatic insouciance that "in praising the effects of religion," Machiavelli "seemeth to maintaine no other thing, then that which most part of the wiser sorte have always affirmed. Viz. that as a bad government is to be preferred before licentiousness, yea even a very tyranny, before a popular confusion; so superstition is better than Atheisme." In a discourse in which the issue at hand is "effects" rather than truth or falsehood, Machiavelli cannot be blamed for not considering the truth of religion. And he echoes the by then usual response to those who are not persuaded by this defense by sending

> them to the bee for better answer, who can gather hony out of those plants, where poison also is taken, and wish them to take heed least their evill conceited opinions grow not either from their want of understanding of that which they reade, or else from that corruption and malignity of their judgements to estimate the same.[61]

Levett's analogy suggests both that the evil in Machiavelli may be a projection on the part of the reader, and that the text that is read in such an evil fashion can also be put to good uses.

A similar defense appears in Edward Dacres's 1636 and 1640 translations of the *Discourses* and *The Prince*.[62] Both works were dedicated to James, Duke of Lennox, a member of Charles I's privy council. In the dedicatory letter prefacing his translation of the *Discourses*, Dacres recommends Machiavelli's "discovery of the first foundations, and analyzing of the very grounds, upon which the Roman Commonwealth was built" as particularly relevant to the present "turbulent times": for "when the times grow perplex'd with perills and difficulties, true worth and experience are sought after, and then of value." In Dacres's view, the *Discourses* show rulers how to maintain a commonwealth, a term he does not equate with a republican form of government.

In his remarks on specific chapters Dacres is particularly concerned to rebut Machiavelli's recommendations about the use of force to establish de facto political power—as he very well might be on the eve of the civil war. In commenting on the *Discourses*, book 1, chapter 9, in which Machiavelli explains that Romulus's murder of Remus was justified by its beneficial effects, Dacres cites book 1, chapter 18, as rebuttal: Romulus's behavior cannot serve as an example for others because only rarely does a good man use evil means for good purposes, or an evil man turn those means to good ends. In commenting on book 1, chapter 58, in which Machiavelli writes "to a mischievous Prince no man can speake, nor is there any other remedy but the sword," Dacres presents the usual biblical arguments for nonresistance to tyrants:

> But this is such a remedy as hath no warrant from divine or humane lawes, especially when that a Tyrant is the true and lawfull Prince of the country, however that by his evill government and administration of the affaires he deservedly be term'd a Tyrant. That of David none is ignorant of, Sam. 1.24, and 5. Where he cut off the lapper of Sauls garment, and therefore was checkt by his owne conscience. And that in the Psalm, 140, Touch not mine anointed, etc. (183)

And he buttresses these arguments with secular passages from Tacitus's *Annals* and *Histories* to the effect that tyrannicide only brings more confusion in its wake, concluding that "The treacle of this venom is prayer and not vengeance," for God permits tyrants "sometimes for chastisement sometimes for tyrall" (184).

Although Dacres prefers the people to exercise the virtue of obedience when it comes to tyrants, he does not want piety and policy, virtue and *virtù*, to be divorced altogether. Like Botero and other Counter-Reformation writers, Dacres rejects Machivelli's argument that Christianity makes for weaker soldiers. And in his gloss on *Discourses*, 3.30, he criticizes Machiavelli's characterization of Moses as a secular soldier who used violence for the purposes of worldly policy and self-aggrandizement, though not for the reasons we might expect. Machiavelli read "the Scriptures only to a politicke end, not so much for the strengthening of his belief, as the bettering of his discourse"; if he had read with faith rather than simply for the purposes of persuading his audience, he would have seen that Moses "behaved not himself either ambitiously or insolently, nor was anything done by his own prowess or policy, but merely by the ordinance of GOD." The effect of such a gloss is to make force the legitimate resource of the providentially sanctioned ruler alone (448–49).

Although Dacres records his caveats, the fact that he translated the *Discourses* and dedicated them to the Duke of Lennox shows that he was chiefly concerned to appropriate Machiavelli's insights for the purposes of salvaging the kingdom. As we have seen, part of this appropriation took the form of arguing against those passages of the *Discourses* that cynically manipulated Scripture and that defended violent innovation and republicanism. In Dacres's reading, the message of the *Discourses* can be read as perfectly compatible with that of *The Prince*, and both, he suggests, can be put to use by royalists in their battle against parliamentary insurgents.

Dacres codifies these principles of interpretation in his 1640 translation of *The Prince*. In his marginal gloss on chapter 15 of *The Prince*, Dacres condemns what he calls Machiavelli's "ambidexterity":

> A second blemish in this our Authours book I find in his fifteenth Chapter: where he instructs a Prince to use such ambidexterity as that he may serve himselfe, either of vertue, or vice, according to his advantage, which in true pollicy is neither good in attaining the Principality, nor in securing it when it is attained. For Politicks presupposes Ethiques, which will never allow this rule: as that a man might make this small difference between vertue, and vice, that he may indifferently lay aside, or take up the one, or the other, and put it in practise as best conduceth to the end he propounds himself. (121)

In rejecting Machiavelli's recommendation of ethical ambidexterity, or what he later calls "suplenesse of disposition" (142), Dacres calls attention to the indeterminate link between politics and ethics that critics of rhetoric have also always condemned. Yet, in his dedication of the translation to the Duke of Lennox, he makes that ambidexterity the grounds of his defense of Machiavelli:

> this book carryes its poyson and malice in it; yet mee thinks the judicious peruser may honestly make use of it in the actions of his life, with advantage. . . . Epictetus the Philosopher sayes, Every thing hath two handles, as the firebrand, it may bee taken up at one end in the bare hand without hurt: the other being laid hold on, will cleave to the very flesh, and the smart of it will pierce even to the heart.

And in the prefatory letter to the reader, he emphasizes the reader's responsibility for taking up the text "without hurt":

> Surely this book will infect no man: out of the wicked treasure of a mans own wicked heart, he drawes his malice and mischiefe. From the same flower the Bee sucks hony, from whence the Spider hath his poyson. And he that means well, shall be here warnd, where the deceitfull man learnes to set his snares. A judge who hath often used to examine theeves, becomes the more expert to sift out their tricks. If mischiefe come here upon, blame not me, nor blame my Authour.

In Dacres's view, Machiavelli's text cannot infect anyone who is not already so infected; but it can teach the well-intentioned reader how to recognize snares and tricks. Here he exculpates Machiavelli from any blame for that which he reports, perhaps implying that description is not prescription but something closer to criticism.

This two-handedness informs Dacres's own reading of *The Prince*. In his comments on individual chapters, he alternately praises and condemns Machiavelli's recommendations, and those that he condemns he renders harmless firebrands. "Till wee come to this seaventh Chapter," he remarks, "I find not anything much blameworthy," but Cesare Borgia is unacceptable as "a paterne to a new prince." And he adds that in this example Machiavelli himself provides the ammunition for arguing against him in purely secular and pragmatic terms. Rather than showing the superiority of Machiavellian *virtù*, examples such as Borgia illustrate its fallibility: "Policy shewd itselfe short-sighted; for hee foresaw not at the time of his Fathers death, he himself should bee brought unto deaths doore also." Like Botero and his contemporaries, Dacres cannot help drawing the theological moral from Borgia's dramatic failure: "And me thinkes the Example might have given occasion to our Author to confesse, that surely there is a God that ruleth the earth" (34).[63]

Other readers explicitly ascribed Dacres's "two-handedness" to Machiavelli, arguing that his irony or rhetorical indirection was in the service of his republicanism. Alberico Gentili, a professor of law at Oxford, defended *The Prince* in his *De legationibus libri tres* (1585), a work that was dedicated to Sir Philip Sidney. Describing Machiavelli as a "laudator democratiae" (eulogist of democracy), he writes:

> Born, educated, and attaining to honors under a democratic form of government, he was the supreme foe of tyranny. . . . It was not his purpose to instruct the tyrant, but by revealing his secret counsels to strip him bare, and expose him to the suffering nations. Do we not know that there have been many princes such as he describes? That is the reason why princes of that type object to the survival and publication of his works. The purpose of this shrewdest of men was to instruct the nations under pretext of instructing the prince, and he adopted this pretext that there might be some hope that he would be tolerated as an educator and teacher by those who held the tiller of government.[64]

According to Gentili, Machiavelli's desire to find employment with the Medici led to the rhetorical indirection of *The Prince*. But he also excuses Machiavelli's discussion of tyranny by noting that even Plato and Aristotle represented the tyrant in their works. In any case, Machiavelli's works should be preserved, particularly his "precious *Observations on Livy*," because Machiavelli is an exemplary reader of history: "In reading history he does not play the grammarian, but assumes the role of philosopher" (156, 157). That is, in determining a course of action he does not simply refer to historical precedents—which always conflict—but is able to discern which is the correct one for the occasion at hand.

John Wolfe, the friend and printer of Gentili, had articulated a similar defense in the preface to the pseudo-Italian 1584 edition of *The Prince* and the *Discourses*. He tells us that he used to think of Machiavelli as diabolical, but reading his works changed his mind:

> The more I read, the more they pleased me, and to speak truly, every hour I discovered new doctrine in them, new sharpness of wit, and new methods for learning the true way of drawing some utility from the profitable reading of histories, and, in brief, I realized that I had learned more from these works in one day about the government of the world, than I had in all my past life, from all the histories I had read. I learned exactly what difference there was between a prince and a tyrant, between government by many good men and government by a few bad ones, and between a well-regulated commonwealth and a confused and licentious multitude.[65]

While Wolfe does not specify the rhetorical features that led to his conversion, his description of what he learned suggests that he read *The Prince* just as he read the *Discourses*. The message of the two works is the same, whether because *The Prince* directly exposes the weakness of tyranny or because, as Gentili argues, it surreptitiously teaches how to subvert it. And, as for Gentili, for Wolfe Machiavelli is the exemplary reader of history, who teaches not only substance but method to his imitators.[66]

Lastly, we find an explicit acknowledgment that simple representation can also serve as condemnation, that description can reveal the internal contradictions that give rise to a critique of the status quo, in James Bovey's *The Atheisticall Politition, A Breife [sic] Discourse concerning Ni. Machiavell* (1642).[67] Bovey defends Machiavelli by explaining that he merely published the maxims according to which princes have secretly acted. Describing the conditions under which Machiavelli composed *The Prince*, he writes:

> No time was fuller of action, nor shewed the instabilities of worldly honours than the occurrences that happened in *Italy* at this time; Now from a man wholly imployed in Court affaires, where it was thought madnesse to looke beyond second causes; worse things might have been with better reason expected, than these so bitterly condemn'd; which are indeed but the Historie of wise impieties, long before imprinted in the hearts of ambitious pretenders, and by him made legible to the meanest understanding, yet he is more blam'd for this faire expression, than they are that daily commit farre greater impiety, than his or any pen else is able to expresse.
>
> It was his profession to imitate the behaviour of Princes were it never so unseemly. (2)[68]

Whereas Machiavelli is treated in sixteenth-century rhetoric and courtesy books as the exemplar of courtly dissembling, he is here seen as a mere imitator of princes and ambitious pretenders. Machiavelli's imitation of the behavior of princes is scandalous not only to the naive reader but also to the princes themselves who "blame the publication of these Maximes, that they may put them in practice with more profit and securitie" (2). In this case, description serves to expose tyranny and thus acts as a weapon against it: "For upon how great disadvantage should a good Prince treat with a bad Neighbor; if [i.e., unless] he were not onely familiar with the paths of wickednesse, but knew other wayes to shun them; and how to counterminde their treacherous practices" (2). In short, Machiavelli's work may be excused not only as a faithful imitation of reality but as "a Grammar for the understanding of Tyrannical government" (7).[69]

When we recall that this text was published in 1642 such remarks acquire greater force: like Machiavelli's imitation of the unseemly behavior of tyrants, Bovey's imitation of Machiavelli serves to criticize the behavior of Charles I.[70] This domestication of Machiavelli is made explicit on the first page of his tract, where Bovey refers to Charles's minister, Strafford, and to Archbishop Laud: "He that intends to expresse a dishonest man cals him a Machiavillian, when we might as justly say a *Straffordian* or a *Cantabirian*." Bovey implicitly returns to Laud and Strafford at the end of the tract, arguing that while kings' ambassadors may use false-hood and deceit in foreign policy, they must not "turne . . . the edge of these qualities towards their owne people to whom they are tyde in a more naturall, and honest Obligation" (7). Finally, while Bovey allows that those who imitate the tyrant Cesare Borgia may prosper in the short run, in the end, like Borgia, "they shall not want impediments, or discon-tents, that shall out-talke the pleasure of their Ambition" (6). Like Machi-avelli himself, Bovey uses description for the purposes of analysis and critique, placing rhetoric in the service of dissent. And, like his own six-teenth-century predecessors, the Machiavelli who interests Bovey is the chronicler of "wise impieites," the grammarian of de facto political power.

Although individual emphases vary, all of the readers we have examined in this chapter were sensitive to the way Machiavelli's rhetoric hovers between description and prescription, a storehouse of commonplaces and a series of recommendations for political conduct, argument *in utramque partem* and critique. In their different ways, Gardiner, Bacon, Ralegh, and Shakespeare understood that the rhetorical dimension of Machia-velli's political thought embraced the stereotypical Machiavel as well as the neutral political analyst, the dissembling rhetorician of political ne-cessity as well as the historian of tyranny. They understood, too, that the distinction was often, for all practical political purposes, hard to main-tain. As we have seen, in their defensive attempt to preserve this distinc-tion, prefatory remarks and occasional comments on *The Prince* and the *Discourses* also illustrate several (often simultaneously held) views of Machiavelli's rhetoric. For Dacres, Machiavelli's work is poisonous but still of use to the "judicious peruser"; for Bovey, Machiavelli is shocking not because he has something new and especially poisonous to say but because he publishes the *arcana imperii*, the secrets of princely rule. Da-cres condemns Machiavelli but suggests that we read him against the grain; Bovey argues that those who condemn Machiavelli have misjudged his rhetoric as prescriptive rather than descriptive. For John Wolfe, Ma-chiavelli is himself an exemplary reader, one who teaches "the true way of drawing some utility from the profitable reading of histories." And for others, such as Gentili, Machiavelli is a sly rhetorician who, in instructing tyrants, instructs also in their removal—whether by informing the people of their methods or by causing such tyrants to bring about their own downfall. In the first case, Machiavelli's rhetoric is interpreted as a kind of argument on both sides of the question; in the second, as irony or an immanent critique of the status quo. As we will see in the following chapter, this flexible political rhetoric—its threatening contingency and its seemingly arbitrary methods—was regularly identified with Machiavelli in the culture at large. Although Machiavelli was not the origin of such "wise impieties," he came to symbolize both the dangers and the resources of rhetorical politics at times of political crisis.

FIVE

MACHIAVELLIAN DEBATES,

1530–1660

Though Justice against Fate complain,
And plead the antient Rights in vain:
But those do hold or break
As men are strong or weak.
—*Andrew Marvell,* "An Horatian Ode upon
Cromwell's Return from Ireland"

WHEN Andrew Marvell sought to describe Cromwell's troubling *virtù* in the "Horatian Ode," he chose a Machiavellian rhetoric of de facto political power, of terrifying natural energy whose capacity to create seemed inextricably linked to its capacity to destroy. He also imitated Machiavelli's own rhetoric, at once dispassionate and critical, with his description of Cromwell as a man who "Could by industrious Valour climbe / To ruine the great Work of Time." Marvell's Machiavellian rhetoric can serve as an emblem of generations of Renaissance Englishmen who identified Machiavelli with political innovation—with ruining and remaking the great Work of Time. In this chapter I explore the topics of Machiavellism as they emerge in response to three moments of political and religious crisis in the English Renaissance. I begin with the crisis precipitated by Henry VIII's break with the Catholic church, focusing on the role of the doctrine of things indifferent in the justification of Henry VIII's Act of Supremacy and in subsequent discussion concerning the proper jurisdiction of church and state. I then turn to the crisis of the civil war, specifically to the debates in the 1640s about episcopacy, and then about the successes of Cromwell and the New Model Army. In conclusion, I discuss the case of conscience known as the Engagement Controversy, when Cromwell and his supporters sought to secure an oath of allegiance to the new government. In each case we see a homology between the rhetoric of Machiavellism and contemporary political and theological concerns, one that contemporaries were aware of and exploited for a variety of rhetorical ends.

The Machiavellian rhetoric analyzed in this chapter does not presuppose the direct influence of Machiavelli. Rather, my goal is to show how the topics of Machiavellism and the figure of the Machiavel crystallized contemporary concerns about sovereignty and obedience, legitimate and illegitimate power, authority and dissent. Just as rhetoric was one locus of anxiety about political relations in the period, so political and theological debates borrowed the language of rhetoric—of persuasion, decorum, and circumstance—to discuss the contingent realm of human affairs in which discretion operates. And just as the Machiavel symbolized the anxieties provoked by rhetorical indeterminacy—the fear of force and fraud—so the use of force and fraud in things left to discretion was described in rhetorical and Machiavellian terms in political and theological debate. Yet, in both cases, Machiavellism could also stand for something more complicated: the sphere of rhetorical politics in which monarchy and republicanism, divine right and individual conscience, are competing arguments.

Here it may be helpful briefly to review one influential account of Machiavellism in order to highlight what is to be gained by a rhetorical approach to English Machiavellism in particular. According to Pocock, it is only in the seventeenth century—with the crisis of sovereignty and the debates about the legitimacy of de facto political power—that the conditions exist for the proper understanding of Machiavelli. As Pocock writes,

> It was the decisive perception of Machiavelli that if all politics was action, all action involved innovating, changing the world, depriving the action of the conditions which had legitimated it without immediately supplying those that would legitimate it in the future. When he employed *virtù* to mean both that by which we maintained ourselves against *fortuna* and that by which we exposed ourselves to her in the first place, he signalised both the restoration of the ideal of action and the peculiar exposure of the republic to time. . . . Machiavelli, then, carried to extremes of his own the perception, common to all inheritors of the civic humanist tradition, that the republic was, of all forms of government, that most challenged by the problem of achieving stability in time. It is consequently not surprising to learn that the vocabulary of the republic was found especially appropriate to the expression of problems of this order. (*JH*, 18–19)

According to Pocock, the Machiavellian language of the mixed constitution "provided apologists for both sides in the First Civil War with a paradigm: a common language or frame of reference" for negotiating conflicting allegiances (22). Yet, while this language served to dramatize the breakdown of the government, it did not necessarily provide the desired solution:

> Englishmen were neither willing nor necessitated to define themselves as naked before *fortuna*, in a moment from which only *virtù* could save them by reconstituting a republic. There were too many vocabularies, casuist, his-

torical, theological or prophetic, of which they could avail themselves to define the moment of institutional collapse, to seek the way out of it, or simply to deny that it had occurred. (23)

One way to resolve the crisis of authority was to appeal to "the arbitration of the sword" (23). Yet for Pocock such an appeal signals that "the problem of contingency [has begun] to appear in its Hobbesian rather than in any Machiavellian form, and the republican vocabulary [is] overlaid by others" (25).

Once we have recovered the link between the rhetorical Machiavelli and Machiavelli the political analyst, however, we see that the rhetoric of Machiavellism encompasses both the "arbitration of the sword" and republicanism, as separate or related arguments in response to the problem of de facto political power. Accordingly, what Pocock says of the language of seventeenth-century republicanism—that it "might be employed both to dramatize the collapse of traditional authority and to propose solutions to the problems it posed" (*JH*, 41)—applies equally to the Machiavellian sword, and for Renaissance readers both were subsumed under the paradigm of Machiavellian rhetoric. Furthermore, as previous chapters have begun to suggest and as I argue more fully below, precisely because this rhetoric is topical rather than simply thematic, it is not incompatible with casuist and theological vocabularies in the sixteenth and seventeenth centuries. Just as these topics are of use in both principalities and republics, so are they equally relevant to religious as well as secular political agents.

The ambivalent rhetoric of Machiavellism allows us to see the continuities not only between seventeenth-century republicanism and millenarianism but also between sixteenth- and seventeenth-century Machiavellism. For the problems that historians of political thought associate with de facto political power in the seventeenth century were discussed in the sixteenth-century debates concerning the jurisdiction of church and state. And just as Machiavellism was a rhetoric for conceptualizing the crisis of legitimacy in the seventeenth century, so in the sixteenth century the Machiavel symbolized anxieties about the use and abuse of power, and about the contingent nature of political authority.

Yet, as we move from the 1530s to the 1650s, we also observe a shift in the arena in which Machiavellian topics receive emphasis, as well as a shift in the topics themselves. In the sixteenth century the rhetoric of Machiavellism is particularly apparent in debates over the rival jurisdictions of pope and king, church and state. In the early seventeenth century this rhetoric appears in the struggle between the king and parliament as well. And, although the availability of Machiavellian topics is a constant from the 1530s to the 1650s, with the beheading of Charles I and Cromwell's rise to power, the topics of persuasion and coercion, and virtue and success, gain particular prominence in debates over the legitimacy of de facto political power.

Henry VIII and the Doctrine of Things Indifferent

The debate over Henrician policy in the 1530s provides us with a particularly salient instance of the intersection of rhetoric, Machiavellism, and theological concerns in the period. Much of the defense of Henry VIII's break with the Catholic church centered on the doctrine of *adiaphora* or things indifferent. In sixteenth- and seventeenth-century theological debate, things indifferent are things (actions, beliefs, ceremonies, objects) which are not necessary for salvation; they are neither commanded nor forbidden by Scripture and are therefore left to discretion. For most writers on the subject, such things are thus "of them-selves . . . neither right nor wrong, but according as they are rightly or wrongly used."[1] The doctrine of indifference thus isolated a realm that was not strictly or necessarily within the jurisdiction of the church. For some, right use was a matter of church discipline though not of doctrine; for others, such as Luther, Melancthon, and Protestant casuists in England, right use was a matter of individual conscience; for still others, it was a matter of royal jurisdiction.[2] It was this last argument that made the doctrine an important cornerstone in the justification of Henry VIII's Act of Supremacy. For Henry's propagandists argued that the sphere of things indifferent was completely under the jurisdiction of secular power.

Although indifference was, strictly speaking, a theological issue, the rhetorical and potentially Machiavellian dimension of the doctrine was apparent to all who commented on it. The fact that indifference was a matter of discretion—even of discretion concerning the ultimate jurisdiction over things indifferent—meant that the realm of things indifferent was subject to rhetorical considerations of context and of decorum. Depending on one's viewpoint, this was either an enabling approach to the sphere of politics or a radically destabilizing one. For some of Henry's advisers "indifference" was not only a way of articulating the rhetorical and Machiavellian problem of action within the contingent realm of human affairs; it also proved to be a response to such contingency. For the very act of isolating a contingent or indifferent realm of "policy" from the pope's spiritual jurisdiction over things necessary for salvation served simultaneously to name and to justify the king's de facto political power over the church in England. The indifferent realm of policy also served as a foundation for an Erasmian *via media* in political and religious affairs. For, as G. R. Elton has noted, "the concept of a *via media* depended on the insistence that not all the demands of religion were equally necessary to salvation: some doctrines had universal and mandatory character, while others would vary in their application with time and place."[3] Yet, for critics of Henrician policy, such considerations of decorum provoked fears concerning the contingency of judgment, whether on the part of the individual or the state; at the worst, such discretion implied the Machiavel's rhetorical force and fraud, deception and manipulation. Thus when things indifferent were seen to be a matter of individual conscience, they raised the specter of antinomianism, libertinism, dissent, and rebellion.[4] And, when the realm of things indifferent was equated with secular power, it gave rise to fears of de facto political power and the arbitrary imposition of authority. Sixteenth-century discussion of the doctrine of things indifferent thus reproduced contemporary attitudes toward rhetoric as either a repertoire of arguments whose use would be determined by context or a dangerous, morally suspect faculty of linguistic force and fraud.

Before turning to the role of the doctrine of things indifferent in the debate over Henry's royal supremacy, it may be helpful to recall that both those who criticized Henrician policy and those who supported it in the 1530s and 1540s associated it at times with Machiavelli. In 1537 Harry Lord Morley sent Thomas Cromwell an Italian text of Machiavelli's *Florentine Histories*, which he recommended as a precursor of Henry's policy:

> The author, it appears, wrote it to Clement VII., late bishop of Rome; you will marvel that he durst, for he so declareth their "petygrew" that one may know their usurpations. He tells of their "jests" from Charlemagne, their frauds, treasons, &c. . . . In the eighth book is the war of the Florentines against the b[isho]p of Rome and Fernando, king of Naples, some 50 years ago. As the King's cause is somewhat like, note how little the Florentines reputed the Romish bishop's cursings. Show the very words to the King; his Majesty will be pleased to see them.

He went on to add: "This book of Machiavelli, *de Principe*, is surely a good thing for your Lordship, and for our Sovereign Lord in Council."[5] In 1540 John Legh wrote in a letter to the Privy Council that Pole had warned him "against reading the story of Nicolo Matchavello, which had already poisoned England and would poison all Christendom."[6]

Ironically, some of the Tudor humanists who defended Henry's Act of Supremacy had frequented Pole's household in Padua, where they may also have become familiar with Machiavelli's works. As Gordon Zeeveld has written, "For young Englishmen of ambition, Pole's household was as much a training school for government service as an academy of letters."[7] In the 1520s and early 1530s, Richard Morison and Thomas Starkey visited Padua. Starkey left Pole's household eventually to become the king's chaplain and to write a defense of royal supremacy that I will examine below. Morison wrote to Cromwell from Padua soliciting government service and was successful in his plea. In 1535, upon his return to England, Cromwell commissioned him to write propaganda in support of Henry's break with the Catholic church. The results were *Apomaxis* (composed 1536, published 1538), a defense of royal supremacy; and three treatises in support of the crown's actions in response to the 1536–37 Pilgrimage of Grace, *A lamentation in whiche is shewed what Ruyne and destruction cometh of seditious rebellion* (1538), *A Remedy for Sedition* (1538), and *An invective against the great and detestable vice, treason* (1539). In *A Remedy* and *An invective*, Morison referred in passing to Machiavelli's *Discourses* and *Florentine Histories*.[8] In 1550 Morison briefly acted as Henry's ambassador to Charles V, during which time Roger Ascham was his secretary. Finally, William Thomas, who was too young to contribute to the formulation of Henrician policy, fulfilled a role not unlike that of Morison and Starkey some twenty years later. He traveled in Italy in the 1540s and returned to England in 1549 to become clerk of the Privy Council. In a letter to Edward VI, he offered political advice on eighty-five topics, most of which are taken from the chapter titles of Machiavelli's *Discourses*.[9]

Thus at least some of the humanists who contributed to the formation of Tudor policy knew Machiavelli's work and appear to have perceived its compatibility with their political agenda. The same is true of their critics. Cardinal Pole's condemnation of Henry's policy as Machiavellian in the 1540s may have been in part a response to the propaganda written by Starkey and Morison in defense of Henry's break with the Catholic church. In any case, Pole condemned the break as Machiavellian not because he was theologically incapable of understanding Machiavellism but because he understood it all too well.[10]

According to Gordon Zeeveld, Starkey was the first to see the importance of the doctrine of things indifferent for Tudor policy.[11] Upon his return from Italy in the early 1530s, Starkey had sought royal preferment. Cromwell, who was then orchestrating Henry VIII's propaganda campaign in defense of the divorce and supremacy, probably asked Starkey to contribute to this campaign; the *Exhortation to Unitie and Obedience* (composed 1534, published 1536) was Starkey's response. By 1535 Starkey was not only the king's chaplain but also his intercessor with Pole, whose favorable opinion on the divorce Henry was eager to have.[12]

In the *Exhortation*, Starkey argued in defense of the king's supremacy that the pope's "superioritie," his jurisdiction over the church in England and elsewhere, was a thing indifferent: it was not necessary for salvation and could be accepted or rejected according to the requirements of "worldly polycie." While papal supremacy may once have been a "convenient"—as opposed to necessary—way of securing unity and agreement within the church, over time the pope "usurped power" (21) and established a "cloked tiranny" (45). For this reason it is necessary to insist on the difference between spiritual concerns and worldly policy, the pope's power of persuasion as opposed to the king's sovereignty (49–51). Papal tyranny must be rejected in favor of Henry's supremacy, for only national supremacy is flexible enough to respond to the requirements of what we might call political decorum:

> for where as in the hole body of Christis churche be so many sondry nations, and therin beside the diversities of tongues and maners, so divers polycies and ordynaunces of lawes, that one man therof to have knowledge and experience, which is required to the ryght judgment of causes, it semeth impossible. . . . for thoughe he were a man of moste hye perfection, and of wysedome most polytyke, seynge that the administration of Justice and equitie standeth a great parte in the knowledge of the particular circumstaunces of causes, howe shuld he to so many nations, of whom he hath no knowledge nor experience, give justice with truth and equitie? (67)

According to this argument, the requirements of policy dictate not only national sovereignty but also royal supremacy.[13] Furthermore, not only does the king judge things indifferent with discretion, according to Starkey; his jurisdiction is approved by "common consent" (69–70, 73). Thus while the pope's power is usurped and therefore illegitimate and merely de facto, the king's power is not only de facto but also de jure because he has the consent of the people. What amounts to coercion and tyranny on the part of the pope is an act of persuasion on the part of the king. Yet precisely because the sovereign exercises his discretion in things indifferent according to common consent, for the individual subject the realm of things indifferent is finally equivalent to "positive law as it was laid down in the King's statutes" (Zeeveld, 151). The subject is required to obey this law and is absolved of any blame for the king's decisions regarding earthly and spiritual policy (88). Starkey's argument for obedience—like Hobbes's and the defenders of the oath of engagement more than a hundred years later—would thus seem to admit the rhetorical realm of decorum and discretion only in order to argue that the individual subject must not concern himself with such controversial matters. His argument also explicitly resolves the "case of conscience" that could conceivably emerge for the individual Christian who obeys the sovereign rather than his own conscience in things indifferent.

In his *De vera obedientia* of 1535, Bishop Gardiner offered a related defense of royal supremacy that also drew on the doctrine of things indifferent. Gardiner argued that priests and rulers have different jurisdictions but that the usual division of ecclesiastical control of spiritual matters and royal control of temporal matters is "a blynde distinccion and full of darkenes."[14] Princes have always been the spiritual guardians of their people. Furthermore, precisely because Christ did not seek an earthly kingdom, the power that priests exercise is one of persuasion—of "teaching and preaching"—rather than of worldly force, which remains the prerogative of the king (131, 149). Accordingly, a priest is

> not to beare rule but to be in subjeccion, not to commaunde princes, but to acknowledge him selfe to be under their power and commaundement, not only when they commaunde thinges indifferent [aequa] and easily to be done, but also when they commaunde thinges not indifferent [iniqua], so they be not wicked [impia]. (131–33)

In the words of his sixteenth-century Protestant translator, Gardiner assumes that "thinges indifferent" are under the jurisdiction of the crown, and then extends this jurisdiction to cover other spiritual matters as well. The effect is to disable the church's claim to temporal power and the pope's claim to obedience over and above that owed to the king.[15]

As Peter Donaldson has noted, although there is no evidence that Gardiner had read Machiavelli at this time, his defense of royal supremacy is consonant with the views expressed in his Machiavellian treatise of 1555. For, in *De vera obedientia*, Gardiner offers

> a theory of kingship in which the secular and sacral aspects of the office were related in a way that provided a model for Gardiner's later attempt to reconcile Machiavelli and sacral kingship. The attempt to work out a defense of Henry VIII's claim to supreme headship of the Church of England led Gardiner to argue not only that kings are providentially chosen, sacred beings but also, paradoxically, that the religious significance of their rule and the basis of their claim to preeminence over priests and popes lay precisely in the secular character of their office.[16]

As we will see, seventeenth-century political thinkers such as Henry Parker would turn similar arguments not against the pope but against the king's and bishops' claim to divinely ordained authority.

As Parker's later critique of absolute sovereignty suggests, Starkey's and Gardiner's justifications of Henry's supremacy are unstable for several related reasons. First, the defense of obedience to the king is a defense of resistance—here to Rome, but potentially to any established authority. This point is brought home in one striking passage in Starkey's *Exhortation*. Describing how the devil creates "blindness" in men's minds, Starkey writes:

> By this blyndenes also he bringeth man to the obedience of his vayne and beastely affectes, by the reason wherof he never tastethe of the swetenes of vertue, and into that gardein he never doth entre, ye or yet if he doo, there he can not tary at all, but streyght way is caste out agayne, to that Eve beynge over obedient. (26)

Starkey is arguing against obedience to the devil and the pope, and for obedience to the king; but by describing the Christian's sin as "over obedience," he also suggests that the posture of the faithful Christian will be one of dissent. Gardiner makes a similar point when, in the conclusion to *De vera obedientia*, he addresses the charge of his own lack of obedience to Rome and claims that if the oath of allegiance to Rome was not good, it is better to break it: obedience to the king now requires dissent from Rome (161). Yet, once it appears that "obedience" from one perspective is dissent from another, it may be harder to argue against the dissenter, such as Pole, who uses the language of obedience to justify his resistance to the status quo.

The second and related reason for the instability of the defense of royal supremacy has to do with the criterion of legitimate dissent. Although Starkey invokes obedience as the limit to the indeterminacy of things indifferent, he also describes obedience itself as a thing indifferent that can itself be performed well or badly. As we have seen, obedience to the king is justified because the king's jurisdiction is approved by common consent; obedience to the pope is not because the pope rules by coercion. Yet once consent is admitted as proof of legitimacy, its absence may be invoked as proof of illegitimacy, as Starkey himself implied in his *Dialogue between Cardinal Pole and Thomas Lupset*, where mixed government on the model of Venice is described as the best weapon against tyranny.[17] Starkey himself was aware of this instability in the argument of the *Exhortation*, for he explicitly argues against the slippery slope of dissent at several points. In the preface to the king, Starkey explains the occasion of his treatise as the "controversie and disobedience lately shewid here among us," that is, the rebellions in the Midlands and the North against Henry's innovations in religion;[18] later he remarks:

> for yf by the pluckynge downe of this authoritie [of the pope] & utter contempt therof, you thynke, that you may by and by, without offence, of your owne heedes trede under foote, all rytes and customes of the churche . . . then shall you falle sone into suche arrogancy, disobedience in hart, & con-

tempt of al lawes both of god and man, that boldly I dare this affirm, that if it were not for feare of worldly punishment, to none you wolde then be obedient. (72–73)

And he goes on to argue in Machiavellian fashion that it is only the "feare of religion," that is, the fear of God's retribution, that keeps us from the "ruyne of all civile order" (73).

Finally, in arguing for a sphere of worldly policy that is governed by considerations of custom, circumstance, and decorum, Starkey and Gardiner expose the historicist and critical potential of the doctrine of things indifferent. For as Arthur Ferguson has noted, the doctrine treated "matters indifferent for practical purposes as expressions of a cultural diversity that had arisen in the course of time and in relation to passing conditions" (174). "Thus, things indifferent, having been established as useful to religion, could, by common counsel, be changed by the same authority" (177). As we see from Henry's break with the Catholic church, the doctrine could be used to argue for change, as well as for the status quo; it thus could be used against the authority of the sovereign, as well as in support of it.

Later critics of Tudor policy absorbed Starkey's and Gardiner's double-edged lessons. Thus, in his *Short Treatise of Politike Power* (1556), the Marian exile John Ponet accepted Starkey's equation of the realm of things indifferent with the king's statutes, but only in order to limit such jurisdiction by restricting the domain of things indifferent:

> True it is, that in maters indifferent, that is, that of themselves be neither good nor evil, hurtfull or profitable, but for a decent ordre: Kinges and Princes (to whom the people have geven their autoritie) maie make suche lawes, and dispense with them. But in maters not indifferent, but godly and profitably ordayned for the common wealthe, ther can they not (for all their autoritie) breake them or dispense with them.[19]

The ruler who does not observe the distinction between necessary and indifferent matters, who treats the former as though they were the latter and so under his jurisdiction, is described in terms that suggest the Machiavel:

> He spoyleth the people of their goodes, either by open violence . . . or craftily under the name of loanes, benevolences, contribuciones, and suche like gaye painted words . . . . [He uses] all kinds of subtilties, deceates, crafts, policies, force, violence, cruelties, and suche like devillishe ways. (Gij-Gii$^\mathrm{v}$)[20]

Like Starkey and Gardiner, Ponet and his co-religionist Christopher Goodman also saw that obedience was a two-edged sword. Ponet argued that proper obedience in the face of such "devillishe ways" would take the form of resistance and dissent: "For if Obedience be to muche . . . in a common wealthe, it causeth muche evil and disordre. For to muche maketh the governours to forget their vocation, and to usurpe upon their subjectes" (Cix). Similarly, in *How Superior Powers Ought to be Obeyed* (1558), Goodman warned against the evils that follow from "unlawful obedience" to the "papistes and their unlawful Quene."[21]

At the close of the sixteenth century, James I adopted a different sort of Machiavellian rhetoric to assimilate the realm of things indifferent to royal prerogative. In *Basilikon Doron* (1598), James appeared to agree with Ponet when he contrasted indifferent things to those that are necessary for salvation:

> But learne wisely to discerne betwixts points of salvation and indifferent things, betwixt substance and ceremonies; and betwixt the expresse commandement and will of God in his word, and the invention or ordinance of man; since all that is necessarie for salvation is contained in Scripture. (17)

Yet, because indifferent things are not necessary for salvation, they are governed by another kind of necessity, by the rhetorical and politic consideration of circumstances: "But as for all other things not contained in the scripture, spare not to use or alter them, as the necessitie of the time shall require" (17). James implied that, because the king is not a "mere laicus" (45), it will be up to him rather than the individual believer to determine the degree of ceremony in the church.[22] Of particular interest here is James's Machiavellian rhetoric of necessity: by arguing that decisions regarding things indifferent will be made "as the necessitie of the time shall require," James shows the dialectical relationship between contingency and necessity, *fortuna* and *virtù*, that made contemporaries associate indifference with Machiavellian rhetoric and with reason of state. Not surprisingly, "necessity" came to signify not only the use of reason of state to preserve the state and guarantee the safety of its citizens but also the rhetorical manipulation of circumstances, the Machiavellian invocation of reason of state, in the interest of personal power.[23]

James made a similar argument for royal jurisdiction over things indifferent in his "Apologie for the Oath of Allegiance" (1607). The oath was required not only of Protestants but also, especially, of Catholics in order to ensure their political allegiance to the crown rather than the Catholic church. James defended the oath by insisting on the separation of civil and spiritual power. Quoting Matthew 22:21, "Give unto Caesar what is Caesars and to God what is Gods" (108), James argued that Catholics owe obedience to the pope in spiritual matters but to the sovereign in civil affairs. Thus he described the office of a Christian king as

assisting the spirituall power with the temporall sword, by reforming of cor-
ruptions, by procuring due obedience to the Church, by judging and cutting
off all frivolous questions and schismes, as *Constantine* did; and finally, by
making *decorum* to be observed in every thing, and establishing orders to
bee observed in all indifferent things for that purpose, which is the onely
intent of our Oath of Supremacie. (108)

Just as the realm of contingency, of rhetorical and practical considerations, was subordinate to the king's politic judgment in *Basilikon Doron*,
so here James used the rhetorical term *decorum* to constrain rather than
encourage the exercise of individual judgment regarding things indifferent. Decorum is what the king decrees. He was particularly critical of the
"new Catholike doctrine" of equivocation, according to which Catholics
might verbally subscribe to an oath which they simultaneously refused
with mental reservations (91). As we have seen, this jesuitical "devil's
craft" (91) was regularly associated with Machiavelli in the Renaissance.[24] Yet, as James's opponents were well aware, his scriptural argument for the separation of religion and the state could have Machiavellian
implications as well: in the "Apologie" James distinguished between temporal and spiritual power only in order to conflate them in a single civil
authority governing temporal or political affairs. Thus he insisted on the
power of the king to "command . . . obedience to be given to the word of
God [and to] reform the religion according to his prescribed will" ("Apologie," 108). He also identified the king's power with the institution of
episcopacy.

In contrast, in his *Treatise of Things Indifferent* (1605), the puritan
divine William Bradshaw defended royal supremacy while criticizing the
king's reliance on episcopacy and the doctrine of things indifferent. In a
striking marginal gloss, he warned against the Machiavellian manipulation of apparent "indifference":

We should be careful since not all indifferent things which appear indifferent
are. Florentines can disguise and color any thing; and it is now adays the
common exercise of the greatest wits of the world to transform good into
evil, evil into good, and both into indifferent; so that in these days scant any
thing is as it appears, or appears as it is.[25]

As Bradshaw was well aware, once matters have been judged indifferent,
they are open to arbitrary figuration or interpretation, which is the vehi-
cle of the arbitrary imposition of church or state authority. He thus described indifference as the fraud perpetrated by the rhetorical Machiavel
who disguises and transforms absolute ethical truths into their opposites
through "colors" or figures of speech.

As these positions illustrate, the doctrine of things indifferent is a touchstone not only for Tudor-Stuart discussions of sovereignty, royal prerogative, and legitimate dissent, but also for the various ways in which Machiavellian rhetoric intersects with theological debate in the sixteenth and seventeenth centuries. For these and subsequent interpreters of the doctrine, a Machiavellian rhetoric of "worldly policy" was used to describe both the problem of and the solution to the realm of indifference. As we have seen, for royalists and Anglicans who assimilated this area of concern to royal prerogative and reason of state, Machiavellian means are justified as a way of controlling Machiavellism more broadly conceived as the contingent sphere of rhetoric and interpretation. Some puritans and, later, parliamentarians, argue in contrast that because matters of religion are never really indifferent, the king's inferiors must have the right to judge according to their consciences in these matters if the king is not to be falsely equated with God.[26] For these critics of the status quo, the doctrine of indifference was associated not only with Anglican episcopacy but also with the sovereign's Machiavellian statecraft, including in some cases perceived leanings toward the pope. Here Machiavellian means are condemned as the logical outcome of any attempt to control arbitrarily the contingent realm of interpretation.

The Civil War and Machiavellian Indifference

The debate concerning the doctrine of things indifferent is still alive in the 1640s, though the context of the debate is no longer the struggle between the king and pope but between the king and his bishops, on the one hand, and parliament, on the other. Recognizing the link between the king's reliance on episcopacy and the doctrine of indifference, puritan critics of the king increasingly argued that "nothing is indifferent"; they appropriated the king's own language of decorum and necessity to argue against his Machiavellian exercise of reason of state.

Robert Greville Lord Brooke's *A Discourse opening the Nature of Episcopacie* (1642), an important precursor of Milton's *Areopagitica*, is representative of the puritan equation of the doctrine of things indifferent with the king's support of episcopacy in the 1640s. Part of Greville's argument was that if the church is given jurisdiction in things indifferent, it will inevitably encroach on the king's power; his ultimate point was not that the king should have jurisdiction in such indifferent matters but that church and state should remain separate, as far as possible.

Greville argued against coercion and for tolerance of nonconformity. He claimed that the bishops had "with the chaines [of] *Indifferency* bound up the Peoples *Liberty*," and gave as an example the "Booke of

Sports" issued by James and Charles but "first invented by [the bishops] themselves" (Haller, 2:59–60, cf. 137). This small treatise, ostensibly written by James, defended recreation on the Sabbath and thus arrogated to episcopacy and the Crown the right to judge what was indifferent or, in Greville's complaint, what was of necessity indifferent. (Milton's *Comus* was written shortly after the reissue of the "Book of Sports" and provides another response to the question of indifference, as I suggest below.) In response to royal and ecclesiastical coercion, Greville first argued that precisely because our behavior in things indifferent has not been determined by Scripture, it should also not be decided by the church:

> For, allow the *Church* hath all the power in *Indifferents*, (which I dare not yet yeeld), who hath made the *Church* a *Judge* (beyond appeale) *what is Indifferent*? Is not this, to bring *necessary* and *indifferent* things all under one notion, If the Church shall judge *indifferent* things to be *necessary*, and *necessary* to be indifferent? which would be to me a sad story.
>
> But you will say, if the Church be not the Judge of what is *Indifferent*; who may be That Judge? (Haller, 2:56)

The answer, according to Greville, was "recta ratio"; but his further comment revealed the infinite regress of such appeals to positive authority: "But who shall tell us what is *Recta Ratio*? I answer, *Recta Ratio*" (2:57). It is at this point that Greville introduced rhetorical considerations of the sort that James mentioned but only in order to do away with the sphere of indifference and thus with the Anglican Church's power in this area. He conceded that, considered abstractly or in its "universall nature, (not cloathed with these and these circumstances)," an action "seemeth to have some *Indifferencie*; and then, if ever, it is in the *Churches* power." But if you consider an action "as it is presently to be put in practise," "If you value and ballance it in this last sense, nothing is indifferent" (2:57). In any given case, right reason will always dictate the one correct course of action. As with James, though to different ends, attention to rhetorical decorum limits rather than enlarges the realm of choice. William Bradshaw scored the same point against episcopacy in his much earlier *A Treatise of Things Indifferent* (1605), when he wrote, "There is nothing absolutely indifferent (as our Divines of State dream) but by some circumstance of time, place, person, use, it may be either very good or very evil" (marginal gloss, 26). Here, too, the rhetorical consideration of circumstances—time, place, person, and use—was directed against the Machiavellian possibilities of rhetoric, represented by episcopacy or the "Churches power." If rhetoric names the sphere of pure contingency or indeterminacy, it can only be controlled by the arbitrary exercise of power. But if at any particular moment context and decorum are defining, as Bradshaw seemed to believe, then contingency disappears and one need not engage the Machiavellian dilemmas of action or of interpretation.

Greville, however, conceded that precisely because human reason is fallible, indifference is sometimes unavoidable in the realm of appearances:

> I conceive that all the *Indifference* (in the world) lies in our Understandings, and the Darkenesse thereof, (which makes them wavering sometimes, and doubtfull whether to doe or not . . .)

> All things, All Acts, are *in Re*, either *Necessary* to be done, or Unlawfull; but to my blind judgment, (while I cannot discerne whether I may Act, or may not) some things *Seeme*, but *are not Indifferent*; and so we thinke (but erroneously) that these may be done, or not, as we please. (Haller, 2:71)[27]

But this kind of indifference or contingency serves to undermine rather than to shore up the authority of the bishops. Given our darkened understanding, dissent and even heresy are inevitable, and any attempt to coerce behavior in things indifferent is more likely to encourage schism than is the free exchange of differing opinions (Haller, 2:130, 136). In rejecting the Machiavellian coercion of king and episcopacy, Greville thus recovered something like the Machiavellian appreciation of contingency as the condition of political action, not to mention freedom of religion.

The association of the doctrine of things indifferent with arbitrary interpretation as an instrument of papist and Machiavellian reason of state appears as well in Henry Parker's *Observations upon some of his Majesties late answers and expresses* (1642). In this pamphlet, considered by some historians to be the most influential pamphlet of the civil war, Parker argued that all political power is "originally inherent in the people" and that God only confirms the consent of the people to their monarch (Haller, 2:167).[28] The king and his followers, however, have lost sight of these truths, and are pursuing "Machavills politicks," according to which "Princes ought to ayme at greatnes, not in, but over their Subjects":

> To be *deliciae humani generis* [the darling of mankind] is growne sordid with Princes, to be publike torments and carnificines, and to plot against those Subjects whom by nature they ought to protect, is held *Caesar*-like, and therefore bloody *Borgias* by meere crueltie & treachery hath gotten roome in the Calender of witty, and of spirited *Heroes*. And our English Court of late years hath drunke too much of this State poyson. (Haller, 2:168–69)

In this description of the court of Charles I, the king and his followers are both Machiavels and the victims of their own Machiavellian poison. One of the forms this poison has taken is the belief that the king has absolute power, by "right of conquest," to interpret the law.[29]

Parker rejected this belief by claiming for civil law the same self-evidence that Luther claimed for Scripture:

> The Parliament claims a right of declaring, and interpreting Law. The King makes this question thereupon? *Is the Law it self subject to your Votes, that whatsoever you say, or do, shall be lawfull, because you declare it so? Am I supream, and yet you above me? Must my power be governed by your discretion?* This is the Popes Arrogance, That all must submit their understanding, and Scripture it self, to His declaring power. . . . In perspicuous, uncontroverted things, the Law is its own interpreter, and there no Judge is requisite. (Haller, 2:201)

Parker went on to admit that "In matters of Law and State both, where ambiguity is, some determination must be supream," but he argued that parliament's judgment is less dangerous to the public interest than the king's "mere discretion" (Haller, 2:202). In a reversal of the royalist fear that subject's discretion in things indifferent will give rise to libertinism, Parker made the king's discretion an instance of Machiavellian usurpation:

> As for the Popes Arrogance, who undertakes to interpret Scripture where it wants no interpreter, And in matters of mere opinion to usurpe over all mens consciences; As if he had infallibility in his sole breast. He is not an instance to be alleaged against Parliaments, as Princes, For tis very probable, That if the Church had not submitted it self to so slavish a condition under one Man, but had been governed by some generall Junto of Divines fairly elected, it had never swerved into such foul idolatry, and superstition, as it has don. (Haller, 2:202)

In words that echo Starkey, Parker cast aspersions on the king's claim to supremacy by comparing it to the Catholic church, specifically to the pope's claim to determine what is necessary and what is indifferent with respect to salvation. He also compared the king's divisive proceedings to "the Florentines wretched Politiques" and to "*Machiavils* rule" (Haller, 2:185, 176), contrasting such rule to "the popular and mixed government" of ancient Rome and modern Venice (2:205).

The Machiavelli who appears in this treatise is the stereotypical Machiavel, but he should not for all that be dismissed. In Cesare Borgia, Parker found a symbol of the iniquity of merely de facto political power—right by conquest—and perhaps also a foreshadowing of Charles's eventual failure. And, like his predecessors, he equates such Machiavellian force not only with "crueltie" but also with arbitrary interpretation, whereas the rule of law is equated with contract, counsel, and consent. He thus highlights the rhetorical dimension of de facto political power as well as of legitimate sovereignty.[30]

In light of the contemporary recognition that the realm of indifference was inseparable from Machiavellian questions of policy and of action in the realm of appearances, Raab's comment on the irrelevance of Machiavelli to most seventeenth-century concerns takes on a new meaning. According to Raab,

> Machiavellian criteria had little to do with most of the general forms into which Englishmen of the mid-seventeenth century crystallized their problems and aspirations. To men who thought in terms of alternative forms of church government, of toleration or a state Church, of the Divine Right of Kings (before 1649), of forms of baptism, of Anglo-Saxon and Norman precedents, of the Common Law of England, or of the right to vote, *The Prince* and *The Discourses* had little to offer. Nor was Machiavelli of much help to those who were groping unsuccessfully for a rationale by which to justify parliamentary sovereignty over monarchical prerogative. It was rather into the gaps left by these unresolved problems in the structure of English thought that Machiavelli's pragmatism seeped and then flowed. (103)

The realm of indifference, like that of rhetoric with which it is coterminous, was just such an "unresolved problem" in the sixteenth and seventeenth centuries. And Machiavelli appeared on both sides of the debate. On the one hand, the king invoked Machiavellian considerations of decorum and necessity to justify his determination of things indifferent; on the other hand, his critics associated such rhetorical politics with the Machiavel and with the arbitrary imposition of royal and ecclesiastical authority. For many writers engaged in the debate, the realm of things indifferent provoked anxiety about the Machiavellian use of force and fraud in the related spheres of politics and religion.

The Civil War: Persuasion and Coercion, Virtue and Success

In the decades leading up to the civil war, Englishmen began to debate the proper jurisdiction, legitimacy, and then finally the necessity of the monarchy. As in the sixteenth century, such debates commonly drew on the distinction between persuasion and coercion to differentiate between legitimate and illegitimate power or between the spheres of ecclesiastical and royal jurisdiction; and, throughout this period, the abuse of rhetoric and the illegitimate exercise of power were stigmatized as Machiavellian. But Machiavellism has a broader relevance to these debates as well. As they struggled first with Charles's abusive exercise of power, and then with Oliver Cromwell's de facto sovereignty over England, seventeenth-century writers were also increasingly drawn into a discussion of the Machiavellian topics of persuasion and coercion, virtue and success. In the following pages, I survey the rhetorical vocabulary of seventeenth-century views of the relationship of church and state in order to show how the language of persuasion inevitably gave rise to fears of Machiavellian force and fraud, coercion and seduction. I then turn to the Machiavellian topic of virtue and success in contemporary discussions of Cromwell and the New Model Army.

The languages of political legitimacy and theological conviction were inseparable from that of rhetoric in the seventeenth century. When Hobbes argued in *Leviathan* that "Faith has no relation to, nor dependence at all upon Compulsion, or Commandement," and when he insisted that Christ's role is not to command obedience but "to perswade,"[31] he was drawing on a distinction between spiritual and worldly power that was central to Anglican and puritan debate from the 1530s to the 1650s. Worldly power could take the form of legitimate force or coercion; spiritual power—the power of the Word or of God—involved persuasion, reformation, and spiritual transformation.

The distinction between persuasion and coercion could be used, as in Hobbes's Erastian argument, to disarm the church's claim to worldly power as Machiavellian and to subordinate the church to the state; or it could be used—as it was by Greville, Milton, Robinson, Parker, and the anonymous author of *The Ancient Bounds*, to argue for greater toleration and for the state's protection of religious dissenters.[32] In Hobbes's argument the sovereign exercise of force is justified in the civil sphere, which means that the sovereign has the right to control his subjects' actions but not their consciences. Those who argued for toleration saw religion not as subordinate to the state but as a separate sphere of activity, in which the use of civil force was Machiavellian and illegitimate.

The distinction between persuasion and coercion did not simply set religious belief apart from the state; it also appeared within the sphere of worldly power in the distinction between legitimate and illegitimate force. Marchamont Nedham was the extreme case in claiming that all governments had their origins in force and that a government erected by the stronger party was as valid de jure as if it had the consent of the whole.[33] Thus baldly stated, this argument was too obviously and stereotypically Machiavellian to be useful in the ideological struggle for legitimacy in the early decades of the seventeenth century. Thus James I, who asserted the right that derives from conquest, also insisted on the original consent of his subjects and "the reciprock and mutuall duetie" between the ruler and the ruled.[34] Like James, Hobbes and his contemporaries shared a preoccupation with legitimating coercion by persuasion or consent, force by representation, whether in the balance of power between king and parliament or in the social contract.

The distinction between persuasion and coercion, legitimate and illegitimate power, appeared within the sphere of religion as well. For Hobbes and many of his contemporaries, precisely because the kingdom of Christ was not of this world, it was up to the civil power to administer temporal affairs. The use of coercion was thus legitimate in civil matters, illegitimate in purely spiritual matters. Yet for those contemporaries— whether Presbyterian, Independent, or sectarian—who did not accept Hobbes's subordination of the church in its institutional form to the state, the belief in the spiritual power of the Word or of grace could easily slide into an emphasis on material effects. The question then arises of how to distinguish the persuasive power of the Word from the rhetorical seduction of the Machiavel; how to tell the difference between divinely inspired, legitimate effects and illegitimate worldly power. Here it becomes clear that the distinction between persuasion and coercion is often not between rhetoric and something else but between two uses of rhetoric, two uses of power.

The rhetorical dimension of true and false religion is everywhere apparent in seventeenth-century treatises, and Satan—the archetypal religious hypocrite—is frequently described in terms that recall the Machiavel. Thus, in *The Soules Conflict*, Richard Sibbes warned against Satan, "a cunning rhetorician" who "enlargeth the fancy, to apprehend things bigger than they are."[35] And Richard Baxter, in "The Vain Religion of the Formal Hypocrite," personified hypocrisy in terms that suggest the rhetorician manipulating arguments to suit his purposes: "It is in the heart that hypocrisy hath its throne, from whence it can command the outward acts into any shapes that are agreeable to its ends; and can use materials of divers natures, as the fuel and nutriment of its malignity."[36] But to the deceptive power of rhetoric Sibbes opposed the legitimate power of religion: "Religion is not a matter of word, nor stands upon words, as wood consists of Trees . . . but . . . of Power, it makes a man able" (Haller, *Rise*, 161). Elsewhere he called this power "a divine kind of rhetoric":

> That which satan would use as an argument to drive us from God, we should use as a strong plea with him. . . . When therefore conscience joining with satan, sets out thy sin in its colours, labour thou by faith to set out God in his colours, in mercy and loving kindness. Here lies the art of a Christian; it is divine rhetorick thus to persuade and set down the soul.[37]

Similarly, John Downame opposed the "flowing eloquence" of men to the forceful rhetoric of the Holy Ghost:

> under the vaile of simple and plaine speech, there shineth such divine wisdom and glorious majestie, that all the humane writings in the world, though never so adorned with the flowers of eloquence, and sharp conceits of wit

and learning, cannot so deeply pearce the heart of man, nor so forcibly worke upon his affections, nor so powerfully incline his will either to the imbracing of that which is good, or avoiding of that which is evill, as the word of God.[38]

For Downame and others, the power of rhetoric or of words was well used as long as it was subordinated to the Word; but the fear remained that this power could be abused or misused, that an individual might arrogate such power to himself and use it to Machiavellian, that is, fraudulent or coercive, ends.

Precisely because rhetoric had both a sacred and a stereotypically Machiavellian use, it appeared on both sides of the question in debates concerning legitimate and illegitimate force in politics and religion. The abuse of rhetoric was associated with Satan, tyranny, coercion, and seduction; rhetoric rightly used was persuasion, the honest exchange of opinions, or sacred eloquence. Yet, in drawing the distinction between legitimate and illegitimate power in terms of persuasion and coercion, seventeenth-century writers necessarily engaged the dilemma of Machiavellism they hoped to avoid. Persuasion is an unstable means of legitimating coercion since the power of rhetoric to persuade is inseparable from its power to coerce and deceive. Furthermore, as we see from the examples below, the threat of Machiavellism narrowly conceived as illegitimate force and fraud proves to be inseparable from Machiavellism broadly defined as the effort to articulate, without conflating, intention and effect, action and success, force and representation, coercion and persuasion.

In *Free-Grace: or, The Flowings of Christs Blood Freely to Sinners* (1645), John Saltmarsh assumed the difference between force and faith when he claimed that free grace "should be that onely principle of power in beleevers," and when he distinguished the rhetoric of "Gospel Commandments" from "Legal Commandments": "The Law commands by promises and threatenings, blessings and curses; the Gospel persuades rather then commands, and rather by promises. . . . by patern [rather] then precept, and by imitation then command."[39] William Dell, like Saltmarsh a preacher in the New Model Army, argued in a similar vein in *Right Reformation* (1646):

> Forceable Reformation is unsutable to Christs Kingdom; For Christs kingdom stands in the Spirit; and the force of flesh and blood can contribute nothing to this.
>
> Again the faithful, the Subjects of this Kingdom, are a Spiritual people, and so they are without the reach of any outward force. . . . [Christ] never used the power of the world, but did all by the power of the Word.[40]

And the anonymous author of *The Ancient Bounds* (1645) argued in favor of toleration: "To make a man of this or that judgment or opinion or faith, to make a man of this or that practice in religion, may not be required by the civil sword; it may be persuaded, induced by exhortation, example, or such means, and that's all."[41] In his later *Treatise of Civil Power* (1659), Milton reiterated this distinction between persuasion and coercion when he stated, "Surely force cannot work persuasion, which is faith" (Hughes, 852).

For Milton, Saltmarsh, Dell, and others, when coercion is used in matters of religion, it simply gives rise to hypocrisy. According to Dell,

> by fear and punishment, may men be brought to say and do, that which they neither beleeve nor understand: and how acceptable such popish faith and obedience is unto God, all spiritual Christians know, and every mans conscience, me thinks, should be convinced.
>
> It maketh men Hypocrites and not Saints; for it forceth the body, and leaves the heart as it was; for the heart cannot be forced by outward power, but by the Inward efficacy of the truth: Now the hearts of men being corrupt, what are all outward duties, they are forced to, but so much Hypocrisie? (121–22)

Milton made the same point in *Of Civil Power*: "Force neither instructs in religion nor begets repentance or amendment of life, but on the contrary hardness of heart, formality and hypocrisy."[42]

Yet if external force gives rise to hypocrisy and fraud, this problem is not solved by making religion a matter of persuasion. To begin with, the puritan emphasis on conversion and its signs or effects also generates hypocrisy. When Saltmarsh, in the passage quoted above, characterizes the Gospel's persuasion in terms of "imitation" rather than "command," he unwittingly points to the problem of mere "outward conformity," that is, to the hypocritical imitation of the signs of faith. In "The Vain Religion of the Formal Hypocrite," Baxter describes this ability of the hypocrite to imitate the signs of piety: "Hypocrisy is natural popery; it filleth the places of worship with images. Instead of prayer, there is the image of prayer; and instead of preaching, hearing, praising God, and other parts of worship, there is the image of worship" (17:29–30). The hypocrite is not distinguished by his outward actions but by his Machiavellian intention: "And now we discern the quality of our enemy, of our snares, of our danger, and of our duty; it is not mere violence, but deceit, that can undo us; not force, but fraud, that we have to resist" (Baxter, 17:7).

Although Baxter singled out fraud as the chief abuse of the habit of reading the signs of election in external events, force and fraud are in practice inseparable. For John Preston "spiritual rebirth" was "not an emptie forme of godlinesse, but an effectual prevalent power" that transforms the life of the believer.[43] This language of power, which was particularly characteristic of the antinomian preachers in the New Model Army, inevitably raised the question of how to tell the difference between legitimate and illegitimate force or success.[44] For example, even as William Dell insists on the difference between godly and ungodly power, persuasion and coercion, his vocabulary of power suggests their likeness. In the passage quoted above—Christ "never used the power of the world, but did all by the power of the Word"—Dell compounds the identification of these two powers with the alliteration and assonance of "world" and "word." Elsewhere he writes to similar effect: "Forceable Reformation makes only Hypocrites and gilded sepulchres, putting a form of godliness upon the outward man, when there is no power of godliness in the inner man, but a power of ungodliness" (122).

The same potential confusion of powers appears in *Smoke in the Temple* (1646), where Saltmarsh defends Independency by arguing that the covenant of God "is a law upon [our] inward parts, sweetly compelling in the consciences with power and yet not with force, with compulsion and yet with consent."[45] In one clause Saltmarsh insists on the distinction between power and force, while in the next he allies compulsion with consent. Similarly, while he distinguishes between civil and church government, he allows that the former

> may be made up of such scripture and prudential materials as may much reform the outward man, even as a mere prudential civil government may do if severely executed. . . . In many civil states, merely from their wholesome policy and administration, excellent and precious flowers spring up, many moral virtues, as prudence, temperance, obedience, meekness, justice, fortitude. Yet all this makes not a government to be Christ's, but only that which is merely the discipline of Christ, and policy of Christ. (184–85)[46]

While Saltmarsh distinguished "imitation" from "command" in a passage cited above, here he identifies it with "discipline," as though to acknowledge that the Machiavellian possibilities of imitation must themselves be constrained to Christian ends. Yet, as the Machiavellian connotations of "policy" suggest,[47] once "discipline" and constraint have been introduced, it may be difficult to tell the difference between the policy of Christ and other kinds of policy. Power must produce effects or signs, and signs inevitably involve the possibility of hypocrisy. Thus, to the extent that one appealed to superior power or success as a sign of divine providence, one could be said to be arguing from the force of circumstances or the status quo.

Hugh Peter, Cromwell's preacher, regularly interpreted the army's successes as a sign of divine favor, as did Cromwell himself in his correspondence and public speeches.[48] Of his victory at Naseby, Cromwell wrote:

I can say this of Naseby, that when I saw the enemy draw up and march in gallant order towards us, and we a company of poor ignorant men, to seek how to order our batle—the General having commanded me to order all the horse—I could not (riding alone about my business) but smile out to God in praises, in assurance of victory, because God would, by things that are not, bring to naught things that are. Of which I had great assurance, and God did it. O that men would therefore praise the Lord, and declare the wonders that He doth for the children of men![49]

Similarly, in *The Tenure of Kings and Magistrates* (1649), Milton remarked on "the glorious way wherein justice and victory hath set [Parliament and the army]—the only warrants through all ages, next under immediate revelation, to exercise supreme power" (Hughes, 752). And, while further qualifying this view in *Eikonoklastes* (1649), he still implied that success was the consequence of virtue and divine favor:

We measure not our cause by our success, but our success by our cause. Yet certainly in a good cause success is a good confirmation, for God hath promised it to good men almost in every leaf of Scripture. If it argue not for us, we are sure it argues not against us; but as much or more for us than ill success argues for them, for to the wicked God hath denounced ill success in all they take in hand. (Hughes, 814)[50]

Yet, when the success is military, what is to distinguish the argument from military success from simple military force or coercion?[51] Even more to the point, queried William Prynne in *The Sword of Christian Magistracy*, can an army chaplain really be against coercion? To Dell's criticism of the use of force in religious matters, Prynne cited the army itself as the best counterargument: "Let him . . . perswade his Armed Saints no more to destroy, hurt, or kill cavaliers, much less any godly ministers . . . unlesse they will likewise permit the Christian magistrate to hurt and destroy obstinate seducing Hereticks."[52]

For many contemporaries, the danger of a Machiavellian appeal to success or superior force as a sign of providence was paralleled by the potentially Machiavellian invocation of necessity. Just as it was difficult in practice to distinguish godly from ungodly force, so was it difficult—and for some, impossible—to distinguish Cromwell's appeals to necessity from "necessity, the tyrant's plea." Judging from his speech to the first parliament of the Protectorate, Cromwell himself was sensitive to this problem:

I would it had not been needful for me to have called you hither to have expostulated these things [concerning the militia etc.] with you, and in such a manner as this is! But necessity hath no law. Feigned necessities, imaginary necessities, are the greatest cozenage that men can put upon the providence of God, and make pretences to break known rules by. But it is as legal and as carnal and as stupid, to think that there are no necessities that are manifest necessities, because necessities may be abused or feigned.[53]

Yet, according to his many critics, Cromwell's appeals to necessity were feigned. In the introduction to this book, I quoted Clarendon's description of Cromwell as "the greatest dissembler living." He may have been referring to the speech just quoted when he went on to describe Cromwell as a man who "never did anything, how ungracious or imprudent soever it seemed, but what was necessary to the design; even his roughness and unpolishedness, which, in the beginning of the parliament he affected . . . was necessary." With typical irony, Clarendon used Cromwell's own language of necessity to drive home the general's artful manipulation of his audience. Marchamont Nedham also charged Cromwell with Machiavellian dissembling in *Mercurius Politicus*.[54] And John Lilburne, who praised Machiavelli in *The Upright Man's Vindication* (1653), condemned Cromwell's Machiavellian treatment of the army in *As You Were* (1652), where he addressed the future Protector as a man who "walks by the Principles of Atheisme & Machiavellisme, and holds it lawful to doe any thing in the world that comes your way, that will most serve your turne, for the accomplishment of your owne ends, be they never so bloody, wicked, or tyrannical."[55] And while Milton continued to support Cromwell during the Protectorate, he too began to register some anxiety about the equation of righteousness with power and success. In the *Second Defense*, Milton wrote to the Lord Protector:

> The work which you have undertaken is of incalculable moment, which will thoroughly sift and expose every principle of your heart, which will fully display the vigor and genius of your character, which will evince whether you really possess those great qualities of piety, fidelity, justice, and self-denial, which made us believe that you were elevated by special direction of the Deity to the highest pinnacle of power. (Hughes, 835)

Although just a few pages earlier, Milton praised Cromwell as "the favored object of divine regard" (Hughes, 833), here he admits that the actual possession of power is not necessarily a sign of virtue and divine favor. In addition, Milton's syntax works against his assertion that the present task will "display" Cromwell's noble character: the correspondence between power and virtue is located in the past and in the realm of belief ("which made us believe"), suggesting that the present evidence of such correspondence is always capable of being "mere counterfeit and varnished resemblance" (Hughes, 836).

As these quotations illustrate, while it was common in the seventeenth century to distinguish between religion and government in terms of persuasion and force, the Machiavellian dyad of force and fraud also constantly reappears within the sphere of religious persuasion. Similarly, the distinction between persuasion and Machiavellian coercion, between rhetoric used well or badly, was a constant feature of political debate. Like Machiavelli's own rhetoric of innovation, the political and religious rhetoric of sixteenth- and seventeenth-century Englishmen repeatedly staged the Machiavellian dilemmas it aspired to solve. And it did so because the very isolation of a sphere of contingency that is open to debate gives rise, again and again, to the question of legitimate authority, of who has the right to judge. This dilemma is illustrated as well by the Engagement Controversy.

The Engagement Controversy

The possibility Milton entertains in the passage quoted above—that actual possession of power may not signify virtue—was at the center of the Engagement Controversy of 1649–52, when parliament sought to secure allegiance to the new government through an oath of "engagement." As with the controversy over Henry VIII's Act of Supremacy, the Engagement Controversy provides a compelling illustration of the intersection of politics, theology, and Machiavellism: it crystallizes more than a century of debate over the Machiavellian topics of legitimacy and force, virtue and success, intention and effect, means and ends; at the same time, some Engagers turned the fear of stereotypical Machiavellism on its head, by refusing to distinguish between persuasion and coercion, conquest and usurpation, and by making that refusal their most compelling argument in favor of the oath. Once again, it is not Machiavelli's republicanism that is crucial in this context but rather his insistence that all power is de facto power. In order to understand the force of the Engagers' emphasis on de facto power, we need to return to the beginning of the seventeenth century.[56]

The relationship between force and legitimacy, virtue and success, was debated not only during the civil war but throughout the first half of the century. Apologists for absolute sovereignty, including James himself, did not simply argue for divine right but also—because the divine right argument was not entirely persuasive to contemporaries—for the right resulting from conquest. Yet, precisely because God could permit—without thereby justifying—the rule of a usurper or tyrant as a way of punishing the sins of a people, the legitimacy of de facto political power was the subject of considerable debate. In particular, the argument from conquest raised the question of how to distinguish between conquest and usurpation, between de facto power that had become legitimate through time, and de facto power that remained illegitimate.

Throughout the first half of the seventeenth century, most political thinkers believed that coercion or conquest required legitimation by consent, contract, natural law, divine right, or by some combination of these. As we have seen, even as James I supplemented the argument from divine right with that of conquest, he insisted on the original consent of his conquered subjects and "the reciprock and mutuall duetie" between ruler and ruled.[57] By the time of the civil war, however, and particularly with the rule of the Rump parliament after the death of the king, the "older" arguments for political legitimacy—arguments from consent, contract, divine or natural law—had lost some of their force.[58] Instead, the Engagers based their argument for obedience on de facto political power, refusing to distinguish not only between conquest and consent but also between conquest and usurpation.[59]

Thus, in his *Considerations Concerning the Present Engagement* (1649), the minister John Dury wrote:

> he to whom God hath committed the plenary administration of publick affairs with unconfrontable power, is God's vicegerent over the society of those to whom his administration doth extend it self, either by vertue of a contract, which makes a law, or by vertue of a conquest, which is bound to no law but the will of the Conqueror.[60]

For Dury, there is no significant difference between contract and conquest, each having equal "vertue"—or "unconfrontable force"—to compel assent. In *The Case of the Commonwealth of England, Stated* (1650), Marchamont Nedham also claimed that "the Power of the Sword is, and ever hath been the foundation of all Titles to Government" (15). In a passage that reads as a Machiavellian gloss on accounts of the origin of society in sixteenth-century rhetoric textbooks, Nedham argued:

> The world, after the Flood, in time grew more populous and more exceedingly vicious, being inclined to rapine, ambition, &c., so that, the *pater familiar* [sic] way of government being insufficient to correct those grand enormities, there was need of someone more potent than the rest that might restrain them by force. Upon which ground it was Nimrod, first of all men, complotted a new and arbitrary way of government, backing it with power by a party of his own, that those crimes which could not be cured by persuasion might be cut off by compulsion and that, by a power seated in his own sword and will, he might oppose the willfullness of others. (15)

In this scenario, force is the necessary supplement to persuasion rather than vice versa. Nedham goes on to admit that Nimrod eventually used his power "but to lay the foundations of idolatry and tyranny"; however, this fact does not contradict the assertion that all governments have their origin in de facto political power. Francis Osborne made a similar point in *A Plea for a Free State compared with Monarchy* (1652), asserting that it is rare for princes "to hold their *Principalities* from a more legitimate Tenure, then *Poyson* or the *Knife*."[61]

In the opinion of many scholars, the argument from de facto power is the chief distinction of arguments for the Engagement.[62] Yet, from a rhetorical point of view, what is striking about these pamphlets is their complicated address to the individual reader. As we will see, many Engagers equate the sphere of policy with the rhetorical and theological realm of things indifferent and with the realm of casuistry, only then to argue, in royalist fashion, that private judgment is inapplicable to the public sphere. As with Hobbes's argument in *Leviathan*, the intended effect of such rhetorical defenses of de facto political power is to remove politics from the realm of persuasion and individual discretion altogether.[63] Yet, even as they present a world in which the notion of political legitimacy has no force and there is no room for individual consent or contract, they appeal to the judgment of the individual reader to swear allegiance to the present government. Thus they call attention to the possible conflict of allegiances, and to the rhetorical sphere of indeterminacy and individual discretion, in the very act of attempting to persuade the reader that there is no conflict and so, no room for choice.[64]

In so doing, the treatises for the Engagement, like *The Prince* and the *Discourses*, present a rhetorical politics in which persuasion must supplement force and de facto political power. They help us to see not only that the argument from de facto political power is one response to the Machiavellian indeterminacy of politics and rhetoric, but also that even de facto political power requires an argument and the consent of the subject. If the stereotypically Machiavellian achievement of these treatises is to replace persuasion with coercion, and to present all power—whatever its origin—as providentially sanctioned, the treatises also call attention to the Machiavellian indeterminacy that is the condition of their appeal. Ironically, it is the apparently unmitigated, stereotypically Machiavellian argument from force that ends up refiguring the instability of the Machiavellian topics most forcefully of all. As in other texts we have explored, here, too, force and indeterminacy, the Machiavel and Machiavelli's rhetorical politics, are the two faces of Renaissance Machiavellism, and need to be analyzed together.

The stereotypically Machiavellian dimension of the argument from de facto political power did not escape critics of the Engagement. William Prynne accused John Dury of being a "Time-serving Proteus and Ambidexter Divine."[65] Others described the Engagers as opportunistic and hypocritical, and worried that the oath was intended to bind the swearer to implied but unexpressed terms of agreement.[66] But it is not only the stereotypical Machiavel who appears in debates concerning the Engagement. Nedham explicitly draws on Machiavelli in his defense of de facto political power. As an example of the power of the sword, he refers us to Machiavelli's account of Cesare Borgia (22–23; see also 35); and in his concluding defense of the republican form of government, he cites Machiavelli's *Discourses*.[67] Nedham, of course, is notorious for having written royalist, as well as parliamentary, propaganda at various points in his life: he is the true time-serving Proteus. But his protean flexibility seems also to have made him particularly receptive to Machiavelli's rhetorical politics, his arguments both for princely rule and for republicanism.[68] This appears to be true of other Engagers as well: Anthony Ascham referred to Machiavelli in his treatise on the Engagement, and Francis Osborne, who wrote a short tract urging allegiance to the new government in 1652, was also the author of *Politicall Reflections upon the Government of the Turks, [and] Nicholas Machiavel . . .* (1656), a work that borrows heavily from James Bovey's favorable treatment of Machiavelli and that is consistent with the politics espoused in Osborne's earlier tract.[69] If, in the eyes of their critics, the Engagers are simply Machiavels, whose rhetoric is an instrument of force and fraud, and whose invocation of circumstances is a Jesuitical cloak for Machiavellian ends, then in the eyes of more sympathetic observers, the Machiavellism of Nedham and others is the product of a rhetorical politics, which aims to negotiate between the conflicting claims on the subject's obedience.[70] We can begin to explore the link between these two faces of Machiavellism by addressing the issue of casuistry.

As John Wallace and others have argued, the Engagement Controversy gave a renewed impetus to casuistry, which sought in the absence of a commonly recognized political authority to adjudicate or resolve the subject's conflicting allegiances to king and parliament.[71] In particular, the new oath was discussed as a case of conscience because the subjects of the commonwealth had previously sworn an oath of allegiance to Charles. The defense of the oath by Engagers, such as Ascham and Dury, allows us to see how the casuistical analysis of circumstances could serve the Machiavellian defense of usurpation or of de facto political power. In his *Discourse, wherein is examined, what is particularly lawfull during the Confusions and Revolutions of Government* (London, 1648), Ascham pressed the consideration of circumstances so far as to identify the whole realm of politics with the realm of theological indifference. He distinguished between natural law, which is not subject to debate, and human law, which is intrinsically debatable and subject to change; he described the latter in a language that suggests the realm of indifference:

> But Civill or Humane actions proceeding from a mutable and various Principle, (the will) cannot alwayes be alike or uniforme: and besides the will within, humane actions without are subjected to different circumstances, and to infinite encounters. . . . And as circumstance hath power to change the matter, so in the forme of the action, it leaves in the middle a latitude and extent, sometimes inclining to one extreme, sometimes to another. (7)

This indeterminacy of things indifferent—which Ascham goes on to call "middle things"—gives rise to "scruples, and doubtings" regarding the correct course of action in any given case (7). Yet, precisely because all rights are disputable if examined closely, and forms of government change according to place, time, and circumstance (22, 70–72), the best right is actual possession and the best reason to obey is in order to guarantee subsistence and physical protection. Ascham thus distinguishes, in Machiavellian fashion, private morality from public interest: "Yea, reason of state is not busied so much about inward piety and vertue, as it is about publique quiet and repose . . . *malus homo potest esse bonus civis* [an evil man can be a good citizen]" (8). One consequence of this distinction between "vertue" and civic *virtù*, individual piety and public repose, is that public deliberation is limited to issues of necessity—such as self-preservation and preservation of the commonwealth—rather than morality. And, as we have seen, the appeal to necessity and the invocation of reason of state were hallmarks of Machiavellism for Ascham's contemporaries.[72]

In *A Perswasive to a Mutuall Compliance under the Present Government* (1652), Francis Osborne also invoked casuistical distinctions between piety and public affairs to justify obedience to the government. He noted that "the *Apostle Paul* commands Christians to *submit* to the *present power*, for *Conscience sake*," even if the present power is entirely "corrupt" (6). For Osborne, conscience was a private matter, a faculty whose judgment does not impinge on public affairs. Thus he remarked with Hobbesian sarcasm, "We never heard newes, till these times, of *State-Martyrs*; the *Primitive Saints* thinking all *Kingdomes* too poore to dye for, but that of *Heaven*" (7). As with Ascham, one consequence of this argument—and a measure of how far we have come from earlier arguments concerning sovereignty and things indifferent—is that the form of government itself has now itself become a thing indifferent. In *A Plea for a Free State compared with Monarchy*, Osborne writes:

> though *Government* may be *by Divine Institute*; yet *This* or *That* is as *indifferent*, as whether your clothes be made after the *Dutch* or the *French fashion*; It being sufficient, if *they* defend us from the injuries of the *Weather*, and *This* protect us against our *enemies*; and prevent *Sin* and *Disorder*, the true *occasions of all Government.* (Plea, 38)

In his later *Advice to a Son* (1656), Osborne made the same point, suggesting that it should be "indifferent to a Wise Man, what Card is Trump; whose Game may possibly prove as fair under Clubs as Diamonds; neither ought he to be troubled whether his Fetters consist of Many Limbs, or but one" (83). Although Osborne went on to argue here and elsewhere for the moral as well as practical superiority of republics to monarchies, his argument for Engagement is based on the purely pragmatic considerations of protection: we should submit to the present government—whatever its form—because it has the power to protect us (*Perswasive*, 10; *Advice*, 87).

Like Ascham and Osborne, Dury opposed private actions involving matters of conscience to the realm of public events, where there are no grounds for distinguishing between God's providence and precepts, that is, between God's merely allowing an event to take place and his sanctioning that event. As Dury reasoned in *A Second Parcel of Objections against the taking of the Engagement answered* (London, 1650), "God's appointment of a power over us, is a just caus [*sic*] to oblige us to submission thereunto, whether hee doth it Providentially or Preceptively; or both waies" (23; cf. Nedham, 18):

> it is true, when you have a precept to walk by, you must not make God's acts of Providence over you a rule, to warrant anie designs which contradict the precepts, which are given you to walk by; but when things are to bee look't upon by you; not as your own, or other men's Actions; but as determined events, which God hath appointed to fall out, in a way of Justice and Judgment; then you ought not to set your self against the same; so of *Absolom's* incest, wee must saie that God's providence ordered it for judgment over *David*, for a punishment of his Adulterie; and in that respect it was good; but as it was the effect of *Achitophel's* wicked Policie to make matters desperate, and a satisfying of *Absolom's* lust, and a dishonor to his Father, and a shameless act, it was evil, and highly to bee condemned; thus in the events of things befallen of us, which are the changes of powers over us; first the King, then the Parliament, then the Armie; and now again the Parliament; these events in themselvs are neither good nor evil to us, as God hath brought them about, and ordered their succession for judgment, they were all good; and everie power in it's [*sic*] own time was to bee submitted unto, by those that were under it, because it was of God for the time over them. . . . Thus Providence, as to events become's [*sic*] a Rule to oblige us, to do things for our selvs good and lawful; and to approve of the same in others. (23–24)

In the realm of policy, the moral valence of an event—including incest and adultery—is ultimately determined not by individual conscience but by God, who can use an evil action to a good end. The "event" or "success" of a given party is thus to be understood as a sign of providence rather than of individual virtue; and, precisely because providence determines events, they are not to be resisted. As I argued in my discussion of Gardiner in chapter 4, this conflation of providence and precept, de facto and legitimate power, makes God the consummate Machiavellian. In doing so, it turns the realm of public, political action into a Machiavellian realm as well, separate from the moral deliberations of individual conscience.

As the preceding remarks have begun to suggest, in the Engagers' arguments for de facto political power, the topics of virtue and success, intention and effect, means and ends, undergo a series of ironic transformations. Whereas previous writers had tried to purge these topics of any suggestion of stereotypical Machiavellism, the Engagers called attention to the inevitability of such Machiavellism in the realm of policy. Thus, for example, when the successes of the New Model Army were invoked as a sign of providential favor, the implication was that the cause was just. Success was interpreted as a sign of virtue by parliamentarians, even though royalists pointed out the stereotypically Machiavellian dimension of such a claim. In the aftermath of the civil war, the stereotypically Machiavellian underside of this claim came to the fore when the parliamentarians themselves argued for the legitimacy of swearing an oath to de facto political power. Success—whether in the past or the present—was now invoked as a sign not so much of virtue as of power. As Thomas Povey remarked presciently in *The Moderator Expecting Sudden Peace or Certaine Ruine* (1642), "The question hereafter will be, not so much, where is the Right? But where is the Power? For the Right of Power must carry the businesse."[73] Povey's surmise was borne out by Ascham, who in his *Discourse* described the civil war as a case of conscience precisely because the success of the contending parties was not clearly related to their virtue or legitimacy:

> I may . . . descend now into the bottom of the question, and speak to the maine parties whether Just or unjust, who by the variety of successe, may one after another command us and our estates, and in both reduce us to the forementioned extreme necessity: In which condition or confusion the question is what is lawfull for us to doe? (22)

The question cannot be decided by an appeal to "right," since right "is a thing alwayes doubtfull, and would be ever disputable in all Kingdomes; if those Governours who are in possession should freely permit all men to examine their Titles" (22). The ironic twist comes when this moment of skepticism regarding the claim to legitimacy provides the solution to the problem of obedience: precisely because right is disputable and there is no obvious connection between virtue and success, Ascham asserts that success or "possession" of power provides the only ground for the subject's obedience: "Possession . . . is generally the strongest title that *Princes* have" (23). Lewis de Moulin made the same point concerning the dissociation of power and virtue when he remarked of de facto political rulers in *The Power of the Christian Magistrate in Sacred Things* (London, 1650), "It ought to suffice us that they governe, and that they have not ascended by their own vertue, but are set over, and appointed by God" (24). And he noted that obedience to "him that had possession *de facto*, though not *de jure*, . . . hath beene always practised in *England* under all the Kings since the Conquest" (27). From the perspective of these quotations, the Machiavellism of the Engagers' argument does not lie in the absolute (stereotypically Machiavellian) denial of any correspondence between virtue and success, but in the assertion that we are incapable of judging such a correspondence and are thus bound to obey those who are in "actual possession" of power. It is precisely the instability of the relationship of ethical virtue and success that provides the best argument for power politics.

As a result, the topics of intention and effect, means and ends, also undergo an ironic transformation. In the casuistical literature of the sixteenth and early seventeenth centuries, intention and context were both viewed as determining the significance of an action. And, initially, the same applied here. In his analysis of "the obligation of words," Ascham condemned equivocation but excused the swearing of an ambiguous oath if the intention of the swearer was good: "Those *words which are not in themselves true, are not alwaies lies*; For they are directed to a Morall and to a pious end, and therefore by that intention are not contrived to deceive or abuse." It was this appeal to intention that excused all parties to the oath of Engagement; for the swearer who intends obedience to the government is free from blame however the words of the oath may be construed. Yet, the ultimate effect of treating the Engagement oath as a case of conscience, involving questions of intention and effect, was to remove it from the realm of casuistry altogether. Concerning the intentions of the present government, Ascham observed, "Other mens actions are as farre out of our power as *winds and tempests are*; to which two as wee contribute nothing, so we cannot properly be scrupulous in our consciences concerning their bad effects"; in short, "we cannot properly scruple at that which is out of our power" (*Discourse*, 62, 36, 31). Dury also argued that because the consequences of our actions are beyond our control—future events are determined by providence—it is inappropriate for individuals to attempt to judge the legitimacy of taking the oath in terms of its probable effects. In *A Second Parcel*, Dury writes,

But your friends will saie perhaps this: but if your entering into the Engagement will establish them [the government] in the power which they abuse, how can you do it with a good conscience? I answer, that whatever is a cleer matter of dutie, ought for conscience sake to bee intended for itself without scrupling the event: because the future accidental effects, and contingent events of humane actions are wholly in God's hand; nor can I know whether my taking of the Engagement shall establish them in the power, which they have or no: and if it doth, whiles I do nothing but my dutie, I must leav that to God. (56)[74]

The realm of contingency—at least the contingent effects of the present government—is now beyond the subject's calculation.[75]

Finally, in the casuistical invocation of circumstances, the Machiavellian topic of means and ends was revised. Because the circumstances governing the original oath of allegiance to the king had changed, the oath was no longer in force. At the same time, because the intention of the oath to the king had been to preserve the commonwealth, the end of that oath was just as well served by the oath of Engagement. Or, to put it another way, the end of preservation remained the same, although the available means of realizing that end had changed. But, rather than calculating the relation of means to ends, the subject was simply invited to use his judgment of discretion to "acquiesce" to the present state of affairs. Thus the individual subject was bound in conscience to obey de facto political power, but he was also bound not to deliberate about the moral legitimacy of such power. While not rejecting appeals to conscience and individual discretion altogether, many Engagers reduced the role of these faculties to that of ratifying a providentially determined state of affairs. The truly Machiavellian achievement of these treatises was to make *virtù* and its concomitant rhetorical politics a function of the superior powers and of God, rather than of the individual subject. At the same time, the Machiavellian underside of these treatises exposed the dialectical relationship between force and indeterminacy, and force and persuasion, in the realm of politics.

In the previous pages I have surveyed a variety of ways in which sixteenth- and seventeenth-century debate concerning questions of legitimate and illegitimate power was suffused with the rhetoric of Machiavellism. To the extent that politics was equated with the sphere of contingency, it gave rise to fears of rhetorical manipulation, that is, the Machiavellian exercise of force and fraud, coercion and deception. As we have seen, the Machiavellian topics of virtue and success, intention and effect, means and ends, also appear in these debates and, while some participants associated a particular interpretation of these topics with the machinations of the stereotypical Machiavel, others—such as the defenders of the Engagement—exhibited a more complicated understanding of the relevance of Machiavelli to contemporary events. Finally, although some of the authors I have discussed appreciated Machiavelli's arguments for republicanism, they were also acutely aware that Machiavelli's rhetorical politics makes republicanism only one possible response to a crisis of sovereignty.[76]

PART THREE

MILTON

MILTON provides one of the best challenges to the usual histories of Renaissance Machiavellism and one of the best examples of the revised definition of Machiavellism proposed in this book. In the usual account, Milton figures as one of the happy few who read Machiavelli as a theorist of republicanism rather than as the arch-hypocrite, rhetorician, and atheist we know as the paradigmatic Machiavel.[1] Among the texts adduced to support this view are Milton's commonplace book, which includes numerous references to Machiavelli's *Art of War* and *Discourses*; the possible allusion to Machiavelli in the sonnet to Vane; the discussions of republics and mixed commonwealths in the prose, such as in *The Ready and Easy Way*; and, finally, Aubrey's much-quoted remark that Milton was a republican because he was "so conversant in Livy and the Roman authors, and the greatness he saw done by the Roman commonwealth."[2] And yet the standard equation of classical republicanism with *secular* political theory would seem to make it inapplicable to Milton above all.[3] Nor can the usual histories of Machiavellism fully account for the fact that the Machiavel and the republican—far from being decorously distinguished—are conspicuously linked in Milton's work, most obviously in the Satan of *Paradise Lost*.

The discussion of the doctrine of things indifferent in part 2 of this book suggests a different approach to Milton's Machiavellism, one that is compatible with his theological and rhetorical concerns. In the following pages I argue that if we take seriously Milton's intervention in the ongoing debate regarding things indifferent, as well as his portrayal of Satan as Machiavel and rhetorician, we are in a better position to understand Milton's republicanism in the later prose works and in *Paradise Lost*. As we will see, Milton was Machiavellian in a way Machiavelli would have appreciated: he understood the rhetorical dimension of politics exemplified by Machiavelli's *Prince* and *Discourses*; and much of his work can be seen as an extended meditation on the relation of rhetoric and faith not only to virtue but also to *virtù*. In turn, Milton the radical puritan and rhetorician helps us further to revise the usual histories of Machiavellism as secular political thought in the English Renaissance.

Specifically, Milton understood that the rhetorical politics embodied in the doctrine of things indifferent was at once a condition of Christian liberty and a threat to its realization. From *Comus* to *Areopagitica* to *Paradise Lost*, Milton enlarged the sphere of indifference in order to enlarge the role of rhetorical debate and individual discretion, as well as the possibilities for individual *virtù*. He thus gradually articulated a defense of Christian liberty, as well as the presuppositions that would eventually lead him to argue in favor of republicanism. At the same time, he was acutely aware of the Machiavellian underside of such a defense. In particular, Milton's conception of truth as "knowledge in the making" seemed at times even to him to be the product of a stereotypically Machiavellian hubris or self-aggrandizement. Two conclusions follow from this analysis. The first is that we need to take the Machiavel seriously if we are to understand Milton's defense of Christian liberty and his republicanism. The second is that the classical republicanism attributed to the later Milton and to other English revolutionaries does not signal a cultural shift to a secular analysis of politics so much as an appreciation of the relevance of Machiavelli's rhetorical politics to the dilemmas of Christian liberty.[4]

SIX

A RHETORIC OF INDIFFERENCE

IN THIS chapter, I consider Milton's intervention in the debate concerning things indifferent in his prose works. As we will see, in enlarging the sphere of things indifferent and giving the individual conscience discretion in such matters, Milton departs from the usual puritan position, according to which "nothing is indifferent." At the same time, he develops the principle of indifference into a rhetoric, thereby dramatizing his awareness that the sphere of indifference is the sphere of rhetoric, in which persuasion and action may take place. Milton's Machiavellism in his prose works is both general and specific. In reflecting on the role of discretion in the life of the believer, Milton takes up the general Machiavellian topics of intention and effect, means and ends, virtue and success; he also confronts the possibility that the assertion of individual agency is indistinguishable from the self-interest, force, and fraud of the Machiavel. In addition, in his later works he declares his republican convictions, his preference for a mixed government such as Machiavelli had discussed in the *Discourses*. If the Machiavellism of the earlier works is broad and topical—a Machiavellism by analogy—the Machiavellism of the later works is specific and republican. In the following pages, my aim is to show how the latter emerges out of and is consistent with the former: Milton's republican convictions are as much an outgrowth of his Machiavellian rhetoric of indifference as they are a specific response to the crisis of sovereignty which we know as the English civil war.

As his commonplace book and his 1658 publication of Ralegh's *The Cabinet-Council* suggest, Milton saw the relevance of Machiavelli's flexible and pragmatic counsel not only to a secular republic but also to a republic of saints. From Ralegh, as we have seen, the would-be ruler or courtier learned the necessity of joining prudence and virtue; the legitimacy of "sembling and dissembling" in pursuit of the good; the error of praising or blaming actions according to their "success"; and the somewhat contradictory error of assuming that individual virtue can succeed without divine favor. In those passages where he recommends a combination of Machiavellian pragmatism, traditional virtues, and Christian reason of state, Ralegh reminds us of Edward Dacres's and the Jesuit Thomas Fitzherbert's objections to the discussion of Cesare Borgia as exemplary ruler in chapter 7 of *The Prince*. As Fitzherbert remarked, "Whether we respect true wisdome, or the common craft and subtiltie of worldlie men (which is now commonly called machiavellian policie) [Borgia] erred in the principles of both."[1] For Dacres, too, the example of Borgia proved that policy without providence must always "show itself short-sighted." But whereas Dacres, Fitzherbert, and Ralegh at times simply assert that worldly prudence can be perfected only by divine grace, Milton continually explores the relation of grace to the possibility of *virtù* or effective political action.

Still more telling for Milton's recognition of the rhetorical and theological implications of Machiavelli's work are his remarks in his commonplace book. Under the rubric "Of Religion, to what extent it concerns the state," Milton wrote:

> Among the most excellent of all mortals are those who instruct the minds of men in true religion, more excellent even than those who have founded, however well, kingdoms and republics by man-made laws. Machiavel. discors Book 1. c[hapter] 10.
>
> That the combining of ecclesiastical and political government (when, that is to say, the magistrate acts as minister of the Church and the minister of the Church acts as magistrate) is equally destructive to both religion and the State, Dante, the Tuscan poet, shows in his Purgatorio. Cant. 16. . . .
>
> The opinions of men concerning religion should be free in a republic, or indeed under good princes. While Machiavelli praises such princes, he says, among other good things, that under them you will see golden times, "where each man can hold and defend the opinion that he wishes." discors Book 1 c[hapter] 10. See the Theological Index, Of Not Forcing Religion.[2]

This entry is significant both because it shows Milton applying Machiavelli's *Discourses* to a republic of saints and because it suggests that Milton recognized the indifference of many of Machiavelli's maxims. Milton does not read Machiavelli simply as a secular theorist; rather, he sees the *Discourses* as compatible with his own argument against "forcing religion." Implicit here, but developed at length in Milton's prose works, is the belief that republics are particularly favorable to the Reformation because they allow the free exchange of opinion and the free exercise of the individual (Protestant) conscience. Yet, while Milton registers Machiavelli's preference for republics over monarchies in the very next entry in his commonplace book, in the passage quoted above he also notes that, according to Machiavelli, the same freedom of opinion that exists in republics may also exist under "good princes." A similar indifference of means is apparent in the fact that the stereotypically Machiavellian means of force and fraud, or what Milton calls "political adroitness" (464), which we associate with the Machiavel, are also necessary for the republican who is "zealous in religion" (465). Taking up the question of "whether it is permissible to kill a tyrant," Milton answers: "Against a bad ruler there is no other remedy than the sword. 'To cure the ills of the people, words suffice, and against those of a prince the sword is necessary.' Macchiavel. discors. c[hapter] 58. Book 1" (456). And under "Of sedition," he notes: "The rebellion of a people has often been the means of their regaining their freedom. . . . Witness Macchiavelli: 'I say that those who condemn the riots between the nobles and the common people thereby, in my estimation, blame those things that were the principle means of keeping Rome free.' . . . discors. Book 1. c[hapter] 4" (505). Milton thus recognizes the flexibility of many of Machiavelli's own arguments and observations—their relevance to principalities and commonwealths—at the same time that he implies, with Machiavelli, that republics are particularly good at protecting the realm of things indifferent, in which individual choices and actions take place. As we will see, in both his prose and poetry Milton elaborates this rhetorical defense of reformation and republicanism, and he does so in part by developing his own rhetoric of things indifferent.

Areopagitica

Milton joins the debate over things indifferent most notably in *Areopagitica* (1644). In his preface to this work, Ernest Sirluck argued that Milton was not interested in the debate before this time, and explained Milton's resort to the language of indifference in *Areopagitica* as rhetorical and strategic.[3] To convince parliament to rescind its order for prepublication licensing, Milton had to divide the Presbyterian majority that supported the order. One way to do this was to appeal to the Erastians among them. Such an appeal could not be made on the basis of the separation of church and state—the usual argument for toleration of free speech—since this is precisely what the Erastians rejected. So Milton made a strategic decision to enlarge the area of indifference, the area in which "Parliament must not violate Christian liberty" (Sirluck, 170).

What Sirluck failed to note is that this strategic decision is inseparable from Milton's rhetorical justification of dissent in *Areopagitica*. For, from a rhetorical point of view, what is striking about this text is Milton's inversion of the usual arguments about things indifferent.[4] As we have seen, both supporters and critics of the status quo equated the realm of things indifferent with the jurisdiction of established authorities. Thus supporters tried to enlarge the area of indifference while dissenters restricted it, often claiming that nothing was indifferent to the individual believer. Milton's intervention in this debate is far more rhetorically sophisticated than the usual positions in that he uses the argument of his

Presbyterian opponents against them: he enlarges the realm of indifference to criticize rather than support episcopacy and he does so by making indifference a matter of individual judgment. This rhetorical inversion of his opponents' arguments has implications for Milton's interpretation of indifference and for the rhetoric of *Areopagitica* as a whole. Not only does Milton dramatize the equation of indifference with the sphere of individual judgment, he also illustrates William Bradshaw's fears— quoted above in chapter 5—of the impossibility of telling the difference between indifference and Machiavellism.

Unlike James I, Bradshaw, and Greville in their different ways, Milton does not argue that rhetorical decorum dictates the one right course of action. Rather, rhetorical indeterminacy is emphasized even to the point of being, at times, conflated with truth itself. In moving away from the contemplation of truth as fixed and absolute to a conception of "knowledge in the making," Milton preserves the judgment and agency of the individual believer, but at the cost of engaging the Machiavellian dilemmas of innovation in the realm of fortune or action in the realm of contingency and appearance. In particular, Milton's treatise shows the difficulty of distinguishing between divine and earthly force and fraud, once one accepts the limitations of human knowledge and the consequent appearance of a realm of indifference. At the same time, because Milton, like Greville, believes that there is an absolute truth though it may be only incompletely known by human agents, the treatise illustrates the tensions between the concept of truth as fixed or absolute and truth as something we know rhetorically and dialectically.

Milton's argument against prepublication licensing moves from a defense of books as good or bad in themselves (either "the image of God" or "blasphemous and atheistical" [720]) to the claim that books are things indifferent that can be used well or badly by the reader. Quoting the divine message sent to Dionysius Alexandrinus, "Read any books whatever come to thy hands, for thou art sufficient both to judge aright and to examine each matter," Milton comments:

> "To the pure all things are pure"; not only meats and drinks, but all kinds of knowledge whether of good or evil; the knowledge cannot defile, nor consequently the books if the will and conscience be not defiled. For books are as meats and viands are—some of good, some of evil substance, and yet God in that unapocryphal vision said without exception, "Rise, Peter, kill and eat," leaving the choice to each man's discretion. (727)

At this point Milton would seem to be arguing against censorship on the basis of an ethic of intention (supported by the antinomian scriptural tag, "to the pure all things are pure"). Prepublication licensing would be futile because the possibility of sin does not lie in the book but in the reader's prior disposition. But the problem with such an exclusive focus on intention is that it seems to make education—the inculcation and exercise of virtue—impossible. If intention or disposition governs the right use of things indifferent, it is important to stress that such usage is itself educated through practice. So in the famous passage criticizing "a fugitive and cloistered virtue," Milton opposes what he calls a "blank virtue" to "a pure" virtue, one that does not exist from the start but emerges from a process of trial or purification. Thus Milton shifts from an antinomian emphasis on right intention to an Arminian one on use and works. As Joan Bennett has argued in a different context,

> For Milton, it was necessary, but not enough, to be pure in heart; one had also to work hard to figure out a way in each circumstance to act efficaciously: "who had not rather follow *Iscariot* or *Simon* the magician, though to covetous ends, preaching, then *Saul*, though in the uprightness of his heart persecuting the gospell?"[5]

In order to guarantee the possibility of efficacious action, the possibility of failure has to be admitted as well. Accordingly, the ever-present possibility of sin is reaffirmed and relocated in the external world:

> the knowledge of good is so involved and interwoven with the knowledge of evil, and in so many cunning resemblances hardly to be discerned, that those confused seeds which were imposed on Psyche as an incessant labor to cull out and sort asunder, were not more intertwined. It was from out the rind of one apple tasted, that the knowledge of good and evil, as two twins cleaving together, leaped forth into the world. And perhaps this is that doom which Adam fell into of knowing good and evil, that is to say, of knowing good by evil. (728)

The passage begins by suggesting a slight difference ("hardly to be discerned") between good and evil as though one had only to look closely to distinguish between them; but as we read further it becomes clear that the occasion of sin is indistinguishable from the occasion of virtue: "Suppose we could expel sin by this means; look how much we expel of virtue: for the matter of them both is the same; remove that, and ye remove them both alike" (733). For Milton in this text knowledge is dialectical; it proceeds by contraries. And this dialectical process is itself described as "incessant labor" or, in the lines that follow, a "race" or "trial."

This emphasis on exercise or trial is dramatized in the rhetorical organization of the text. Just as the realm of things theologically indifferent allows for the exercise of virtue, so rhetorical figures are things indifferent which can be used in a variety of ways by the author and the reader. The indeterminacy or instability of certain words and metaphors serves as an illustration of the author's, and occasion of the reader's, exercise of virtue. Thus the same thing may be described in contrary ways and the same figures may be applied to different things or concepts. For example, Milton describes truth as both an organic body and an architectural building. In the first case, "hewing" refers to the hacking of the limbs of truth (742); in the second to the carving of cedars for the "temple of the Lord" (744). An analogous distinction is made between "dividers of unity" (742) and the "dividing of one visible congregation from another, though it be not in fundamentals" (747); between "the fiercest rent and disunion" (747) and the "many schisms and dissections [necessary] . . . ere the house of God can be built" (744). As Machiavelli does, Milton draws a distinction between faction and productive conflict. Differences are necessary "while things are not yet constituted in religion" (739) because they generate progress toward the truth or "knowledge in the making" (743); though the fact that the same words and images are used to describe these two different conceptions of difference also suggests that progress is never so obvious that one can rest with a simple assertion or "think to make a staple commodity of all the knowledge in the land" (737). Here the metaphor of trade, which in another context might convey an ongoing process of intellectual exchange, is used to condemn a conception of knowledge as a fixed commodity, an object that can be transferred from one person to another without regard for intention or right use.

Milton's anxiety about the relation of such intention to the truth is registered in his own ambivalent rhetoric when discussing human agency. In the dialectic of the argument, as soon as he stresses individual agency and the exercise of individual judgment, he draws back to assert the existence and efficaciousness of objective truth.[6] When his rhetoric of indifference seems to imply a rhetorical and therefore unstable "ground" of virtue, when it implies that virtue is simply a matter of individual judgment responding to particular circumstances, he then argues that judgment and rhetoric must themselves be "licensed" by reference to the truth.[7] Yet, this check on the free exercise of individual judgment is beset with difficulties, for although truth is absolute, it must not be coercive; nor can it be a matter of mere "implicit faith" (739). Such passive believers are rather "heretic[s] in the truth" (739). Furthermore, not only can truth be held incorrectly by an individual but truth itself may look like heresy. Thus Milton writes, "If it come to prohibiting, there is not aught more likely to be prohibited than truth itself; whose first appearance to our eyes bleared and dimmed with prejudice and custom, is more unsightly and unplausible than many errors" (748).

Milton's anxiety about the rhetorical "ground" of virtue is particularly apparent in his use of personification, a preeminent rhetorical figure of agency.[8] On the one hand, Milton describes the heresy of the "implicit" believer in terms of a process of personification: this believer transfers his own agency to "some factor . . . some Divine of note and estimation," and "makes the very person of that man his religion" (740). As a result, religion is itself personified, that is, alienated and reified:

> So that a man might say his religion is now no more within himself, but is become a dividual movable, and goes and comes near him, according as that good man frequents the house. He entertains him, gives him gifts, feasts him, lodges him. His religion comes home at night, prays, is liberally supped, and sumptuously laid to sleep . . . his religion walks abroad at eight, and leaves his kind entertainer in the shop trading all day without his religion. (740)

In this passage, as in the earlier one, personification is the rhetorical equivalent of implicit faith or mere outward conformity.

On the other hand, personification is the figure Milton uses to negotiate the problematic relationship of individual agency and truth. Thus after the image of "the temple of Janus with his two controversal faces," which suggests a bellicose version of humanist argument on both sides of a question, Milton argues that truth is not simply the desired object of such discussion but one of the warriors: "Let [Truth] and Falsehood grapple; who ever knew Truth put to the worse, in a free and open encounter" (746). We need not worry about—or license—such encounters because the outcome is guaranteed by the personified agency of truth. The next two paragraphs enact a similar shift from the agency of the individual to that of truth. Milton first describes "a man [who] hath been laboring the hardest labor in the deep mines of knowledge, [and] hath furnished out his findings in all their equipage, drawn forth his reasons as it were a battle ranged . . . in the wars of Truth" (746–47). But lest the wars of truth prove inconclusive, he again hastens to argue that they are only a mock battle. "Truth is strong [and] . . . needs no policies." However, as in the work of the royalists and parliamentarians cited in chapter 5, the emphasis on the agency or power of truth has its own liabilities. In the end, the personification of truth raises the problem of antinomianism it was designed to address.

Just as the antinomian tenet "to the pure all things are pure" threatens the distinction between law and grace, man and God, so does the personification of—the attribution of human agency to—truth. For once truth is personified—one might even say, once truth enters the realm of representation—it engages the Machiavellian dilemma of how to distinguish between the force of truth and the force of its fraudulent representation. Although truth's power is a check on the weakness of individual judgment and the indeterminacy of the rhetorical "wars of Truth," very quickly this reassertion of the force of truth proves to be indistinguishable from that of falsehood. In a logical extension of the earlier passage on implicit faith, where personification symbolizes the (unethical) alienation of agency, here the ability to alienate is figured as deliberate and strategic misrepresentation on the part of truth:

> For who knows not that Truth is strong, next to the Almighty. She needs no policies, nor stratagems, nor licensings to make her victorious—those are the shifts and the defenses that error uses against her power. Give her but room, and do not bind her when she sleeps, for then she speaks not true, as old Proteus did, who spake oracles only when he was caught and bound, but then rather she turns herself into all shapes except her own, and perhaps tunes her voice according to the time, as Micaiah did before Ahab, until she be adjured into her own likeness. (747)

The passage begins by distinguishing between the direct force of truth and the fraud or dissemblance of error. In this dichotomy, licensing is a Machiavellian tactic, a "policie" or "strategem." But immediately truth herself is described as capable of deception when so constrained. In a mirror image of the Proteus who speaks true when bound, bound truth speaks falsely. Thus the "shifts and defenses that error uses against [Truth's] power" are also the defenses that truth uses against the power or "licensing" of error. The reference to the prophet Micaiah further complicates the initial distinction between the force of truth and fraud, since Micaiah "warned Ahab that other prophets were inspired by 'a lying spirit' (1 Kings xxii, 23)" (Hughes, 747 n. 264). He thus points to the fact that divine inspiration may be feigned. Personification—here construed as God speaking through man—is the figure not only of true prophecy but also of false impersonation.

Then, in a further reversal of the metaphor, one that develops the implication of this chiasmus of Proteus and truth, truth herself is described as protean in an approved sense:

> Yet it is not impossible that she may have more shapes than one. What else is all that rank of things indifferent wherein Truth may be on this side, or on the other, without being unlike herself? What but a vain shadow else is the abolition of those ordinances, that handwriting nailed to the cross; what great purchase is this Christian liberty which Paul so often boasts of? His doctrine is, that he who eats, or eats not, regards a day, or regards it not, may do either to the Lord. (747)

In identifying truth with Proteus and with "all that rank of things indifferent" the passage enacts the appropriation of the rhetorical power of metaphor—of indirection, disguise, and conversion from one shape to another—for truth, but at the price of making the "likeness" of truth indistinguishable from its "unlikeness."[9] Thus Milton dramatizes the rhetorical or dialectical core of truth even as he seems to be arguing for a positive conception of truth as simply different from coercion and false-hood. It is precisely this conflation of truth with the realm of things indif-ferent that allows for the exercise of individual judgment but also threat-ens to undermine the notion of truth itself. And if truth is undermined or uncertain, then the license of individual judgment can only be rhetorical, in the sense of appealing to a contingent configuration of circumstances and interests. Milton does not resolve this Machiavellian dilemma here or in his later work; rather, he dramatizes it again and again.

Machiavellian Topics

The topics and dilemmas of Machiavellism also appear in Milton's later treatises on the relationship of spiritual to temporal power. Like his con-temporaries, Milton takes up the Machiavellian topics of persuasion and coercion, intention and effect, virtue and success, in the realm of religion and politics; and, like them, he expresses a fundamental tension between the authority and power of divine providence and the power of human agency. At the same time he dramatizes the ever-present danger of their conflation—whether in an antinomian emphasis on individual conscience or an Arminian emphasis on works. As in *Areopagitica*, Milton shows that he is aware both of the stereotypical Machiavellism of confusing the power of the individual with divine power, and of the Machiavellian di-lemmas of preserving a realm of active virtue in a world governed by providence or—as Machiavelli would say—by fortune.

As we saw in chapter 5, in the late 1640s and 1650s Milton appeals to the successes of Cromwell and the parliamentary army as a sign of provi-dential favor; but he is also wary of such a stereotypical Machiavellian justification of the status quo. Thus, in *The Tenure of Kings and Magis-trates*, he first describes the tyrant's being brought "to the trial of justice, which is the sword of God, superior to all mortal things, in whose hand soever by apparent signs his testified will is to put it"; and he exhorts his readers to assist "the present parliament and army in the glorious way wherein justice and victory hath set them—the only warrants through all ages, next under immediate revelation, to exercise supreme power" (Hughes, 751, 752). Yet, later in the tract, he qualifies the implicit jus-tification of de facto power in the hendiadys of "justice and victory" by paraphrasing Thomas Smith's *De republica anglorum* (1583): "Sir Thomas Smith also, a protestant and a statesman, in his *Commonwealth of England*, putting the question whether it be lawful to rise against a tyrant, answers that the vulgar judge of it according to the event and the learned according to the purpose of them that do it" (763). Here, Milton rejects judging simply according to victory or success. And he does so in part because he is aware of the indifference of worldly power. Commenting on Romans 13, which was regularly cited by royalists to justify kingly power and absolute obedience to the crown, Milton remarks:

> "There is no power but of God," saith Paul (Rom. xiii), as much as to say God put it into man's heart to find out that way at first for common peace and preservation, approving the exercise thereof; else it contradicts Peter, who calls the same authority an ordinance of man. It must also be understood of lawful and just power, else we read of great power in the affairs and kingdoms of the world permitted to the devil: for saith he to Christ (Luke iv, 6), "All this power will I give thee and the glory of them, for it is delivered to me, and to whomsoever I will, I give it:" neither did he lie, or Christ gainsay what he affirmed; for in the thirteenth of the Revelation, we read how the dragon gave to the beast "his power, his seat, and great authority:" which beast so authorized most expound to be the tyrannical powers and kingdoms of the earth. (758–59)

In this passage Milton employs his characteristic rhetorical strategy of enlarging the area of human discretion, even to the point of making the much-cited, authoritative Romans 13 subject to debate. That is, Milton does not simply rebut his opponents' interpretation by proposing a thematic paraphrase of his own; rather, his interpretation of this passage is that it is open to interpretation. "There is no power but of God" is not simply a statement of fact but a test of human judgment, an exercise in deliberating about the best way to achieve "common peace and preservation." And such exercise is necessary because power is indifferent, and may be used well or badly. To illustrate this point, Milton refers to the passage in Luke where Satan offers Christ worldly power; he insists that Satan's offer was genuine, because to deny Satan power would be to deny that tyrants have the power to oppress their subjects. At issue is not the possession of power but its right interpretation and right use. Only power that is correctly used may be correctly described as "ordained of God" (759).

In asserting the compatibility of Romans 13 and Peter—of divine and human ordinance—Milton makes the whole realm of politics coextensive with that of things indifferent. In striking contrast, for example, to James I, who in his discussion of things indifferent in *Basilikon Doron* distinguished between the express commandments of God and the invention and ordinance of man, Milton equates them: the power ordained by God is the power ordered by man. He then develops the implications of this analysis by calling attention to the rhetorical dimension of sovereignty. Just as Romans 13 is open to interpretation, so the rule of a sovereign is open to interpretation by the people, who create legitimacy by their linguistic act of consent. Politics is the sphere of things indifferent in the sense that it is a matter of human discretion and so is continually open to reinterpretation and renegotiation. Thus, if Romans 13 may be cited to support submission to kings, it may also be cited to support resistance; similarly,

> if the people's act in election be pleaded by a king as the act of God and the most just title to enthrone him, why may not the people's act of rejection be as well pleaded by the people as the act of God and the most just reason to depose him? So that we see the title and just right of reigning or deposing, in reference to God, is found in scripture to be all one: visible only in the people, and depending merely upon justice and demerit. (759)

Here it may be helpful to contrast this passage with William Bradshaw's suspicion that indifference was a Machiavellian invention. According to Bradshaw, the Machiavel isolates a sphere of indeterminacy which is then vulnerable to coercive interpretation or figurative "coloring" in the service of his own interests. For Milton, in contrast, the indifference of worldly power—and of the scriptural warrants of such power—provides an occasion for the exercise of virtue and allows the rhetorical transactions that create and unmake the sovereign. In equating the realm of politics with the sphere of things indifferent, and in emphasizing the rhetorical dimension—and popular source—of secular power, Milton draws near to Machiavelli's rhetorical politics.

Milton pursues the implications of the doctrine of things indifferent and of a rhetorical politics in *A Treatise of Civil Power in Ecclesiastical Causes* (1659). In this work Milton distinguishes, as his contemporaries did, between the use of force in civil matters and of persuasion in spiritual matters. He again refers to Romans 13, arguing against those who interpret this passage as giving "power to the magistrate both of civil judgment and punishment in causes ecclesiastical" (844). The only judge of spiritual matters is the conscience of the individual believer. And he goes on, in a passage reminiscent of *Areopagitica*, to equate the realm of things indifferent with individual Christian liberty rather than with episcopacy or "Erastus and state tyranny" (845). To those who argue that certain things "are indifferent, but for that very cause by the magistrate may be commanded," Milton comments sardonically:

> As if God of his special grace in the gospel had to this end freed us from his own commandments in these things, that our freedom should subject us to a more grievous yoke, the commandments of men. As well may the magistrate call that common or unclean which God hath cleansed, forbidden to St. Peter, Acts x, 15; as well may he loosen that which God hath straitened or straiten that which God hath loosened, as he may enjoin those things in religion which God hath left free, and lay on that yoke which God hath

taken off. For he hath not only given us this gift as a special privilege and excellence of the free gospel above the servile law, but strictly also hath commanded us to keep it and enjoy it: Gal. v, 13: "You are called to liberty." I Cor. vii, 23, "Be not made the servants of men." (850)

This passage seems to confirm the fears articulated by men such as Thomas Wilson who, in *The Rule of Reason*, cautioned against interpreting "freedom" in the New Testament to mean political as well as spiritual equality.[10] As in *The Tenure of Kings and Magistrates*, Milton's interpretation of spiritual freedom in things indifferent has consequences for his view of the state even as he argues for the separation of civil and ecclesiastical power. Although worldly force must not be applied to matters of religious "convincement" or persuasion, it is the proper function of the magistrate to "defend things religious settled by the churches within themselves" (848). Similarly, although "Christ rejects outward force in the government of his church . . . to show us the divine excellence of his spiritual kingdom, able without worldly force to subdue all the powers and kingdoms of this world," "a Christian commonwealth may [still] defend itself against outward force in the cause of religion as well as in any other" (847). As in the debates concerning the successes of the parliamentary army, here, too, force is a thing indifferent that may be used to defend as well as subvert religion. There is a further implication as well. For the corollary of Milton's defense of spiritual freedom is an attack not only on "state tyranny over the church" but on any form of tyranny that makes us "servants of men."[11] Implicit here is the claim that the assertion of individual freedom in things indifferent leads logically to a preference for a republican form of government—an argument that is the theological equivalent of Machiavelli's defense of republics in the *Discourses*. Just as Machiavelli claimed that republics were better able to respond to the contingencies of fortune, so Milton claims that republics are better able to preserve the realm of contingency in which individual conscience may be exercised and individual virtue may prosper.

This claim is clearly stated in *The Ready and Easy Way to Establish a Free Commonwealth* (1660). "The whole freedom of man," Milton writes, "consists either in spiritual or civil liberty," and both dictate a republican form of government. Regarding the first, Milton argues: "This liberty of conscience, which above all other things ought to be to all men dearest and most precious, no government [is] more inclinable not to favor only, but to protect, than a free commonwealth, as being most magnanimous, most fearless, and confident of its own fair proceedings" (895–96). He goes on to note that, although Queen Elizabeth was "accounted so good a protestant," she recognized that further "reformation would diminish regal authority" (896). Francis Osborne had made a similar argument in *A Plea for a Free State compared with Monarchy* (1652), when he wrote, "though experience proves by *this State*, and the *Catholique Cantons*, &c. that the *Roman profession* may sute, in some measure, with *all kinds of Government*, yet undeniable *Reason of State* renders *Monarchy most acceptable to the Pope*, as it doth *the Reformation to Free States*" (28). In both cases, republics or commonwealths are thought to be particularly conducive to reformation because they allow for the free exercise of conscience and judgment in things indifferent.

Yet, if freedom of conscience in things indifferent is best protected by a free commonwealth, freedom of conscience and individual judgment are also the source of the backsliding that Milton regularly condemns from *The Tenure of Kings and Magistrates* onward. One of the most powerful of such condemnations appears in the conclusion to *The Ready and Easy Way*, in a passage that seems to echo, in part, Machiavelli's discussion of *fortuna* and *virtù* in chapter 25 of *The Prince*:

> I trust I shall have spoken persuasion to abundance of sensible and ingenuous men; to some, perhaps, whom God may raise of these stones to become children of reviving liberty, and may reclaim, though they seem now choosing them a captain back for Egypt, to bethink themselves a little and consider whither they are rushing; to exhort this torrent also of the people not to be so impetuous, but to keep their due channel; and at length recovering and uniting their better resolutions, now that they see already how open and unbounded the insolence and rage is of our common enemies, to stay these ruinous proceedings, justly and timely fearing to what a precipice of destruction the deluge of this epidemic madness would hurry us, through the general defection of a misguided and abused multitude. (898–99)

In *The Prince*, Machiavelli compared Fortune to "one of those torrential streams which, when they overflow, flood the plains, rip up trees and tear down buildings"; but urged that men take "countermeasures while the weather is still fine, shoring up dikes and dams, so that when the waters rise again, they are either carried off in a channel or confined where they do no harm." In Milton's description, the people have themselves become the torrential streams of fortune that are not keeping their due channel, because no one is exercising *virtù*. The Machiavellian vision of this passage is complicated by biblical allusions to John the Baptist prophesying salvation (Luke 3:8: "God is able of these stones to raise up children unto Abraham"), to Ezekiel who imagines his audience as dry bones that revive as he prophesies (Ezekiel, 37), and to the deluge or flood, which was a consequence of "the general defection of a misguided and abused multitude." Milton seems here both to be urging his contemporaries to active virtue with a prophetic rhetoric that mingles his own voice with that of God (syntactically, it is God who exhorts the torrent), and to be excusing the imagined failure of his rhetoric to persuade and of his contemporaries to "become children of reviving liberty." On the one hand, the failure of *virtù* is moralized and theologized by Milton as a failure of virtue and a reenactment of the fall. Still, virtue, like *virtù*, is intended to have effects in the world of politics and of contingent human affairs. If Milton is Machiavellian in his effort to restore *virtù* to virtue, he is also Machiavellian in his acute awareness of the contingency—the indifference—that is the condition of free will. It is perhaps for this reason that Milton's own rhetorical performance is made dependent on divine inspiration but is not equated with success. His audience must be capable of backsliding if they are to be capable of reviving liberty.

SEVEN

VIRTUE AND *VIRTÙ* IN *COMUS*

> Therefore, if wise men will needs send their sons into Italy, let
> them do it wisely, under the keep and guard of him who, by his
> wisdom and honesty, by his example and authority, may be
> able to keep them safe and sound in the fear of God, in Christ's
> true religion, in good order and honesty of living; except they
> will have them run headlong into over-many jeopardies, as
> Ulysses had done many times, if Pallas had not always gov-
> erned him; if he had not used to stop his ears with wax, to bind
> himself to the mast of his ship, to feed daily upon that sweet
> herb Moly, with the black root and the white flower, given
> unto him by Mercury to avoid all the enchantments of Circes.
> —*Roger Ascham,* The Scholemaster

BORROWING from J.G.A. Pocock's description of Machiavelli's *The Prince* as "an analytic study of innovation and its conse-quences" (*MM*, 156), we can describe *Comus* as an analytic study of virtue and its consequences or, to rephrase this in the humanist vocab-ulary of the time, of virtue and power (*virtus* and *vis*). In *Comus* the problems of agency we observed in *Areopagitica* are signaled in two ways. On the one hand, the conflict between the Lady and Comus can be read as the allegorical opposition of Virtue to Force and Virtuosity, with the result that virtue comes to seem "unexercised and unbreathed." On the other hand, as in *Areopagitica*, the "indifferent" rhetoric of the text suggests Milton's effort to reunite—without conflating—virtue and power, intention and effect, in a single faculty analogous to Machiavel-lian *virtù*. Thus, as Angus Fletcher has noted, in *Comus* the genre of the masque is in conflict with itself: while invoking the allegorical conven-tions of its Stuart predecessors, Milton's work also resists its own allegor-ical impulse.[1] In this resistance Milton dramatizes both the strengths and the dilemmas of his own Machiavellian interpretation of virtue.

In the following pages I rehearse the topics of Machiavellism with an eye to the issues that will concern us in the discussion of *Comus*. In partic-ular, the topics of intention and effect, virtue and success, will be recast in terms of the dilemmas of epideictic poetry. For, as many readers have noted, the problem of agency we observed in *Areopagitica* appears in *Comus* not only as a theological issue but also as a poetic one: the issue of the poet's agency, his poetic virtuosity. I then turn to the Machiavellism of the two Stuart masques most often cited as precursors of *Comus*: Jonson's *Pleasure Reconcil'd to Virtue* and Carew's *Coelum Britannicum*. As Stephen Orgel has argued, the Stuart masque is ideologically both Platonic and Machiavellian: Platonic because it presents an ideal, hierarchical world and an image of the good to which the audience is supposed to aspire; Machiavellian "because its idealizations are designed to justify the power they celebrate."[2] In these masques, the poet's aim is to justify the ways of the king to men by arguing that royal power is a sign of royal virtue. But, if these masques are stereotypically Machiavellian in the way Orgel suggests, they also engage the topics of Machiavellism more generally by asking us to reflect on the complicated relationship of virtue to success, intention to effect, both at court and in the writing of epideictic poetry. The Machiavellism of these masques can then help us understand Milton's innovations in *Comus*.

Of particular importance in this context is that Jonson's *Pleasure Reconcil'd to Virtue* served as an ideological justification of James's "Declaration of Sports," the proclamation that Sabbath entertainment is a thing indifferent and thus a matter of royal and ecclesiastical jurisdiction; also of note is that *Comus* was performed shortly after the reissue of the declaration by Charles I in 1633. Although Milton certainly recognized the self-serving (and in this sense Machiavellian) motives of the royal masque, *Comus* also dramatizes a different sort of Machiavellism, one that is manifest in his own rhetoric of things indifferent and his attempt to link virtue to *virtù*. While from one perspective this might be construed as Milton's justification of the power he celebrates (ostensibly Bridgewater's, finally God's), from another equally important perspective *Comus* provides a rhetorical justification of dissent. For, in contrast to the intended equation of royal power with virtue, Milton tries to make individual virtue itself the locus of power, without thereby sacrificing a Machiavellian interest in effects. *Comus* thus provides an important link to Milton's subsequent meditation on republican virtue in *Paradise Lost* for it allows us to see more clearly than *Areopagitica* the poetic implications of contemporary debates concerning the agency of the individual believer and the political dissenter. It also shows us that well before *Areopagitica* Milton was exploring the question of indifference—and its rhetorical implications—in his poetry.

Virtù and Virtuosity

We can begin to address the issue of poetic virtuosity by noting that the Renaissance poet and courtier shared a concern with the conspicuous display of *virtù* or virtuosity.[3] As I briefly suggested in part 2 of this book, in presupposing a flexible faculty of judgment, *virtù* is in some respects like the *sprezzatura* of Castiglione's courtier. Neither is intrinsically related to the conventional virtues though—or precisely because—in each case the virtues may be assumed for the sake of appearances. Just as the Machiavel was characterized in terms of his amoral or, in Christian terms, immoral manipulation of appearances, so a similar anxiety attended the social upstart, specifically the low-born individual who assumed the manners and appearance of a noble or courtier and who, as a result, was often described as Machiavellian. The fear was that a supposedly innate condition such as social status could be achieved or feigned. Here we have a stereotypically Machiavellian version of the trope of virtue and success, according to which "virtue" is the rhetorical effect of success rather than vice versa.

An apparently benign, poetic version of this trope appears in Renaissance discussions of epideictic rhetoric, that form of rhetoric in which the poet praises or blames in order to incite to ethical action. While pretending to mirror the virtues of his addressee, the poet aspires to produce the effect of virtue as the result of his successful (persuasive) representation. As Jonson writes in his poetic epistle to Selden:

> Though I confess (as every muse hath erred,
> And mine not least) I have too oft preferred
> Men past their terms, and praised some names too much,
> But 'twas with purpose to have made them such.

(ll. 19–22)

Hyperbole—here, the representation of virtue as already achieved—is the means of ethical persuasion.

But epideictic rhetoric may also raise the specter of Machiavellian self-interest. The social insubordination of the Machiavel, who manipulates appearances to his own ends, finds a poetic equivalent in the insubordination of the poet, who uses rhetoric not to persuade to the good but rather to seduce or simply to display his own poetic virtuosity. In the traditional tripartite division of rhetoric, it is epideictic discourse that is most prominently associated with this self-reflexive capability of rhetoric and poetics. According to contemporary treatises, the epideictic poem does not merely praise or instruct; it is also the genre of self-display, the genre that allows the poet to give a virtuoso performance. The traditional anxiety about the orator's ability to defend evil as well as good here finds an analogue in the anxiety about—and the love of—appearances for their own sake or, more accurately, for the sake of poetic self-aggrandizement. Poetic virtuosity thus becomes a trope for virtuosity at court or in politics more generally.[4] As with the ambivalence attending the figure of the courtier, here too the fear is that the relationships of virtue to success, and means to ends, will be inverted: rather than subordinating aesthetic display to ethical ends, the ethical instruction of the text is the occasion of poetic virtuosity and self-aggrandizement.

As we will see, this anxiety about appearances and virtuosity—about "works"—was complicated for some poets writing in the 1630s by the conflict between Archbishop Laud's perceived emphasis on ritual or cere-mony and his puritan critics. Those puritans who believed in strict pre-destination tended to see Laudian innovation as Arminian, as stressing the *achievement* of salvation through ritual rather than seeing salvation or damnation as a fixed condition. Conversely, those puritans who were sympathetic to Arminianism, with its belief in free will and individual effort, condemned Laudian ritual as a kind of institutionalized inertia or theological defense of the social and political status quo.[5]

As the previous chapters have suggested, there are a variety of re-sponses to the ambivalence about virtuosity or the power of appearances in the Renaissance. One prominent one is to moralize rhetoric by appeal-ing to some extrarhetorical standard, such as natural law, innate virtue, or divine grace. Another response is to rhetoricize virtue, to make of it a practice rather than a thing—in short, to dereify it. In the first case, the praise of virtue may take the form of grounding it in, for example, natural law or divine right; in the second, virtue is inseparable from the play of rhetoric or figuration. In its revision of the Stuart masque, *Comus* drama-tizes both responses, and thus registers an ambivalence about virtuosity in a particularly salient way. A look at Jonson's *Pleasure Reconcil'd to Virtue* and Carew's *Coelum Britannicum* can help us understand Mil-ton's own Machiavellian virtuosity, his attempt to reappropriate *virtù* for his own poetic and political ends.

Jonson and Carew

The problems faced by the author of a masque are the problems of epi-deictic rhetoric, whether he aims to justify or to instruct: in the first case, the poet must make the activity of praise seem like inactivity, like the mere reflection of reality; in the second, the poet's praise must encourage the activity of imitation on the part of the viewer. These problems reappear in the rhetoric of the masque which, in anatomizing royal virtue, also comments on the conditions of representing it. Insofar as it is already achieved, such virtue is best represented by the spectacular, hieratic, and symbolic elements of the masque. But insofar as the goal is also to drama-tize the power or efficaciousness of royal virtue, the masque requires some action. The danger here is that an active virtue will suggest the mu-tability of royal virtue, the instability of royal power. In form and theme the Stuart masque thus registers those anxieties about the vulnerability of ritual and status to innovation and individual effort, which contemporaries associated with Machiavellism.

Orgel comments on the problem of representing royal virtue in his analysis of *Pleasure Reconcil'd to Virtue*: although the explicit argument of the masque is that virtue must be active, the main character, Hercules, is conspicuously inactive.[6] As the figure of Hercules illustrates, one way both to represent virtue as active and to contain the threatened association of activity with mutability and indeterminacy is to relegate such activity to the past (Hercules's choice has already been made, his labors already achieved). Another way is to represent activity as "wholly mental": "The two antimasque episodes tell us that a virtuous and constant mind will triumph over the forces of evil." But, as Orgel notes, activity as mutability resurfaces in the conclusion of the masque, suggesting a possible critique of virtue at court. *Pleasure Reconcil'd to Virtue* deliberately registers "the strains of idealization" and in so doing criticizes the status quo.[7]

Carew's *Coelum Britannicum* displays a similar conflict in its representation of royal virtue. Jennifer Chibnall has argued that the masque tries to negotiate between two conflicting ideologies, an older "aristocratic code of hospitality and paternalism in a stable society with 'clear class distinctions'" and "the new 'capitalist/Protestant ethic' of self-improvement, thrift, hard work and competition."[8] One need not accept Chibnall's equation of an ethic of self-improvement and competition with emergent capitalism to agree that *Coelum Britannicum* registers a conflict between virtue as an innate, already achieved condition, and virtue as the product of effort or labor.[9] Thus the figure of Plutus refers to "the daily sacrifice / Brought to my Temple by the toyling rout" (ll. 298–99), but this effort on behalf of "gainfull trade" (l. 508) is rejected as incompatible with true virtue. Yet, true virtue requires an effort of its own:

> we advance
> Such vertues onely as admit excesse,
> Brave bounteous Acts, Regall Magnificence,
> All-seeing Prudence, Magnanimity
> That knowes no bound, and that Heroicke vertue
> For which Antiquity hath left no name,
> But patternes only, such as *Hercules*. . . .
>
> (ll. 559–65)

Commenting on Mercury's rejection of "Falsly exalted passive Fortitude" in favor of aristocratic "Heroicke vertue," Chibnall defines the paradoxical position of the Stuart aristocrat in the following way: "A virtue that could know a 'bound' cannot satisfy the aspiration of the aristocrat who must define his place as above all servility. This place cannot be static yet must be stable" (87; see also 82–83). The contrast between two kinds of effort is summed up in Mercury's address to Charles:

> The growing Titles of your Ancestors,
> These Nations glorious Acts, joyn'd to the stocke
> Of your owne Royall vertues, and the cleare
> Reflexe they take from th' imitation
> Of your fam'd Court, make Honors storie full,
> And have to that secure fix'd state advanc'd
> Both you and them, to which the labouring world,
> Wading through streames of blood, sweats to aspire.
>
> (ll. 848–55)

Although "glorious Acts" are a part of royal virtue, the appearance of effortful imitation is mitigated by the rhetoric of reflection: such acts are "the cleare reflexe" of the court, which is why the effort of advancing does not threaten the "fix'd state" of royal virtue. In contrast, "the labouring world" seems to expend all its effort merely aspiring to the condition of action.

The paradox of advancing to fixity is further illustrated in the conclusion to the masque when Genius asserts that the fame of Charles and Henrietta-Maria "shall flye / From hence above, and in the Spheare / Kindle new Starres, whilst they rest here" (ll. 993–95). Chibnall comments, "The resolution of the contradiction between ideal stability and real action is thus achieved by creating a separation between the real and ideal self that can yet be united in mutual influence" (90). Here virtue is ideally reconciled to meritorious effort while being distinguished from mere aspiration: Charles's reign is one "Where faire Desert, and Honour meet" (l. 1117).

If *Coelum Britannicum* illustrates the conflict between Neoplatonic virtue and individual *virtù*, fixity and advancement, *Pleasure Reconcil'd to Virtue* stages this conflict with specific reference to the doctrine of things indifferent. As a number of critics have remarked, *Pleasure Reconcil'd to Virtue* provides a kind of metacommentary on the ideological function of the court masque: in this work, Jonson defends James's policy regarding the indifference of recreation on the Sabbath, including the recreation of the masque. Yet, in taking as his subject royal jurisdiction over things indifferent, Jonson also comments on the Machiavellian instability of equating royal virtue with "faire Desert."

In the view of James and his bishops, recreation on the Sabbath was to be allowed to those who attended the Anglican church services and forbidden to those who did not. The declaration also served as an implicit defense of Anglican ritual and court ceremony for, at the time it was issued, James was trying to bring the Scottish church into conformity with the Church of England.[10] In his proclamation James singled out for special rebuke those "Papists and Puritans" who opposed his policy and whose opposition was creating unrest in the countryside. Speaking of his travels through Lancashire, James wrote:

> We heard the general complaint of our people, that they were barred from all lawful recreations and exercise upon the Sunday's afternoon, after the ending of all divine service, which cannot but produce two evils: the one the hindering of the conversion of many, whom their priests will take occasion hereby to vex, persuading them that no honest mirth or recreation is lawful or tolerable in our religion, which cannot but breed a great discontentment in our people's hearts, especially of such as are peradventure upon the point of turning; the other inconvenience is, that this prohibition barreth the common and meaner sort of people from using such exercises as may make their bodies more able for war, when His Majesty or his successors shall have occasion to use them.[11]

Jonson's masque provided a justification of James's proclamation, arguing that "though [Virtue's] sports be soft, / her life is hard" (ll. 300–301). Here, too, recreation is a thing indifferent which, while it may be abused, may also be used to consolidate the authority of church and state. This point was forcefully dramatized by the masquers who, according to the report of the Venetian ambassador, wore the red robes and mitres of Anglican bishops. At a time when James's innovations in Scotland were accused of being "idolatrous," Jonson praises James's pleasures as a sign of labor and of virtue.[12]

This dual justification of pleasure is registered in a dual rhetoric: a Neoplatonic rhetoric of vision and a rhetoric of labor and *virtù*. On the one hand, the threatening indifference of pleasure is controlled by the oversight of royal virtue; on the other, pleasure is not only the "crowned reward" of "godlike travail" (ll. 90, 116) but is itself a kind of labor. Thus, in Mercury's speech, which echoes the passage just quoted from the "Declaration of Sports," pleasure itself becomes a kind of labor: "Since in [Virtue's] sight and by her charge all's done, / Pleasure the servant, Virtue looking on" (ll. 191–92). Just as the "common and meaner sort of people" will become more serviceable or useful to the king through sport, so here pleasure remains virtue's—that is, James's—servant. As Milton clearly saw, however, the justification of royal virtue and the royal policy regarding things indifferent by an appeal to right usage and "labor hard" (l. 91) is unstable: it introduces the indeterminacy and contingency of choice into the Neoplatonic allegory of virtue (l. 274), and so exposes the Neoplatonic rhetoric of vision as a verbal and interpretive effect.

In the beginning of the masque, Jonson implies that sight or vision is itself a form of action, thus reconciling the conflicting claims of action and inaction. After Hercules awakes, the choir sings:

> Wake, Hercules, awake: but heave up thy black eye
> 'Tis only asked from thee to look and those
>   [pygmies] will die,
>   Or fly.
>   Already they are fled,
> Whom scorn had else left dead.
>   (ll. 140–44; see also ll. 170, 191, 202)

Mercury drives the point home doubly in the next line: "*Rest* still, thou *active* friend of Virtue" (my emphasis). Rest is here a sign of activity, and this oxymoron is contained as well in "still," meaning "without motion" and "continually." Even when Daedalus's songs make it clear that vision does not produce meaning unless an activity of reading or interpretation intervenes (ll. 195–201), the threat of such activity is contained by presenting the labor of choice and interpretation as already having taken place in the past. Jonson thus builds into the representation of choice an invulnerability to risk or danger; legibility becomes a figure for the security of morality in the present. The quibble on figure in the following lines illustrates this nicely:

> Come on, come on; and where you go,
>   So interweave the curious knot,
> As ev'n th' observer scarce may know
>   Which lines are Pleasure's and which not.
> First, figure out the doubtful way
>   At which awhile all youth should stay,
> Where she and Virtue did contend
>   Which should have Hercules to friend.
>   (ll. 224–31)

"Figure out" is a command to the dancers to trace out or represent the scene of Hercules at the crossroads and only secondarily an injunction to reenact Hercules's choice—precisely because the choice is represented as already having occurred. At the same time, this displacement of the labor of choice makes the dancers' motions (the "lines" of line 227) legible, like lines of poetry, in the present:

> So let your dances be entwined,
>   Yet not perplex men unto gaze;
> But measured, and so numerous too,
>   As men may read each act you do.
>   (ll. 234–37)

Yet, as with the earlier demonstration that pleasure may be abused, so here the poet acknowledges that vision may be as well. Seeing may perplex, as well as inform, the gaze: it may not be possible to tell "which lines are Pleasure's and which not." Accordingly, the final lines of the song declare that vision is not enough: the beholder must also have the "power" to rise to the occasion. By the time we have reached the third song, choice and interpretation are located in the present rather than the past—"Go choose" Daedalus urges—and while "what is noble should be sweet," "wantonness" is still a possibility (ll. 282–83). This emphasis on power and choice looks forward to the last song of the masque, which comments on the earlier displacement of effort by reintegrating labor into the present. Although the argument of the masque up to this point has been that one need not choose between pleasure and virtue (they are reconciled in James's reign), in these final lines pleasure is forcefully placed in a subordinate position:

> But she [virtue] will have you know
>   That though
> Her sports be soft, her life is hard.
>   You must return unto the hill,
>   And there advance
> With labor, and inhabit still
>   That height and crown
> From whence you ever may look down
>   Upon triumphèd Chance.
>
> (ll. 299–307)

These concluding lines are far more ambivalent than the body of the masque regarding the possibility of reconciling pleasure and virtue. The emphasis instead is on labor and, to make matters worse, a labor that does not necessarily or usually find its reward on earth. "Place" is not a guarantee of merit; virtue must be its own reward. Once the necessity of effort is acknowledged in the present rather than narrated in the past tense, the ambiguities of *virtù* come to the fore. Thus, although these lines can be read as Jonson the stoic criticizing the facile virtue of some courtiers and reminding us that true virtue means sovereignty over oneself ("inhabit still / That height and crown"), they also articulate something like a Machiavellian sense of the relation of virtue to *virtù*: *virtù* is the faculty of innovation that allows one to respond to *fortuna*, ideally "to advance / With labor, and inhabit still," that is, to create "stillness" out of motion, stability out of instability, order out of disorder. But *virtù* can also take the form of assuming a virtue if one has it not. Here the labor of *virtù* may allow one to achieve a higher place in—thereby threatening the fixity of—the social and political order. In such a world, virtue is its own reward (l.298) or will find its reward in heaven precisely because on earth labor is not correlated in any direct way with moral results *or* intentions (cf. *Jonsonian Masque*, 184–85). The final lines of the song comment, "only she [virtue] can make you great, / Though place here make you known" (ll. 316–17). The ultimate threat in such a world is that virtue itself will be displaced to heaven, that, in the Neoplatonic rhetoric of vision, one can only "look down" on "triumphèd chance" from a position of exile or impotence.

The problem of justifying power as virtue in the Stuart masque might now be summarized as the problem of how to make inaction look like action (and vice versa), and how to make status look like (or even claim that it should involve) achievement without threatening the status quo. Yet, from our brief analysis of *Pleasure Reconcil'd to Virtue* and *Coelum Britannicum*, it appears that the rhetoric of virtue is inseparable from that of *virtù*, and that the latter may serve either to uphold or undermine royal authority. In Milton's masque the tension between status and activity is also manifest in two conflicting notions of virtue: virtue as innate and virtue as created in the activity of choice, deliberation, action, or works. As we will see, *Comus* rings its own changes on the relation of virtue to effects and of innovation to authority.

Comus

Just as *Pleasure Reconcil'd to Virtue* was produced shortly after James's "Declaration of Sports," so *Comus* followed on Charles I's reissue of the declaration in 1633. Unlike the "Papists and Puritans" who rejected the royal policy regarding sports altogether, Milton turns such policy on its head: as he would in *Areopagitica*, in *Comus* Milton appropriates the royal and ecclesiastical rhetoric of things indifferent in order both to expose the Machiavellism of the Anglican establishment and to anatomize and justify the *virtù* of the individual Christian and poet. My aim in the following pages is to enlist the masque as further evidence of Milton's pervasive Machiavellism.

We can begin to characterize the Machiavellism of *Comus* in a preliminary way by noting that the Attendant Spirit's description of Comus's genealogy (ll. 46ff.) recalls Ascham's warning against Italianate courtiers in *The Scholemaster*.[13] Comus is a virtuoso rhetorician (the Lady refers to his "dear Wit and gay Rhetoric," l. 790), just as he is the Machiavel or Vice conspiring to undermine the Lady's virtue. And Comus's own rhetoric suggests both the magical force and the fraud of rhetoric, alternating as it does between the cadences of Shakespeare's Puck and Ariel (e.g., ll. 94–144), and the deceptiveness of the courtly figure of Puttenham's *allegoria*:

> I under fair pretense of friendly ends
> And well-plac't words of glozing courtesy,
> Baited with reasons not unplausible,
> Wind me into the easy-hearted man,
> And hug him into snares. When once her eye
> Hath met the virtue of this Magic dust,
> I shall appear some harmless Villager
> Whom thrift keeps up about his Country gear.
>
> (ll. 160–67)

Like Archimago in book 1 of *The Faerie Queene*, who "well could file his tongue as smooth as glass" (*FQ*, 1.1.35, l.7), or Despaire whose alliterative style anticipates Comus's "well-plac't words" (*FQ*, 1.9.38–47), Comus's courtliness or courtesy is fraudulent ("glozing"). Comus thus combines the indirect power of fraud with the direct rhetorical force Milton associated with Shakespeare, who affects the reader in the same way Comus affects the Lady. Just as Comus makes the Lady "a statue" (l. 660), in "stony fetters fixt and motionless" (l. 819), so Milton had earlier described Shakespeare's power to "make us Marble with too much conceiving" ("On Shakespeare," Hughes, 64).

Comus's Machiavellism is also brought home by his association with "revelry" (l. 103). Like Jonson's Comus in *Pleasure Reconcil'd to Virtue*, Milton's Comus is a figure of court entertainment or sport (ll. 103, 128), and thus the embodiment of royal and ecclesiastical policy concerning things indifferent. Just as William Bradshaw saw indifference as the rhetorical cover for political Machiavellism, so Comus's Machiavellian rhetoric has obvious political connotations: like the bishops who, in Greville's words, bind "up the Peoples *Liberty*" "with the chaines [of] *Indifferency*," Comus has used "baits and guileful spells" (l. 537) to chain up unwary forest travelers.[14] In *Eikonoklastes* Milton would make Charles himself a Comus figure, one who uses "glozing words" and "deceavable Doctrines" to "captivate and make useless that natural freedom of will in all other men but himself," whereas his idolatrous subjects are described as "men inchanted with the *Circaean* cup of servitude."[15]

In its allusions both to Milton's predecessors and to royal and ecclesiastical policy, Comus's language directs us once again to the analogy between the right use of things indifferent and rhetorical activity. On the one hand, *Comus* dramatizes the problem of how to engage in "sports"—including masques—without seconding royal and ecclesiastical policy.[16] On the other, it points to the related problem of Milton's own poetic agency or virtuosity: how to make room for poetic innovation while still refuting the association of rhetorical power with demonic—or royal—force and fraud. Although part of the analytical task of the masque would seem to be to distinguish the chaste virtuosity of the Christian poet from the seductive *virtù* of the Machiavel, that generations of readers have referred to Milton's masque by the name of its Machiavellian protagonist suggests that the poet and the Machiavel may simply be two sides of the same indifferent coin. Comus is the obvious embodiment of *virtù* and rhetorical virtuosity in the masque; in his resemblance to the courtly Machiavel and his anticipation of Satan in *Paradise Lost*, Comus raises the question of whether all virtuosity is not in some way Machiavellian or demonic in a world ruled by God.

Both the occasion of *Comus* and the rhetoric of the Attendant Spirit's opening speech raise questions of right government, obedience, and authority, which are associated with the masques at court. *Comus* was performed for the Earl of Bridgewater in honor of his appointment as head of the Council of the Marches in Wales. The performance took place on Michaelmas, a liturgical holiday associated with the investiture of magistrates and governors.[17] Yet, although the Attendant Spirit in his opening speech equates virtue and *virtù* in the figure of Bridgewater—"A noble Peer of mickle trust and power," who is also "mindful of the Crown that Virtue gives"—once we descend to earth, the relation of virtue to *virtù* is no longer celebrated but rather open to question. The virtuous "fair offspring" of the Earl require the external aid and protection of the Spirit. From this point on, the focus of the masque appears to narrow considerably. We are no longer dealing with obvious questions of political sovereignty but, as with the end of *Pleasure Reconcil'd to Virtue*, with sovereignty over the self. Or rather, the question of political sovereignty is relocated to the self. Furthermore, compared to the initial celebration of magistracy, the problem is now analogous but reversed. The question is no longer how to present (and justify) the magistrate's power as virtuous but how to present individual virtue itself as a source of power.[18] That the Lady is eventually arrested by Comus's spell then emerges as the interpretive crux of the masque: is the Lady's stasis a form of action or inaction, willed obedience or the inability to will (to go forward)? Is the Lady tempted and, if not, has her virtue been tested? And if not, is it virtue? In Machiavellian terms, what is the relation of virtue to *virtù*, that is, what is the relation of virtue to power and to the skillful manipulation of the realm of indifference?

In posing such questions, *Comus* comments on and revises the Neoplatonic and Machiavellian rhetoric of the Stuart masque. As we will see, Milton criticizes a Neoplatonic rhetoric of vision, associated, according to some critics, not only with divine right but also with a Laudian emphasis on ritual and spectacle. But, in offering a puritan critique of such *visibilia*, Milton does not decisively reject justification by works.[19] He does not divorce ethics from effects—as would, for different reasons, a simple ethics of intention or a stereotypically Machiavellian emphasis on effects. Rather, *Comus* dramatizes the conflict between faith and works, between an antinomian emphasis on grace and an Arminian belief in human agency; and it does so by staging a conflict between what I will call the allegorical and rhetorical plots of the masque. If the allegorical plot, concerning the Lady's triumph over Comus, locates the *virtù* of virtue in divine grace, the rhetorical plot shows that for a genuine trial of virtue to take place there can be no simple correspondence between *virtù* and grace, means and ends, intention and effect. In recovering a sense of the contingency of human action, this plot restores *virtù* to the poet (and thus, indirectly, to the individual Christian), but at the price of admitting its indifference: its vulnerability and moral ambiguity. As in *Areopagitica*, here too rhetorical indifference gives rise to the dilemmas of Machiavellism that it is designed to control. The stereotypical Machiavellism of illegitimate force and fraud proves to be inextricable from Machiavellism conceived as the effort to join, without conflating, intention and effect, *virtù* and success. In the tension between the allegorical and rhetorical plots, Milton gives us an anatomy of the possible relationships of virtue to *virtù*, and dramatizes the conflict we saw in *Areopagitica* between absolute truth and "knowledge in the making" (Hughes, 743). As in *Areopagitica*, so in *Comus* rhetoric proves to be the locus of agency and of resistance to external authority, even the authority of Truth or God.[20]

The initial opposition of Comus and the Lady provides us with the lineaments of the allegorical plot. As we have seen, Comus is associated with sport, revelry, dazzling spells and rites—all of which suggest episcopacy and the royal interpretation of the doctrine of things indifferent. He also speaks of "the virtue of this Magic dust" that will deceive the Lady into thinking he is "some harmless Villager" (ll. 165–66), thereby reducing virtue to *virtù* or power in the fashion of the stereoytypical Machiavel. In contrast, the Lady appears as a figure of virtue, whose *virtù* is not her own but the result of divine intervention. In her very first speech, she summarizes the allegorical conflict of the masque:

> A thousand fantasies
> Begin to throng into my memory,
> Of calling shapes and beck'ning shadows dire,
> And airy tongues that syllable men's names
> On Sands and Shores and desert Wildernesses.
> These thoughts may startle well, but not astound
> The virtuous mind, that ever walks attended
> By a strong siding champion Conscience.——
> O welcome pure-ey'd Faith, white-handed Hope,

> Thou hov'ring Angel girt with golden wings,
> And thou unblemish't form of Chastity,
> I see ye visibly, and now believe
> That he, the Supreme good, t' whom all things ill
> Are but as slavish officers of vengeance,
> Would send a glist'ring Guardian, if need were,
> To keep my life and honor unassail'd.
>
> (ll. 205–20)

In the allegorical plot, evil is associated with the "thousand fantasies" that call to mind Comus's "dazzling Spells . . . / Of power to cheat the eye with blear illusion" (l. 155). In contrast to the *virtù* of the evil Machiavel, which yields powerful—if deceptive—effects, virtue is represented as a matter of intention, of faith and conscience, whose *virtù* is the result of divine aid. In the Lady's anticipation of her trial, the moral of the allegory is that the virtuous mind will be rewarded in times of trouble with the assistance of divine *virtù*. Yet, both the representation of this crisis later in the masque and the intervening dialogue register some discomfort with the allegorical plot.

The exchange between the Lady's two brothers provides a commentary on the allegorical plot, for the questions they debate are precisely those that the reader confronts: what kind of trial could the Lady, as an allegorical figure of virtue, possibly undergo, and what would such a trial reveal about the relationship of virtue to *virtù*? In the Second Brother's eyes, the ethic of intention that the Lady expresses leaves her entirely vulnerable to the dangers of the forest. In the eyes of the Elder Brother, the Lady is completely protected by her own innate virtue. In the first case, the exclusive focus on inner light means that experience is merely contingent and potentially harmful; in the second case, the emphasis on inner virtue means that there is no contingency of experience at all. This debate then receives its own ironic comment, as the Elder Brother is gradually forced to admit that the "virtuous mind" does need external aid in the form of divine protection. If we now retrace this exchange in detail, we will see that it prepares the reader to be skeptical not only of the brothers' theoretical approach to the meaning of virtue but also of the Lady's own abstract and theoretical virtue—a virtue that in the language of *Areopagitica* we might call "blank" (Hughes, 728).

In response to the Second Brother's fears for the Lady's safety, the Elder Brother first argues that there is no need to anticipate ("forestall") or seek out evil, especially if such anticipation is due to the illusions of the imagination:

> Peace brother, be not over-exquisite
> To cast the fashion of uncertain evils;
> For grant they be so, while they rest unknown,

> What need a man forestall his date of grief,
> And run to meet what he would most avoid?
> Or if they be but false alarms of Fear,
> How bitter is such self-delusion?

(ll. 359–65)

Yet, while the Elder Brother advises restraint, he also insists, like Spenser's Redcrosse, on the self-sufficiency of virtue:

> I do not think my sister so to seek,
> Or so unprincipl'd in virtue's book
> And the sweet peace that goodness bosoms ever,
> As that the single want of light and noise
> (Not being in danger, as I trust she is not)
> Could stir the constant mood of her calm thoughts,
> And put them into misbecoming plight.
> Virtue could see to do what virtue would
> By her own radiant light. . . .

(ll. 366–71; cf. *Faerie Queene*, 1.1.12, 9)

These arguments are two sides of the same coin: if virtue is innate and self-sufficient, there is no need to test or strengthen it in active confrontation with evil. But here, as in Eve's argument for tending the garden alone in *Paradise Lost* (*PL*, 9.322–41), the wording is strangely vexed. How self-sufficient is virtue if it must put off ("forestall") its "date of grief" or its recognition of self-delusion?

A similar question emerges with the Elder Brother's characterization of wisdom, which follows on the assertion of the self-sufficiency of virtue:

> And Wisdom's self
> Oft seeks to sweet retired Solitude,
> Where with her best nurse Contemplation
> She plumes her feathers, and lets grow her wings
> That in the various bustle of resort
> Were all to-ruffl'd, and somtimes impair'd.
> He that has light within his own clear breast
> May sit i'th' center, and enjoy bright day,
> But he that hides a dark soul and foul thoughts
> Benighted walks under the midday Sun;
> Himself is his own dungeon.

(ll. 375–84)

In the last five lines of this speech the Elder Brother equates Wisdom with the "inner light," the assurance of faith or the knowledge of one's right intention, rather than with the activity or trial of "knowledge in the making." In this equation, genuine trial or danger is forestalled—

both anticipated and precluded—since the external world is simply a reflection of one's ethical predisposition. Yet, the description of Wisdom as impervious to experience is undermined by the prior characterization of Wisdom as vulnerable to the challenges of the active life. Although the Elder Brother asserts that his sister is not "so to seek" (so at a loss) that she would be disturbed by her experience in the woods, Wisdom is described as "seek[ing] . . . sweet retired Solitude" (l. 375) in order to recover from "the various bustle of resort" (l. 379). The Elder Brother's rhetoric thus contradicts his assertion of the self-sufficiency of virtue by suggesting that the contemplative life is not a self-sufficient condition but rather a momentary withdrawal from the exertions of the active life.

The Second Brother seems to have anticipated the problems with equating Virtue and Wisdom with an ethic of intention or the inner light when, to the Elder Brother's argument that there is no real danger, he replies that there is no defense. As with Spenser's analysis of pride and despair in book 1 of *The Faerie Queene*, the two views dialectically imply each other; neither allows for the genuine interaction of virtue and experience. This eclipse of experience is represented here by the Second Brother's use of the concept of opportunity:

> You may as well spread out the unsunn'd heaps
> Of Miser's treasure by an outlaw's den,
> And tell me it is safe, as bid me hope
> Danger will wink on Opportunity,
> And let a single helpless maiden pass
> Uninjured in this wild surrounding waste.
>
> (ll. 398–403)

In these lines opportunity is not equivalent to the rhetorical notion of occasion as that which can be used well or badly, but is instead described simply as an occasion for danger. The rhetorical effect is a kind of inversion or parody of Machiavelli's description of fortune as a woman who may be mastered by the prince's *virtù*: in the shifting analogy between the miser's treasure, opportunity, and "a single helpless maiden," the Machiavellian prince is reduced to a virgin who is certain to be raped by occasion.

In response to this concern, the Elder Brother gives us a slightly revised account of the relationship of virtue to *virtù*. While agreeing with the younger brother that the Lady may rely on the "strength of Heav'n" (l. 417), he also gives her a power of her own. In words that echo the Lady's first speech about her imperviousness to the "airy tongues that syllable men's names / On Sands and Shores and desert Wildernesses," he remarks:

> 'Tis chastity, my brother, chastity;
> She that has that, is clad in complete steel,
> And like a quiver'd Nymph with Arrows keen
> May trace huge Forests and unharbor'd Heaths,
> Infamous Hills and sandy perilous wilds.

And he goes on to compare the power of chastity to the Gorgon:

> What was that snaky-headed *Gorgon* shield
> That wise *Minerva* wore, unconquer'd Virgin,
> Wherewith she freez'd her foes to congeal'd stone,
> But rigid looks of Chaste austerity
> And noble grace that dash't brute violence
> With sudden adoration and blank awe?
>
> (ll. 420–24, 447–52)

This speech concerning the tremendous power of chastity then receives an ironic comment in the Elder Brother's offer to use his sword to defend his sister—something that would not be necessary if she were really capable of freezing her foes to stone—and in the Spirit's rebuff that something of more "divine effect" (l. 630) is needed. It also ironically anticipates the very next scene, in which the Lady appears "chain'd up in Alabaster" by Comus's spell. What the Elder Brother's speech suggests is that chastity's most powerful Gorgon effect may be to freeze the Lady herself into a position of vulnerability rather than strength.[21]

The culmination of the allegorical plot, in which Virtue is rescued by divine *virtù*, is also a turning point in which divine intervention is revealed to be disturbingly like the "force . . . and wile" of Comus. To begin with, in rebuffing the Elder Brother, the Spirit proposes remedies that recall Comus's "virtue of some Magic dust":

> Care and utmost shifts
> How to secure the Lady from surprisal,
> Brought to my mind a certain Shepherd Lad
> Of small regard to see to, yet well skill'd
> In every virtuous plant and healing herb.
>
> (ll. 617–21)

Like Comus, the Spirit resorts to "shifts" and "virtuous" plants to work his magic. Furthermore, in asking Sabrina to save the Lady from her Machiavellian opponent, the Spirit calls attention to the similarities between divine grace and Machiavellian force:

> Goddess dear
> We implore thy powerful hand
> To undo the charmed band

Of true Virgin here distrest,
Through the force and through the wile
Of unblest enchanter vile.

(ll. 902–907)

As in the passages from Dell, Saltmarsh, and others, which were examined in chapter 5, here, too, force can be a sign of faith or of fraud: it may
take the form of Sabrina's "powerful hand" or Comus's force and wile.
The indifference of force is only further accentuated by the Spirit's speaking in the same cadences and with the same Shakespearean rhetoric as
Comus. The question this passage raises is, what are we to make of this
indifference of rhetoric and force?

This passage is exemplary because it dramatizes the conflict between
the allegorical and rhetorical plots of the masque. The culmination of the
allegorical plot is also the moment of greatest resistance to it, since the
indifference of rhetoric and force points to the similarity between
Comus's spells and the action of grace. This similarity can be interpreted
in one of two ways. On the one hand, the rhetoric of power suggests that,
like Comus's spells, grace may be coercive and preclude the genuine exercise of virtue. In this construction, while Milton allegorizes divine intervention, he also resists the explicit moral of the masque by calling attention to the coerciveness of grace. On the other hand, that Sabrina and
Comus are both creatures of *virtù* and speak the same iambic quadrime-
ter verse directs our attention to the rhetorical plot of the masque, in
which the same means and same rhetoric can be used to different ends
and different effects. In doing so, it helps us recapture a sense of Christian
liberty as active rather than passive, and of a *virtù* that is the expression
of individual virtue.

The conclusion of the masque dramatizes a similar conflict between the
allegorical and rhetorical plots, and between the force of grace and the
force of individual virtue:

Mortals that would follow me,
Love virtue, she alone is free,
She can teach ye how to climb
Higher than the Sphery chime;
Or if Virtue feeble were,
Heav'n itself would stoop to her.

(ll. 1019–24)

These lines present the Lady's and the Elder Brother's conviction that the
virtuous mind is self-sufficient, and that when virtue is feeble, she will be
aided by divine grace. As we have seen, these two views are dialectically
related: the Lady's absolute belief in her virtuous mind leads to her abso-

lute dependence on divine intervention: internal strength is simply supplanted by external strength. While this reliance on divine grace is theologically sound from one perspective, from another it concedes too much. It denies the Lady the *acquisition* of virtue, as well as its active exercise. It is for this reason, I suggest, that the concluding lines are phrased in the subjunctive: although Sabrina has freed the Lady, the poet's language preserves our sense that the relationship of *virtù* to virtue and Christian liberty is still unresolved or is itself conditional.

It is the conditional nature of this connection between virtue and *virtù* that informs what I have called the rhetorical plot of *Comus*. In this plot the deus ex machina intervention of Sabrina is precisely what the poet wants to avoid. Here a different relation between virtue and *virtù* is proposed: rather than assuming the freedom of virtue from moral danger or securing virtue by external power, virtue is exemplified in the appropriation of that power for one's own use. Thus, if we return to the opening of the masque, we can see that, although *Comus* begins with an image of the heavenly sphere, we quickly find ourselves in a Spenserian wood of Error, a world in which there is no simple ascent by analogical reasoning to a Neoplatonic realm of forms or to heaven, no necessary descent of grace, and no necessary correspondence between aesthetic appearance or literary allusion and ethical import. In each case, the guaranteed correspondence of virtue and success would amount to an eclipse of individual agency, including that of the poet. To this forcible equation of virtue and effects, Milton opposes an uncertain equation, one that preserves the possibility of effective action in time. Like *Areopagitica*, *Comus* dramatizes the doctrine of things indifferent in its rhetoric and, in doing so, stages a counterplot to its own explicit moral. Whereas in the latter, virtue is weak unless aided by grace, in the former the emphasis is on works, specifically the work of reading. Poetic virtuosity thus becomes a trope for political and religious *virtù*.

The Attendant Spirit's description of "perplex't paths of this drear Wood" initially suggests the Wood of Error in *The Faerie Queene*. Yet, when the Lady first appears she reads the woods (like Una and Redcrosse) in two contradictory ways. They seem both "kind, hospitable" and threatening and "thievish."[22] Thus from the outset, there is no obvious, legible correspondence between appearances and ethics. Virtue is not simply a matter of vision but of right judgment, here represented by the sense of hearing; the Lady's first words are "This way the noise was, if mine ear be true, / My best guide now" (ll. 170–71).[23] Yet, the Lady's conviction that the virtuous mind is unassailable creates a dilemma. If the woods cannot be misread or misused, then there is no possibility of error or seduction; but neither is it possible to tell the story of redemption. If this story is to be told, not only must the woods' appearance be subject to interpretation, it must be possible to err. Like the Elder Brother, the Lady compromises by asserting both that the woods are the occasion of startling "fantasies" and that virtue can be seen in the present as though it were an allegorical emblem ("And thou unblemish't form of Chastity / I see thee visibly"). However, her subsequent lines once again provide an ironic comment on this rhetoric of vision:

> Was I deceiv'd, or did a sable cloud
> Turn forth her silver lining on the night?
> I did not err, there does a sable cloud
> Turn forth her silver lining on the night,
> And casts a gleam over this tufted Grove.
>
> (ll. 221–24)

The internal echo of these lines is dramatized and, possibly, ironized in the Song to Echo that immediately follows, for it is hard to imagine how one could receive a genuine response from Echo. The Lady inquires of "Sweet Echo, sweetest Nymph that liv'st unseen":

> Canst thou not tell me of a gentle Pair
> That likest thy *Narcissus* are?
> O if thou have
> Hid them in some flow'ry Cave,
> Tell me where,
> Sweet Queen of Parley, Daughter of the Sphere.
>
> (ll. 236–41)

It may be that the reference to Echo's Narcissus is intended as a further gloss on the Lady's speech, as though to comment on the barren narcissism of a virtue that can never be astounded, that cannot in principle err. From this ironic perspective, her "I did not err" articulates a different view of virtue: it shows that virtue must be achieved in time and that only a specific encounter with temptation can be narrated in the past tense.[24] The state of "having chosen" must be continually earned. The fact that the woods can be read in two ways and that deception is always possible ("Was I deceived . . .?" [l. 220]) then determines the figurative logic of the masque. *Comus* is not structured by simple dichotomies, according to which Comus is Shakespeare, song, rhetoric, and magic, the Lady Spenser, reason, and logic. The aim is not to cast out fantasies, rhetoric, or Shakespeare but to appropriate and use them correctly.

This point is dramatized in the appearance of the same disguises and rhetorical powers on both sides of the debate. Thus to Comus's disguise we can counterpoint the Attendant Spirit's, and to Comus's association with Bacchus we can oppose the Spirit's with Orpheus. (As Fletcher has noted, the name of the Attendant Spirit, "Thyrsis," is also the name of

Bacchus's staff.) Comus's song is answered by Sabrina's, as are his implied powers of transformation. He changes himself into a shepherd and his captives into beasts, and Sabrina is described as having undergone "a quick immortal change" into "Goddess of the River" (ll. 841–42). Finally, the Lady, who rejects Comus's rhetoric and fantasy for the inviolability of the virtuous mind, is depicted as a powerful rhetorician almost in spite of herself. Her first song has a ravishing effect on both Comus and the Attendant Spirit (ll. 245–70, 555–67), both of whom describe it in language that suggests *A Midsummer Night's Dream*. And, although the Lady's initial rejection of Comus's flattering response—"ill is lost that praise / That is addrest to unattending Ears; / Not any boast of skill, but extreme shift / How to regain my sever'd company, / Compell'd me to awake the courteous Echo" (ll. 271–75)—suggests that she is unwilling to recognize the power of her own rhetoric, in her final exchange with Comus she demonstrates her understanding that there is a right use of rhetoric, in particular of epideictic.

Like the dialogue between the two brothers, the debate between Comus and the Lady provides a metacommentary on the masque. As we have seen, the genre of the masque was intrinsically bound up with praise of the sovereign or of the noble family that had commissioned it. This epideictic task in turn generated a series of anxieties and dilemmas: the poet must subordinate the aesthetic display of the masque to the ethical end of representing and teaching virtue. To this point in the masque, Comus has been the figure most prominently associated both with rhetorical display and with the courtly milieu of the masque, whereas the Lady has symbolized a rejection of masquing and revelry. In this final exchange, however, the Lady explicitly appropriates the power of rhetoric as her own. Comus begins the debate by introducing the question of the use of nature's gifts:

> Why should you be so cruel to yourself,
> And to those dainty limbs which nature lent
> For gentle usage and soft delicacy?
> But you invert the cov'nants of her trust,
> And harshly deal like an ill borrower
> With that you receiv'd on other terms,
> Scorning the unexempt condition
> By which all mortal frailty must subsist,
> Refreshment after toil, ease after pain,
> That have been tir'd all day without repast,
> And timely rest have wanted; but, fair Virgin,
> This will restore all soon.
>
> (ll. 679–90)

For Comus, the Lady's chaste refusal of "all the pleasures / That fancy can beget on youthful thoughts" (ll. 668–69) amounts to ingratitude, a refusal of the obligation of praise: "If all the world / Should in a pet of temperance feed on Pulse, / Drink the clear stream, and nothing wear but Frieze, / Th' all-giver would be unthank't, would be unprais'd" (ll. 720–23). In a rhetoric that looks forward to the serpent's in *Paradise Lost*, Comus urges both the self-display that is characteristic of epideictic discourse—"beauty is nature's brag, and must be shown / In courts, at feasts, and high solemnities / Where most may wonder at the workmanship" (ll. 745–47)—and the "mutual and partak'n bliss" associated with the *carpe diem* poem (l. 741). At the same time, Comus's language—which echoes that of Despaire in *The Faerie Queene* (1.9.38–47)—alerts the reader to the deadly narcissism of his own vision of epideictic rhetoric. In response, the Lady redefines the problem as one not simply of use but of right use:

> I hate when vice can bolt her arguments,
> And virtue has no tongue to check her pride:
> Impostor, do not charge most innocent nature,
> As if she would her children should be riotous
> With her abundance; she, good cateress,
> Means her provision only to the good
> That live according to her sober laws
> And holy dictate of spare Temperance.
>
> (ll. 760–67)

Only when nature's blessings are evenly dispensed is the giver "better thank't, / His praise due paid" (ll. 775–76). In this speech, the Lady redefines nature as a realm of things indifferent. At the same time she shows that epideictic rhetoric is also a thing indifferent, a means that need not be identified with the self-aggrandizing ends of Comus or of the court. In contrast to her first speech, in which she imagined virtue being rescued by the intervention of divine *virtù*, here the Lady exercises her virtue by defending it and thus recovers what Comus calls "a superior power" (l. 801). It is significant in this context that, although the Lady imagines drawing on a "sacred vehemence" to counter Comus's "dear Wit and gay Rhetoric" (ll. 790, 795), the invocation of divine aid remains a mere possibility:

> Thou art not fit to hear thyself convinc't;
> Yet should I try, the uncontrolled worth
> Of this pure cause would kindle my rapt spirits
> To such a flame of sacred vehemence,
> That dumb things would be mov'd to sympathize,

And the brute Earth would lend her nerves, and shake,
Till all thy magic structures rear'd so high,
Were shattered into heaps o'er thy false head.

(ll. 792–99)

What is striking about the Lady's lines is that sacred vehemence—which alludes to the advent of the Spirit at Pentecost (the "sonus tanquam advenientis spiritus vehementis" of Acts 2:2)—is not employed but simply imagined.[25] The conditional "Yet should I try" functions in much the same way as the Attendant Spirit's concluding "Or if Virtue feeble were": in both cases the intervention of superhuman power and the consequent eclipse of human agency are delayed by the conditional or subjunctive phrasing.[26]

While the next scene allegorizes divine intervention in the figure of Sabrina, it also preserves human agency on the level of its rhetoric. Here, as in the exchange between Comus and the Lady, rhetoric is a thing indifferent that can be used well or badly. Thus Sabrina speaks the language of Puck and Ariel earlier associated with Comus, and the Spirit's final vision of nature's bounty appropriates and revises Comus's *carpe diem* through its allusion to Spenser's erotically charged Garden of Adonis (*FQ*, 3.6.44–52).[27] If we now read the epilogue in terms of the second rhetorical plot of the masque we can also see that right use (of Spenser and Shakespeare, of eros) is connected not simply with intention but also with effects. Fixity and innovation, intention and action, are united rather than being ascetically divorced. As William Kerrigan has remarked, the epilogue "tries to achieve what the children and their spiritual guardians could not: the capture of the magician in the navel of the woods and the appropriation of his power. Imagination finds what vigilance lost" (61).[28] It is this emphasis on use as the appropriation of power that destabilizes virtue and makes of it an activity that is concerned with effects as well as intentions. In the poet's rhetoric, the pleasures of the imagination and of epideictic poetry are reconciled not only to virtue but also to *virtù*.

Milton could thus be said to rewrite the conclusions of *Pleasure Reconcil'd to Virtue* and *Coelum Britannicum*. If, in the former, Jonson registers doubts about the reconciliation of virtue and pleasure on earth, he also proposes the stoic consolation that virtue can take pleasure in itself. If efficacious action is not possible and heavenly aid is not forthcoming, at least the man of virtue can look down on earth and scorn those who claim "place" as the sign of their virtue and their reward. In *Coelum Britannicum*, place and merit, status and activity, are reconciled on earth in the examples of Charles and Henrietta-Maria, who then become a pattern for the reformation of heaven. In Milton's masque, the Spirit's initial equation of virtue and *virtù*, stasis and action, is part of the Neoplatonic allegory of the masque, according to which the Lady is the embodiment of virtue, which can be "assailed but never hurt." Such virtue would from the outset be free from moral danger, secure in the knowledge of "having chosen" the right path.[29] However, Milton does not simply represent but also analyzes the moral implications of the past participle "having chosen": he criticizes the rhetoric of the Stuart masque by insisting on the temporal dimension—the Machiavellian contingency—of this drama of the will, a drama that is incompatible with the belief that one has already chosen, once and for all. To this end, Milton ironizes the conflict between activity and passivity that we saw in the masques of Jonson and Carew: in fixing the Lady to Comus's chair, he literalizes the stasis of allegorical virtue in order to suggest that the Lady's and Elder Brother's sense of freedom from moral danger is the real threat, whereas the "force and . . . wile" (l. 906) of Comus's virtuosity, demonic flexibility, and aesthetic play are a potential source of strength. Thus, while the Lady's fixity serves as an ironic comment on the claims of "place" or "status" as a guarantee of virtue, the possibility of efficacious action is not only preserved by the conditional tense of the concluding lines but exemplified in the rhetoric of the masque as a whole. While the masque allegorizes divine intervention the rhetoric defers it, in order to make room for the poet's own virtuoso performance. To the Lady's power of passive resistance the poet opposes his own active appropriation and use of Comus's power. In contrast to Jonson, who presents the doctrine of things indifferent as an argument not only for the subservience of pleasure to virtue but also for the obedience of subject to king, indifference here becomes the locus of resistance to external authority. And this includes the resistance of the individual Christian not only to royal and ecclesiastical policy but also the resistance to—or in the language of the Nativity Ode, the "prevention" of—divine intervention.

The question the masque poses but does not answer is what is the relationship between this resistance and the usual modes of legitimating such resistance by reference to positive principles of authority: God, right reason, or natural law? What is the relation of *virtù* and rhetorical virtuosity to providence? According to Milton's rhetoric of indifference, this question has no single answer, and it is precisely in this indifference that the threat of Machiavellism resides. Once the criterion of right use becomes a matter of individual conscience and discretion—of individual *virtù*—it may be impossible to tell the difference between Comus and Sabrina, between a satanic and divine rhetorical power.

EIGHT

MACHIAVELLIAN RHETORIC IN *PARADISE LOST*

> Such an one was that *Macchiavile*, who perswaded men to
> governe in this world, partly by fraud, partly by force, and
> partly by fortune: and not by the divine providence, whereat
> hee jested immitating therein, not only *Julian* and those pro-
> phane heathens which said of the Israelites, *Where is now*
> *theyr God* (making mocke of theyr religion) but also (and that
> effectually) that cankered Serpent, which hearing that God had
> forbidden *Adam* and *Heva* the Tree of Knowledge of good and
> evil, scoffed at Gods word, and saide: *Tush, it is nothing so:*
> *yee shall not die, but ye shall be as Gods.*
> —*John Carpenter,* A Preparative to Contention

BETTER than any other single figure, Satan in *Paradise Lost* exemplifies the intersection of rhetoric, theology, the Machiavel, and
the republican that we have been exploring in this book.[1] Perhaps
the most famous nondramatic Machiavel of the Renaissance, Satan is a
skillful orator and casuist, who uses rhetorical force and fraud to wheedle
and coerce his fellow fallen angels. Not surprisingly, the topics of Machiavellism—the relation of *virtù* or virtue to success, means to ends, persuasion to coercion, force to consent—appear regularly in his speeches. What
is surprising, or truly diabolical, however, is the way Satan attributes the
stereotypically Machiavellian understanding of these topics to God.
While in his use of force and fraud and his pretensions to absolute rule
Satan resembles the Machiavellian Charles I, his republican rhetoric suggests that God is as coercive and manipulative as the Stuart monarch. In
a kind of ironic comment on the mutual appropriation of each other's
arguments by royalists and parliamentarians, Satan speaks the language
of republicanism in order to cast God as the Machiavel.[2]

Milton's decision to have Satan the Machiavel occasionally speak as a
republican has given rise to a number of interpretations. For some readers, Satan represents not only Charles I but also Milton's disillusionment
with Cromwell, the hypocritical puritan. Satan may also reflect Milton's
own doubts concerning the revolutionary cause or the adequacy of a secular language of politics.[3] For other readers, Satan's obvious misuse of
republican language, along with his own tyrannical behavior, shows that
the language of earthly politics is inapplicable to heaven and vice versa.
Satan is wrong to expect heaven to be a republic; rather, heaven is the

only legitimate absolute monarchy, and kings act hubristically when they style themselves as God.[4] Still other critics argue, conversely, that the human language of absolutism is inapplicable to divine rule, which proves on examination to be a meritocracy based on virtue rather than force.[5] Here it turns out that an analogy can be drawn between divine and human rule, precisely the one Satan refuses to recognize.

In the following pages I suggest a different approach to the issue of Satan's republican rhetoric. Rather than seeing the conjoining of the Machiavel and the republican as evidence of Milton's disillusionment with the revolutionary cause, I believe Satan is one of Milton's best arguments for its validity. Just as Machiavelli argues for building a republic on the assumption of human corruption and for a rhetorical politics that integrates the resources of force and fraud into the arsenal of persuasion, so Milton begins *Paradise Lost* with Satan in order to show that rhetorical and political indeterminacy, which his contemporaries stigmatized as Machiavellian, is also the condition of free will. As Mary Ann Radzinowicz has argued, "Satan's rebellion is political as well as spiritual, no mere subplot but part of a repeated pattern, a design in which failure itself enforces the doctrine of free choice."[6] Satan does not speak as a republican simply to illustrate that the language of republicanism—of virtue, debate, consensus, and dissent—can be appropriated for evil purposes, but also to show that it must be capable of being so appropriated for virtue to be meaningful. Furthermore, Christian virtue here is not the simple opposite of Machiavellian *virtù*, but rather structurally analogous to it in that both aim to articulate, without equating, intention and effect, virtu(e) and success. And, just as the force and misrepresentation of the stereotypical Machiavel are part of the rhetorical politics of the mature Machiavellian, so too Milton aims to make the resources of the Machiavel part of his own politics, as well as of his Machiavellian justification of the ways of God to men. What Satan stigmatizes, in the language of the Machiavel, as force and fraud, turns out to be the condition of virtue and knowledge in the making. In the following pages I analyze Milton's exploration of the indifferent resources of the Machiavel, by looking briefly at Satan's rhetoric in Books 1 and 2 of *Paradise Lost*, and then in greater detail at his encounter with Sin and Death, and his rhetoric in prelapsarian Eden.

Satan's Rhetoric in Books 1 and 2

Satan's rhetoric consistently asks us to rethink the relationship between the stereotypical *virtù*—or force and fraud—of the Machiavel, republican *virtù*, and Christian virtue. Although Satan the Machiavel initially seems the opposite of the republican and the puritan saint, who share a concern with virtuous—in the sense of ethically responsible as well as effective—political action, it gradually emerges that force and fraud are not only an instrument but also a condition of republican and Christian virtue. Here we begin to see how the Machiavel and the republican are not simply mutually exclusive for Milton—not only because the republican will on occasion use the Machiavellian tools of force and fraud but also because the Machiavel and republican are two possibilities of the rhetorical politics that Milton and Machiavelli share to different degrees.

In Satan's account, God is a Machiavel who fraudulently concealed his power in order to trick the angels into rebelling; once they did, he revealed himself as the de facto ruler by virtue of his greater power (1.91–124). Although Satan acknowledges God as the de facto "Conqueror (whom I now / Of force believe Almighty . . .)" (1.143–44) and hopes to use similar "force or guile" to wage war against God in return, he also rejects—when it serves his purposes—the argument for the legitimacy of de facto power: "That Glory never shall his wrath or might / Extort from me" (1.110–11). In rationalizing his defeat, Satan contrasts God's rule by coercion and fraud to his own leadership and the "united force" of the devils, which are the result of "free choice," "merit," and "consent" (2.19–24, 388). Here Satan rehearses the republican interpretation of the Machiavellian topics of force and consent, virtue and success, opposing the de facto arguments for the Engagement as well as for absolute, monarchical power. In this account, the force and fraud of the stereotypical Machiavel are antithetical to republican virtue, and this antithesis is only confirmed when we recognize that it is not God but Satan who is the hypocritical Machiavel, using republican rhetoric merely to advance his own tyrannical ends.

Yet, if Satan appears to suggest the incompatibility of Machiavellian *virtù* and republican virtue, a more complicated picture soon begins to emerge from his overdetermined rhetoric. Like Machiavelli, Milton plays with classical and Christian meanings of virtu(e), not in order to separate them completely but rather to explore the various possible relations between them. For example, when Satan refers to the fallen angels' "wearied virtue" (1.320), he implies that *virtù* is not equivalent to success; if it were, he would be God and the fallen angels his followers in heaven. Yet, he also suggests that the fallen angels are physically weary (wearied *virtù*) because they are ethically weak (wearied virtue). He thus implies in spite of himself that ethical virtue is the basis of God's power, that, in God's case at least, virtue does guarantee success.

In a later passage, the narrator plays with the meanings of "virtue" in order to explore the relation between *creaturely* virtue and *virtù*; he describes the fallen angels who bend toward Satan,

> With awful reverence prone; and as a God
> Extol him equal to the highest in Heav'n:
> Nor fail'd they to express how much they prais'd,
> That for the general safety he despis'd
> His own: for neither do the Spirits damn'd
> Lose all thir virtue; lest bad men should boast
> Thir specious deeds on earth, which glory excites,
> Or close ambition varnisht o'er with zeal.
>
> (2.478–85)

Here, too, the meaning of "virtue" is overdetermined, hovering between *virtù* and Christian virtue. At first glance, the meaning seems clear: the fallen angels praise Satan's heroic valor or *virtù*, not his Christian virtue. Yet, the next lines can be construed in at least two ways. The first is that, precisely because even the fallen angels demonstrate *virtù* in deeds excited by glory or ambition, no creature on earth is able to boast of similar deeds: all such claims to agency are diabolical and thus merely "specious"; the specious deeds of *virtù* are no sign of Christian virtue.[7] Here we already begin to see how *virtù* might not be simply the opposite of ethical virtue: for if human action is "specious" and Christian virtue takes the form of faith alone, then *virtù* comes to stand for the supposed achievement of deeds with ethical consequences.

This brings us to the second possible interpretation of the passage, according to which Milton wishes to preserve rather than deny the element of *virtù* in Christian virtue. For, as I have already suggested in the previous chapter, Milton rejects the Lutheran argument against freedom of the will and the possibility of working toward salvation. In this light, the devils' actions are not specious; their responsibility for their deeds is precisely what allows them to be "damn'd." (Perhaps here we might even understand the opposition between the fallen angels and "bad men" to suggest that whereas the devils preserve some "virtue," "bad men" are those who pretend to deeds that are not their own.) Accordingly, when the devils complain later in book 2 that their "free virtue" is enthralled "to Force or Chance" (2.551), we understand that they have freely chosen to enthrall themselves. Similarly, when Satan declares the inefficacy of divine force—"That Glory never shall his wrath or might / Extort from me"—he takes responsibility for his own actions and thus justifies God's behavior and his own damnation: God will not extort praise, not because he is incapable of exercising such power but because true praise—like virtue—cannot be coerced. "Spirits damn'd" are still possessed of "virtue," in the sense of the free will to alter their own condition. Thus, if there is no necessary connection between Christian virtue and *virtù*, neither are they simply opposed.

Abdiel's response to Satan in book 6 similarly complicates the relationship of virtue to *virtù*:

> O Heav'n! that such resemblance of the Highest
> Should yet remain, where faith and realty
> Remain not; wherefore should not strength and might
> There fail where Virtue fails, or weakest prove
> Where boldest; though to sight unconquerable?
> His puissance, trusting in th' Almighty's aid,
> I mean to try, whose Reason I have tri'd
> Unsound and false; nor is it aught but just,
> That he who in debate of Truth hath won,
> Should win in Arms, in both disputes alike
> Victor; though brutish that contest and foul
> When Reason hath to deal with force, yet so
> Most reason is that Reason overcome.
>
> (6.114–26)

Here Abdiel notes Satan's fraudulent likeness to God, as well as Satan's "puissance . . . to sight unconquerable," at the same time that he expresses the faith that virtue and success, virtue and *virtù*, will correspond. He thus calls attention to the existence of force and fraud, and the necessity of angelic force to combat Satan's troops, even as he asserts that God's power is on the side of the angels. Abdiel tries to negotiate, as Milton does in *Areopagitica*, between the exercise of virtue in the realm of appearances and of things indifferent, and the conviction that "Truth is strong . . . [and] needs no policies" (Hughes, 747). And, as Milton does in *Areopagitica*, he suggests that the likeness of Truth and Error, of Satanic *virtù* and Christian *virtù*, as well as the lack of necessary correspondence between virtue and success, intention and effect, are an inevitable aspects of action in the realm of appearances. Yet, Abdiel also implies by his syntax that the indifference of *virtù* is divinely ordained: "His puissance, trusting in th' Almighty's aid / I mean to try" locates the origin of satanic as well as angelic power in God. He thus makes the realm of things indifferent a gift of God, in which virtue may be achieved only because it may also fail.

Milton similarly complicates the relationship between the stereotypically Machiavellian *virtù* of force and fraud and Christian virtue in Satan's description of God in his final address to the fallen angels in book 1. Here Satan unwittingly shows that what is stereotypically Machiavellian from one perspective is Christian from another:

O Myriads of immortal Spirits, O Powers
Matchless, but with th' Almighty, and that strife
Was not inglorious, though th' event was dire,
As this place testifies, and this dire change
Hateful to utter: but what power of mind
Foreseeing or presaging, from the Depth
Of knowledge past or present, could have fear'd
How such united force of Gods, how such
As stood like these, could ever know repulse?
For who can yet believe, though after loss,
That all these puissant Legions, whose exíle
Hath emptied Heav'n, shall fail to re-ascend
Self-rais'd, and repossess thir native seat?

(1.622–34)

Here Satan rehearses his earlier description of God's fraudulent concealment of his superior power, but with a difference. Once again he claims
that the cause of defeat was insufficient knowledge; but he also reveals
that even absolute knowledge would have been insufficient in the circumstances: "what power of mind / Foreseeing or presaging, from the Depth
/ Of knowledge past or present" could have anticipated Satan's defeat?
The following line—"For who can yet believe, though after loss"—reads,
at first glance, as a gloss on those that precede it, as though to suggest that
even the actual experience of the fall can't make the fall believable to
Satan. Yet, in shifting from knowledge to belief, Satan implicitly acknowledges that what is insufficient knowledge from one perspective is
the occasion of faith from another; that what the Machiavel and his critics would call fraud—the intentional discrepancy between appearance
and reality or, in the case of God, between free will and foreknowledge—
is the condition of human action. As Satan admits, it is precisely because
experience does not provide conclusive evidence, that he can believe in,
and act on, his ability to "re-ascend."

As this brief discussion of Satan's rhetoric suggests, the *virtù* of the
Machiavel is not simply opposed to republican or Christian virtue.
Rather, *virtù* is a thing indifferent, whose force, fraud, and concern with
effective human action are both instruments and conditions of Christian
virtue. If we now turn to Satan's encounter with Sin and Death in book 2
of *Paradise Lost*, we can analyze more closely how Milton exploits the
indifference of rhetorical figures to anatomize human agency and justify
the ways of God to men. Here, too, the Machiavel and the republican
prove to be related.

The Allegory of Sin and Death

Like *Comus*, Satan's encounter with Sin and Death allegorizes Milton's own fears regarding the stereotypical Machiavellism of rhetorical virtuosity, his fears that poetic power might be allied to the forces of rebellion rather than true revolution. At the same time, in its rhetorical form and its biblical allusions, the episode aims to justify Milton's poem by illustrating that the resources of the Machiavel may also be appropriated by the Machiavellian republican: "for neither do the Spirits damn'd / Lose all thir virtue" (2.482–83). The episode not only invites us to think about the Machiavellian topics of force and consent, means and ends, but also illustrates the inseparability of Milton's rhetoric of indifference from his defense of Christian liberty. The stereotypically Machiavellian indeterminacy of rhetorical figures here becomes a justification of free will. In dramatizing that the force and fraud of allegory, and the indeterminacy of rhetoric, are conditions of republican *virtù*, Milton turns the culture's fear of Machiavellian rhetoric on its head and makes the fallen Machiavel the best argument for a republic of saints. As with the other texts analyzed in this book, the rhetorical form of this episode needs to be taken seriously if we are to understand Milton's Machiavellism.[8] In the following pages I focus first on the allegory of Sin and Death and then on the critical reception of the episode as an example of Miltonic sublimity. As we will see, Milton's allegory criticizes allegory from within, at the same time that his sublime defense of agency dramatizes the Machiavellian underside of sublimity.

In considering how the allegory of Sin and Death helps us meditate on the Machiavellian dilemmas of action in the realm of indifference, it may be useful to recall both Angus Fletcher's remarks about the daemonic Machiavellism of allegorical agency and George Puttenham's about the Machiavellism of allegory. Together, their comments begin to suggest why Satan the Machiavel tends toward allegory, and why allegory should be a particularly powerful rhetorical device for meditating on the paradoxes of agency, both Machiavellian and Christian.

Fletcher uses the term *daemonic* in a morally neutral sense, to describe a world in which "supernatural energies and consuming appetites are the sole means to existence." And he draws an explicit parallel between the daemonic agent and the stereotypical Machiavel: "Like a Machiavellian prince, the allegorical hero can act free of the usual moral restraints, even when he is acting morally, since he is moral only in the interests of his power over other men."[9] Yet, while free from moral restraints, the allegorical agent seems not only possessed *of* an intellectual or physical *virtus*

(41), but also possessed *by* external force, driven by an "appetite of dominion" (52). He thus combines the appearance of "unrestrained will" with "a maximum of restraint" (68–69). Allegorical fixity is simply the other side of daemonic agency. Satan the Machiavel is such a daemonic hero: in assuming a radically contingent universe, one governed by *fortuna* and susceptible to the machinations of his own unrestrained will, he makes himself into a "fixed mind" (*PL*, 1.97). He also gives rise to allegorical figures who reflect his own reified sense of agency. If, according to Fletcher, the allegorical hero often seems to operate in a world of daemonic powers, a world in which mental functions are compartmentalized and personified, it is not all that surprising that the daemonic hero appears, conversely, to generate allegorical figures from his own forehead.

In his *Arte of English Poesie*, Puttenham offers a slightly different account of the Machiavellism of allegory but one that is equally important for understanding Satan's encounter with Sin and Death. For Puttenham, allegory or "false semblant" is a figure that depends on force and fraud, the wresting of signification and the resulting "dissimulation":

> And ye shall know that we may dissemble, I meane speake otherwise then we thinke, in earnest aswell as in sport, under covert and darke termes, and in learned and apparant speaches . . . and finally aswell when we lye as when we tell truth. To be short every speach wrested from his owne naturall signification to another not altogether so naturall is a kinde of dissimulation, because the wordes beare contrary countenaunce to th' intent.[10]

Allegory thus raises the question of the relationship of force and signification. Puttenham implies that every trope that wrests signification disguises meaning under a false appearance, regardless of whether one is lying or telling the truth. He thus suggests that the forceful breach of allegory, which opens a space between words and intent, language and meaning, makes the attainment of truth contingent upon the possibility of falsehood. Without this split produced by dissimulation, neither truth nor falsehood would be possible. Allegory, for Puttenham, may be termed the "chief ringleader and captaine of all other figures, either in the Poeticall or oratorie science" (197), "as it is supposed no man can pleasantly utter or perswade without it" (196). Thus if Fletcher's allegory is a figure of force and compulsion, Puttenham suggests that allegory's forceful wresting of signification—or fraud—is a condition of meaning in general.[11]

Satan's encounter with Sin and Death dramatizes both aspects of allegory: the episode does not simply allegorize Satan's force and fraud and thereby equate force and fraud with allegory; it also stages a critique of such an equation by showing that the possibility of Machiavellian force and fraud is a condition of all signification and agency. Allegory comes to signify a false conflation of interpretation with perception, and—as in

Areopagitica and *Comus*—the false delegation of ethical responsibility; at the same time, it also embodies a structure of linguistic difference that is the condition of meaningful human action. In its ambivalent rhetoric—at once parodic and sublime—the episode dramatizes the indeterminacy or indifference that is a condition of interpretation and free will.

We can begin to get at the indifference—the ambivalence and poly-semousness—of this allegory by noting its high degree of self-reflexivity. This self-reflexivity is apparent first of all in the descriptions of Sin and Death. Traditionally, allegory was seen both as the representation of what is by nature obscure to human understanding and as itself an obscure form of representation. We can only know God or divine truths indirectly or allegorically but, in accommodating these truths to human understanding, allegory also presents them under a veil. Thus Demetrius in his *On Style* associates allegory with darkness and night, and Vossius writes that "by its obscurity [allegory] resembles the darkness of night, which easily terrifies the fearful."[12] The obscure representation of Sin and Death thus functions as a kind of allegorical parody of allegory. That is, in personifying the unknowable or unrecognizable, the descriptions should make Sin and Death clearer to us, but the descriptions themselves merely double the original obscurity of these terms. This is especially true of Death, "the other shape / If shape it might be called that shape had none" (2.666–67). Obscurity and darkness also attend Satan's conception of Sin: "dim [his] eyes, and dizzy swum / In darkness" (2.753–54).

Sin's narration of her birth is another self-reflexive, parodic moment of the allegory; her account alludes to one prominent allegory of the birth of Christ in the Renaissance, at the same time that it anatomizes the production of allegorical figures as a process of projection and, to use Fletcher's vocabulary, compartmentalization of functions:

> Hast thou forgot me then, and do I seem
> Now in thine eye so foul, once deem'd so fair
> In Heav'n, when at th' Assembly, and in sight
> Of all the Seraphim with thee combin'd
> In bold conspiracy against Heav'n's King,
> All on a sudden miserable pain
> Surpris'd thee, dim thine eyes, and dizzy swum
> In darkness, while thy head flames thick and fast
> Threw forth, till on the left side op'ning wide,
> Likest to thee in shape and count'nance bright,
> Then shining heav'nly fair, a Goddess arm'd
> Out of thy head I sprung: amazement seiz'd
> All th' Host of Heav'n; back they recoiled afraid
> At first, and call'd me *Sin* and for a Sign

Portentous held me; but familiar grown,
I pleas'd, and with attractive graces won
The most averse, thee chiefly, who full oft
Thyself in me thy perfect image viewing
Becam'st enamor'd, and such joy thou took'st
With me in secret, that my womb conceiv'd
A growing burden.

(2.747–67)

On one level, Sin's description of her birth is a parody of God's generation of the Son, since the latter was traditionally allegorized as the birth
of Athena in the Renaissance.[13] But Sin also describes the moment of her
birth as the projection of Satan's thoughts of rebellion and conspiracy,
force and fraud: Sin springs out of Satan's head as he and his fallen angels
are joining together "In bold conspiracy against Heav'ns King" (ll. 750–
51). As Kenneth Knoespel has informed us, the Hebrew word for sin,
pesha, means rebellion. Thus the generation of Sin from Satan's conspiracy serves not only to dramatize etymology[14] but also conversely to gloss
the independent or self-regarding activity of the imagination, with its concomitant claim to unmediated agency, as sinful rebellion.[15]

The passage just quoted provides a further allegorical comment on the
relation of linguistic mediation to rebellion. As a number of critics have
remarked, the birth not only dramatizes etymology but also gives rise to
a "linguistic event" of its own: "amazement seiz'd / All th' Host of
Heav'n; back they recoil'd afraid / At first, and call'd me *Sin*, and for a
Sign / Portentous held me" (2.758–61).[16] Sin seems unfamiliar and this
unfamiliarity is tied to recognizing Sin as a sign of something else, a warning. It is familiarity or habit, here described as a narcissistic identification
("Thyself in me thy perfect image viewing / Becam'st enamor'd" [2.764–
65]), which leads to a misrecognition of Sin's otherness, that is, to the
deepest sin: "familiar grown, / I pleased, and with attractive graces won
/ The most averse" (2.761–63).[17] In these lines Milton allegorizes rebellion as the refusal to recognize the mediation of signs, as the narcissistic
desire to conflate self and other. Thus what is an allegory of narcissism and identification on the one hand proves to be an allegory of the
necessity of allegory—of linguistic mediation and difference—on the
other.

This point can be clarified by turning to some of the analogues and
subtexts of Sin's narrative. To begin with, Satan's response to Sin suggests the familiar Augustinian distinction between signs that are to be
used and those that are to be enjoyed. For Augustine, "all things are to be
used (*uti*), that is, treated as though they were signs, God only to be enjoyed (*frui*), as the ultimate signification. To enjoy that which should be
used is reification, or idolatry."[18] Satan's enjoyment of Sin involves an

idolatry of the sign rather than a recognition of the signified—a form of self-reflection that precludes genuine engagement with the text or the external world. When we take into account Sin's seduction of Satan, we could say that allegory panders to the reader, and thus obstructs the kind of rational exercise of the will which is the precondition of right reading and of virtue. In not leaving room for the reader's own activity, this pandering might just as easily be described as a kind of violence or coercion, a violence that is later dramatized in Death's rape of Sin. From this perspective, the passage can be read not only as a critique of the allegorical reification of meaning but also as a defense of reading allegorically; such a defense of allegory is also a defense against it, for to read allegorically is to take the figure of Sin as a sign, a warning.

Satan's "enjoyment" or lust may parody the dangers of antinomianism as well. It is significant in this context that excessive allegorizing was associated with antinomian tendencies in the seventeenth century, and that antinomianism was often conflated with libertinism by its critics. As James Turner has written, "In mid-seventeenth-century polemic . . . radical 'enthusiasm' was associated with the abuse of Genesis and the attempt to recover an Adamite relation to the body. This was supposed to involve either naturalistic sexual freedom or ascetic hatred of the flesh, and sometimes both at once." At times such "paradisal antinomianism" took the form of engaging in sex or sin in order to cast it out (a kind of parody of the Miltonic "trial by what is contrary").[19] The incestuous coupling of Satan and Sin would thus figure in particular the antinomian abuse of— or refusal to be constrained by—the "letter" or sign (*PL*, 2.760) with its attendant dangers of libertinism. Satan's coupling with Sin would also figure the way in which the assumption of radical indeterminacy or immediacy turns into its opposite: the bondage of the will.

Here we can further clarify the dialectical implications of Milton's self-conscious allegory of allegory by examining his biblical source. The genealogy of Sin and Death from lust derives from the Epistle of James, whose canonical status was controversial in the Renaissance not least of all because of its Pelagian or, in seventeenth-century discourse, Arminian argument for justification by works and thus for free will.[20] The passage reads:

> Let no man say when he is tempted, I am tempted of God: for God cannot be tempted with evil, neither tempteth he any man: But every man is tempted, when he is drawn away of his own lust, and enticed. Then when lust hath conceived, it bringeth forth sin: and sin, when it is finished, bringeth forth death. (1.13–15)

In his preface to the epistle, Luther objected, "Flatly against St. Paul and all the rest of Scripture, [James] ascribes righteousness to works. . . . [and] does nothing more than drive to the law and its works; He calls the law a 'law of liberty,' though St. Paul calls it a law of slavery, of wrath, of death and of sin."[21] As John Tanner has argued, however, it is precisely the Pelagian emphasis on individual responsibility in the passage from James that serves to condemn Satan in our eyes:[22] the autogeneration of Sin from Satan's forehead figures the responsibility of the sinner for his fall (as Adam says of man in book 9 of *Paradise Lost*, "within himself / The danger lies, yet lies within his power: / Against his will he can receive no harm" [9.347–49]); Satan's failure to recognize Sin is a failure to recognize his own responsibility. It is also a failure to recognize that what is the law of death and sin from one perspective is the law of liberty and of works from another, and that if sin takes the form of a sign, it is signs, conversely, that allow for the recognition of sin.

Satan's error lies, paradoxically, in his refusal to read, to accept the necessity of interpretation and the possibility of error. He thus substitutes, both structurally and thematically, determinism for freedom, fate for faith and free will. Here, too, "fixed mind" and force or compulsion coincide.[23] Signs that should ideally point to something else simply point back to themselves. Precisely because Satan's narcissistic identification with the allegorical figure of Sin precludes genuine recognition of otherness, allegory in relation to Satan figures the danger of seduction by and idolatry of literature rather than, as it was traditionally presumed to do, providing armor against it. The episode could thus be said to perform its own immanent critique of the idea of an autonomous cultural realm of literature: the claim to unmediated imaginative activity is itself a form of violence, of reification and rebellion.

The preceding analysis has suggested the way the allegory of Sin and Death functions as a thing indifferent that may have positive as well as negative implications or uses in the poem. If the episode represents the stereotypical Machiavellism of allegory, it also criticizes such force and fraud as well. In so doing, it points to an alternative mode of reading the obscurity and failed referentiality we have noted in the representation of Sin and Death and in Sin's account of her encounter with Satan. Borrowing from the more appreciative critics of the poem, we can redescribe this indifference in terms of the rhetorical category of the sublime. My aim in doing so is to situate the previous analysis in relation to the critical reception of the episode from the seventeenth century onward, and to show how even the encomiastic category of the sublime refigures the Machiavellian indifference of allegory.

In "On Paradise Lost," prefaced to the 1674 edition of the poem, Marvell recorded how he feared Milton would "ruin . . . / The sacred Truths to fable and old Song," and "perplex . . . the things he would explain"; yet, in the end he was "convinc'd," and commended Milton's "verse created like [his] Theme sublime" (Hughes, 209–10). Later readers followed suit, often singling out the perplexity of the Sin and Death episode as one of the chief examples of the Miltonic sublime. Commenting on the line, "Rocks, caves, lakes, dens, bogs, fens and shades of death" (*PL*, 2.621), Burke wrote:

> This idea or affection caused by a word ["death"], which nothing but a word could annex to the others, raises a very great degree of the sublime; and it is raised yet higher by what follows, a *"universe of death."* Here are again two ideas not presentable but by language; and an union of them great and amazing beyond conception. Whoever attentively considers this passage in Milton . . . will find that it does not in general produce its end by raising the images of things, but by exciting a passion similar to that which real objects excite by other instruments.[24]

And Coleridge, commenting on the description of Death in *Paradise Lost*, argued in a similar vein:

> The grandest efforts of poetry are where the imagination is called forth, not to produce a distinct form, but a strong working of the mind, still offering what is still repelled, and again creating what is again rejected; the result being what the poet wishes to impress, namely, the substitution of a sublime feeling of the unimaginable for a mere image.[25]

Burke's and Coleridge's comments nicely capture the ambivalence of the sublime. On the one hand, it seems as though the poet's deliberate failure of representation allows greater freedom to the reader's imagination; on the other hand, the reader's failure to imagine anything precisely serves to refer the reader to what is described by Coleridge as "a sublime feeling of the unimaginable" but has been described by other theorists of the sublime as an identification with a higher power, one that transcends the faculties of perception and imagination. Luther's description of the law in his *Commentary on Galatians* provides one example of the religious experience of the sublime: "Wherefore this is the proper and absolute use of the law, by lightning, by tempest and by the sound of the trumpet (as in Mt. Sinai) to terrify, and by thundering to beat down and rend in pieces that beast which is called the opinion of righteousness."[26] The abasement of the sinner proves to be an uplifting experience insofar as it makes him aware of his own sinfulness and thus receptive to divine grace. From this perspective the sublime descriptions of Satan, Sin, and Death serve as a counterplot to their infernal activities, by inviting the reader to contemplate his own divine nature. Similarly, according to Marvell, Milton's sublime style effectively transforms his potentially satanic poetic activity into divinely inspired prophecy: "Just Heav'n thee like *Tiresias* to requite / Rewards with Prophecy thy loss of sight."

Milton may have intended the sublime allegory of Sin and Death to convey an explicitly republican message as well. As Annabel Patterson and others have recently reminded us, Longinus's discussion of the sublime—which was available to seventeenth-century readers in English translation, as well as in Latin and Greek—explicitly linked the sublime to political liberty and to democracy. Marvell, in particular, seems to have noted the republican dimension of the Miltonic sublime in his prefatory poem to *Paradise Lost*. As Patterson has observed, Marvell's image of Milton as "a latter-day Samson braced to bring down the pillars of his society upon the heads of its leaders" "reverberates with Milton's invocation in the *First Defence* of the 'heroic Samson,' who 'still made war single-handed on his masters, and . . . slew at one stroke not one but a host of his country's tyrants.' "[27] In the preceding pages we have seen how the generation of Sin allegorizes the illegitimate rebellion of the individual sinner and of the self-regarding imagination; I would now like to suggest that Satan's confrontation with Death be read as a related critique of monarchical authority. For, like Machiavelli, Milton's aim here and elsewhere in *Paradise Lost* is not simply to stage the indifference of rhetorical figures but also to show how they may be appropriated by the religiously motivated republican.

Satan's challenge to Death is represented as a repetition and parody of his rebellion against God's throne. When Death first appears, it "seem'd his head / The likeness of a Kingly Crown had on" (2.672–73). And, when Satan refuses to recognize Death's authority, Death surmises he is "that Traitor Angel . . . / Who first broke peace in Heav'n and Faith, till then / Unbrok'n, and in proud rebellious Arms / Drew after him the third part of Heav'n's Sons / Conjur'd against the Highest" (2.689–93). Both in his revolt against heaven and in his encounter with Death, Satan's assumption is that kingly power is merely de facto political power that may be challenged by equal and opposing power. This assumption is dramatized in the lines in which Satan and Death—like allegorical figures from *The Faerie Queene*—are indistinguishable in battle:

> Each at the Head
> Levell'd his deadly aim; thir fatal hands
> No second stroke intend, and such a frown
> Each cast at th' other, as when two black Clouds
> With Heav'n's Artillery fraught, came rattling on.
>
> (2.711–15)

Unlike Satan's challenge to God, Satan's contest with Death is merely a conflict of equal powers. As such, the passage looks forward to the War in Heaven and to Abdiel's remarks, discussed above, on the indifference of reason, arms, and military *virtù* (6.114–26). And, as in Abdiel's speech, so here the narrator implies that this indifference is itself divinely ordained: both fight with "Heav'n's Artillery."[28]

The fact that Death is an allegorical projection of Satan's own desire for absolute rule may also suggest that Milton intends for us to see kingship as a deadly, allegorical projection and alienation of the subject's true freedom. In *The Reason of Church Government* (1642), Milton had written that the authority of the civil magistrate seems originally "to have been placed, as all both civil and religious rites once were, only in each father of family" (Hughes, 678), but that in time magistracy was grounded in reason and persuasion. And, in *The Tenure of Kings and Magistrates* (1649), Milton argued against Filmer that "the law was set above the magistrate," and that eventually kings and magistrates

> received allegiance from the people, that is to say, bond or covenant to obey them in execution of those laws which they, the people, had themselves made or assented to. And this ofttimes with express warning, that if the king or magistrate proved unfaithful to his trust, the people would be disengaged. (Hughes, 755)

In a later passage already mentioned, Milton rebutted Filmer's and others' coupling of 1 Peter 2:13 with Romans 13:

> Therefore kingdom and magistracy, whether supreme or subordinate, is without difference called "a human ordinance" (1 Pet. ii, 13, &c.), which we are there taught is the will of God we should alike submit to, so far as for the punishment of evildoers and the encouragement of them that do well. "Submit," saith he, "as free men." But to any civil power unaccountable, unquestionable, and not to be resisted, no, not in wickedness and violent actions, how can we submit as free men? "There is no power but of God," saith Paul (Rom. xiii), as much as to say God put it into man's heart to find out that way at first for common peace and preservation, approving the exercise thereof; else it contradicts Peter, who calls the same authority an ordinance of man. It must also be understood of lawful and just power. (Hughes, 758–59)

In juxtaposing Satan's illegitimate "conspiracy against Heav'n's King" (2.751) with his initial refusal to recognize the kingly authority of his son, Milton calls attention to the indifference of dissent. What is illegitimate dissent from God becomes legitimate dissent from an allegorical figment of absolute authority. As in the passage just cited from *The Tenure of Kings and Magistrates*, where Milton asserts that the power to contract is the power also to disengage, so here the power to alienate agency is also the power to reassume it. The allegorical conflict of Satan and Death both dramatizes and ironizes the royal fiction of absolute, patriarchal authority. It thus indirectly provides a defense of republicanism.

Yet, in the end, Milton's indifferent rhetoric touches the category of the sublime as well. Although from one perspective the sublime may be equated with true prophecy and republicanism, from another the sublimity of Sin and Death simply replays the problem posed by the Machiavellian indifference of the allegory in a higher key. For, according to some modern critics, in the experience of the sublime, reason "stages" a failure of that form of representation that assumes an analogy between cognition and vision, understanding and the phenomenal world, in order to make room for the nonphenomenological activities of reading and writing—of prophecy in the seventeenth-century sense of exegesis.[29] The imagination fails to comprehend nature, but this failure allows reason to recognize its independence from nature. As Donald Pease has written, "Instead of locating the source of the sublime in its former locus, i.e., in external nature, the imagination redirects Reason to another locus, within Reason itself, where Reason can re-cognize astonishment as its own power to negate external nature."[30] In doing so, however, reason simply displaces to this ostensibly higher level, "within Reason itself," the question of its own authority. Like allegory, the literary category of the sublime raises questions concerning the relation of authority and interpretation, free will and determinism, which are central to Milton's theological and political concerns: if sublimity can be staged, how does one tell the difference between a satanic or Machiavellian self-aggrandizement and divinely inspired prophecy or poetry? How does one tell the difference between legitimate and illegitimate dissent?[31] In confronting the reader with the Machiavellian possibilities of its indifferent rhetoric, the episode looks forward to dilemmas faced by Adam and Eve in books 4, 8, and 9 of *Paradise Lost*.

Machiavellism in Eden

Satan's encounter with Sin and Death has usually been perceived as something of an anomaly in *Paradise Lost*. From the eighteenth century on, the allegory was regularly praised as sublime while being criticized as inappropriate to the otherwise nonallegorical epic. Although admitting that "the descriptive part of this allegory is . . . very strong and full of sublime ideas," Addison complained, "I cannot think that persons of such a chimerical existence [Sin and Death] are proper actors in an epic poem." Samuel Johnson irritably echoed this complaint in his *Life of Milton*: "This unskilful allegory appears to me one of the greatest faults of the poem."[32] And, although modern readers have preferred to see the "fault" of allegory as a deliberate rhetorical strategy, they have also isolated the episode by associating allegory exclusively with a fallen mode of language.[33] Rather than being a form of sublimely inspired language or divine accommodation, allegory in this case is a satanic, parodic version of the Word.

The preceding pages have begun to suggest, in contrast, that the structures of linguistic difference and indifference that we observed in the Sin and Death episode—the emphasis on the mediation of signs and the varied uses of rhetorical figures—are constitutive of prelapsarian experience as well.[34] The fact that the Sin and Death episode can be described both as an allegory and as a critique of allegory is thus part of the larger argument of the poem. Yet, if linguistic mediation exists in Eden, the poet still wants to distinguish between true and false versions of it. Thus the distinction that Christianity has traditionally marked with the fall Milton places within Eden itself, though this does not mean that Adam and Eve are somehow fallen before their acts of disobedience. In particular, *Paradise Lost* shows that the structure of the prohibition not to eat of the Tree of Knowledge is the same as that of the law of postlapsarian experience (the prohibition is already a law), and that the differential structure articulated by the law is a condition of freedom as well as slavery. Whether the law is perceived as enabling or not is a function of reading, which in either case depends on the law in order to negate it.

This point may be clarified by returning to Luther's objections to the Epistle of James. The Lutheran view of the law as a law of slavery consequent upon the fall would seem to underlie any strict differentiation between pre- and postlapsarian experience. Although Pelagius might suffice for a description of the original fall, as fallen creatures we are incapable, according to Luther, of willing freely. Yet, in *Paradise Lost*, Milton takes issue with this Lutheran position. That Sin is first a sign means conversely that signs (linguistic mediation) allow for the recognition of the possibility of sin. In glossing the genealogy of Sin and Death in the Epistle of James, Milton's allegory thus suggests that sin shares a linguistic structure not only with the postlapsarian law but with the prelapsarian prohibition, and that, in both cases, this linguistic structure is a condition of virtue. In the following pages I consider the command not to eat from the Tree of Knowledge as an example of linguistic mediation and the linguistic constitution of virtue in prelapsarian Eden; I then analyze Satan's Machiavellian rhetoric in book 9 in similar terms. Just as the divine prohibition exemplifies the linguistic mediation that is a condition of virtue, so Milton uses the disjunction between intention and language in Satan's rhetoric—his Machiavellian fraud—to explore the way in which the wresting of signification is a condition of all agency and meaning.

It is significant that we first see the Tree of Knowledge from Satan's vantage point, for the poet's description emphasizes that "virtue" is tied to right use:

> Thence up he [Satan] flew, and on the Tree of Life,
> The middle tree and highest there that grew,
> Sat like a Cormorant; yet not true Life
> Thereby regain'd, but sat devising Death

To them who liv'd; nor on the virtue thought
Of that life-giving Plant, but only us'd
For prospect, what well us'd had been the pledge
Of immortality.

(4.194–201)

The narrator uses "virtue" to mean the power of the Tree of Life—just as in book 9 Eve will refer to the virtue of the Tree of Knowledge and of other plants in the garden. But "virtue" also retains its ethical sense as the faculty that governs and is a consequence of right use. It is right use that converts the Tree of Life from a mere object to a "pledge" or sign of God's promise of immortality. The ethical indifference of the Tree—that it can be used well or badly, that it can be construed as a pledge or a mere plant—is thus a condition of virtue in both senses of the word. As in the Sin and Death episode, Satan's literal-minded perception is reflected in his "devising Death": in scriptural terms, the letter killeth but the spirit giveth life.

Like the Sin and Death episode, this passage on the Tree of Life prepares us for Adam's description of God's command against eating from the Tree of Knowledge. Adam describes the prohibition in a way that explicitly ties its linguistic structure to the possibility of virtue. Two aspects of his account are important to note: first, the prohibition signifies that the recognition of sin is a linguistic rather than a merely perceptual activity; second, as a sign, the prohibition is intended to establish the difference between coercion and persuasion. God "requires," Adam tells Eve,

From us no other service than to keep
This one, this easy charge, of all the Trees
In Paradise that bear delicious fruit
So various, not to taste that only Tree
Of Knowledge, planted by the Tree of Life,
So near grows Death to Life, whate'er Death is,
Some dreadful thing no doubt; for well thou know'st
God hath pronounc't it death to taste that Tree,
The only sign of our obedience left
Among so many signs of power and rule
Conferr'd upon us, and Dominion giv'n
Over all other Creatures that possess
Earth, Air, and Sea. Then let us not think hard
One easy prohibition, who enjoy
Free leave so large to all things else, and choice
Unlimited of manifold delights:
But let us ever praise him, and extol

His bounty, following our delightful task
To prune these growing Plants, and tend these Flow'rs,
Which were it toilsome, yet with thee were sweet.

(4.420–39)

Here it is clear that although Adam does not understand the word "death," he does understand the prohibition as a test of obedience.[35] The partial obscurity of the prohibition is thus analogous to the obscurity of Sin and Death; in both cases it functions as a boundary or limit. The sign is thus, in a curious way, performative rather than cognitive. It refers Adam and Eve to the limits of cognition but recuperates this failure of cognition ("whate'er Death is / Some dreadful thing no doubt") in the recognition of the task of obedience to God's word: "for well thou know'st / God hath pronounc't it death to taste that Tree." As Milton intimates in the homophones of Raphael's later warning, "Know to know no more" (4.775), knowledge is predicated on negation, on the knowledge of limits. Furthermore, this limit is of ethical as well as epistemological importance, for absolute knowledge would itself be coercive and thus preclude virtue. At the same time, the prohibition itself is clearly a sublime obstacle, a limit that tempts one to "think hard"—that is, beyond the boundary it establishes; and to think of that activity as hard which formerly—that is, without thought—was easy and so without virtue. Negation makes thought possible, at the same time that it makes the closure of absolute knowledge impossible, for us. But this impossibility is the condition of virtue. Just as the Mosaic law is given to fallen man to allow for the recognition of sin (12.287–308), so the prohibition is given to Adam and Eve as a sign which, as it articulates difference, allows for genuine choice, reason, and obedience. And this articulation of difference is itself predicated on the doctrine of things indifferent. As Milton writes in *Christian Doctrine*,

> it was necessary that something should be forbidden or commanded as a test of fidelity, and that an act in its own nature indifferent, in order that man's obedience might be thereby manifested. For since it was the disposition of man to do what was right, as a being naturally good and holy, it was not necessary that he should be bound by the obligation of a covenant to perform that to which he was of himself inclined; nor would he have given any proof of obedience by the performance of works to which he was led by a natural impulse, independently of the divine command. (Hughes, 993)

In Milton's analysis, the Tree of Knowledge is itself a thing indifferent, and it is this indifference that makes possible the test of virtue constituted by the prohibition. Or, to put it another way, as in the passage on divine ordinance and human order in *The Tenure of Kings and Magistrates*,

Milton diminishes the difference between God's command and human discretion in things indifferent by making the former a test of the latter.

If the prohibition establishes the fact of linguistic mediation in prelapsarian Eden, it is not surprising that Adam and Eve's prelapsarian experience in book 9 of *Paradise Lost* rehearses many of the issues we saw dramatized in Satan's encounter with Sin and Death. Satan's narcissistic refusal to recognize the mediation of signs is refigured in book 9 as Eve's narcissistic blindness to Satan's fraud. Yet, if Milton allegorizes stereotypical Machiavellism in the Sin and Death episode as the unwarranted claim to self-origination and imaginative power, in book 9 of *Paradise Lost* Machiavellism appears as well in its more familiar form of rhetorical deception and hypocrisy. Even more than in books 1 and 2, Satan appears in book 9 as the archetypal hypocrite, using fraud and malice (9.55) to wage war against Adam and Eve. And, as in those earlier books, part of Satan's Machiavellism involves ascribing the stereotypically Machiavellian use of force and fraud to God himself, while claiming in his own case and that of the fruit that appearances are truthful. As with Satan's speeches to the fallen angels in books 1 and 2, here too Milton implies that what is rhetorical force and fraud from one perspective is the condition of virtue from another.

Satan is the original of Bradshaw's Machiavel, who manipulates the realm of appearances so that "scant any thing is as it appears, or appears as it is."[36] In addition, in a particularly diabolical twist, Satan makes even those things that appear as they are seem different. Debating about the proper means to serve his ends, Satan

> Consider'd every Creature, which of all
> Most opportune might serve his Wiles, and found
> The Serpent subtlest Beast of all the Field.
> Him after long debate, irresolute
> Of thoughts revolv'd, his final sentence chose
> Fit Vessel, fittest Imp of fraud, in whom
> To enter, and his dark suggestions hide
> From sharpest sight: for in the wily Snake,
> Whatever sleights none would suspicious mark,
> As from his wit and native subtlety
> Proceeding, which in other Beasts observ'd
> Doubt might beget of Diabolic pow'r.
>
> (9.84–95)

Satan's deliberations lead him to the conclusion that suspicious behavior in a creature one expects to be suspicious will not be suspicious. This reasoning simultaneously parodies and illustrates Machiavelli's remark that "men in general judge more by the sense of sight than by the sense of touch, because everyone can see but only a few can test by feeling. Everyone sees what you seem to be, few know what you really are" (*P*, 51). "Sharpest sight" will be its own undoing, because its suspicion takes the form of perceiving, that is, trusting the appearance of, "sleights" and "fraud."

Once he has assumed the form of the serpent, Satan's rhetoric consists of making distinctions between appearance and reality, intention and effect, means and ends, *virtù* and success, only in order then to argue for their correspondence on the basis of apparent evidence or sense certainty. In particular, according to Satan, physical sight guarantees intellectual insight. In fact, all of Satan's arguments in book 9 can be organized around the sense of sight in a way that makes his rhetoric an elaborate pun. Thus the serpent appeals throughout book 9 both to Eve's sight and to her desire to be seen. He calls attention to the shallowness or superficiality of mere sight as opposed to the depth of insight (9.544: "Beholders rude, and shallow to discern"). In this way, his rhetoric turns sight into desire and thus into a sense of absence (9.535–36: "gaze / Insatiate"). At the same time, he asks Eve not to think or be on guard: "Wonder not, sovran Mistress, if perhaps / Thou canst, who are sole Wonder, much less arm / Thy looks." Then, having established the difference between two kinds of looks, fairness, and perception (9.538, 605–606), the serpent argues for their identity by referring to himself as evidence:

> Queen of this Universe, do not believe
> Those rigid threats of Death; ye shall not Die:
> How should ye? by the Fruit? it gives you life
> To Knowledge. By the Threat'ner? look on mee,
> Mee who have touch'd and tasted, yet both live,
> And life more perfet have attain'd than Fate
> Meant mee, by vent'ring higher than my Lot.
> Shall that be shut to Man, which to the Beast
> Is open? or will God incense his ire
> For such a petty Trespass, and not praise
> Rather your dauntless virtue, whom the pain
> Of Death denounc't, whatever thing Death be,
> Deterr'd not from achieving what might lead
> To happier life, knowledge of Good and Evil;
> Of good, how just? of evil, if what is evil
> Be real, why not known, since easier shunn'd?
> God therefore cannot hurt ye, and be just;
> Not just, not God; not fear'd then, nor obey'd:
> Your fear itself of Death removes the fear.

(9.683–702)

What is interesting about this passage is the way Satan argues inconsistently both for the truth of sense evidence and for God's Machiavellian use of fraud. He appeals to the evidence of his own appearance—"Look on me"—to suggest both that God's "rigid threats of Death" are fraudulent, and that the Machiavellian use of force would disable any claims to legitimacy: "God . . . cannot hurt ye, and be just." The same is true of the divine prohibition construed as a threat: Eve's "fear itself of Death removes the fear," because such fear is construed as evidence of coercion. Yet, in describing God as a Machiavel, Satan admits the possibility of deception that undermines any strict claim for the correspondence between appearance and reality. In so doing, he betrays the Machiavellism of his pretension to unmediated experience.

Satan's rhetoric also makes clear that the appeal to sense evidence is tied to a particular interpretation of "virtue" as natural strength or innate power. As in books 1 and 2, Milton plays with the word *virtue* in a way that invites us to reflect on the relationship between the natural virtue of herbs, plants, and fruit in the Garden, and the ethical virtue of obedience, which is dependent upon the linguistic intervention of God's prohibition. Thus Satan describes the orbs of heaven, whose "known virtue appears / Productive in Herb, Plant, and nobler Birth / Of Creatures animate" (9.110–12); and, reflecting on why God created the Earth, he wonders if God's "virtue spent of old now fail'd / More angels to create" (9.145–46). In both cases "virtue" may be construed as productive power. In a similar vein, the fruit of the Tree of Knowledge is repeatedly described as possessed of, in Eve's words, a "virtue . . . / Wondrous indeed, if cause of such effects" (9.616, 649–50). Just before the fall, Eve praises the Tree's "Virtues" (9.745); in describing the Tree as both "Fair to the eye" and "of virtue to make wise" (9.778, 779), she once again suggests that the appeal to sense evidence and the construction of "virtue" as a natural power and unfailing cause of specific effects are two sides of the same coin.

Yet, as Milton argues in the passage quoted above from his *Christian Doctrine*, and as Eve herself implies in the "separation colloquy" when she presents Milton's argument in *Areopagitica* ("What is Faith, Love, Virtue unassay'd" [9.335]), such natural or innate "virtue" is itself a thing indifferent, one that needs to be tested or tried before it can be called Christian virtue. The prohibition provides for just such a denaturalization of virtue through the mediation of signs. Even Satan suggests as much when he urges Eve to show an epic *virtù* or "dauntless virtue" by trespassing God's prohibition (9.694). He thus implies, in spite of himself, that the natural "virtue" of the Tree is nothing compared to the virtue Adam and Eve exercise by being obedient to—or disobeying—God's command.

The linguistic play with "virtue" helps us to understand Milton's Machiavellian defense against the force and fraud of the Machiavel. Such defense takes the form of arguing not that force and fraud are simply evil, or that appearances are merely deceptive, but rather that the possibility of deception means that appearances must be interpreted, and that the activity of interpretation is itself an occasion of free will. Or, to put it another way, "virtue" must be denaturalized so that it no longer appears as an object of perception but rather as an activity of interpretation. Accordingly, all of book 9 is governed by an opposition between knowledge construed as cognition of an object (knowledge as possession) and knowledge construed as an activity of choice. The first kind of knowledge is associated with perception and with reasoning by analogy. The second kind is identified with obedience to God and faith, for which there can be no merely perceptual evidence. The impossibility of such evidence might seem to guarantee the harmlessness—the inefficacy—of deceptive appearances or, to use Puttenham's words for the trope of *evidentia*, "counterfait representation." Yet, if appearances—and the realm of things indifferent—are reasoned away, learning and the right exercise of virtue are impossible.

Thus the problem that Eve faces when confronted with Satan disguised as "mere serpent in appearance" (9.413) is the same problem faced by the postlapsarian Redcrosse in book 1 of *The Faerie Queene*: the problem, that is, of Puttenham's "false semblant." In a garden that includes both the "fair appearing good" (9.350) that is the snake and the "fair appearing good" that is Adam, no single rule of interpretation (whether according to analogy or the inversion of simple irony) will suffice. Rather, it is precisely the absence of such an a priori rule that makes reading (construed not as the possession of knowledge but as the activity of choice) possible. Eve's error does not arise from the entirely rational assumption of the snake's good intentions (she has every right to expect the "subtle" snake to be as innocuous as the "mazy error" of the streams of paradise) but from her subjection of faith and of the divine prohibition to the serpent's view of human reason—from a reading for knowledge that refuses to accept the knowledge of human limitations. Accordingly, with the serpent's help, Eve reasons in contradictory fashion, both analogically and ironically. For, once she assumes with the serpent that she can accede to divine knowledge by reasoning analogically from appearances, she leaves herself open to (the misconstruction of) a mere Outside. Milton's nonallegorical poetic is not at all designed to solve the ethical and epistemological problems dramatized by Spenserian allegory or by the allegory of Sin and Death; for what is allegory by one name is *enargeia* or *evidentia* by another.

Fittingly, Milton conveys his criticism of a phenomenological approach to reading not only thematically but also intertextually. If we return to the scene of seduction, we can see that although the pleasing appearance of the serpent dazzles Eve even before it speaks, Milton's allusive style seems to place the reader in a different position. For the comparison of the serpent to a ship (9.513) recalls Virgil's description of the Trojan horse. We are reminded of the sliding—or falling (*lapsus*)— wheels that allow the horse to slip into the city (*inlabitur urbi*), and the approach of the Greek ships, whose departure from Tenedos (*Aeneid*, 2.254–67) recalls a similar departure of the snakes (*Aeneid*, 2.203, 225) who devoured Laocoon. The reader is thus tempted to think that the cognoscenti of Virgil are in a position of superior knowledge in comparison with Eve, and that their knowledge of Virgil provides them with proof of why Eve should not have fallen: that is, the snake is a Trojan horse. But allusion here also functions as a trope of evidence and, in doing so, undermines the reader's supposed superiority: if we do not remember that Virgil, like Homer, is an "erring" narrator (*PL*, 1.747), we should note that the Virgilian passages to which Milton alludes do not tell a story of simple deception (according to which appearances are in ironic contradiction to what they really signify) but rather of a double misreading—for the Trojans believe Sinon's lies but they do not believe Laocoon's truth. We are thus gradually forced in book 9 to confront the fact that knowledge per se, knowledge of allusion, knowledge of the deceptiveness of appearances (and one is tempted to add aesthetic knowledge in particular—as the model of disinterested, independent inquiry) is not a guarantor of virtue.

Yet, while Satan's rhetoric plays with the unreliability of appearances and so undermines the possibility of a phenomenological account of reading, it also makes it clear that deceit and misrepresentation are not the invention of the devil: they are not created *ex nihilo*. If conventional signs are distinguished from natural signs insofar as the former involve the "will to signify" (as Augustine argues in *On Christian doctrine*), Satan does not introduce conventional signs into Eden.[37] He simply makes explicit what was already a potentiality of human language: the possibility of misrepresentation is a constitutive part of representation just as the possibility of choosing wrongly is a constitutive part of free will. In other words, all human language is arbitrary, which is to say, in the root sense of the word, willful. The question is, whose will is being served? Satan's sin, then, is not in using language arbitrarily but rather in turning that arbitrary language into an object: by making language seem to signify "naturally," in short, by arguing that knowledge can be acquired as, or in the form of, a natural object (the Tree of Knowledge), and so reifying it. Like Augustine, Milton makes clear that the first wrong choice is the choice to think of language and of Christian knowledge as objects rather than as activities of choice.

That Milton aims to defeat Satan and his "rebellious rout" not by denying the conventionality of signs but by admitting it—and then by arguing that this conventionality is itself an assertion of free will (and thus a justification of God's ways)—is apparent in the treatment of Adam's fall. Since Adam falls neither by force nor by fraud, he undermines this stereotypical Machiavellian paradigm (itself associated with Satan's rhetoric throughout books 1 and 2): the fall is not primarily a problem of external misrepresentation but of self-deception. Eve is righter than she knows when she says of her fall to Adam:

> who knows
> But might as ill have happ'n'd thou being by,
> Or to thyself perhaps: hadst thou been there,
> Or here th' attempt, thou couldst not have discern'd
> Fraud in the Serpent, speaking as he spake;
> No ground of enmity between us known,
> Why hee should mean me ill, or seek to harm.
>
> (9.1146–52)

Although Eve claims to be reading (eating) for knowledge, her remarks here betray her necessary ignorance (the necessary limits of knowledge), an ignorance Adam accepts only in order to *choose* to reject it. When he warns Eve "not to taste that only Tree / Of Knowledge, planted by the Tree of Life, / So near grows Death to Life, whate'er Death is, / Some dreadful thing no doubt; for well thou know'st" (4.423–26), the syntax of the lines dramatizes the inseparability of knowledge and ignorance. Yet, in the end, "he scrupl'd not to eat / Against his better knowledge, not deceiv'd" (9.997–98). Milton's aim in both scenes of the fall is to shift the definition of reading from reading for the acquisition of cognitive knowledge to reading as the activity of choice, a choice that if correctly made presupposes a different kind of knowledge as its foundation. Thus, whereas Satan argues (9.756) that "good unknown / Sure is not had" (knowledge as possession), Milton replies with Eve that "In such abundance [of the yet unknown] lies our choice" (9.619–20).

I have argued that the Sin and Death episode is an exemplary instance of Milton's ambivalent or, in theological terms, indifferent rhetoric. In Sin's narration of her encounter with Satan, we are offered an allegorical parody of allegory; and in Satan's encounter with Death, we are offered an allegory and critique of monarchical power. From one perspective (which we can identify with Sin's description of Satan's response), allegory implies a fallen mode of reading since it reifies signification and precludes any genuine encounter with otherness, any genuine exercise of deliberation and choice among possible meanings. From another perspective, the episode provides an allegorical critique of reading allegorically and so dramatizes the indifference of this rhetorical mode. From this second perspective, allegory exemplifies a structure of signification that characterizes pre- as well as postlapsarian experience. One burden of the episode is thus to show that signs, including prohibitions and laws, are not simply a consequence of the fall but the precondition of any genuine ethical choice: language itself is a thing indifferent that can be used well or badly.

Milton thus uses what contemporaries stigmatized as the Machiavellian indeterminacy of language, its potential for force and fraud, as an argument for free will. In so doing, as we have seen, he provides us with a rhetorical theology and rhetorical politics, both more concerned to stage than to resolve the paradoxes of Christian doctrine.[38] Like the rhetoric of *The Prince*, Milton's rhetoric dramatizes the dilemmas of agency in a world in which our actions are partially governed by *fortuna*—or entirely foreseen by God. Furthermore, like Machiavelli's allegorical figure of Fortune as a woman, Milton's allegorical critique of allegory aims to dramatize—and to free virtue from—the threat of reification in the face of pure contingency (fortune) or pure determinism (the Calvinist God). In both cases, the critical or enabling aspect of such allegory might be described as a mode of reading or reasoning, in which the failure of immediate perception gives way to an elevating activity of interpretation, one that restores to the subject the conviction of free will.

In this light, Milton's remark in *Areopagitica*—"Reason is but choosing," a remark that describes the activity of Adam, Eve, and the reader of *Paradise Lost*—is the exemplary Miltonic narrative in little: it posits the passage between epistemology and ethics. Faced with the limits of human cognition, the reader exercises judgment in the realm of things indifferent and in so doing performs his or her divinely ordained ethical task. The problem, of course—and it is the problem of Reformation hermeneutics—is how does one tell the difference between the satanic self-aggrandizement of "perfect, self-originating agency"[39] and those decisions and actions that do not simply claim to be but are obedient to a higher power? Here we are reminded of the possibility that reason might act as a stage Machiavel, pretending a failure of knowledge in order narcissistically to "discover itself freshly in an attitude of awe."[40] Satan's narcissism in his encounter with Sin enacts this theatrical possibility. As Milton was well aware, if ethical discretion in things indifferent can be staged or parodied, this also raises questions concerning Milton's own rhetorical defense and education of the reader's ethical judgment. We know not only from the Sin and Death episode but also from the poet-narrator's self-descriptions, which frequently echo earlier descriptions of Satan, that Milton was himself sensitive to this dilemma. Milton stages the plot and counterplot of allegory in the Sin and Death episode not only to try to distinguish between legitimate and illegitimate dissent, reformation and rebellion, but also to meditate on the satanic and Machiavellian dimension of justifying the ways of God to men. Just as *fortuna* was for Machiavelli both the occasion of *virtù* and the threat to its realization, so for Milton the satanic Machiavel signifies the realm of indifference that is both a threat to, and the occasion of, virtue. Not least disturbing in the conflation of truth and the realm of things indifferent is the suggestion that the exercise of Christian virtue may be inseparable from a self-aggrandizing stereotypically Machiavellian *virtù*. But, for Milton, this possibility is the risk one must take in order to reunite virtue and *virtù* in the proper exercise of Christian liberty.

In contrast to those many critics who have asserted that Milton was only interested in the Machiavelli of the *Discourses*, the preceding pages have shown that Milton was fully aware that the Machiavel and the republican theorist are two aspects of rhetorical politics, and that what contemporaries stigmatized as the indeterminacy or indifference of rhetoric in the figure of the Machiavel is also the condition of political virtue. Like the proponents of the oath of Engagement, Milton exacerbated this indeterminacy in the rhetoric of his prose and poetry, not in order to argue as they did for the necessity of allegiance to the arbitrary authority of de facto political power, but rather to insist on the exercise of deliberation and action in the contingent world of political affairs. Like Machiavelli, Milton was aware that the indeterminacy of rhetoric could serve as a dialectical critique of the status quo, a means of unmooring custom and ideology and making room for a republic of virtuous citizens or saints. Like the critics of Machiavelli, Milton knew that the cost of such indifference was the Machiavel.

CODA

RHETORIC AND THE CRITIQUE OF IDEOLOGY

THIS BOOK began as a study of the "other" tradition of Renaissance rhetoric—not the tradition of dialogue, debate, and consensus but of conflict, disunion, and dissent. Familiar with the argument that Machiavelli courted and then mocked the assumptions of humanist political discourse, I assumed Machiavelli was disturbing to Renaissance readers in part because of his attack on the humanist rhetoric of consensus. And I assumed that Renaissance readers of Machiavelli would accordingly identify him both with the subversive or critical potential of rhetoric and with political dissent. I was not sure whether I agreed with Pocock that "the truly subversive Machiavelli was not a counselor of tyrants, but a good citizen and patriot," that is, a republican (*MM*, 218); but I believed I knew Machiavelli was subversive. In the course of writing this book I had to learn the lesson of my first book all over again—the lesson of argument on both sides of a question.[1] While many readers did of course see Machiavelli precisely in terms of republican disunion or dissent, many more saw him as providing a rhetoric of de facto political power—a rhetoric of theatrical violence, sembling and dissembling, whether in the service of the commonwealth (to use a Renaissance term that is not equivalent to our *republic*) or in the interests of the self-aggrandizing tyrant. Although for some readers Machiavelli's rhetorical politics was truly innovative, for others, beginning with Guicciardini, Machiavelli was not the radical critic of humanism he represented himself as being but something more like an armchair theorist, excessively enamored of ancient examples. For still other, more charitable readers, Machiavelli was simply a good observer of "wise impieties," not a shockingly original political thinker. In short, Machiavelli was himself read *in utramque partem*.

I believe this complicated reception of Machiavelli is responding to the complexity of Machiavelli's own political vision, not least of all his vexed relation to the humanist tradition. And I believe it is not only refreshing but right to be reminded of the armchair Machiavelli—the Machiavelli who, after all, wrote a commentary on Livy and who thought that modern commerce was detrimental to civic virtue. But I also think that Renaissance readers of Machiavelli knew what the reception of Machiavelli in succeeding centuries has borne out: Machiavelli was quite simply a great writer, and his eloquence was not ancillary but central to his understanding of politics.

Although I have analyzed the variety of responses to Machiavelli's rhetorical politics in this book, it is important in concluding to say the obvious: that Machiavelli *was*, among other things, a republican thinker—a thinker who believed that republicanism was the best *argument* not only for preserving the state but also for generating *virtù* among its citizens. And although I have stressed, throughout this book, Machiavelli's acute sense of the possible failure of this argument (a failure he experienced with the return of the Medici to Florence), in concluding I would like to focus on the success of Machiavellian rhetoric as a critique of ideology.

As we have seen, although Machiavelli's critics perceived amoral argument on both sides of a question as immoral, some of his admirers and defenders perceived in Machiavelli's rhetoric not only a method that was exemplary in its flexible response to contingency, but also a dialectical mode of analysis that was at once descriptive and subversive. For these admirers, Machiavelli offered a rhetoric not only for constituting but also for challenging the status quo: rhetorical politics served as a critique of ideology.[2] In this coda, I wish to explore in more general terms the intersection of rhetoric and ideology, not in order to rehearse the argument of this book but rather to indicate some of the modern critical issues that have informed my analysis. My brief remarks should also suggest how research in the history of rhetoric and of reading may contribute to contemporary debates in literary theory.[3]

The terms of abuse applied to rhetoric in the Renaissance—in particular, the association of rhetoric with "force and fraud"—suggest that it was viewed the way critics now view ideology. Paul Ricoeur has defined ideology in part as "the distortion . . . [of] the symbolic structure of social life" in the service of class interests. Ideology involves both "the impact of violence in discourse, [and] a dissimulation whose key eludes consciousness."[4] So rhetoric was accused of being an instrument of deception, an expression of particular interests, or a potentially coercive system of symbolic interaction. Yet, as we have seen, Renaissance writers were concerned not only with the potential abuse of rhetoric or with the ideological functions of the humanist tradition itself; they were also aware of the power of rhetoric to subvert established authority. Elaborating this analogy between rhetoric and ideology will help us further to see—as Machiavelli and his admirers did—how Renaissance rhetoric provided the tools not only of ideological manipulation but also of the critique of ideology; it will also allow us to revise the place of the humanist tradition in modern critical debate.

Ricoeur's argument that ideology and critique are two sides of the same coin provides a useful analogy to the ideological and critical functions of Renaissance rhetoric. According to Ricoeur, the pejorative theory of ideology as distortion of "the symbolic system of social life" (8) presupposes a "neutral" definition of ideology as the cultural symbolic system or a rhetoric that is constitutive of human understanding.[5] For distortion could not occur if we were not already operating within a symbolic system: as Ricoeur remarks,

> If social reality did not already have a social dimension, and therefore, if ideology, in a less polemical and less negatively evaluative sense, were not constitutive of social existence but merely distorting and dissimulating, then the process of distortion could not start. Only because the structure of human life is already symbolic can it be distorted.[6]

Yet this notion of ideology poses a further problem, that of the connection between ideology as symbolic system and ideology as distortion (12). The answer according to Ricoeur is to be found in a third function of ideology as the legitimation of authority:

> Ideology enters here because no system of leadership, even the most brutal, rules only by force, by domination. Every system of leadership summons not only our physical submission but also our consent and cooperation. . . . Ideology's role as a legitimating force persists because, as Weber has shown, no absolutely rational system of legitimacy exists. (13)

The function of ideology is to bridge the gap between the claims to legitimacy and the beliefs held by members of society. And, in doing so, ideology "moves beyond mere integration to distortion and pathology. . . . Ideology tries to secure integration between legitimacy claim and belief, but it does so by justifying the existing system of authority as it is" (14).

Yet, for Ricoeur, the gap between authority and domination, which requires the supplement of ideology, has a critical function as well: "Is it not because a credibility gap exists in all systems of legitimation, all authority, that a place for utopia exists too?" (15). It is here that the critical potential of the concept of ideology becomes apparent. For the power of ideology to distort and the power of the imagination to construct critical utopias are two sides of our irreducibly imaginative and, in a neutral sense, ideological relation to the world (see 145).

Just as ideology in its pejorative meaning is the modern equivalent of Renaissance attacks on rhetoric, so ideology in a neutral sense has its equivalent in Renaissance rhetorical practice. Like the distortions of ideology, the force and fraud of rhetoric—its deviation from the norms of communication and representation—can only be charted against an already irreducibly rhetorical relation to the world. The pejorative sense of rhetoric presupposes a "neutral" sense of rhetoric as a system of symbolic action that is not parasitic on but constitutive of human experience. The rhetorician's abuse of power presupposes a notion of language that does not simply represent but rather constructs the world as we know it. (Representation in this analysis is an effect of a preexistent symbolic system or rhetoric.) In providing us with the means of force and fraud, and of legitimation of the status quo, such rhetoric simultaneously gives us the power to dissent.

This view of rhetoric as an instrument not only of ideological manipulation but also of critical dissent allows us to revise the place of the humanist rhetorical tradition in contemporary debate concerning the critique of ideology. The debate between Gadamer and Habermas concerning the relationship of hermeneutics to critique is particularly pertinent since both authors identify hermeneutics with the humanist tradition from the Renaissance to the present, while the critique of ideology becomes the preserve of the critical social sciences. Yet, as Ricoeur has argued and as I suggest below, this opposition between hermeneutics and critique depends on a monolithic view of the humanist tradition, one that is belied by the humanists' ambivalence about rhetoric, an ambivalence that was facilitated by their rhetorical training *in utramque partem.*

Gadamer insists on the priority of hermeneutics to any critique of ideology, arguing that our relation to the past is fundamentally mediated not only by our "prejudices" but by a preexistent tradition: we are always already within a symbolic system. In this sense the "dialogue" with the past always takes place within a preestablished consensus. For Gadamer this hermeneutical situation does not preclude a critical attitude toward the past: the authority of tradition presupposes recognition, not blind obedience. Yet, as Paul Ricoeur has noted, the language in which Gadamer describes this relation to the past is more subservient than critical: "That which has been sanctioned by tradition and custom has an authority that is nameless, and our finite historical being is determined by the fact that always the authority of what has been transmitted . . . has power (Gewalt) over our attitudes and behaviour."[7] In terms of one recent typology of humanist imitators, Gadamer's attitude toward tradition is more reverential than ambivalent or dialectical.[8]

Habermas, in contrast, is suspicious of the coercive force (Gewalt) of tradition. Like those Renaissance humanists who reject the authority of the past as ideologically coercive, Habermas argues that Gadamer's textual and hermeneutical orientation precludes genuine criticism of the status quo. For although hermeneutical criticism or philology allows for the correction of accidental textual errors, it is incapable, according to Habermas, of dealing with "systematic distortion," that is, with ideology. Instead of conversing with the past, the critic of ideology must propose a "regulative ideal" of nonideological symbolic interaction ("communicative action") against which ideological distortion can be measured. Yet, in doing so, Habermas goes to the opposite extreme from Gadamer: if Gadamer runs the risk of conflating tradition with the coercive power of rhetoric or the constraints of imitation, Habermas's ideal of "unconstrained communication" runs the danger of isolating reason from rhetoric and imitation altogether.

Like Ricoeur, I think the opposition between hermeneutics and the critique of ideology is too stark. First, hermeneutics has a critical dimension, as my brief discussion of Renaissance theories of rhetoric and imitation in the early chapters of this book has suggested. It involves a recognition of historical distance and of anachronism. Furthermore, Renaissance philologists were sometimes capable of recognizing systematic, ideologically motivated textual distortions—as Valla did in his analysis of the Donation of Constantine. Second, the critique of ideology necessarily involves interpretation and relation to an authoritative past: as Ricoeur remarks, "critique is also a tradition," as is the case with Exodus ("Hermeneutics," 99). Familiarity with the past is necessary in order to reimagine the future: "He who is unable to reinterpret his past may also be incapable of projecting his interest in emancipation" (97). Thus whereas Gadamer gives priority to interpretation and Habermas stresses the necessity of critique, I want to insist with Ricoeur on the intersection of these two. Both in the Renaissance and in current critical debate this intersection deserves the name "rhetoric." Rhetoric is an instrument not only of force and fraud but also of the critical distance and reflection that is necessary for the critique of ideology. As Machiavelli and his best Renaissance readers recognized, the possibility of the former is the precondition of the latter.

APPENDIX

A BRIEF NOTE ON RHETORIC AND REPUBLICANISM IN THE
HISTORIOGRAPHY OF THE ITALIAN RENAISSANCE

THE QUESTION of the relationship between humanist rhetoric and republicanism is a venerable topos in the historiography of the Italian Renaissance, and in Machiavelli studies in particular. The most influential recent interpretations of Machiavelli—those by political historians such as J.G.A. Pocock and Quentin Skinner—are couched in the terms of this debate. For this reason, the debate deserves special consideration here. Both Pocock and Skinner accept the argument that humanist rhetoric contributed to the development of civic humanism and that Machiavelli was the inheritor of this civic ideology. Yet, while Pocock and Skinner represent the current consensus regarding the influence of humanist rhetoric on Machiavelli, Machiavelli is still read and analyzed as though his own rhetoric were irrelevant to his political thought. In the following pages I suggest that both the debate and the recent consensus have important—but unrealized—methodological implications for the interpretation of Machiavellism in particular and for the relationship of rhetoric to political theory in general. Both suggest that Machiavelli's own work needs to be read and analyzed rhetorically.

The following brief history of the debate provides a topology of approaches to the question of rhetoric and civic humanism, and thus helps to situate my own rhetorical approach. The historians discussed below conceive of rhetoric variously as a tool of argument in the service of political ideas, an ideologically neutral technique of argument on both sides of a question, or as a mode of debate and dialogue that is both formal and critical. It is this last definition of rhetoric that informs my own rhetorical analysis of Machiavelli and that helps to explain the tensions and the ties between the Machiavel and the republican Machiavelli.

Although scholars agree that the quattrocento saw a burgeoning of humanist defenses of *libertas*, the explanations for this phenomenon vary. In *The Crisis of the Early Italian Renaissance* Hans Baron argued that the Florentines developed an ideology of civic humanism under the pressure of the Visconti threat to the Florentine republic in 1401–1402.[1] Before this time, according to Baron, humanism was essentially a literary endeavor, unrelated to the exigencies of political life. Fourteenth-century humanists, "compounding medieval ascetic ideals with stoic precepts, believed that the true sage ought to keep aloof from society and public duties." Petrarch's intermittent interest in the active life was an exception: for Baron he was "a Moses, led to see a new land, but not granted to enter it."[2] And Salutati, while very much engaged in the active life as chancellor of the republic on the eve of the Florentine crisis, did not integrate his political experience with his humanist literary and intellectual pursuits. If he had, according to Baron, he could never have defended Caesar's tyranny and condemned the republican Brutus in *De tyranno* (165–66). For all these reasons, it took the political crisis of the early quattrocento to channel the humanists' rhetorical skills into the defense of republicanism and the active life.

In a series of articles addressing Baron's claims, Jerrold Seigel argued that humanist defenses of *libertas* in the quattrocento were not simply responses to a political crisis but rather the products of a humanist rhetorical culture that encouraged arguments pro and contra a given topic. *Pace* Baron, there is no clear alliance between humanist rhetoric and republicanism in the early quattrocento, nor is there a sharp "break between the literary humanists of the fourteenth century and the 'civic humanists' of the fifteenth" (7–8). Drawing on Kristeller's definition of the humanists as professional rhetoricians, Seigel claimed instead that Petrarch and Bruni shared the culture of Ciceronian rhetoric, one that would dispose them to defend both the active and the contemplative lives at different points in their careers.

Ironically, then, although Baron and Seigel differed concerning the conditions that gave rise to the defense of republicanism, they agreed on the merely contingent relation of rhetoric to these values. For Baron, the decisive factor in the transformation of literary humanism into civic humanism was the political threat from the Visconti; for Seigel, humanist rhetoric was no more conducive to republican than to other political values since it was still essentially a literary exercise in the early quattrocento. In both cases rhetoric is conceived of as a neutral technique of argument that for professional or political reasons may be allied to particular substantive arguments.

Eugenio Garin offered a different analysis of the import of rhetorical training for Renaissance culture and politics. In contrast to Seigel, Garin stressed the discontinuity between medieval and humanist study of the ancients. And although he acknowledged with Baron the importance of political circumstances for the development of humanism, he focused instead on the political implications of the *studia humanitatis* as forms of knowledge. Drawing on humanist works of the fifteenth and sixteenth centuries, Garin argued that humanist philology involved a new, disinterested critical study of the past, and that rhetoric for the humanists entailed a theory of historical change and of the kinds of knowledge most appropriate to civic or political life.[3] In addition, he showed the frequent association of oratory with times of political crisis or republicanism. Patrizi, for example, credited Petrarch with reawakening the spirit of the ancient orators buried by monarchs and barbarians; and Brocardo, in Speroni's dialogue on rhetoric, remarked that he did not see "why rhetoric should be banished from republics, seeing that it is the art which has as its object human actions, from which republics arise."[4] According to Speroni, republics are especially subject to change, to history, and thus to considerations of decorum; conversely, because the laws of the republic are made "with reference to time, place, utility, one's own power and that of others, they often change form and appearance."[5] It is important to see that Garin's—and Speroni's—point here is not simply a thematic one. Rhetoric does not simply take politics as its subject matter but is uniquely suited in its form and method, its sensitivity to context and audience, to dealing with political issues and facilitating civic participation. Here the formal techniques of rhetorical argument both allow for a critique of the status quo and encourage positive political commitment.

Garin's work helped to create a consensus concerning the importance of humanist rhetoric for the development of civic consciousness among those historians, such as Quentin Skinner and J.G.A. Pocock, who sought to mediate between Baron's emphasis on political conditions of republicanism and Seigel's on the humanists' professional training.[6] However, this consensus has not yielded the attention to the rhetoric of political theory that Garin's analysis would seem to dictate.

While not rejecting the importance of political circumstances for the formation of republican political theory, Quentin Skinner argued for the contribution of "a new and self-conscious humanist form of rhetorical theory, which was imported into Italy from France in the second half of the thirteenth century" (*Foundations*, 1:35). He thus objected that,

> in treating the crisis of 1402 as "a catalyst in the emergence of new ideas," Baron has underestimated the extent to which the ideas involved were not in fact new at all, but were rather an inheritance from the City Republics of medieval Italy. . . . The other problem is that, in emphasising the special qualities of "civic" humanism, Baron has also failed to appreciate the nature of the links between the Florentine writers of the early *quattrocento* and the wider movement of Petrarchan humanism which had already developed in the course of the fourteenth century. (1:71)

Like Seigel, then, Skinner stressed the continuities between medieval and Renaissance rhetorical defenses of liberty; but like Garin, he insisted that these defenses were not mere rhetorical exercises but the genuine rhetorical expression of civic consciousness.[7] Yet, while Skinner acknowledged that humanist rhetorical theory enjoined the imitation of the classics and transformed "the prevailing conventions of the *Ars Dictaminis*," his argument concerning the connection between humanist rhetoric and republicanism is finally thematic: the study of the classics was important because it led to a familiarity with classical political arguments for republican government and against tyranny (1:35). Not surprisingly, Skinner's analysis of Renaissance works of political thought also is entirely thematic, focusing on abstract ideas (sometimes called "vocabulary") rather than the literary or rhetorical dimension of humanist culture. It thus falls short of his own methodological claims, as well as the important methodological implications of Garin's remarks on the humanist conception of rhetoric, both of which require some attention to the form of the works Skinner is summarizing. This is particularly striking in his analysis of Machiavelli whom he sees as both continuing and criticizing the earlier humanist tradition. Machiavelli emerges as a republican thinker who distances himself from an earlier humanist rhetoric of consensus by emphasizing the benefit of political conflict and dissension. But his achievement as a republican theorist is divorced from the rhetoric of his texts and summarized thematically. This misses a crucial element in Machiavelli's political theory, as well as a reason for the wide readership of his works.[8]

In *The Machiavellian Moment*, as we have seen, J.G.A. Pocock viewed Machiavelli as an example of that moment in the Renaissance in which secular, republican political theory emerged in response to the perception of historical contingency. For Pocock, humanist rhetoric is one facet of this complex historical moment. Yet, while Pocock saw rhetoric as contributing to the "emergent historicism" (3) of Renaissance republicanism, he finally subordinated it to the more impressive achievement of a genuinely secular political theory. "Machiavelli" in this analysis names the way in which politics displaces or supersedes humanist rhetoric, just as the historical Machiavelli moves beyond the assumptions of civic humanism. This displacement describes both Pocock's historical narrative and his method. In his discussion of the work of Machiavelli, Guicciardini, and others, rhetoric as a topic and a method of analysis has fallen by the wayside. A close look at Pocock's discussion of the Baron-Seigel debate will illustrate why this is the case.

While conceding Seigel's point about the internal constraints of the humanist rhetorical culture, Pocock also insisted that civic humanism did exist, whether or not it was genuinely espoused by its humanist defenders. Echoing Garin, he noted: "Since rhetoric was both civic and active, it was possible for the rhetorician—or the humanist *qua* rhetorician—to provide a language in which to articulate a civic consciousness he might or might nor share" (59). This participation might take the form of republicanism but need not, since the "affinity" between rhetorician and citizen "ran far deeper than that" (60): "The rhetorician and the citizen were alike committed to viewing human life in terms of participation in particular actions and decisions, in particular political relationships between particular men" (59–60). For Pocock, as for Garin, this concern with particulars explains the similarities between "philological and political humanism." Elaborating on the analogy between "the conversation with the ancients" and "the conversation among citizens" (61–62), he argued:

> The humanist stress on communication was enough to raise the question of how particular men, existing at particular moments, could lay claim to secure knowledge. The answer could not be given in terms of the simple cognition of universals, or the intellectual animal would be thrust back into the universe of the scholastics, the political animal into that of the imperial hierarchies; to give it in terms of the simple accumulation of experience would be similarly fatal to humanist and citizen alike. Yet an answer must be given somehow, or Petrarch would be unable to read Livy, Florence unable to govern itself. How might a conversation between particulars be capable of organized rationality? The rhetoric of philology, or of politics, might provide the answer; but politics was more than rhetoric. (62–63)

In the end, although Pocock and Skinner agree on the contribution of humanist rhetoric to the development of Renaissance republicanism, they see this rhetorical moment as one superseded by a properly political analysis. Rhetorical attention to particulars—whether in a republic or principality—eventually gives way to republican theory. As an art for dealing with contingency, rhetoric thus provides Pocock and Skinner with an analogue for the republican response to political crisis; but it does not provide a tool of analysis of republican texts.

There are several costs to this supersession of rhetoric when we come to Machiavelli's work. The first is a neglect of one of the dominant languages available to Renaissance writers for conceptualizing the sphere of contingency and the problem of innovation within this sphere. According to Pocock, politics is more than rhetoric because the rhetorical resources for the articulation of a given mode of civic consciousness may exist without being exercised; that exercise requires favorable political conditions, as well as the language to conceptualize them. Yet, in focusing on these conditions, Pocock distanced himself from the humanists' usual understanding of their own activity. Although some humanists reflected on the social and political conditions necessary for civic liberty and the appropriation of the past in the economic and institutional terms that we would recognize, most tended—as Pocock's analogy between reading and governing in the quotation above suggests—to assimilate these historical conditions to the philological study of ancient texts and the rhetorical standard of decorum: the study of classical languages and ancient history was necessary for the proper understanding and editing of classical texts, and the recognition of historical change was necessary to determine what in the classical work could speak to—and was worth imitating in—the present. Notoriously, it was not only Petrarch who read Livy and for whom the ability to read Livy was related to the possibility of Florentine self-government, but also Machiavelli.

The second problem with the neglect of rhetoric is the unproblematic assimilation of Machiavelli the author of *The Prince* to the republican theorist of the *Discourses*, and the consequent refusal to take seriously the reception of Machiavelli as rhetorician and Machiavel. Thus, although Skinner notes in passing the ironic treatment of humanist virtues and what he misrepresents as Machiavelli's shocking silence about religion in *The Prince*, he tends to focus instead on such similarities as the shared concern with "greatness" and "the government of cities" in Machiavelli's two major works of political thought. For Skinner, Machiavelli is "essentially . . . an exponent of a distinctive humanist tradition of classical republicanism."[9] Pocock also emphasizes the continuities between *The Prince* and the *Discourses* as "analytic stud[ies] of innovation and its consequences." As Pocock writes in one of his characteristic dismissals of the reception of Machiavelli as Machiavel, "the truly subversive Machiavelli was not a counselor of tyrants, but a good citizen and patriot" (*MM*, 218). For both Pocock and Skinner, *virtù* is assimilated to classical virtue, and the problem of the relation of *The Prince* to the *Discourses* is resolved in favor of classical republicanism. In neglecting the humanist rhetorical tradition and the hyperbolic rhetoric of Machiavelli's texts, this vision of classical republicanism domesticates what is most disturbing and innovative in Machiavelli's work.

NOTES

INTRODUCTION

1. *Clarendon: Selections from "The History of the Rebellion" and "The Life by Himself"*, ed. Gertrude Huehns (Oxford: Oxford University Press, 1978), 304–305.

2. In the coda to this book, I consider the implications of my argument for contemporary discussion of the relationship between rhetoric and the critique of ideology.

3. On Garin, see the appendix. Rhetoric was linked to imitation and to politics broadly conceived as the realm of civic affairs in most Renaissance theory and practice. To begin with, like the rhetorical notion of decorum, the term *imitation* could have both a literary and an ethical or political valence: depending on the text, it could refer not only to the literary imitation of previous authors or the artist's representation of nature but also to the audience's response. In this last case, imitation is simply another name for the rhetorical effect of the text. Renaissance poetics was thus rhetorical in that it aimed not only to delight but also to move and instruct the audience; rhetoric, both as the codification of schemes and tropes as well as a theory of persuasive argument, was the model for poetics. Conversely, rhetoric involved an element of imitation because the skills of persuasion were acquired by imitating the ancients and because the orator learned to represent himself in a compelling way to his audience. Furthermore, as with poetry, the reader or hearer of a rhetorical performance was invited to imitate the examples in the text or speech and his response was judged to have ethical and political consequences.

On the centrality of the terms *decorum* and *imitation* to both humanist rhetoric and moral philosophy, see Hannah Holborn Gray, "Renaissance Humanism: The Pursuit of Eloquence," *Journal of the History of Ideas* 24 (1963): 497–514, esp. 506; and Thomas M. Greene, *The Light in Troy: Imitation and Discovery in Renaissance Poetry* (New Haven, Conn.: Yale University Press, 1982), chaps. 3, 4, and 9.

4. On classical republicanism see Zera S. Fink, *The Classical Republicans* (Evanston, Ill.: Northwestern University Press, 1945); Caroline Robbins, *The Eighteenth-Century Commonwealthman* (Cambridge, Mass.: Harvard University Press, 1959); and the introduction to her edition of *Two English Republican Tracts* (Cambridge: Cambridge University Press, 1969); Felix Raab, *The English Face of Machiavelli: A Changing Interpretation 1500–1700* (London: Routledge and Kegan Paul, 1964), who tends rather to identify Machiavellism with secular political thought; J.G.A. Pocock, " 'The Onely Politician': Machiavelli, Harrington, and Felix Raab," *Historical Studies, Australia and New Zealand* 12 (1965): 265–95; *The Machiavellian Moment: Florentine Political Thought and the Atlantic Republican Tradition* (Princeton, N.J.: Princeton University Press, 1975); and the introduction to his edition of *The Political Works of James Harrington* (Cambridge: Cambridge University Press, 1977), esp. 15–42. Pocock has over time

revised his equation of Machiavellism with *secular* republicanism. See note 7 below. Finally, see Blair Worden, "Classical Republicanism and the Puritan Revolution," in *History and Imagination: Essays in Honor of H. R. Trevor-Roper*, ed. Hugh Lloyd-Jones, Valerie Pearl, and Blair Worden (New York: Holmes and Meier, 1981), 182–200. Although Worden acknowledges that many classical republicans were Arminians, he nevertheless tries to maintain a separation between classical republicanism, which rejected the political goals of the puritans, and what he calls puritan republicanism.

There are, of course, important exceptions to the secular-republican reading of Machiavelli, and I have been influenced by these studies; but the authors have not generally discussed the Renaissance reception of Machiavelli's work and so have not seen the implications of their focus on the other Machiavelli—the Machiavelli of force and fraud, the analyst of political necessity—for the history of Machiavellism. See, among others, Gennaro Sasso, *Niccolò Machiavelli: Storia del suo pensiero politico* (1958; Bologna: Il Mulino, 1980); Leo Strauss, *Thoughts on Machiavelli* (Chicago: University of Chicago Press, 1958); Joseph Anthony Mazzeo, *Renaissance and Seventeenth-Century Studies* (New York and London: Columbia University Press and Routledge and Kegan Paul, 1964), 90–144; Federico Chabod, *Machiavelli and the Renaissance*, trans. David Moore (New York: Harper and Row, 1958), and *Scritti su Machiavelli* (Turin: Einaudi, 1964); Mark Hulliung, *Citizen Machiavelli* (Princeton, N.J.: Princeton University Press, 1983). One important author who has discussed the Renaissance reception of this dimension of Machiavelli's thought is Friedrich Meinecke, *Machiavellism: The Doctrine of Raison d'Etat and Its Place in Modern History*, trans. Douglas Scott (1924; Boulder, Colo.: Westview, 1984). Yet none of these authors, including Meinecke, makes the rhetorical tradition central to his interpretation.

5. The claim that the Machiavel signals an uninformed reading is supported by the well-known fact that the condemnation of "Machiavel" did not depend on firsthand knowledge of Machiavelli's texts, and is often difficult to separate from Tacitism or Senecanism in the Renaissance. On Tacitus, see Peter Burke, "Tacitism," in *Tacitus*, ed. T. A. Dorey (New York: Basic Books, 1969), 149–71; Mary F. Tenney, "Tacitus in the Politics of Early Stuart England," *Classical Journal* 37 (1941): 151–63; Kenneth C. Schellhase, *Tacitus in Renaissance Political Thought* (Chicago: University of Chicago Press, 1976); Giuseppe Toffanin, *Machiavelli e il tacitismo* (Padua, 1921); André Stegmann, "Tacitisme: Programme pour un nouvel essai de définition," in *Machiavellismo e antimachiavellici nel cinquecento* (Florence: Olschki, 1969), 117–30; Arnaldo Momigliano, "Tacitus and the Tacitist Tradition," in *The Classical Foundations of Modern Historiography* (Berkeley and Los Angeles: University of California Press, 1990), 109–31; J.H.M. Salmon, "Stoicism and Roman Example: Seneca and Tacitus in Jacobean England," *Journal of the History of Ideas* 50 (1989): 199–225; and Richard Tuck, *Philosophy and Government, 1572–1651* (Cambridge: Cambridge University Press, 1993). Not all of these works discuss the relation of Machiavellism to Tacitism; but the features characteristic of Tacitism and the attacks and defenses of Tacitism in this period are identical to those of Machiavellism. Supposed anti-Machiavellians such as Botero, Lipsius, and Boccalini regularly link Tacitus and Machiavelli. I discuss this link in chapter 3.

6. See, for example, Emile Gasquet, *Le Courant machiavélien dans la pensée et la littérature anglaises du XVIᵉ siècle* (Paris: Didier, 1975), esp. the conclusion, 415–20. The literature on the Machiavel in Elizabethan and Jacobean literature is extensive; see, among others, Edward Meyer, *Machiavelli and the Elizabethan Drama* (Weimar: Emil Felber, 1897); Mario Praz, "Machiavelli and the Elizabethans," *Proceedings of the British Academy* 13 (1928): 49–97; W. A. Armstrong, "The Influence of Seneca and Machiavelli on the Elizabethan Tyrant," *Review of English Studies* (Oxford: Clarendon Press, 1948), 19–35; Daniel C. Boughner, *The Devil's Disciple: Ben Jonson's Debt to Machiavelli* (New York: Philosophical Library, 1968); Jonas Barish, *The Antitheatrical Prejudice* (Berkeley and Los Angeles: University of California Press, 1981); Margaret Scott, "Machiavelli and the Machiavel," *Renaissance Drama*, n.s. 15 (1984): 147–74, who argues correctly that the Machiavel is not a misreading of Machiavelli's work; Julia Lupton, "Truant Dispositions: *Hamlet* and Machiavelli," *Journal of Medieval and Renaissance Studies* 17 (1987): 59–82; and Rebecca W. Bushnell, *Tragedies of Tyrants: Political Thought and Theater in the English Renaissance* (Ithaca, N.Y.: Cornell University Press, 1990).

Some historians also comment on the emergence of classical republican ideas in literary texts. Whereas Raab and Pocock only briefly mention literary figures in their accounts, Zera Fink, Caroline Robbins, and Blair Worden all note that "classical republicanism of the Puritan revolution is a literary as well as a political phenomenon" (Worden, "Classical Republicanism," 190). In their accounts, what is literary about the republicanism of these authors is that republican tenets—faith in reason, the belief that "all power derived originally from the people and could be resumed by the people" (Worden, 193)—appear as themes in their literary works. I challenge this purely thematic reading in the chapters on Milton below. On delegitimized politics, see *MM*, 163; cf. Raab, 118.

7. In *JH*, Pocock maintains the equation of Machiavellism with republicanism but seems to have recognized the inadequacy of the equation of republicanism with secular political thought. He notes that Marvell mixes the language of Machiavellism with that of millenarianism and biblical prophecy in his depiction of Cromwell in "An Horatian Ode"; even Harrington "seems to have discerned messianic and apocalyptic possibilities for his republic." In the course of the seventeenth century the language of Machiavellism came to be used in puritan religious debate as well. In Pocock's revised analysis, the problem faced by both secular and religious thinkers of the seventeenth century was that of legitimating authority in a world of de facto political power. Although the language of republicanism was less suited to this task than were millenarian beliefs, it was nevertheless "available" (33). In a witty remark that Machiavelli might have appreciated, Pocock admits, "The Florentine secretary was also among the prophets, who had interested him" (*JH*, 41). I take up the theological context of Machiavellism particularly in chapters 3 and 5. For an important argument for the compatibility of Machiavellian republicanism and Christianity in Italy, see William J. Bouwsma, *Venice and the Defense of Republican Liberty: Renaissance Values in the Age of the Counter Reformation* (Berkeley and Los Angeles: University of California Press, 1968), esp. chap. 1.

8. In his many programmatic statements about the historiography of political

discourse, Pocock suggests that a political language is, by definition, a locus of ideological conflict: a political language is spoken by more than one speaker, often to heterogeneous ends. See, for example, "Introduction: The state of the art," in J.G.A. Pocock, *Virtue, Commerce, and History* (Cambridge: Cambridge University Press, 1985), 1–34; and J.G.A. Pocock, "The concept of language and the *métier d'historien*: some considerations on practice," in *The Languages of Political Theory in Early-Modern Europe*, ed. Anthony Pagden (Cambridge: Cambridge University Press, 1987), 19–38. In this second essay, Pocock also stresses "the antinomian use of language: . . . the use by the ruled of the language of the rulers in such a way as to empty it of its meanings and reverse its effects. Appropriation and expropriation are important aspects of what we have to study" (24). He even imagines a history of a "Machiavellian or anti-Machiavellian rhetoric," which would consider "how it became an idiom or language available for the purposes of others besides Machiavelli" (35). Individual speech acts ("paroles" rather than "langues," in Pocock's Saussurean vocabulary) are also potentially heterogeneous, capable of drawing on or participating in a variety of different languages (23, 30). Yet, Pocock's reading of Machiavelli's speech act—for all its interest in the formal character of *virtù*—is remarkably univocal. Conflict and ambivalence become a function of the *reception* of Machiavelli rather than, as I argue, a function of Machiavelli's own ambivalent rhetoric. It is telling in this context that, when Pocock argues in the introduction to *Virtue, Commerce, and History* that "political language is by its nature ambivalent," he is referring to "the *generalized* language of discourse at any time," that is, the sum total of available discourses at a given moment; here, too, ambivalence seems to be located between discourses rather than in a *specific* political discourse (8; my emphasis). I believe this discrepancy between methodological principle and practice may be observed in Quentin Skinner's work as well. A selection of Skinner's essays on methodology and of responses by his critics is collected in *Meaning and Context: Quentin Skinner and His Critics*, ed. James Tully (Cambridge: Cambridge University Press, 1988). For a brief discussion of my objections to Skinner's reading of Machiavelli, see the appendix.

9. See Cicero, *De officiis*, 3, 47.

10. I have discussed these assumptions in chapter 2 of *Rhetoric, Prudence, and Skepticism in the Renaissance* (Ithaca, N.Y.: Cornell University Press, 1985).

11. See Meinecke, *Machiavellism*, 30; and Felix Gilbert, *Machiavelli and Guicciardini: Politics and History in Sixteenth-Century Florence* (Princeton, N.J.: Princeton University Press, 1965). Of the crisis in political thinking in Florence in the late fifteenth century, Gilbert writes: "In these years, as men were altering their opinions about the qualities needed by a successful leader, there was also a change in the views about the means by which man could control the course of events. Force, which previously had been thought to be just one of the several factors which determined politics, now came to be regarded as the decisive factor" (128–29); see also Quentin Skinner, "Political Philosophy," in *The Cambridge History of Renaissance Philosophy*, ed. Charles B. Schmitt, Quentin Skinner, Eckhard Kessler, and Jill Kraye (Cambridge: Cambridge University Press, 1988), 432: "As we have seen, the early humanists had often drawn a strong contrast between *virtus* and *vis*, between manly qualities and sheer brute force. By

contrast, Machiavelli treats the willingness to exercise force as an absolutely central feature of good princely government."

12. I owe this sentence to an incisive critique of a draft of this chapter by Lorna Hutson of the University of London.

PART ONE
MACHIAVELLI

1. One of the best examples of this recognition is provided by Agostino Nifo, who plagiarized Machiavelli's *Prince* before it was published in 1532 in a work entitled *De regnandi peritia* (1523). As a number of critics have noted, Nifo restored the signs of a typical humanist treatise on politics by adding references to authoritative classical authors, such as Cicero and Aristotle, and by writing a final chapter in which he recommends the traditional virtues to the prince. He also excused his examples of tyrannical behavior by offering moralizing conclusions and by saying that he was describing both the poison of tyranny and the remedy of virtuous behavior. In short, he revised *The Prince* to make it look as much like a traditional mirror of princes as possible. The Latin text and a French translation of Nifo's treatise exist in a modern edition: *Une Reécriture du Prince de Machiavel: Le De regnandi peritia de Agostino Nifo*, ed. and trans. Simone Pernet-Beau and Paul Larivaille, Documents du Centre de Recherche de Langue et Littérature Italiennes (Paris: Université Paris X-Nanterre, 1987). On Nifo, see Procacci, 3–26; and Robert Hariman, "Composing Modernity in Machiavelli's *Prince*," *Journal of the History of Ideas* 50 (1989): 3–29.

2. In a letter to Benedetto Varchi, quoted in Luigi Firpo, "Le origini dell'antimachiavellismo," in *Machiavellismo e antimachiavellici nel cinquecento* (Florence: Olschki, 1969), 27. In his edition of *Il Principe* (Oxford: Clarendon Press, 1891), L. Arthur Burd argues that Busini is reporting his own view in 1549 rather than Florentine opinion in 1527.

3. *Considerazioni intorno ai Discorsi del Machiavelli sopra la prima deca di Tito Livio*, in Francesco Guicciardini, *Scritti politici e Ricordi*, ed. Roberto Palmarrochi (Bari: Laterza, 1933), 33.

4. Francesco Guicciardini, *Ricordi* (Milan: Garzanti, 1975), ricordi C110 and C117; translation by Mario Domandi, *Maxims and Reflections of a Renaissance Statesman* (New York: Harper and Row, 1965), 69, 71.

5. See Mario Martelli, "Schede sulla cultura di Machiavelli," *Interpres* 6 (1985–86): 283–330, esp. 287–88; and Carlo Dionisotti, "Machiavelli letterato," in *Machiavellerie* (Turin: Einaudi, 1980), 227–66; reprinted in *Machiavelli and the Discourse of Literature*, ed. Albert Russell Ascoli and Victoria Kahn (Ithaca, N.Y.: Cornell University Press, 1993), 17–51.

6. On Machiavelli's humanist education and learning, see the appendix in Felix Gilbert, *Machiavelli and Guicciardini: Politics and History in Sixteenth-Century Florence* (Princeton, N.J.: Princeton University Press, 1965), 318–22; Armando Verde, "Niccolò Machiavelli studente," *Memorie domenicane*, n.s. 4 (1973): 404–408; Quentin Skinner, *Machiavelli*, Past Masters Series (New York: Hill and Wang, 1981). Skinner conjectures that this humanist education helped Machiavelli gain the post of second chancellor of Florence: "The prevalence of

these [humanist] ideals [in Florence] helps to explain how Machiavelli came to be appointed at a relatively early age to a position of considerable responsibility in the administration of the republic. For his family, though neither rich nor highly aristocratic, was closely connected with some of the city's most exalted humanist circles. . . . It is also evident from Bernardo's *Diary* that, in spite of the large expense involved—which he anxiously itemised—he was careful to provide his son with an excellent grounding in the *studia humanitatis*" (4, 5).

7. On the relationship of *The Prince* to the mirror of princes, see, in particular, Felix Gilbert, "The Humanist Concept of the Prince and the 'Prince' of Machiavelli," *Journal of Modern History* 11 (1939): 449–83; and Allan H. Gilbert, *Machiavelli's Prince and Its Forerunners* (Durham, N.C.: Duke University Press, 1938). On Machiavelli's attack on the humanist rhetoric and politics of consensus, see chapter 2 below.

8. I borrow the phrase "immanent critique" from Adorno and Horkheimer who used it to describe a mode of dialectical thinking that exposes the internal contradictions of a given ideology, historical situation, or philosophical system. Specifically, an immanent critique confronts "the existent, in its historical context, with the claim of its conceptual principles, in order to criticize the relation between the two" (Max Horkheimer, *The Eclipse of Reason* [New York: Continuum, 1987], 182).

9. On the rhetorical dimension of Machiavelli's political thought see, among others, Eugene Garver, *Machiavelli and the History of Prudence* (Madison: University of Wisconsin Press, 1987); Michael McCanles, *The Discourse of 'Il Principe'* (Malibu, Calif.: Undena Publications, 1983); Timothy Hampton, *Writing from History: The Rhetoric of Exemplarity in Renaissance Literature* (Ithaca, N.Y.: Cornell University Press, 1990), 62–80; John D. Lyons, who discusses Machiavelli's use of examples in *Exemplum: The Rhetoric of Example in Early Modern France and Italy* (Princeton, N.J.: Princeton University Press, 1989), 35–71; A. J. Parel, "Machiavelli's Use of Civic Humanist Rhetoric," *Rhetorica* 8 (1990): 119–36; Wayne Rebhorn, *Foxes and Lions: Machiavelli's Confidence Men* (Ithaca, N.Y.: Cornell University Press, 1988), who discusses Machiavelli's rhetoric in particular on pages 113–16 and 192–227; Barbara Spackman, "Machiavelli and Maxims," *Yale French Studies* 77 (1990): 137–55; John F. Tinkler, "Praise and Advice: Rhetorical Approaches in More's *Utopia* and Machiavelli's *The Prince*," *Sixteenth Century Journal* 19 (1988): 187–207; William E. Wiethoff, "Machiavelli's *The Prince*: Rhetorical Influence in Civil Philosophy," *Western Speech* 38 (1974): 98–107; and the collection of essays by Italian and English scholars in *Machiavelli and the Discourse of Literature*, ed. Albert Russell Ascoli and Victoria Kahn (Ithaca, N.Y.: Cornell University Press, 1993). In thinking about Machiavelli's rhetoric, I have benefited in particular from Nancy Struever's unpublished paper, "Machiavelli and the Critique of the Available Languages of Morality in the Sixteenth Century," published in a revised version in her *Theory as Practice: Ethical Inquiry in the Renaissance* (Chicago: University of Chicago Press, 1992), 147–81. With the exception of a few pages in Struever, these critics have not extended their insights to the history of Renaissance Machiavellism.

Despite the above bibliography, some historians of Machiavelli still neglect the rhetorical dimension of his work. August Buck usefully surveys recent interpretations of Machiavelli's work in *Machiavelli*, Erträge der Forschung, vol. 226 (Darmstadt: Wissenschaftliche Buchgesellschaft, 1985), and, with the exception of a brief discussion of the mirror of princes, does not mention humanist rhetoric.

10. Kenneth Burke, in *A Rhetoric of Motives* (1950; Berkeley: University of California Press, 1969), 158–66, and Garver, in *Machiavelli and the History of Prudence*, also analyze Machiavelli's works in terms of rhetorical topics, though not the ones I isolate here. Whereas Garver focuses on Machiavelli's relation to Cicero's and Aristotle's topics, I am chiefly concerned with the topics that emerge in the Renaissance reception of Machiavelli.

11. Garver, in *Machiavelli and the History of Prudence*, also argues that rhetorical problems cannot be solved by applying fixed moral principles or brute force (71, 88), and notes the connection between political innovation and rhetorical invention (27).

CHAPTER ONE
THE PRINCE

1. Sheldon Wolin, *Politics and Vision* (Boston: Little, Brown, 1960), 224.

2. Idealism and instrumentalism are complementary, for the ideal or absolute makes all action merely instrumental to its realization. Eugene Garver also notes this connection in *Machiavelli and the History of Prudence* (Madison: University of Wisconsin Press, 1987), 3–26. Garver also discusses Machiavelli's critique of ideology (see his index), as does Joseph Anthony Mazzeo, *Renaissance and Seventeenth-Century Studies* 104, 107, 114–15. I take up the relationship between rhetoric and the critique of ideology in the coda below.

3. In *Machiavelli and the History of Prudence*, Eugene Garver discusses Machiavelli's inclusion of atechnical arguments within his political rhetoric. Also relevant to this discussion of Machiavelli's inclusion of force within his rhetorical paradigm is Michael McCanles's discussion of Machiavelli's "textualizing" of the realm of politics in *The Discourse of 'Il Principe'*, xv, 7, and passim.

4. Recent interpretations of *The Prince* in the context of the humanist notion of imitation include Eugene Garver, *Machiavelli and the History of Prudence*; Mark Hulliung, *Citizen Machiavelli* (Princeton, N.J.: Princeton University Press, 1983), esp. 130–67; Hanna Pitkin, *Fortune Is a Woman* (Berkeley and Los Angeles: University of California Press, 1983), 268ff.; Thomas M. Greene, "The End of Discourse in Machiavelli's 'Prince,'" *Yale French Studies* 67 (1984): 57–71; Quentin Skinner, *The Foundations of Modern Political Thought*, 2 vols. (Cambridge: Cambridge University Press, 1978), 1: 152–86; Gennaro Sasso, *Niccolò Machiavelli: Storia del suo pensiero politico* (Naples, 1958; rev. ed. Bologna: Il Mulino, 1980); Giuseppe Toffanin, *Il Cinquecento* in *Storia della letteratura d'Italia*, 6th ed. (Milan: F. Vallardi, 1960), 388–89. For earlier discussions of Machiavelli's relation to humanism, see Felix Gilbert, *Machiavelli and Guicciardini: Politics and History in Sixteenth-Century Florence* (Princeton, N.J.: Princeton University Press, 1965), and the introduction to part 1, note 7. On exemplarity in Machiavelli, see the introduction to part 1, note 9.

5. Machiavelli's use of *prudente* and *prudenzia* is almost as frequent as his use of *virtù* and has a similar effect of subverting the traditional humanist moral

connotations of the term. The two terms are also frequently linked in a single phrase. See, in addition to the passage cited in the text, the Italian text of *P*, 3.22 ("della virtù e prudenzia loro"); 7.34 ("uno prudente e virtuoso uomo"); 8.50 ("uno principe prudente"); 9.55 ("Paolo Vitelli . . . uomo prudentissimo"); 15.66; 16.67; 18.72; 21.92; 22.93; 23.95–96; 24.97; 25.98–101. As contemporaries did, Machiavelli sometimes gave the name *astuzia* to this demoralized concept of prudence. For a similar argument about Machiavelli's "demoralization" of prudence, see Martin Fleischer, "A Passion for Politics: The Vital Core of the World of Machiavelli," in *Machiavelli and the Nature of Political Thought*, ed. Martin Fleischer (New York: Athenaeum, 1972), esp. 139. On Machiavellian prudence, see also Garver, *Machiavelli and the History of Prudence*.

6. On ruse, see the discussion by Pierre Manent, *Naissances de la politique moderne: Machiavel, Hobbes, Rousseau* (Paris: Payot, 1977), 19.

7. See Garver, *Machiavelli and the History of Prudence*, 87, for a different reading of this image.

8. On the link between imitation and self-knowledge, see Thomas M. Greene, *The Light in Troy: Imitation and Discovery in Renaissance Poetry* (New Haven, Conn.: Yale University Press, 1982), 142, 172, 184.

9. Sheldon Wolin, *Politics and Vision*, 227, and Joseph Anthony Mazzeo, *Renaissance and Seventeenth-Century Studies* (New York: Columbia University Press; London: Routledge and Kegan Paul, 1964), 95, also comment on Machiavelli's conception of the intrinsic irony of politics.

10. The refusal to act in the face of such ironies Machiavelli called literature; see *Florentine Histories*, book 5, chap. 1; in Hulliung, *Citizen Machiavelli*, 137.

11. As Hulliung (*Citizen Machiavelli*, 158–59) and Sydney Anglo (in *Machiavelli* [New York: Harcourt, Brace, and World, 1969], 244–49) have remarked, Machiavelli's rejection of *mediocritas* or the middle way is also reflected in his antithetical, either/or style of arguing. I take up the question of Machiavelli's antitheses in the following chapter on the *Discourses*.

12. See Quintilian, *Institutio Oratoria*, 8.6.5; 9.2.44–47.

13. Nancy Struever also discusses the dereification of *virtù* in *Theory as Practice*, 155. See also Mazzeo, *Renaissance and Seventeenth-Century Studies*, 92.

14. Alfredo Bonadeo, *Corruption, Conflict and Power in the Works and Times of Niccolò Machiavelli* (Berkeley and Los Angeles: University of California Press, 1973), 82; J. H. Whitfield, *Machiavelli* (Oxford: Oxford University Press, 1972), 80, 108; Claude Lefort, *Le Travail de l'oeuvre Machiavel* (Paris: Gallimard, 1972), 376, though Lefort remarks on the "réserve troublante" that qualifies Machiavelli's condemnation. Another representative of this first position is Jerrold Seigel, "*Virtù* in and since the Renaissance," in *Dictionary of the History of Ideas*, 5 vols. (New York: Scribner, 1968), 4:476–86.

15. See Gennaro Sasso, *Niccolò Machiavelli*, 296ff; Gabriele Pepe, *La politica dei Borgia* (Naples: Ricciardi, 1945), 281–82; and Ugo Dotti, *Niccolò Machiavelli: La fenomenologia del potere* (Milan: Feltrinelli, 1979), 179ff. for the first position; for the second, see Pocock, *MM*, 152, 167.

16. Greene, "The End of Discourse in Machiavelli's 'Prince,'" notes the tenuousness of the distinction between Borgia and Agathocles (65) but sees this as

evidence of a breakdown in the concept of *virtù* rather than as a deliberate strategy; Manent, *Naissances de la politique*, 16, however, sees the distinction as deliberately false. See also Nathan Tarcov, "Quentin Skinner's Method and Machiavelli's *Prince*," in *Meaning and Context: Quentin Skinner and His Critics*, ed. James Tully (Princeton, N.J.: Princeton University Press, 1988): 194–203, esp. 201 on Agathocles.

17. Russell Price, "The Theme of *Gloria* in Machiavelli," *Renaissance Quarterly* 30 (1977): 588–631.

18. See Machiavelli's *Vita di Castruccio Castracani da Lucca*, where Castruccio is described as equaling Philip of Macedon and Scipio, even though he rose from an obscure beginning (Niccolò Machiavelli, *Tutte le opere*, ed. Mario Martelli [Florence: Sansoni, 1971], 615, 628). It is also notable that Machiavelli describes himself as "uno uomo di basso et infimo stato" (a man of low social rank) in his prefatory letter to *The Prince* (13, 3).

19. See chapter 12 on the pseudo-distinction between laws and arms, as well as chapter 19 on arms and friends.

20. Struever also discusses the conflation of the ethical good and the amoral well in *The Prince* in *Theory as Practice*, 157; McCanles, *The Discourse of 'Il Principe'*, 63–65, discusses Machiavelli's deliberate invocation of two registers of "bene" in this passage.

21. Discussing prudence in the *Nicomachean Ethics*, Aristotle writes: "It is this kind of deliberation which is good deliberation, a correctness that attains what is good" (*NE*, 1141b 20; trans. Martin Ostwald [New York: Bobbs Merrill, 1962]). My definition of *virtù* as functional excellence is taken from Hulliung's discussion of the similarity between *virtù* and *aretē*: "Since the Latin word *virtus* meant almost exactly what *aretē* had meant in popular Greek usage, simply to use the Latin language as it had always been used had the effect, whether intended or unintended, of undoing the Platonic and Aristotelian effort of reworking and philosophizing pagan values. Once again, 'excellence' was synonymous with all that is heroic, noble, warlike, great" (*Citizen Machiavelli*, 136–37). Other readers of Machiavelli have also drawn the analogy between *virtù* and *aretē*: see Bernard Crick in his preface to the Penguin edition of the *Discourses*, 59. On Machiavelli's critique of stoicism, see Hulliung 195ff., 253, and passim, as well as Quentin Skinner's discussion of Machiavelli's relation to Cicero in *Machiavelli*. For an argument that Cicero is a proto-Machiavellian, see Marcia Colish, "Cicero's *De officiis* and Machiavelli's *Prince*," *Sixteenth Century Journal* 9 (1978): 81–93.

22. This opposition is taken from J. H. Whitfield, *Machiavelli* (Oxford: Blackwell, 1947), 117.

23. Roland Barthes, "Le Discours de l'histoire," *Social Science Information* 6 (1967): 6. I owe this reference to Struever, "Machiavelli and the Available Languages." See also Tinkler, "Praise and Advice," on Machiavelli's replacing of the usual demonstrative rhetoric of handbooks for princes with a deliberative approach, with its consideration of *utilitas*, and its emphasis on the topos of necessity (195–201). For a reading of chapter 8 similar to the one offered here, see McCanles, *The Discourse of 'Il Principe'*, 59–69.

24. In *Foxes and Lions*, Wayne Rebhorn also discusses Machiavelli's manipulation of his audience, although he does not discuss Agathocles; see 118–23, 212–27.

25. Felix Gilbert, *Machiavelli and Guicciardini*, 120.

26. Garver, *Machiavelli and the History of Prudence*, 84, also discusses how *virtù* confounds the distinction between means and end.

27. Hulliung also makes this point in *Citizen Machiavelli*, 56, 82, 231. See also Leo Strauss, *Thoughts on Machiavelli* (Chicago: University of Chicago Press, 1958), 288–89; Manent, *Naissances de la politique*, 19–25; and *The Prince*, chapter 9 on the necessity of relying on the people, and chapter 19 for Machiavelli's remarks on the origin of the French parliament. In *MM*, Pocock discusses the prince as a man of *virtù* without fellow citizens (157).

28. See Manent, *Naissances de la politique*, 9–10, 35–39, for a more positive reading of the willing of necessity in *The Prince*.

29. Pitkin makes this point in *Fortune Is a Woman*, 292.

30. Angus Fletcher, *Allegory: The Theory of a Symbolic Mode* (Ithaca, N.Y.: Cornell University Press, 1964).

31. On parataxis in *The Prince* see Fredi Chiappelli, *Studi sul linguaggio del Machiavelli* (Florence: Le Monnier, 1952). See also McCanles, *The Discourse of 'Il Principe'*, 13.

32. On the sublime "inciting to action," see Fletcher, *Allegory*, 249, 246. Fletcher quotes Schiller: "For the sublime, in the strict sense of the word, cannot be contained in any sensuous form, but rather concerns ideas of reason, which, although no adequate representation of them is possible, may be excited and called into the mind by that very inadequacy itself which does admit of sensuous presentation" (251–52). See also Immanuel Kant, *Critique of Judgment*, trans. J. H. Bernard (New York: Macmillan, 1951), 88, 101 (paragraphs 25, 28). The Machiavellism of Milton's use of allegory and of the sublime is discussed in chapter 8.

33. Pocock makes a similar point in *MM*, 171: "We must not say that divine inspiration is being lowered to the level of *realpolitik* without adding that *realpolitik* is being raised to the level of divine inspiration." See Lefort, *Le Travail de l'oeuvre*, 447, on chapter 26 as Machiavelli's example to the Medici of the kind of rhetoric that is useful when addressing the people.

34. In "Machiavelli's Gift of Counsel" (in *Machiavelli and the Discourse of Literature*, ed. Albert Russell Ascoli and Victoria Kahn [Ithaca, N.Y.: Cornell University Press, 1993]: 219–57), Albert Russell Ascoli argues that in chapter 26 of *The Prince* Machiavelli acknowledges that his treatise "is likely to prove no more effective in reshaping history than Petrarch's *canzone*," four lines of which appear as the last words of *The Prince*. "The real message of the final clash between prudent pragmatism and utopian prophecy in *The Prince*, however, is . . . another. . . . Once the wide gap between Machiavelli's foresight and the Medici princes' power has been recognized, once his own hidden identification with the Savonarolian *profeta disarmato* has become apparent, once he admits that 'what is' matters to him far less than 'what (could and) should be,' a fundamental mystification inherent in his conceptual and rhetorical pragmatism is made appar-

ent. . . . 'Pragmatism' is itself profoundly utopian" (256). On the collapse of Machiavelli's treatise into literary idealism, see Thomas M. Greene, "The End of Discourse in Machiavelli's *Prince.*"

35. Theodor Adorno, *Minima Moralia*, trans. E.F.N. Jephcott (London: Verso, 1978), 126–27.

CHAPTER TWO
THE DISCOURSES

1. On original sin, see Pocock, *MM*, 167: "On the one hand *virtù* is that by which we innovate, and so let loose sequences of contingency beyond our prediction or control so that we become prey to *fortuna*; on the other hand *virtù* is that internal to ourselves by which we resist *fortuna* and impose upon her patterns of order, which may even become patterns of moral order. This seems to be the heart of Machiavellian ambiguities. It explains why innovation is supremely difficult, being formally self-destructive; and it explains why there is incompatibility between action—and so between politics defined in terms of action rather than tradition—and moral order. The politicization of virtue had arrived at the discovery of a politicized version of original sin." See also Felix Gilbert, *Machiavelli and Guicciardini: Politics and History in Sixteenth-Century Florence* (Princeton, N.J.: Princeton University Press, 1965), on the *Discourses* as Machiavelli's "political utopia" (192). Describing the superior judgment of the people as compared to a prince, Machiavelli writes, "Not without good reason is the voice of the populace likened to that of God" (*D*, 1.58.264, 255).

2. For Machiavelli's use of the words *reducere, reducersi*, and so forth, see also, in the Italian edition, pages 131, 142, 155, 160, 177, 179, 185, 193, 224, 233, 265, 293, 340, 379, 381, 385, 450; in a negative sense, see 215. The lawyers' and doctors' methodical codification of decisions may have suggested rhetoric to contemporaries. In *Ramus: Method and the Decay of Dialogue* (Cambridge, Mass.: Harvard University Press, 1958), Walter J. Ong, S.J., argues that Renaissance medicine was "shot through with rhetoric, partly . . . because in the Hippocratic writings and elsewhere medical lore was preserved and studied in aphorisms (Bacon's interest in method and his interest in aphorisms go together)" (226). I take up the issue of method and its relation to aphorisms in chapter 4.

3. Throughout the *Discourses* Machiavelli emphasizes the availability of examples for use on both sides of a question; see 3.21 and 3.22. On Machiavelli's examples, see Felix Gilbert, *Machiavelli and Guicciardini*, 167; and the introduction to part 1, note 9.

4. I discuss the humanist rhetoric of consensus in *Rhetoric, Prudence, and Skepticism in the Renaissance* (Ithaca, N.Y.: Cornell University Press, 1985). On the institutional equivalent of such rhetoric of consensus, see John M. Najemy, *Corporatism and Consensus in Florentine Electoral Politics, 1280–1400* (Chapel Hill: University of North Carolina Press, 1982), especially the introduction and epilogue. Najemy suggests a quattrocento analogue for Machiavelli's rhetoric of conflict in the political practice of the Florentine guilds. See also his two articles: "'Arti' and 'Ordini' in Machiavelli's *Istorie*," in *Essays Presented to Myron P.*

Gilmore, ed. Sergio Bertelli and Gloria Ramakus, vol. 1: *History* (Florence: La Nuova Italia, 1978), 161–91, esp. 167–68; and "Machiavelli and the Medici: The Lessons of Florentine History," *Renaissance Quarterly* 35 (1982): 551–76. For examples of the contemporary rhetoric of political union or consensus, see the remarks from the Florentine *Pratiche* (meetings of citizens to advise the Great Council and the Council of Eighty), quoted by Felix Gilbert in "Florentine Political Assumptions in the Period of Savonarola and Soderini," *Journal of the Warburg and Courtauld Institutes* 20 (1957): 187–214. Gilbert argues that Florence in the sixteenth century was "a society deeply riven by personal rivalries, by difference in wealth and education, and torn by internal conflicts. These dissensions came up for discussion in many meetings of the Pratiche. The inability to grasp their significance was reflected in the manner in which the question about which the advice of the Pratica was sought was formulated: 'Che modi e vie siano da tenere circa l'unione dei cittadini a fargli concordi insieme' " (212–13). See also the passages quoted by Gennaro Sasso in *Niccolò Machiavelli: Storia del suo pensiero politico* (1958; Bologna: Il Mulino, 1980), 476 n. 46. Also exemplary is Bernardo Rucellai's discussion of the necessity of civic concord in his *De bello italico*, and his condemnation of the sedition that arises when the people ("plebi") are allowed to participate in government. The relevant passages are cited by Mario Santoro, *Fortune, ragione, e prudenza nella civiltà letteraria del cinquecento*, rev. ed. (Naples: Liguori, 1978), 175–76.

5. On Machiavelli's reading of Livy, and his misunderstanding of Livian *fortuna* as chance, see Mark Hulliung, *Citizen Machiavelli* (Princeton, N.J.: Princeton University Press, 1983), 46.

6. This interpretation is also carried out through Machiavelli's counterpointing of Livy and Polybius. As many readers have noted, in explaining Rome's transition from a monarchy to a republic with a mixed constitution, Machiavelli invokes the Polybian theory of natural cycles of government; but he reduces nature to fortune in the case of Rome. In so doing, he criticizes one strain of classical political theory and thereby makes the active assumption of responsibility possible both in reading and in politics (since not everything is determined by nature, there is room for human deliberation and action). But Machiavelli does not stop with the Livian attribution of Roman excellence to *fortuna* (interpreted as chance), since in the act of reducing Polybian nature to chance, he also redefines chance as disunion. By this circuitous route Machiavelli ends up subscribing to Polybius's theory of the mixed constitution. On Machiavelli's reading of Polybius, see Harvey C. Mansfield, Jr., *Machiavelli's New Modes and Orders: A Study of the "Discourses on Livy"* (Ithaca, N.Y.: Cornell University Press, 1979), 35ff.; Paul Larivaille, *La Pensée politique de Machiavel* (Nancy: Presses Universitaires de Nancy, 1982), 101ff.; Gennaro Sasso, "La Teoria dell'anacyclosis," *Studi su Machiavelli* (Naples: Morano, 1967), 161–222, esp. 199.

7. Giovanni Villani, *Cronica*, ed. Giovanni Aquilecchia (Turin: Einaudi, 1979), book 1, chap. 28; see also book 8, chap. 39.

8. Niccolò Machiavelli, *Florentine Histories*, trans. Laura F. Banfield and Harvey C. Mansfield, Jr. (Princeton, N.J.: Princeton University Press, 1988), preface, 7. Machiavelli's attitude toward Florentine factions is ambivalent in this preface since he distinguishes Florentine divisions from those that contributed to the

continuance of ancient Rome but argues that Florence's survival of these divisions testifies to its power.

9. See Quentin Skinner, *Foundations of Modern Political Thought*, 2 vols. (Cambridge: Cambridge University Press, 1978), 1:58–59.

10. See Guicciardini's remarks on the *Discourses*, 1.4, in his *Considerazioni intorno ai Discorsi del Machiavelli*, in Francesco Guicciardini, *Scritti politici e Ricordi*, ed. Roberto Palmarocchi (Bari: Laterza, 1933), 10–11.

11. For a Renaissance reading of these chapters, which reproduces Machiavelli's arguing on both sides of the question and his finally settling on Rome, see Antonio Brucioli, *Dialogi* (Rome, 1538), "Dialogo della repubblica"; and Procacci's discussion of Brucioli's borrowings from Machiavelli, 29–43. On Brucioli, see also Delio Cantimori, "Rhetoric and Politics in Italian Humanism," *Journal of the Warburg and Courtauld Institutes* 1 (1937): 83–102; Carlo Dionisotti, "La testimonianza del Brucioli," in his *Machiavellerie: Storia e fortuna di Machiavelli* (Turin: Einaudi, 1980), 193–226, and Maurizio Viroli, *From Politics to Reason of State* (Cambridge: Cambridge University Press, 1991), 201–209.

12. In *D*, 1.58.264, 255, Machiavelli describes the superior prudence of the people as compared to a prince in rhetorical terms: "Quanto al guidicare le cose, si vede radissime volte, quando egli [il popolo] ode duo concionanti che tendino in diverse parti, quando ei sono di eguale virtù, che non pigli la opinione migliore, e che non sia capace di quella veritù che egli ode" (With regard to [the people's] judgment, when two speakers of equal skill are heard advocating different alternatives, very rarely does one find the populace failing to adopt the better view or incapable of appreciating the truth of what it hears).

13. Machiavelli could thus be said to use the collapsible distinction between Rome and Sparta as the chief rhetorical paradigm of his text. For, as in *The Prince*, so in the *Discourses* Machiavelli sets up a variety of oppositions (e.g., force/fraud; states that expand/states that do not; *fortuna/virtù*, etc.), only then to show that the opposition is contained within each term. The most important of these is that between Florence and Rome: while Machiavelli begins by distinguishing between the two in terms of the corruption of the first and the lack of corruption of the second, as we read further we see that no state is completely lacking in corruption and that a completely corrupt state would be incapable of regeneration (see 1.16.173–74, 154). For even republican Rome required an individual of *virtù* periodically to remind the corrupt citizens of the original principles of government, whereas in a completely corrupt state no such individual could exist. One effect of this demystification of Rome, as Claude Lefort has argued, is to make Rome a more suitable object of imitation for Florence (*Le travail de l'oeuvre Machiavel*, 585).

14. Relevant here is Machiavelli's discussion of Manlius Torquatus as an example of civic *virtù*. Manlius's "way of behaving was entirely in the public interest and was in no way affected by private ambition, for it is impossible to gain partisans if one is harsh in one's dealing with everybody and is wholly devoted to the common good, because by doing this one does not acquire particular friends or—as I have just called them—partisans" (3.22.452, 469).

15. In the introduction to his translation of *The Discourses of Niccolò Machiavelli*, 2 vols. (New Haven, Conn.: Yale University Press, 1950), Leslie Walker

sums up this tension within Machiavelli's method when he writes that Machiavelli "does not give advice to tyrants because he likes tyranny, for he makes it perfectly plain that he loathes tyranny. . . . He advises all and sundry because he desires to convince his readers that his new method is universal in its applicability" (1:73).

With the examples of Numa and especially Brutus we can begin to see how Machiavelli's *Discourses* could be assimilated, along with *The Prince*, to Renaissance Tacitism. For Guicciardini's insight about Tacitus in the *Ricordi* applies equally well to Machiavelli: "Cornelius Tacitus teaches those who live under tyrants how to live and act prudently; just as he teaches tyrants ways to secure their tyranny" (*Maxims and Reflections*, trans. Mario Domandi [New York: Harper Torchbooks, 1965], C18, 45). My analysis in this and the preceding chapter should suggest that Renaissance readers saw Machiavelli as Tacitean because Machiavelli read Livy the way Renaissance readers, including Guicciardini, read Tacitus.

CHAPTER THREE
RHETORIC AND REASON OF STATE:
BOTERO'S READING OF MACHIAVELLI

1. See Adolph Gerber, *Niccolò Machiavelli, Die Handschriften, Ausgaben und Ubersetzungen seiner Werke im 16. und 17. Jahrhundert*, ed. Luigi Firpo, 3 parts (Gotha: Andreas Perthes, 1912; Turin: Bottega D'Erasmo, 1962), part 2, 3–4, 22–27.

2. For an introduction to reason of state, see Meinecke, *Machiavellism*, and note 5 below; Rodolfo de Mattei, *Il problema della 'ragion di stato' nell'età della Controriforma* (Milan and Naples: Ricciardi, 1979); and Peter Burke, "Tacitism, scepticism, and reason of state," in *The Cambridge History of Political Thought, 1450–1700*, ed. J. H. Burns with Mark Goldie (Cambridge: Cambridge University Press, 1991), 479–98. Burke reminds us that the term had positive as well as negative connotations in the Renaissance: true reason of state was sometimes defined as political prudence in conformity with ethical or religious norms, false reason of state as reasoning in "the pursuit of self-interest" (480). See also Michel Senellart, *Machiavélisme et raison d'état* (Paris: Presses Universitaires de France, 1989), who is particularly concerned to recover the economic dimension of reason of state in the sixteenth and seventeenth centuries; Maurizio Viroli, *From Politics to Reason of State* (Cambridge: Cambridge University Press, 1991), who provides useful English paraphrases of many Italian treatises on reason of state; and Richard Tuck, *Philosophy and Government, 1572–1651* (Cambridge: Cambridge University Press, 1993), which appeared when the present book was in press.

3. In *Storia dell'età barocca in Italia* (1929; Bari: Laterza, 1946), Benedetto Croce argued that Botero was by temperament "incapable of producing a science, which requires precise distinctions and definitions of concepts" (80). For other derogatory comments about Botero, see Federico Chabod, *Giovanni Botero* (Rome: Anonima Romana Editoriale, 1934), 56–57, 67; Rodolfo de Mattei, *Il problema della 'ragion di stato'*, who refers to Botero's lack of philosophical dis-

cipline (54); Luigi Firpo, in his introduction to Giovanni Botero, *Ragion di stato* (Turin: Unione Tipografico-Editrice Torinese, 1948). See also William F. Church, *Richilieu and Reason of State* (Princeton, N.J.: Princeton University Press, 1972), 63ff. For an acute evaluation of Botero in the context of Counter-Reformation discussions of reason of state, see William J. Bouwsma, *Venice and the Defense of Republican Liberty: Renaissance Values in the Age of the Counter Reformation* (Berkeley and Los Angeles: University of California Press, 1968), esp. 293–338, 444–49. In *The Holy Pretence: A Study in Christianity and Reason of State from William Perkins to John Winthrop* (Oxford: Blackwell, 1957), George L. Mosse provides a complimentary, brief discussion of the importance of Botero for the analysis of reason of state in English Protestant treatises on casuistry. Quentin Skinner also has a few kind words for Botero in *The Foundations of Modern Political Thought*, 2 vols. (Cambridge: Cambridge University Press, 1978), 1:248–49.

4. This point is well made by Salvo Mastellone, "Antimachiavellismo, machiavellismo, tacitismo," in *Cultura e scuola* 9 (1970): 132–36; although Mastellone argues that, for this reason, Machiavellism should not be confused with a legitimate reading of Machiavelli's works.

5. In Meinecke's view, sixteenth-century discussions of reason of state grew out of Machiavelli's discourse of necessity, his analysis of the way in which abstract moral rules are modified and justified by the consideration of historical circumstances. Counter-Reformation readers correctly saw that Machiavelli's openness regarding the dictates of necessity gave rise to an ambiguity regarding appropriate means and an indeterminacy of Machiavellian ends. Sixteenth-century readers were thus right to see Machiavelli as a theorist of reason of state—even if such readers then went on to distinguish between a good reason of state (which is subordinate to religious ends) and a bad, Machiavellian reason of state (which is not). They took a wrong turn, however, according to Meinecke, when they lost sight of the idealism implicit in Machiavelli's notion of *virtù*, his hope for the regeneration of the Florentine republic. While preserving Machiavelli's insights into the role of necessity in the maintaining of state power, sixteenth- and seventeenth-century writers one-sidedly condemned Machiavelli for "having prepared the poison of autocracy" (45).

6. As this formulation suggests, and as a number of critics have pointed out, Machiavelli's vision of politics is, to some extent, compatible with Saint Augustine's. In *Venice and the Defense of Republican Liberty*, William Bouwsma writes, "The central problem of Renaissance politics was precisely how to survive in the earthly city. Those who, like Machiavelli, preferred 'politics' to 'principle' (as the issue would be disparagingly represented by spiritual authority) were thus, perhaps, in an important sense on the side of Augustine. On a certain level, therefore, the essential difference between medieval and Renaissance politics may be seen as a conflict over the implications of the Augustinian dichotomy" (28–29).

7. Meinecke's description of reason of state as an ambiguous, dualistic concept, situated at the convergence of what he called *kratos* and *ethos*, or power politics and ethics, expediency and the good, suggests the rhetorical dimension of Machiavelli's politics and of subsequent reflection on Machiavelli's work; yet, Meinecke did not analyze the way in which reason of state emerges from and

articulates a crisis in the assumptions of humanist rhetoric and imitation. See, however, Robert Bireley, *The Counter-Reformation Prince: Anti-Machiavellianism or Catholic Statecraft in Early Modern Europe* (Chapel Hill: University of North Carolina Press, 1990). Bireley argues, as I do, that the Counter-Reformation reception of Machiavelli was basically on target; he analyzes reason-of-state literature in terms of a series of topics, or common themes: (1) the relationship between virtue, reputation, and power; (2) the uses of deceit; (3) economic development; (4) war and the role of the military; (5) the place of religion and toleration in the state; (6) the role of fortune or providence in history (x). He does not, however, connect his thematic analysis to the humanist rhetorical tradition as I do here. Nor does he provide a close rhetorical analysis of treatises on reason of state.

8. See de Mattei, *Il problema della 'ragion di stato'*, chap. 5, "Obbiezioni e correzioni secentesche alla 'Ragion di Stato' del Botero." On the comparison to Tasso, see Carlo Morandi, ed., *Della ragion di stato; Delle cause della grandezza delle città* (Bologna: Cappelli, 1930), xxxviii. In *Counter-Reformation Prince*, Bireley writes that Botero's "*Reason of State* was an immediate and undoubted success from its publication in 1589. Fifteen Italian editions appeared before 1700, ten before the death of the author in 1617. Translations followed, into Spanish (Madrid, 1591; six editions by 1606), French (Paris, 1599–1606), Latin (Altdorf, 1602; three more editions by 1666), and, much later, German (Frankfurt, 1657–1664). From 1589 on, . . . [Botero's] the *Causes of Greatness of Cities* was often printed with it, and after 1598 the *Additions to the Reason of State*, five essays elaborating on themes of the *Reason of State*, was added" (50). On the knowledge of Botero's works in England, see chapter 4, note 11, below.

9. In *La fine dell'Umanesimo* (Milan: Fratelli Bocca, 1920), Giuseppe Toffanin notes that Aristotle's *Poetics* became an instrument in the Counter-Reformation struggle against Renaissance humanism and the Reformation (1–15). I follow here the account of Marc Fumaroli, *L'Age de l'éloquence: Rhétorique et "res literaria" de la Renaissance au seuil de l'époque classique* (Geneva: Droz, 1980), esp. 116–61, who also notes that Counter-Reformation writers turned to Aristotle's *Rhetoric* and *Poetics* to reformulate the relationship of rhetoric and Catholic theology after the Council of Trent; but he stresses the continuities between Counter-Reformation and humanist rhetoric (116–40). For related arguments for continuity, see the history of Jesuit education in the sixteenth century by François de Dainville, *La Naissance de l'humanisme moderne* (Paris: Beauchesne, 1940), esp. chap. 2; Debora K. Shuger, *Sacred Rhetoric: The Christian Grand Style in the English Renaissance* (Princeton, N.J.: Princeton University Press, 1988), chap. 2, esp. 79; and John Monfasani, "Humanism and Rhetoric," in *Renaissance Humanism: Foundations, Forms, and Legacy*, ed. Albert Rabil, Jr., 3 vols. (Philadelphia: University of Pennsylvania Press, 1988), 3:171–236.

10. Quoted in Bernard Weinberg, *A History of Literary Criticism in the Italian Renaissance*, 2 vols. (Chicago: University of Chicago Press, 1961; Midway reprint, 1974), 1:10. For quattrocento arguments for the civic dimension of rhetoric and poetics, see also the appendix below, as well as Monfasani, "Humanism and Rhetoric"; Danilo Aguzzi-Barbagli, "Humanism and Poetics," in *Renaissance*

Humanism, 3:85–169; and Victoria Kahn, *Rhetoric, Prudence, and Skepticism in the Renaissance* (Ithaca, N.Y.: Cornell University Press, 1985), chap. 2.

11. Giacopo Mazzoni, *On the Defense of the Comedy of Dante, Introduction and Summary*, trans. Robert L. Montgomery (Tallahassee: University Presses of Florida, 1983), 101, 91. Francesco Patrizi made the same point in his *Discussiones peripateticae* (1571), cited in Weinberg, *History*, 1:21.

12. Weinberg, *History*, 1:17.

13. The whole passage reads: "Since the civil faculty seeks to implant in the minds of humble citizens obedience to their superiors, so that out of desire for novelties they should not be moved to disobedience and rebellion, and so that they should always remain content with their condition, it gave birth to comedy, in which the humble life is shown to be happy, fortunate, and capable of infinite solace. On the other hand, since the more powerful and all those raised to the mastery of others have not had to pay too much attention to their fortune, and consequently have become insupportable and insolent in their rule, the civil faculty wished to create tragedy, which would function as an adequate counterweight to the insolence of prosperous fortune. Hence all those who find themselves in such a condition will be able to extract useful instruction in moderating the pride characteristic of their state. . . . We can conclude that those two kinds of poems are directed by the civil faculty to the extinguishing of sedition and the preservation of peace" (*On the Defense of the Comedy of Dante*, 105–106). For a similar argument about the classification of genre according to its ability to reinforce social hierarchy, see Giason Denores, *Discorso*, in *Trattati di poetica e retorica del cinquecento*, ed. Bernard Weinberg, 4 vols. (Bari: Laterza, 1970–74), 3:377ff.

14. See Baxter Hathaway, *The Age of Criticism: The Late Renaissance in Italy* (Ithaca, N.Y.: Cornell University Press, 1962; repr. Westport, Conn.: Greenwood, 1972), 205–302, on the debate over catharsis. Two interpretations of catharsis were popular in this period: the Mithradatic interpretation of Robertello, according to which tragedy inures the spectator to changes of fortune by means of the purgation of pity and fear, and the interpretation associated with Vincenzo Maggi, according to which pity and fear are not purged, but used to provide object lessons about other passions, such as wrath and lust (221–23, 243).

Hathaway argues that the debate was influenced by Trissino's *Poetica*, books 5 and 6 (composed in the 1540s, published 1563), which related Aristotle's discussion of catharsis in the *Poetics* to his discussion of the political uses—and dangers—of pity and fear in the *Rhetoric*. And, along with Allan Gilbert, he detects in Trissino an "exploration of the ethics of self-interest," and of the uses of catharsis to control such self-interest, that is reminiscent of Machiavelli (211, n. 10). See Allan Gilbert, *Literary Criticism, Plato to Dryden* (New York: American Book Company, 1940), on the similarity between Trissino's discussion of fear and those of "Italian political writers of the fifteenth and sixteenth centuries, above all Machiavelli" (218 n. 10).

15. Giason Denores, *Discorso*, in Weinberg, *Trattati*, 3:391; Lodovico Castelvetro, *Poetica d'Aristotele vulgarizzata e sposta*, ed. Werther Romani, 2 vols. (Bari: Laterza, 1978), 1:85.

16. See Baxter Hathaway, *The Age of Criticism*, 230; see 233 on Speroni's view of purgation as having "civil utility." It is interesting to see that Speroni used the concept of catharis to defend himself against charges of heresy: "When, in his old age, Speroni was hailed before the Inquisition in Rome to defend himself against charges that the dialogues he had published thirty-five years before were full of heresies and immoralities, he on three occasions referred to literary effects as purgation and obviously intended his judges to understand that he was defending his dialogues because of their purgative value" (232).

17. Quoted by Monfasani, "Humanism and Rhetoric," 210. The list in the next sentence is taken from Monfasani, 209, who points out that these treatises are all published in Bernard Weinberg's *Trattati di poetica e retorica del cinquecento*.

18. On sacred rhetoric, see Monfasani, "Humanism and Rhetoric"; Shuger, *Sacred Rhetoric*; and Fumaroli, *L'Age de l'éloquence*. Monfasani notes: "Without question, the Jesuits created the most successful school system of the early modern period, with 306 colleges in 1608 and more than 600 colleges by 1710 in Europe, America, and even the Far East. In the master plan, the *Ratio studiorum*, of the Jesuit colleges, rhetoric held a privileged place as the culminating subject in the curriculum after grammar and 'the humanities.' Not only was great stress laid on declamation and other oratorical practices, but the rhetoric that the Jesuits taught was essentially classical in structure. A leading textbook of the Jesuit colleges, *De arte rhetorica libri tres ex Aristotele, Cicerone, et Quintiliano praecipue deprompti* by Cypriano Soarez, S.J. (first printed in 1562) was premised on the view that rhetoric was the art of persuasion and not merely of style ('Rhetoricae officium est dicere apposite ad persuasionem, finis persuadere dictione')" (204–205). See also de Dainville, *La Naissance*, chap. 2.

19. On Segni, see Weinberg, *History*, 1:404–406. The information in this paragraph is paraphrased from Procacci, 47–51. On comparisons between Machiavelli and Aristotle, see also de Mattei, *Il problema della 'ragion di stato'*, chaps. 3 and 5.

20. The relevant passage in book 5 of Aristotle's *Politics* is 1314a 30–1315b 10. Rebecca W. Bushnell discusses the pertinence of the *Politics* to Renaissance discussions of mimesis and theatricality in *Tragedies of Tyrants: Political Thought and Theater in the English Renaissance* (Ithaca, N.Y.: Cornell University Press, 1990), chaps. 2 and 3. I quote from pages 27–28. Bushnell notes that ambivalence about the stage was often linked to the fear of tyranny both in antiquity and the Renaissance. Plato describes the tyrant as a figure of passion and a hypocritical dissembler—an actor who misrepresents himself as well as the interests of the state. Plato's view of the tyrant is thus intimately linked to his anxieties about imitation, its ability to stir up the passions and to seduce through misrepresentation. His moral censure of tyranny is an attempt to distinguish in ethical terms what cannot be distinguished in the realm of mimesis. For the tyrant is capable of appearing to be good. In contrast, Aristotle's *Politics* "at once adopts and completely undermines Plato's sexual and theatrical model of the tyrant" (26). Aristotle does not censure mimesis nor does he see the tyrant in simple moral terms. Rather, a king is distinguished from a tyrant only in coming "to power by either succession or election" (26).

21. Le Roy and Botero cited in Procacci, 50, 55.

22. Casuistry was the art of applying general moral principles to specific cases or adjudicating between conflicting moral principles, such as the prohibitions against lying and against abjuring one's faith. As J. P. Sommerville writes, "The task of the casuists was to construct a means whereby a man could at once avoid lying and prevent the harmful results which truth or silence would bring" ("The 'New Art of Lying': Equivocation, Mental Reservation, and Casuistry," in *Conscience and Casuistry in Early Modern Europe*, ed. Edmund Leites [Cambridge: Cambridge University Press; Paris: Editions de la Maison des Sciences de l'Homme, 1988], 166–67). Although the casuists condemned lying, they argued that the Christian was justified in exploiting the ambiguity of language to mislead an interlocutor; to qualify or subvert mentally a verbal statement was also permissible. Although both Protestants and Catholics wrote treatises on casuistry, the casuistical doctrines of verbal equivocation and mental reservation came to be associated particularly with the Jesuits—and with Machiavellism—in the sixteenth and early seventeenth centuries. Although opponents of the Jesuits sometimes allowed verbal ambiguity, they condemned mental reservation as a Machiavellian instrument of reason of state. Sommerville observes that there was some truth to this: "Catholic casuists abhorred Machiavelli, the atheist politician; but working within a tradition quite separate from Renaissance 'reason of state,' they reached conclusions not that far from the Florentine's" (167). On the connection between casuistry and reason of state, see also George L. Mosse, *Holy Pretence*. I take up the issue of casuistry in part 2 below.

23. Perez Zagorin, *Ways of Lying: Dissimulation, Persecution, and Conformity in Early Modern Europe* (Cambridge, Mass.: Harvard University Press, 1990), 169. Zagorin discusses Navarrus on pages 153–85. See also Sommerville, "The 'New Art of Lying,' " 173–74; and de Mattei, " 'Ragion di Stato' e 'Mendacio,' " in *Il problema della 'ragion di stato'*, 187–214.

24. Zagorin, *Ways of Lying*, 93–94; see also Rita Belladona, "Aristotle, Machiavelli, and Religious Dissimulation: Bartolomeo Carli Piccolomini's *Trattati nove della prudenza*," in *Peter Martyr Vermigli and Italian Reform*, ed. Joseph C. McLelland (Waterloo, Canada: Wilfred Laurier University Press, 1980), 29–41. The *Trattati* were written sometime in the mid-cinquecento and were not published. Belladona calls attention to Carli's secular description of prudence, which is much closer to Machiavelli's prudence than to Aristotle's: "For [Carli] prudence and dissimulation form the basis of outward ethical behavior; they also regulate the prudent man's attitude toward official religion, which is viewed as an exclusively socio-political phenomenon and, as such, becomes a source of fraud. In the religious context, as in all other spheres of life, the *prudente* can survive the surrounding corruption by using simulation, while at the same time preserving and guarding the secrecy of his own private inner world" (36).

25. I quote from the partial Italian translation by Luigi Firpo, in *Il pensiero politico del Rinascimento e della Controriforma* (Milan: Mazorati, 1966), 616. Later in the century the Jesuit Antonio Possevino condemned Machiavelli in similar terms in his *Iudicium* (1592, printed with the Telius Latin translation of *The Prince* [Ursellis, 1600]). Possevino appears not to have read Machiavelli but to have borrowed his attack from Innocent Gentillet's *Discours contre Machiavel* of

1576 (Latin translation, 1577), at the same time that he condemned the Huguenot Gentillet as himself a Machiavellian. Referring to the *Discours*, Possevino remarks, "In that work, the author educes certain arguments from ancient history, which may be used to combat Machiavelli: but where he attacks the Catholic church, or gives occasion to do so, he easily equals or surpasses Machiavelli in blasphemy" (202).

26. Jeronimo Osorio, *The Five books . . . of Civill and Christian Nobilitie*, trans. William Blandie (London, 1576), 89, 97–98, 109. In general, Osorio's point, like Augustine's in *The City of God*, is that Christianity is not responsible for the fall of the Roman Empire, and that Christianity does not lead to martial meekness.

27. I quote from the English translation of William Jones, *Six Bookes of Politickes or Civil Doctrine, Written in Latine by Iustus Lipsius* (London, 1594), book 4, chap. 1, p. 60.

28. In contrast, in *Atheismus triumphatus* (Atheism Conquered; published 1631, I quote from the Paris edition of 1636), Tommaso Campanella used the vocabulary of rhetoric to condemn Machiavelli's rhetorical politics. Campanella considered the use of "simulatio," "opinio," and lying, and rejected the argument that Machiavelli's teaching on these matters in *The Prince* and the *Discourses* conforms to Aristotle's in book 5 of the *Politics* and Thomas Aquinas's. According to Campanella, Aristotle and Aquinas did not recommend tyrannical behavior; they simply described it in order to teach how it may be ameliorated. In contrast, Machiavelli teaches neither an art nor "prudentia politica" but "astutia scelerosa." Campanella then went on to insist that although all arts, including that of politics, can be used well or badly, the criteria of right use—of praise or blame—are part of the art; hence the condemnation of tyranny is, strictly speaking, what the classical rhetoricians would call an "artistic" or intrinsic argument (251). See Campanella, "Argumenta admiratoris contra reprehensores Macchiavellismi" and "Responsio" (Arguments of the admirer against the detractors of Machiavellism and Response), 240–41, 243.

29. Bireley, *Counter-Reformation Prince*, 79. On "Lipsius Proteus," see Mark Morford, *Stoics and Neostoics: Rubens and the Circle of Lipsius* (Princeton, N.J.: Princeton University Press, 1991), 136. The frequent accusation of inconstancy punned on the title of Lipsius's other important treatise, *De constantia* (1584).

30. Lodovico Zuccolo, *Della ragione di stato* (1621), in *Politici e moralisti del seicento*, ed. Benedetto Croce and Santio Caramella (Bari: Laterza, 1930), 27–28; see 39 on interests. De Mattei discusses Zuccolo and those who held similar positions in *Il problema della 'ragion di stato'*, 109–28. In Zuccolo's treatise we begin to see the connection between reason of state and historicism: reason of state is not a norm, but a means of reasoning about particular historical conditions, historically particular states. That Machiavellism gave rise to historicism is one of the themes of Meinecke's *Machiavellism*.

31. This biographical material is drawn from Bireley, *Counter-Reformation Prince*, 46–47; and from Fumaroli, *L'Age de l'éloquence*, 142. Francesco Patrizi was the author of a commentary on Aristotle, *Discussiones peripateticae* (Venice, 1571), as well as of several works on poetics, including *Della poetica di Francesco*

Patrici la deca disputata (Ferrara, 1586). On the relevance of this treatise to Botero, see note 38 below. In the following pages I quote from the Italian edition of *Ragion di stato*, ed. Luigi Firpo (Turin: Unione Tipografico-Editrice Torinese, 1948), and then from *The Reason of State*, trans. P.J. and D.P. Waley (London: Routledge and Kegan Paul, 1956). Parenthetical references are to chapter and page in the Italian text, and to page in the English translation.

32. For the linking of Machiavelli and Reformers, see, in addition to Possevino's *Iudicium* and Osorio's *De nobilitate christiana*, Tommaso Campanella, *Atheismus triumphatus*, preface, where Machaivelli is associated with Calvin, "heretics . . . pseudopoliticians"; and Pedro de Ribadeneyra, *Tratado de la religión y virtudes que dever tener el Príncipe, para governar y servar sus Estatos. Contro lo que Nicolas Machiavelo y los Politicos deste tiempo enseñan* (Madrid, 1595), preface, where Machiavelli is linked not only with the teachings of Tacitus and Bodin but also with French Huguenots such as Duplessis Mornay and de la Noue. A partial English translation exists by George Albert Moore, *Religion and the Virtues of a Christian Prince* (Washington, D.C.: Country Dollar Press, 1949).

33. Thomas Hobbes, *Leviathan*, ed. C. B. Macpherson (Harmondsworth, England: Penguin, 1975), book 1, chap. 10, pp. 150–51.

34. Significantly, this argument from interest became more prominent in the second edition of the treatise. In the first edition, Botero insisted that the prince be guided by prudential considerations of interest: "Tenga per cosa risoluta, che nelle deliberazioni de' prencipi l'interesse è quello che vince ogni partito" (It should be taken for certain that in decisions made by princes interest will always override every other argument [2.6.104, 41]); but, in a later chapter in the same edition, he condemned interest as astuteness rather than prudence:

> First [the prince] must make a reputation for prudence rather than astuteness, prudence being a virtue whose function is to seek and to find convenient means to bring about a given end. Astuteness has the same object, but differs from prudence in this: in the choice of means, prudence follows what is honest rather than what is useful, astuteness takes nothing into account but interest. (2.8.114 n. 2, 49 n.)

Botero deleted this passage in subsequent editions, thereby tacitly acknowledging that the criterion of effective representation in the realm of politics is inseparable from the concept of interest. Such a deletion also suggests that Botero found the distinction between prudence and astuteness in terms of means impossible to maintain. For both make use of imitation and rhetoric, of misrepresentation and coercion; both take interests into account. The difference must rather be one of ends and of results. The effect of this deletion was to highlight the pragmatic argument for the superior effectiveness of Christianity in the realm of practical politics. In *Storia dell'età barocca in Italia*, Benedetto Croce notices this shift in Botero's argument but takes it as evidence of his intellectual sloppiness (87). Peter Burke, in "Tacitism," notes that for many Renaissance writers *interest* was synonymous with reason of state (482).

35. In *Counter-Reformation Prince*, Bireley calls this kind of argument "in-

trinsic pragmatism," which "argued from the nature of the act itself, apart from any divine intervention. Moral action by its very nature was useful; immoral action was counterproductive" (31). Gentillet made the same argument in his *Discours contre Machiavel*, as did English Renaissance critics of Machiavelli.

36. Rhetorical politics makes even real piety and real virtues appear in quotation marks. Thus when Botero recommends that the prince seek the guidance of religious counselors before pursuing any policy, it is difficult to know exactly how to interpret his comments:

> A prince should never bring a matter before a Council of State without first submitting it to a spiritual Council. . . . Nor should this seem strange; the Romans never undertook anything without first examining the auspices and auguries, and the Turk today never declares war or makes any important decision without consulting the Mufti and obtaining written advice from him. Why then should a Christian prince close the door of his secret council-chamber against Christ and the Gospels and set up a reason of State contrary to God's law, as though it were a rival altar? (2.15.135, 64)

In the *Discourses* Machiavelli had discussed the Roman use of auspices and auguries to deceive the people into accepting reason of state as divine reason. Here, it is impossible to tell whether Botero is recommending a similar pragmatic use of religion, or whether he is suggesting that, while reason of state is a supplement to reason tout court (1.1), it is underwritten by a divine sovereign who is a true Machiavel, or both.

37. The Italian text is taken from *Della riputatione del prencipe*, in *Della ragion di stato libri dieci . . . accresciuti di diversi Discorsi* (Venice, 1659). The English translations are from Giovanni Botero, *Practical Politics* trans. George Albert Moore (Washington, D.C.: Country Dollar Press, 1949), 221–46. Parenthetical page references are to the Italian text first, then to the English translation.

38. On the use of the term *sublime* in Renaissance treatises on rhetoric, see Fumaroli, *L'Age de l'éloquence*, 148–52 (a discussion of Botero's *De praedicatore verbi dei*); and Shuger, *Sacred Rhetoric*, for whom the Christian "grand style" is essentially a sublime style, with the characteristics of forcefulness, emotional intensity, grandness of conception, plainness (in contrast to the classical grand style), and sometimes harshness. See also Aguzzi-Barbagli, "Humanism and Poetics," who points out that Longinus's treatise on the sublime was translated by Robortello in 1554, and who notes that Botero's acquaintance, Patrizi, demonstrates familiarity with Longinus in his *Della poetica* ("Humanism and Poetics," in *Renaissance Humanism* 3:157 n. 151). Patrizi may have communicated this knowledge to Botero.

39. See Castiglione, *The Book of the Courtier*, trans. Charles Singleton (New York: Anchor Books, 1959), book 1, pp. 43, 46, for a similar discussion of the difficulty of understanding the ease with which the effect of sprezzatura (the courtier's graceful behavior) is produced.

40. The history of Machiavellian reason of state in Italy illustrates this. See William J. Bouwsma, *Venice and the Defense of Republican Liberty*; J. Ferrari, *Histoire de la raison d'état* (Paris: Michel Levy, 1860), chap. 4, "Revanche des républicains de Venise, 1576–1649"; and Richard Tuck, *Philosophy and Gov-*

ernment, 94–104. Ferrari and Tuck discuss the appropriation of Machiavellian reason of state by writers such as Sarpi and Paruta.

41. Cited in Etienne Thuau, *Raison d'état et pensée politique à l'époque de Richilieu* (Paris: Armand Colin, 1966), 403.

PART TWO
ENGLISH MACHIAVELLISM

1. *Epistolarum Reginaldi Poli, Pars I* (Brescia, 1744), 136; quoted in L. Arthur Burd, ed., *Il Principe* (1891; Oxford: Oxford University Press, 1968). Although Pole's text was not printed until the eighteenth century, the letter is summarized in detail in contemporary diplomatic correspondence; see *Letters and Papers (Foreign and Domestic) of the Reign of Henry VIII*, ed. J. S. Brewer, James Gairdner, and R. H. Brodie, 21 vols. (London: Longmans, 1862–1910), vol. 14 (1), no. 200. The Latin text of the chapters on Machiavelli appears as an appendix in Heinrich Lutz, *Ragione di Stato und Christliche Staatsethik in 16. Jahrhundert* (Münster: Aschendorrfer Buchdruckerei, 1961), 48–62. In *The Counter-Reformation Prince* (Chapel Hill: University of North Carolina Press, 1990), Robert Bireley writes that Pole did not actually read *The Prince* until a later visit to Florence (15). On Pole's account of his conversation with Cromwell, see also Peter S. Donaldson, "Machiavelli and Antichrist: Prophetic Typology in Reginald Pole's *De Unitate* and *Apologia ad Carolum Quintum*," in his *Machiavelli and Mystery of State* (Cambridge: Cambridge University Press, 1988), 1–35.

2. See also *Letters and Papers*, vol. 10, nos. 974 and 975 (a summary of Pole's *De unitate ecclesiastica*, in which Pole compares Henry to Nero and Domitian). For an English translation of this text, see *Pole's Defense of the Unity of the Church*, trans. Joseph G. Dwyer (Maryland: Westminster, 1965).

3. *The Acts and Monuments of John Foxe*, ed. Stephen R. Cattley (London: Seeley and Burnside, 1838), 6:56, 7:585–97.

4. The difference here is one of emphasis or degree rather than kind. On the lesser influence of humanist doctrines of imitation in England than on the continent, and the correspondingly greater influence of rhetorical argument by topic or commonplace, see Mary Thomas Crane, *Framing Authority: Sayings, Self, and Society in Sixteenth-Century England* (Princeton, N.J.: Princeton University Press, 1993). English anxiety about rhetoric has been treated extensively by, among others, Daniel Javitch, *Poetry and Courtliness in Renaissance England* (Princeton, N.J.: Princeton University Press, 1978), who notes that rhetorical figures are often discussed in terms of social and political relations—the chief rhetorical figure for Puttenham is the "courtly" figure of *allegoria* or "false semblant"; Jonas Barish, *The Antitheatrical Prejudice* (Berkeley and Los Angeles: University of California Press, 1981), who discusses the Machiavel in chapter 4; Frank Whigham, *Ambition and Privilege: The Social Tropes of Elizabethan Courtesy Theory* (Berkeley and Los Angeles: University of California Press, 1984), who also ties the anxiety about rhetoric to an anxiety about social mobility; Patricia Parker, *Literary Fat Ladies* (London: Methuen, 1987), esp. chaps. 6 and 7; Wayne A. Rebhorn, " 'The Emperour of Mens Minds': The Renaissance Trickster as *Homo Rhetoricus*," in *Creative Imitation: New Essays on Renaissance Litera-*

ture in Honor of Thomas M. Greene, ed. David Quint et al. (Binghamton, N.Y.: MRTS, 1992), 31–66.

5. George Puttenham, *The Arte of English Poesie*, A Facsimile Reproduction (Kent, Ohio: Kent State University Press, 1970), 308. On the distinction between moral art and immoral technique, and the corresponding fear of the abuse of rhetoric, see also Henry Peacham, *The Garden of Eloquence (1593)* (Gainesville, Fla.: Scholars' Facsimiles & Reprints, 1954), who cautions on almost every page against the moral and social abuse of rhetorical figures; and Thomas Wilson, who, in *Wilson's Arte of Rhetorique*, ed. G. H. Mair (Oxford: Clarendon Press, 1909), discusses rhetoric as a morally neutral technique in the prologue to the reader, the preface, and the discussions of disposition; but he also insists that eloquence is linked to right reason (preface) and that "the wicked can not speake wel" (222). On the equation of rhetorical abuse and political and religious subversion, see Patricia Parker, *Literary Fat Ladies*, 100–101; Steven Mullaney, "Lying like Truth: Riddle, Representation and Treason in Renaissance England," *ELH* 47 (1980): 32–47, on the association of the figure of amphibology or ambiguous speech with treason. This conflict was later taken up by Jonson and Hobbes. See Ben Jonson, *Timber, or Discoveries* in *Ben Jonson*, ed. C. H. Herford and Percy and Evelyn Simpson, 11 vols. (Oxford: Clarendon Press, 1925–52), 8:593; and Thomas Hobbes, *De cive* in *English Works*, ed. Sir Thomas Molesworth, 11 vols. (London: J. Bohn, 1839–45), 2:xiii, as well as *Leviathan*, chap. 17.

On courtesy books (including those translated from the Italian, such as Castiglione's *Il Cortegiano*), see Whigham, *Social Tropes*, who notes their Machiavellian aspects. Specifically, the "vocabulary of combat" one finds in these treatises "operates in a social region of conflict, rather than in the moral and epistemological realm of truth and falsehood" (145) and can thus be characterized as an "investigation in the rhetorical foundations of value." On the courtier's *virtù*, see 48, 93, 98.

6. Roger Ascham, *The Scholemaster*, ed. R. J. Shoeck (Don Mills, Ontario: Dent, 1966), 70. The following passage also illustrates the association of the abuse of eloquence with the Italianate courtier:

> Our English Italians [are] . . . common discoursers of all matters, busy searchers of most secret affairs, open flatterers of great men, privy mislikers of good men, fair speakers with smiling countenances, and much courtesy openly to all men; ready backbiters, sore nippers, and spiteful reporters privily of good men. And being brought up in Italy in some free city, as all cities be there; where a man may freely discourse against what he will, against whom he lust, against any prince, against any government, yea, against God himself and his whole religion; where he [is] . . . always compelled to be of some party, of some faction, he shall never be compelled to be of any religion: and if he meddle not overmuch with Christ's true religion, he shall have free liberty to embrace all religions, and become if he lust, at once, without any let or punishment, Jewish, Turkish, papish, and devilish. (72)

Whigham, *Social Tropes*, 176, calls our attention to Gabriel Harvey's "Speculum Tuscanismi" as another portrayal of the Italianate Englishman, described as a "peerlesse . . . Discourser for Tongue . . . and Lynx, to spie out secretes, and privities of States" (*Spenser's Poetical Works*, ed. J. C. Smith and E. de Selincourt [Oxford: Oxford University Press, 1924], 626). The lineaments of Ascham's and Harvey's rhetorical Machiavel are still apparent much later in John Melton's *A Sixe-folde Politician together with a Sixe-folde Precept of Policy* (London, 1609), for example. According to Melton, whereas the good politician follows the rule of decorum and policy, adapting his actions "as the necessitie and circumstance of time, place, and persons do require" (117), the bad politician is one who, like Richard III, engages in "fox-like windings and turnings" (15, 20) and uses rhetoric to deceive. In this, he is like the poet who uses rhetorical indirection to convey political messages (37).

By the second half of the sixteenth century, Machiavelli's Italian origins had become an even greater liability than before. His pragmatic political counsel was read in terms of the perceived papal (Catholic) threat to English sovereignty and was thus increasingly allied with the defense of idolatry, tyranny, or illegitimate and immoral rule. As Whigham notes, "The queen's excommunication in 1570 and the later discovery of the role played by the Florentine Ridolfi in the Norfolk conspiracy were contemporaneous with the publication of Ascham's work" (*Social Tropes*, 177).

7. On casuistry, see Camille Wells Slights, *The Casuistical Tradition in Shakespeare, Donne, Herbert and Milton* (Princeton, N.J.: Princeton University Press, 1981); George L. Mosse, *The Holy Pretence: A Study in Christianity and Reason of State from William Perkins to John Winthrop* (Oxford: Blackwell, 1957); Johann P. Sommerville, "The 'New Art of Lying': Equivocation, Mental Reservation and Casuistry," in *Conscience and Casuistry in Early Modern Europe*, ed. Edmund Leites (Cambridge: Cambridge University Press; Paris: Editions de la Maison des Sciences de l'Homme, 1988), 159–84, on Barnes, Morton and Mason; and the works cited in note 12 below.

8. *A Treatise of Treasons against Q. Elizabeth and the Croune of England . . .* (n.p., 1572), "The Preface to the Reader." The author of this treatise in defense of Mary, Queen of Scots, claims not to impugn Elizabeth's authority while associating recent "mutations" and "innovations" in government with Machiavellian tendencies.

9. Slights, *The Casuistical Tradition*, 15, and, quoting Perkins, 15–16.

10. According to Slights, in *The Casuistical Tradition*, one "fundamental assumption of the Renaissance English casuist is that the circumstances of human affairs are so varied that no action can be defined categorically as sinful or virtuous. The infinite variety of cases is due to differences in circumstances and not to moral relativity. What is just for one man would be just for all men in like circumstances." According to Jeremy Taylor, these circumstances include an individual's "own acts and relations, . . . [and] understanding" (15).

11. Giovanni Botero, *The Reason of State*, trans. P. J. and D. P. Waley (London: Routledge and Kegan Paul, 1956), 3.

12. Ames is cited by Mosse, *Holy Pretence*, 73. Mosse discusses God as a Machiavellian politician on pages 42, 103, and 140–41. In "The 'New Art of Lying,'" Sommerville takes issue with Mosse's view that casuistical argument involved justifying Machiavellian means by Christian intentions on page 180, note 40. Yet, on page 181 he seems to qualify this point by arguing that there was

substance to the charge that Jesuits followed "Machiavellian rules." Also in this volume, see Margaret Sampson, "Laxity and liberty in seventeenth-century English political thought," 72–118; as well as John M. Wallace, *Destiny His Choice: The Loyalism of Andrew Marvell* (Cambridge: Cambridge University Press, 1968), chap. 1, on the importance of casuistry during the Engagement Controversy; and Perez Zagorin, *Ways of Lying: Dissimulation, Persecution, and Conformity in Early Modern Europe* (Cambridge, Mass.: Harvard University Press, 1990). In chapter 5 I take up in greater depth the theological and political uses of casuistry and the doctrine of indifference.

13. Thomas Fitzherbert, *The First Part of a Treatise concerning Policy and Religion* (Douai, 1606), title page; see also chaps. 25–27, 36; and chap. 4 below, note 64.

14. The role of theater and of theatricality in creating or undermining sovereignty is now something of a commonplace in Renaissance studies. See, among others, Stephen Orgel, *The Illusion of Power: Political Theater in the English Renaissance* (Berkeley and Los Angeles: University of California Press, 1975); Stephen Greenblatt, *Renaissance Self-Fashioning: From More to Shakespeare* (Chicago: University of Chicago Press, 1980); Jonas Barish, *The Antitheatrical Prejudice*; Jonathan Goldberg, *James I and the Politics of Literature* (Baltimore, Md.: The Johns Hopkins University Press, 1983); Gordon Braden, *Renaissance Tragedy and the Senecan Tradition: Anger's Privilege* (New Haven, Conn.: Yale University Press, 1985); Leonard Tennenhouse, *Power on Display: The Politics of Shakespeare's Genres* (London: Methuen, 1986); Timothy Murray, *Theatrical Legitimation* (New York: Oxford University Press, 1987); Rebecca W. Bushnell, *Tragedies of Tyrants: Political Thought and Theater in the English Renaissance* (Ithaca, N.Y.: Cornell University Press, 1990); and the works on the Machiavel cited in the introduction to this book, note 6.

15. Plato and Aristotle offer classical precedents for these two views of the Machiavellian dimension of the theater. See chap. 3 above, note 20.

CHAPTER FOUR
READING MACHIAVELLI, 1550–1640

1. The *Art of War* was translated by Peter Whitehorne and dedicated to Queen Elizabeth in 1560, and *The Florentine Historie* was translated by Thomas Bedingfield and dedicated to Christopher Hatton in 1595.

2. The quotation, from Harvey's *Letter-Book*, is cited in Christopher Morris, "Machiavelli's Reputation in Tudor England," *Machiavellismo e antimachiavellici nel cinquecento* (Florence: Olschki, 1969), 88–105, from which I have drawn much of the information in this paragraph. Harvey owned Wolfe's 1584 edition of the *Discourses* and the *Art of War*, and may have owned an earlier Italian edition of Machiavelli's work. (His annotated copy of Machiavelli's *Art of War* is now in the Rare Books collection of Princeton University's Firestone Library.) We know that he read Machiavelli along with Livy in the early 1580s, with Thomas Preston at Trinity Hall; his marginal comments in the text of Livy occasionally refer to Machiavelli's *Discourses*. Harvey also referred to the *Discourses* in his

commonplace book, and made extensive marginalia in the 1573 edition of Peter Whitehorne's translation of the *Art of War*. On Harvey, see also note 33 below.

3. On Wolfe, see Napoleone Orsini, "Le traduzioni elisabettiane inedite di Machiavelli," in *Studii sul Rinascimento italiano in Inghilterra* (Florence: Sansoni, 1937), 4, who writes that censorship explains the false publication information. Raab, 52, writes that the editions of *The Prince*, *Discourses*, and *Art of War* "were illicit being unlicensed; for [the *Florentine History* and *L'Asino d'oro*] Wolfe obtained licenses in the normal way. The ban on Machiavelli in England in the sixteenth century seems to have taken the form of a refusal to license the printing of *Il principe* and *I Discorsi*. I have been unable to find any evidence of a positive prohibition on reading him to parallel his inclusion in the Pauline *Index*, confirmed at the Council of Trent." Christopher Morris, "Machiavelli's Reputation in Tudor England," 89, also argues that the false publication information was devised in order to evade the censors. But in *Bibliografia Machiavelliana* (Verona: Edizioni Valdonega, 1979), Sergio Bertelli argues that Wolfe produced these editions for Italian rather than English consumption (lxxviii). On the Wolfe editions, see also Adolph Gerber, "All of the Five Fictitious Italian Editions of Writings of Machiavelli and Three of Those of Pietro Aretino Printed by John Wolfe of London (1584–1588)," *Modern Language Notes* 22 (1907), 2–6, 129–35. A chapter on Wolfe also appears in Peter S. Donaldson, *Machiavelli and Mystery of State* (Cambridge: Cambridge University Press, 1988), 86–110.

On manuscript translations, see, in addition to the study by Orsini cited above, Napoleone Orsini, "Elizabethan Manuscript Translations of Machiavelli's *Prince*," *Journal of the Warburg Institute* 1 (1937–38): 166–69; Hardin Craig, ed., *Machiavelli's 'The Prince': An Elizabethan Translation* (Chapel Hill: University of North Carolina Press, 1944); Emile Gasquet, *Le Courant machiavélien dans la pensée et la littérature anglaises du XVIᵉ siècle* (Paris: Didier, 1974), Appendix C. There seem to have been at least five manuscript English translations of *The Prince*, based on three separate translations, and four of the *Discourses*, based on three separate translations.

4. The Telius translation and editions are discussed by Adolph Gerber in *Niccolò Machiavelli, Die Handschriften, Ausgaben und Ubersetzungen seiner Werke im 16. und 17. Jahrhundert* (Gotha: Friedrich Andreas Perthes, 1912–13; reprint, Turin: Bottega d'Erasmo, 1962), part 3, 60–75. See also the brief discussion by Hardin Craig in the introduction to *Machiavelli's 'The Prince'*, xv–xvi.

5. Gerber, *Niccolò Machiavelli*, part 3, 67 n. 1. Gerber judges from Stupanus's dedication to the Counter-Reformation Bishop Blarer that Stupanus was not aware of the content of the Huguenot works (see 68 n. 2). On Perna's defense of Machiavelli, see Gerber, part 3, 68–69, n. 2: "What if kings go mad, and rule republics badly and tyrannically, did they learn anything from Machiavelli, [was Machiavelli] the cause and teacher of this crime? as if the doctor were the cause of death." Yet, Perna goes on to describe the texts bound with *The Prince* as antidotes for those who do feel that Machiavelli is poisonous: "Those who judge him poisonous have an antidote for curing poison." Agostino Nifo first put forward the "antidote" way of dealing with Machiavelli in the preface to his 1523 *De regnandi peritia* (the first four books of which translate much of *The Prince*). As

these brief remarks indicate, the Telius editions deserve a separate study of their own.

6. See Pierre Lefranc, *Sir Walter Ralegh, Ecrivain* (Paris: Armand Colin, 1968), 229.

7. "The Epistle Dedicatorie" (1577) also appeared in the English Renaissance translation: *A Discourse upon the Meanes of Wel Governing and Maintaining in Good Peace, A Kingdome, or other Principalitie*, trans. Simon Patericke (London, 1602). In "Machiavelli, Satan, and the Gospel," *Yearbook of Italian Studies* (1971): 156–77, Antonio D'Andrea suggests that the letter was written by a French Huguenot, probably Lambert Daneau, who had met Hastings and Bacon in Geneva. Edward Bacon was the half brother of Francis Bacon; Francis Hastings was also of a prominent Elizabethan family. D'Andrea documents the Protestant beliefs of both and their relations with Huguenots in Geneva.

8. Innocent Gentillet, *Discours contre Machiavel*, ed. A. D'Andrea and P. D. Stewart (Florence: Casalini Libri), preface to part 1. I quote from the Renaissance English translation. Gentillet comments on Machiavelli's method of arguing from maxims: "Yet although the Maximes & general rules of the Politike Art, may something serve to know well to guide and governe a publicke estate (whether it bee principalitie or free cittie:) yet can they not bee so certaine as the Maximes of the Mathematicians, but are rules rather very dangerous, yea, pernitious, if men cannot make them serve and apply them unto affaires, as they happen to come, and not to apply the affaires unto these Maximes and rules. For the circumstances, dependences, consequences, and the antecedents of every affaire and particular businesse, are all for the most part divers and contrarie: insomuch, that although two affaires be like, yet must not men therefore conduct and determine them by one same rule or Maxime, because of the diversitie and difference of accidents and circumstances: For experience teacheth us, that in one same act, that which is good in one time, is not in another, but rather hurtfull: and that which is convenient for some nations, is not good for others; and so of other circumstances" (Ai-Aij). In Gentillet's account, Machiavelli is guilty of insufficient attention to historical and political circumstances, and thus of one-sided maxims: "*Nicholas Machiavell* . . . understood nothing or little in this Politicke science whereof we speake: and . . . he hath taken Maximes and rules altogether wicked, and hath builded upon them, not a Politicke, but a Tyrannical science" (Aij). I discuss Gentillet's reading of Machiavelli in "Reading Machiavelli: Innocent Gentillet's Discourse on Method," *Political Theory* (Fall, 1994).

9. N. W. Bawcutt makes this point in his excellent "Machiavelli and Marlowe's *Jew of Malta*," *Renaissance Drama*, n.s. 3 (1970), 14. Bawcutt argues, as I do, that the learned and popular reception of Machiavelli in England often intersected. He also makes the point that Renaissance readers read Machiavelli in ways that were different from, but not necessarily inferior to, our own. This article came to my attention after I had come to similar conclusions.

10. Cited in Nadja Kempner, *Raleghs staatstheoretische Schriften* (Leipzig: Tauchnitz, 1928), 30. Kempner also quotes from a 1579 letter of Gabriel Harvey: "His [Aristotle's] oeconomicks and politicks on oath by rote. You can not stept into a schollars studye but (ten to on) you shall litely finde open ether 'Bodin de Republica' or 'Le Royes Exposition upon Aristotle's Politiques' or sum other like

Frenche or Italian 'Politique Discoursed' " (30 n. 4). On Englishmen's knowledge of Le Roy, see also J.H.M. Salmon, *The French Religious Wars in English Political Thought* (Oxford: Clarendon Press, 1959), 24, 167–68.

As Bawcutt notes, John Case also argued, in his *Sphaera civitatis* (1588), that Machiavelli borrowed from Aristotle's discussion of tyranny in book 5 of the *Politics*. Similar arguments were made by Italian critics of Machiavelli; see Procacci, 45–75.

11. Lipsius's *Politics* were printed in Latin in 1590 and translated into English as *Sixe Bookes of Politickes or Civil Doctrine* by William Jones in 1594. I discuss one important passage on Machiavelli in chapter 3 above, 67–68. On the knowledge of Botero's works in England, see George L. Mosse, *The Holy Pretence: A Study of Christianity and Reason of State from William Perkins to John Winthrop* (Oxford: Blackwell, 1957); Richard Tuck, *Philosophy and Government, 1572–1651* (Cambridge: Cambridge University Press, 1993), 116–17; and note 36 below. Mosse shows that Botero was translated by the Protestant Sir Richard Etherington in the late sixteenth century; the manuscript was dedicated to Sir Henry Hobart, Chief Justice of the Court of Common Pleas (35; see also Raab, 275). Mosse traces the influence of Botero on English Protestant and Catholic casuists, including the Jesuits Robert Parsons and Thomas Fitzherbert (39–40). He also notes that "Botero's thesis did not go unchallenged in England": in *A Sermon Against Self-Policy* (London, 1624), the Protestant Isaac Bargrave condemned Botero for his casuistical defense of Machiavellian reason of state and self-interest. One passage, in particular, gives an indication of how Bargrave read Botero:

> But if we would have passed the Alpes for our Divinity, wee might have learned, not from hellish *Machiavel* alone, for private interest to doe things against faith, charity, and Religion, but even those our very accusers, *Possevine* and *Ribadeynira* in their *Antimachiavels*, would have taught us, that it is a poynt of conscience to equivocate in a poynt of State, and that as against the sting of Vipers we may use Triacle; which is made of Vipers flesh: so 'tis Religion, against dissemblers to use dissimulation. And thus *Boterus*, that common brander of our *English* and *Scottish* Nations, and for that happely so much esteemed among the *Romanists*, he hath it among his *Capi di Prudenza* for a resolute Principle, that *1. Interesse è quello che vince Ogni partito*, that all friendship, leagues, affinitie, all bands of communion whatsoever, are to be measured by this *Sibi*, by the line of our owne Interest and commodity. And what is this, but an absolute forsaking of GOD, to sacrifice in the house of *Mammon*? (*A Sermon*, 30–31)

12. *A Machiavellian Treatise* by Stephen Gardiner, ed. and trans. Peter Samuel Donaldson (Cambridge: Cambridge University Press, 1975). This edition contains both the original Italian text and a modern English translation; page numbers refer first to the Italian text, and then to the English translation. On Gardiner, see Donaldson, *Machiavelli and Mystery of State*, 36–85. Scholars are currently divided concerning Gardiner's authorship of the treatise. In his edition of the work, Peter Donaldson argues for Gardiner. In his review of the work in *The Historical Journal* 19 (1976): 1019–23, Dermot Fenlon argues that Gardiner's

authorship has not been definitively established but makes the pertinent point that, regardless of the author, the treatise is still an important example of English Machiavellism.

13. Donaldson, Introduction to *A Machiavellian Treatise*, 30. In the quotation concerning alterations the Italian word is *accaduti*; in the next sentence Stephano refers to the *changes* (*mutationi*) in the governance of England.

14. In his introduction to *A Machiavellian Treatise* Donaldson calls attention to the fact that Foxe, in his *Book of Martyrs*, accuses Gardiner of plotting the assassination of Elizabeth (33). As I noted in the introduction to part 2, in this work Gardiner appears as the archetypal Machiavel.

15. Donaldson, in the introduction to *A Machiavellian Treatise*, 18–19, notes that Gardiner openly discusses the conflict between religious and political considerations but does not develop the implications of this observation.

16. There are other echoes of Machiavelli's description of Agathocles. Hengest is described as one of those who "seek by cunning and passage of time to bring to pass that which cannot be done by open force at the first rush"; who "did not omit any kind of cruelty or tyranny that was ever used by Nero or Domitian" (37–38, 116–17).

17. In his introduction to *A Machiavellian Treatise* Donaldson observes that Gardiner borrows from both *The Prince* and the *Discourses* and "where they differ . . . he attempts synthesis" (20).

18. Note also Stephano's historicist argument, his claim that Alphonso's arguments are quite out of date. As I noted earlier, Meinecke argues that Machiavellism functions as a nascent historicism in the sixteenth and seventeenth centuries in England and on the continent.

19. In *Machiavelli and Mystery of State*, Donaldson tentatively makes a similar argument: "That Nifo, Rosello, and Gardiner all relate Machiavelli's discussion of whether it is better to be feared or loved to the polarity of the divine attributes [fear and love, mercy and justice] shows . . . that some interpreters of Machiavelli in the sixteenth century could not divorce their reading of Machiavelli from their commitment to this central principle of sacred kingship. They do not take God to be a tyrant, but in their attempt to justify the harsher aspects of Machiavelli's theories by analogy to the divine nature, they press the principle of analogy to, and perhaps beyond, its limits" (82).

20. Such violence is normalized when, at the end of the dialogue, Stephano links William the Conqueror and Philip II by means of lineal succession:

> Hora non mi resta altro da dire di questa materia havendo monstrato quale era il modo di Guilhelmo nel soggiogare il realme d'Inghilterra, et lasciarlo in fede a li suoi successori, fin all'advenimento del potente et clementissimo Philippo figliolo del Carlo quinto imperatore. Questo io non chiamo mutatione, ne alteratione del regno ma successione legitima, confirmata per tutti gli ordini, alla restitutione della religione, honore del regno, et utile delli popoli. (97)

> Now nothing remains for me to say on this subject, having shown how William subjugated the realm of England and left it in trust to his successors until the coming of the powerful and most merciful Philip, son of the Em-

peror Charles V. This I do not call change or alteration in the kingdom, but legitimate succession, confirmed by all orders, for the restoration of religion, the honor of the kingdom and benefit of the people. (149–50)

In the fuzzy antecedent of "This" ("This I do not call change or alteration"), Stephano conflates the alteration of the Norman conquest with the legitimate succession, by marriage, of Philip II. The argument works as much to question the notion of legitimacy, as it does to erase the sense that all power is de facto power.

21. This secular reading of Moses suggests that Gardiner understood the irony of Machiavelli's reverent treatment of Moses as divinely inspired in chapter 6 of *The Prince*. As Donaldson notes in his introduction to *A Machiavellian Treatise*, anti-Machiavellians regularly criticized Machiavelli for his treatment of Moses as a secular prince (18).

22. In *MM*, Pocock makes a similar observation in commenting on Fulke Greville's *Treatise of Monarchy*: "The way is now open to say that because the king shares the imperfection of intellect with his subjects, he should take counsel of their laws and customs and of themselves in occasional and regular assemblies; but that because that authority is, under God, his alone, he can never be obliged to take counsel of law or parliament and does so only because prudence enjoins it" (353). In commenting on Greville, Pocock also provides a gloss on Gardiner's account of legitimate tyranny: "In a fallen world, even divinely commanded authority has the character of praxis rather than of pure norm. What makes the king's power absolute is the fact of moral imperfection, and the conclusion seems inescapable that it may share in moral imperfection itself. Through the king, God commands it so; but even the king may not know why. The distance between the king as God's deputy executing his judgments and the conqueror as God's scourge executing his punishments is great but not unbridgeable" (*MM*, 353).

23. Thus Stephano distinguishes Philip from other "new princes," not only because his succession was "legitimate" (by marriage) but also because the goal of his reign was "restoration of religion" (149).

24. On the knowledge of Machiavelli's work by Essex and his circle, see Blair Worden, "Classical Republicanism and the Puritan Revolution," in *History and Imagination: Essays in Honor of H. R. Trevor-Roper*, ed. Hugh Lloyd-Jones, Valerie Pearl, and Blair Worden (New York: Holmes and Meier, 1981), 188–90. The phrase "commonwealth of expansion" appears on page 197. Also relevant to an understanding of the political beliefs of the Essex circle, and of Tacitism in Tudor-Stuart political thought, are J.H.M. Salmon, "Stoicism and Roman Example: Seneca and Tacitus in Jacobean England," *Journal of the History of Ideas* 50 (1989): 199–225; Alan T. Bradford, "Stuart Absolutism and the 'Utility' of Tacitus," *Huntington Library Quarterly* 46 (1983): 127–55; Mary F. Tenney, "Tacitus in the Politics of Early Stuart England," *Classical Journal* 37 (1941): 151–63; and Richard Tuck, *Philosophy and Government, 1572–1651* (Cambridge: Cambridge University Press, 1993), 105–19.

25. See Irving Ribner, "Machiavelli and Sidney: The *Arcadia* of 1590," *Studies in Philology* 47 (1950): 152–72. Ribner does not make the case for the direct influence of Machiavelli on Sidney, claiming instead that "the ideas of Machiavelli were a part of the Elizabethan intellectual milieu out of which the philosophy

of Sir Philip Sidney inevitably proceeded" (155). See also Ribner, "Machiavelli and Sidney's *Discourse to the Queenes Majesty*," *Italica* 26 (1949): 177–87.

26. Lipsius recommended Tacitus's *Annals* as "a seminary of morall, and a magazine of pollitique discourses, for the provision and ornament of those, that possesse some place in the managing of the world," and Causabuon attacked readers of Tacitus who did not realize that "ill Examples hurt us" (Bradford, "Stuart Absolutism," 128–29).

27. On sixteenth-century debates about rhetorical and dialectical method, see Wilbur Samuel Howell, *Logic and Rhetoric in England, 1500–1700* (New York: Russell and Russell, 1961), esp. 146–281; Walter J. Ong, S.J., *Ramus, Method, and the Decay of Dialogue* (Cambridge, Mass.: Harvard University Press, 1958); Neal W. Gilbert, *Renaissance Concepts of Method* (New York: Columbia University Press, 1960); Cesare Vasoli, *La dialettica e la retorica dell'umanesimo: 'Invenzione' e 'metodo' nella cultura del XV e XVI secolo* (Milan: Feltrinelli, 1968); Anthony Grafton and Lisa Jardine, *From Humanism to the Humanities: Education and the Liberal Arts in Fifteenth- and Sixteenth-Century Europe* (Cambridge, Mass.: Harvard University Press, 1986), esp. 122–61. I have also discussed the increasing interest in methodizing the teaching of rhetoric in "Humanism and the Resistance to Theory," in *Literary Theory/Renaissance Texts*, ed. Patricia Parker and David Quint (Baltimore, Md.: The Johns Hopkins University Press, 1986), esp. 381–88.

Grafton and Jardine note that " 'Method' was the catchword of promoters of humanist education from the 1510s onward. This practical emphasis on procedure signals a shift in intellectual focus on the part of pedagogic reformers, from the ideal end-product of a classical education (the perfect orator, perfectly equipped for political life), to the classroom aids (textbooks, manuals and teaching drills) which would comparmentalise the *bonae litterae* and reduce them to system. It marks a genuinely transitional stage in the institutionalising of Renaissance humanism. It is part of the gradual shift of humanism as the practice of an exemplary individual, to humanism as an institutionalised curriculum subject—a distinctive discipline in the arts" (*From Humanism to the Humanities*, 124).

28. Grafton and Jardine, *From Humanism to the Humanities*, 136. On Agricola's topical logic, see also Ong, *Ramus*, 98–130; Terence Cave, *The Cornucopian Text: Problems of Writing in the French Renaissance* (Oxford: Clarendon Press, 1979), 12–18; Lisa Jardine, *Francis Bacon: Discovery and the Art of Discourse* (Cambridge: Cambridge University Press, 1975), 29–35.

29. Neal Gilbert, *Renaissance Concepts of Method*, 108. Agricola, Erasmus, and Melancthon were associated with a Christian lay piety that was particularly attractive in England after Henry VIII's break with the Catholic church. When "Henry VIII's quarrel with the canon lawyers in the 1530s made a replacement curriculum an urgent necessity, an Erasmian liberal arts program was seized upon by the Tudor Establishment (with the support of Thomas Cromwell) as a politically appropriate substitute for scholasticism in the statutes of Oxford and Cambridge" (Grafton and Jardine, *From Humanism to the Humanities*, 141). See also James Kelsey McConica, *English Humanists and Reformation Politics* (Oxford: Clarendon Press, 1965) on the influence of Erasmian humanism in the reigns of

Henry VIII and Edward VI. On Henry's break with the Catholic Church, see chapter 5 below.

30. On topics and commonplaces in English Renaissance rhetoric and culture more generally, see Mary Thomas Crane, *Framing Authority: Sayings, Self, and Society in Sixteenth-Century England* (Princeton, N.J.: Princeton University Press, 1993).

31. Grafton and Jardine, *From Humanism to the Humanities*, chap. 7; Kahn, "Humanism and the Resistance to Theory."

32. In *The Advancement of Learning*, Bacon writes: "Another error of diverse nature from all the former, is the over-early and peremptory reduction of knowledge into arts and methods; from which time, commonly, sciences receive small or no augmentation. But as young men, when they knit and shape perfectly, do seldom grow to a further stature; so knowledge, while it is in aphorisms and observations is in growth; but when it once is comprehended in exact methods, it may perchance be further polished and illustrated, and accommodated for use and practice; but it increaseth no more in bulk and substance" (quoted in Gilbert, *Concepts of Method*, 114). As I show below, Bacon associates aphoristic knowledge with Machiavelli.

33. Stubbes is quoted by Raab, 58; Harvey by Lisa Jardine and Anthony Grafton, " 'Studied for Action': How Gabriel Harvey Read His Livy," *Past and Present* 129 (1990): 61. As Jardine and Grafton note, Harvey was particularly interested in "aphoristic history, as crucially policy-forming for the politician; and this is consistent with his commitment to Bodin, Daneau, Hotman and others, associated with contemporary moves to reform the legal systems and political structures of modern states using ancient models" (60). On Harvey's marginalia, see T. H. Jameson, "The 'Machiavellianism' of Gabriel Harvey," *PMLA* 56 (1941): 645–56; Virginia F. Stern, *Gabriel Harvey: His Life, Marginalia and Library* (Oxford: Oxford University Press, 1979), who mentions Harvey's reading of Machiavelli along with Livy (150). Grafton and Jardine discuss Harvey's reading of Machiavelli along with Livy on pages 42–44, and date this activity to 1584. Jameson also discusses the references to Machiavelli in Harvey's *Musarum lachrymae* and *Gratulationes Valdinenses*.

34. Thus in his marginalia to *The Art of War*, Gabriel Harvey regularly notes the relevance of Machiavelli's maxims and examples to contemporary political and military affairs. See Jardine and Grafton, " 'Studied for Action,' " 69.

35. I will call the author of both works "Ralegh" for the sake of convenience. See Raab, 71, who assumes Ralegh's authorship of *Maxims of State* but not of *The Cabinet-Council*; Procacci, 214–20, who records the doubts about Ralegh's authorship of *The Cabinet-Council* but proceeds to analyze it as an important document in the history of English Machiavellism; Mario Praz, "Un Machiavellico Inglese: Sir W. Ralegh," in *Machiavelli in Inghilterra ed altri saggi*, 2d ed. (Rome: Tuminelli, 1941), 158, who argues that *Maxims of State* is later than *Cabinet-Council* and a palinode for Ralegh's activities in Ireland, as well as a general critique of Machiavellism; Antonio D'Andrea, "Aspiring Minds: A Machiavellian Motif from Marlowe to Milton," *Court, Country and Culture: Essays on Early Modern British History in Honor of Perez Zagorin* (Rochester: Univer-

sity of Rochester Press, 1992), who defends Ralegh's authorship of *Maxims of State* (217); Ernest Albert Strathmann, *Sir Walter Ralegh* (New York: Columbia University Press, 1951), 161–68, who argues for Ralegh's authorship of both works; and Lefranc, *Sir Walter Ralegh*, 64–70, who rejects Ralegh's authorship of both works. In "A Note on the Ralegh Canon," *Times Literary Supplement* 15 (April 1956): 228, Strathmann revises his earlier opinion and argues that the author of *The Cabinet-Council* may be Thomas Bedingfield, translator of the *Florentine Histories*.

36. Ralegh used another commonplace book in composing both works, Sansovino's *Concetti politici*, translated into English in 1590 as *The Quintessence of Wit*. Sansovino borrowed many of his maxims from Machiavelli and Guicciardini. See Nadja Kempner, *Raleghs staatstheoretische Schriften*; and Vincent Luciani, "Ralegh's *Cabinet-Council* and Guicciardini's Aphorisms," *Studies in Philology* 46 (1949): 20–30. In *Philosophy and Government*, Richard Tuck discusses Ralegh's borrowings from Botero (116–17). See also Strathmann, *Ralegh*, who remarks that Ralegh translated extracts of Botero's *Delle cause della grandezza e magnificenza delle città* (1589) as *Causes of the Magnificency and Opulency of Cities* (12); and Kemper, *Ralegh*, who notes that Ralegh cited the Latin translation of Botero's *Ragion di stato* in *History of the World* (41 n. 6). References to *Maxims of State* and *The Cabinet-Council* are to *The Works of Sir Walter Ralegh, Kt.*, 8 vols. (Oxford: Oxford University Press, 1829), vol. 8.

37. See Napoleone Orsini, "'Policy' or the Language of Elizabethan Machiavellianism," *Journal of the Courtauld and Warburg Institutes* 9 (1946): 122–34. Kempner believes that *Maxims of State* is the expanded edition of *The Cabinet-Council* and suggests that the title was borrowed from French usage; she notes that Botero's *Ragion di stato* was translated into French as "Maximes d'estat, militaires et politiques" (2d ed., 1602) (21 n. 1). Perhaps more relevant is Innocent Gentillet's extended discussion of Machiavelli's method of arguing by "maxims" in his *Discours contre Machiavel* (1576). See note 8 above.

38. Bawcutt, "Machiavelli and Marlowe," also makes this point. I agree as well with Pierre Lefranc's observation in *Sir Walter Ralegh, Ecrivain*, 241: "Ralegh clearly perceived that the essential issue for Machiavelli is less a matter of doctrine than method, that this method is the same in the two works, and that it leads to the discovery of the same components and the same forces in a monarchy and a republic."

39. *Maxims of State* was published in 1642 and then in the *Remains of Sir Walter Raleigh* (London, 1657).

40. On page 8, Ralegh writes, "Mysteries, or sophisms of state, are certain secret practices, either for the avoiding of danger, or averting such effects as tend not to the preservation of the present state, as it is set or founded." The term *sophism* or *sophismata* appears in Aristotle's *Politics* 1297a 35 (book 4, chap. 13), among other places, where it is often translated as "devices."

41. This pragmatic constraint on tyrannical power reemerges in the conclusion to the work, where the author surveys the causes of change in government. Here he warns that sedition is such a cause but may itself be caused by "covetousness or oppression by the magistrate or higher power" (32).

42. Procacci, 218–19, notes Ralegh's application of chapter 3 of *The Prince* to

England's conquest of Ireland and draws the obvious comparison to Spenser's *A Vewe of the Present State of Ireland*.

43. This is true for the subject as well as the prince: like Bacon, the author sees the special relevance of Machiavelli's advice to courtiers, and moves easily from discussing the necessity of prudent counselors to the circumspection needed by ministers of state in dealing with their rulers.

44. Procacci argues that Ralegh sees in Machiavelli the description of new absolute forms of government in the West, in contrast, for example, to the Turks; see 213, 219–20. I think Ralegh's work demonstrates the corollary as well: that politics is rhetorical, in the sense of being dependent on interests and persuasion, as well as on force and fraud, rather than based on natural or divine law.

45. Bacon figures prominently in most histories of Machiavellism for his "unequivocally secular approach to political affairs": according to Raab, Bacon was not an atheist by modern standards, but like Machiavelli he "realized the patent unreality of a system of theory which attempted to relate political behaviour to a Will of God which was never expressed clearly" (Raab, 76). This is true as far as it goes; but it neglects Bacon's concern with Machiavelli's method.

Paolo Rossi also makes this argument about Bacon's extending his rhetorical reading of politics to the natural world in *Francis Bacon: From Magic to Science*, trans. Sacha Rabinovitch (Chicago: University of Chicago Press, 1978), 192–214. Machiavelli's influence on Bacon is discussed by Napoleone Orsini, *Bacone e Machiavelli* (Genoa: Emiliano degli Orfini, 1936); Vincent Luciani, "Bacon and Machiavelli," *Italica* 24 (1947): 26–40; Lisa Jardine, *Francis Bacon*, 163–68; Emile Gasquet, *Le Courant machiavélien dans la pensée et la littérature anglaises du XVIe siècle*, 391–412.

46. *The Advancement of Learning*, ed. G. W. Kitchin (London: J. M. Dent, 1973), 122.

47. Helpful discussions of Bacon's debt to and criticism of Ramus's views of rhetoric and logic can be found in Wilbur Samuel Howell, *Logic and Rhetoric in England, 1500–1700*, 364–75; Rossi, *Francis Bacon*, 195–201; Jardine, *Francis Bacon*, 66–75, 169–78, 216–26.

48. Jardine, *Francis Bacon*, 75. In *From Humanism to the Humanities*, Grafton and Jardine argue that Ramism "opened the prospect that the purpose of education was to purvey information and skills" (170), and that Ramism involved the separation of the art or technique of rhetoric from the early humanists' ideal of the *vir bonus dicendi peritus* (good man skilled in speaking [189–93]). This description of Ramism has obvious affiliations with Machiavellism. I am arguing, however, that Bacon does not need to be a Ramist to be a Machiavellian. For a different account of Ramism, which insists on the ethical dimension of Ramist logic, see Cesare Vasoli, *La dialettica e la retorica*, esp. 392–95, where Vasoli describes how, for Ramus, the arts are not only instruments but ways to divine knowledge. See also Perry Miller in *The New England Mind: The Seventeenth Century* (Boston: Beacon Press, 1939), 300–62. Miller argues that Ramus was a decisive influence on puritan attitudes toward rhetoric: his subordination of rhetorical invention to logic provided the ethical constraint on the rhetorical appeal to the passions that the puritans feared.

49. For a corrective against the anachronistic understanding of "induction" in

Bacon, see Margaret L. Wiley, "Francis Bacon: Induction and/or Rhetoric," *Studies in the Literary Imagination* 4 (1971): 65–79.

50. In "Rhetoric and Action in Francis Bacon," *Philosophy and Rhetoric* 14 (1981): 212–33, Marc Cogan makes a different but related argument about the political dimension of Bacon's views of rhetoric, arguing that, for Bacon, rhetoric "deals with the composition and arrangement of statements where the ultimate purpose is action" (213).

51. I have discussed Erasmus's method in "Humanism and the Resistance to Theory." For Ramus, examples have the status of illustration; see his *Logike*, book 2, chap. 16, pp. 56–58.

52. See Bacon's dedication of *The Advancement of Learning* to James I, where Bacon equates imitation with servility and so describes James I as inimitable: "For, if we note it well, speech that is uttered with labour and difficulty, or speech that savoureth of the affectation of art and precepts, or speech that is framed after the imitation of some pattern of eloquence, though never so excellent; all this hath somewhat servile, and holding of the subject. But your Majesty's manner of speech is indeed prince-like, flowing as from a fountain, and yet streaming and branching itself into nature's order, full of facility and felicity, imitating none and inimitable by any" (2).

53. References to the translation of *De Augmentis* (*Of the Dignity and Advancement of Learning*) are to *The Works of Francis Bacon*, 15 vols., ed. James Spedding, Robert Leslie Ellis, and Douglas Denon Heath (London: Longmans, 1870), here 5:58, 66.

54. For an extended reading of this essay, see Stanley E. Fish's chapter on Bacon in *Self-Consuming Artifacts* (Berkeley and Los Angeles: University of California Press, 1972), 101–108.

55. Anne Barton, "Livy, Machiavelli, and Shakespeare's 'Coriolanus,'" *Shakespeare Survey* 38 (1985): 115–29. In *"Coriolanus" in Context* (Lewisburg, Pa.: Bucknell University Press, 1971), Clifford Chalmers Huffman discusses the Italian sources for *Coriolanus*, including Machiavelli's *Discourses*. In his analysis of the play, however, he does not refer to Machiavelli, and does not make any special claims for Machiavelli's influence on Shakespeare's representation of political strife in the play. More recently, Annabel Patterson has argued that Shakespeare drew on Machiavelli for a sympathetic representation of the Roman people, and by analogy, the popular 1607 Midlands uprising. See her "'Speak, speak!' The Popular Voice and the Jacobean State," in *Shakespeare and the Popular Voice* (London: Blackwell, 1989), 120–53.

56. See *Wilson's Arte of Rhetorique*, ed. G. H. Mair (Oxford: Clarendon Press, 1909), preface, where Wilson distinguishes between physical coercion and rhetorical persuasion:

When Pirrhus King of the Epirotes made battaile against the Romaines, and could neither by force of armes, not yet by policie winne certaine strong Holdes: He used commonly to send one Cineas (a noble Orator, and sometimes Scholer to Demosthenes) to persuade with the Captaines and people that were in them, that they should yeeld up the saide Hold or Townes without fight or resistaunce. And so it came to passe, that through the pithie eloquence of this noble Orator, divers strong Castelles and Fortresses were peaceably given up into the handes of Pirrhus, which he should have found very hard and tedious to winne by the sworde. (Aij)

This anecdote, which depicts eloquence as a peaceful substitute for "force" and "policie," is then followed by a story of the origin of human society in rhetorical coercion.

57. Also relevant is Thomas Heywood's reference to common theatergoers as "the throng who come rather to see than to heare," and similar remarks by Ben Jonson, cited by Andrew Gurr, *Playgoing in Shakespeare's London* (Cambridge: Cambridge University Press, 1987), chap. 4. I owe this reference to Oliver Arnold.

58. Kenneth Burke, "Coriolanus and the Delights of Faction," in *Language as Symbolic Action* (Berkeley: University of California Press, 1966), 89–90.

59. For a compatible analysis of Shakespeare's *Julius Caesar* in terms of the rhetorical dimension of political power, see Timothy Hampton, *Writing from History: The Rhetoric of Exemplarity in Renaissance Literature* (Ithaca, N.Y.: Cornell University Press, 1990), 205–36.

60. In his *Apologia*, Cardinale Pole reports the view that Machiavelli wrote *The Prince* only to mislead the Medici and bring about their downfall, but he rejects this defense of Machiavelli as unconvincing.

61. Levett's preface is reprinted in Napoleone Orsini, *Studii sul Rinascimento italiano in Inghilterra* (Florence: Sansoni, 1937), 46–47. The date of the preface is 1599. This image may be borrowed from the preface to the 1532 Giunta edition of *The Prince*. See Niccolò Machiavelli, *Il Principe*, ed. L. Arthur Burd (1891; Oxford: Clarendon Press, 1968), 36, where the Giunta passage is quoted. See also Julia Lupton, "Truant Dispositions: *Hamlet* and Machiavelli," *Journal of Medieval and Renaissance Studies* 17 (1987): 59–82.

62. Niccolò Machiavelli, *Machiavels Discourses upon the first decade of T. Livius*, trans. E. D. (London, 1636), and *Nicholas Machiavel's Prince*, trans. E. D. (London, 1640). Dacres's comments appear in the margins of his translation of the *Discourses* and at the end of some chapters of *The Prince*.

63. A similar pragmatic and theological reading of chapter 7, among others, of *The Prince* appears in the Jesuit Thomas Fitzherbert's *The First Part of a Treatise concerning Policy and Religion* (Douai, 1606). Like Dacres, he claims to refute Machiavelli on his own terms, "by reason of state, without the consideration of Gods justice" (381), although he also moralizes his pragmatic critique of examples such as Borgia by glossing their failures as divine punishment. Of Borgia he writes, "Whether we respect true wisdome, or the common craft and subtletie of worldlie men (which is now commonly called machiavellian policie) he erred in the principles of both" (27). Machiavellian reason of state will fail, whereas "reason of religion," or true Christian "policy" will most often succeed (preface).

64. *De legationibus libri tres*, trans. Gordon L. Laing, 2 vols. (New York, 1924), 2:156; cited, in part, by Peter S. Donaldson, in "John Wolfe, Machiavelli, and the republican arcana," in *Machiavelli and Mystery of State* (Cambridge: Cambridge University Press, 1988), 89. The first edition of this text was printed in London, 1585. After commenting on Machiavelli's examples of failed *virtù* in his *Treatise concerning Policy and Religion*, Thomas Fitzherbert also tells us that

Machiavelli's friends explained his ineptness as a deliberate republican strategy. According to his friends, *The Prince* is a masterpiece of rhetorical indirection, designed to lure the Medici to imitate unworkable examples of political behavior and thus to cause the downfall of the Medici and the reestablishment of the Florentine republic:

> some Florentines of no meane judgement his owne cuntrymen, and frends, who in their ordinary discourses concerning his pollicies, doe not stick to confesse that he him selfe knew them to be contrary to true reason of state, and pernicious to princes, & that neverthelesse desiring to overthrow those of the house of *Medices* which opprest the commmonwealth of *Florence* in his tyme, he published his pestilent doctrine, hoping that they wold embrace it & ruine theymselves by the practise thereof, whereby the state of *Florence* might returne to the ould *Democracy* or popular government wherin it had continued many yere before.
>
> Thus say his frends; but how they befrend him in their excusing him of folly, & excusing him of mallicious impietye, I leave it to the judgment of the discret reader. (412)

While Fitzherbert finds this ironic interpretation of *The Prince* unconvincing, the fact that he felt the need to refute it suggests that it still had some currency in the early seventeenth century. For a modern version of the argument that Fitzherbert refutes, see Stephen M. Fallon, "Hunting the Fox: Equivocation and Authorial Duplicity in *The Prince*," PMLA 107 (1992): 1181–95. In *The Scholemaster* (1570), ed. R. J. Shoeck (Ontario: Dent, 1966), Roger Ascham argues that the carping rhetoric of the Machiavel is the product of a free city, that is, an Italian republic. He thus suggests, perhaps in spite of himself, that dissembling is less the Machiavel's natural mode of discourse than it is the form republicanism takes at court (72). In his *Discourses upon Cornelius Tacitus*, trans. Richard Baker (London, 1642), Virgilio Malvezzi refers to "expert Politicians [living in commonwealths] laying aside Tacitus . . . to write Discourses upon Livy. . . . But now that we are under Princes [we should] learne things of this nature; as the conditions of Princes, the cunning of courtiers, and such like. All this Tacitus expresseth." Malvezzi suggests that Tacitus provides Machiavellian (republican) insights for those living under princes.

65. "Lo stampatore al benigno lettore," fol. 2 in *I Discorsi di Nicolo Machiavelli, sopra la prima deca di Tito Livio . . . in Palermo appresso gli heredi d'Antoniello degli Antonielli*, bound with *Il Prencipe di Nicolo Machiavelli . . . con alcune operette*; translation modified. The passage is translated in Donaldson, *Machiavelli and Mystery of State*, 93, who misinterprets the plural as the singular and so thinks the preface is only addressed to the *Discourses* rather than to both *The Prince* and the *Discourses*. Wolfe speaks throughout the preface of "gli scritti," "queste opere." On Wolfe, see in addition to the chapter in Donaldson, H. R. Hoppe, "John Wolfe, Printer and Publisher, 1579–1601," *The Library*, 4th series, 14 (1933): 242–87; S. L. Goldberg, "A Note on John Wolfe, Elizabethan Printer," *Historical Studies, Australia and New Zealand* 7 (1955): 55–61.

66. In *Ignatius his Conclave*, Donne gives us two versions of Machiavelli's two-handedness: "Machiavelli" acts the Machiavel when he praises equivoca-

tion, but then goes on to argue that his texts only superficially defend tyranny, while indirectly serving as a weapon against it: "I did not only teach those wayes, by which, through *perfidiousnesse*, and *dissembling of Religion*, a man might possesse, and usurpe upon the liberty of free *Commonwealths*; but also did arme and furnish the people with my instructions, how when they were under this oppression, they might safeliest conspire, and remove a *tyrant*, or revenge themselves of their *Prince*, and redeem their former losses; so that from both sides, both from *Prince* and *People*, I brought an aboundant harvest, and a noble encrease to this kingdome" (cited in Praz, "Machiavelli and the Elizabethans," 89). In a comment that echoes Renaissance interpretations of Tacitus, Donne's Machiavelli provides political weapons *in utramque partem*. In his *Ricordi*, Guicciardini writes of Tacitus, "Cornelius Tacitus teaches those who live under tyrants how to live and act prudently; just as he teaches tyrants ways to secure their tyranny" (Francesco Guicciardini, *Maxims and Reflections of a Renaissance Statesman*, trans. Mario Domandi [New York: Harper and Row, 1965], C18, 45).

67. [Anon.], *The Atheisticall Politition* (n.p., n.d.). On the authorship and publishing history of this tract, see Raab, 120–23, 264–66. The text is dated November 23, 1642, by Thomason. The anonymous author of the English tract entitled *Machiavel's vindication of himself and his writings against the imputation of Impiety, Atheism, and other high Crimes . . .* also calls attention to the complicated rhetoric of *The Prince*. In this text "Machiavelli" denies that he is recommending tyranny: "If I have been a little too punctual in describing [tyrants] . . . and drawn them to the life in all their lineaments and colours, I hope mankind will know them the better, to avoid them, my treatise being both a satire against them and a true character of them" (cited in Burd, ed., *Il Principe*, 62, who gives as the date of the letter April 1, 1537). The tract appears in the Harleian Miscellany, vol. 1 (1808). The same letter appears as "Nicholas Machiavel's Letter in Vindication of Himself and His Writings," the afterword to the 1674 edition of *The Works of the Famous Nicholas Machiavel*. Raab (Appendix B) argues that the letter, and perhaps the new translations of Machiavelli's works in this volume, are by Henry Neville, who also defends Machiavelli in his *Plato Redivivus* (London, 1679).

68. Bovey may have drawn this passage from Traiano Boccalini's *I Ragguagli di Parnasso* (1612), where "Machiavelli" argues in his own defense that his error has not been hypocrisy but excessive candor:

> Now I ask you, what justice, what reason is there that they who invented that furious and desperate political process described by me should be held sacrosanct, while I, who have simply described it, am called a scoundrel and an atheist? I certainly can't see any rationale for adoring the original of a thing as sacred, and denouncing the copy as execrable.

This passage, quoted in Niccolò Machiavelli, *The Prince*, trans. and ed. Robert M. Adams (New York: Norton, 1977), 263, does not appear in the English translation of Boccalini by J. Florio and others, entitled *The new-found politike* (London, 1626).

69. *The Atheisticall Politition*, 1. Bovey's argument is repeated practically verbatim by Francis Osborne in his *Politicall Reflections upon the Government of the Turks, Nicholas Machiavel, etc.* (London, 1656). Like Bovey, Osborne repre-

sents Machiavelli as a disinterested "historian" of the practices of rulers. Furthermore, although acknowledging that Machiavelli teaches tyranny, he argues that
the means he recommends can be used to Christian ends: "*Worldly wisdome* is
recommended to us in the person of the *unjust steward*. . . . Neither are the *Rules*
[Machiavelli] layes down, waved by the best of men, if wise" (138).

70. Raab, 120–23, discusses Bovey's use of Machiavelli as a secular yardstick
against which to measure the failings of Charles I.

CHAPTER FIVE
MACHIAVELLIAN DEBATES, 1530–1660

1. James I, *Basilikon Doron*, in *The Political Works of James I*, ed. Charles
Howard McIlwain (Cambridge, Mass.: Harvard University Press; London: Oxford University Press, 1918), 4. All further citations of James's work are from this
edition. In "Things and Actions Indifferent: The Temptation of Plot in *Paradise
Regained*," *Milton Studies* 17 (1983): 163–85, Stanley Fish reminds us that the
notion of *adiaphora* is stoic in origin:

> Generally speaking, the doctrine of things indifferent comes into two ver-
> sions, although they are not always precisely differentiated. The first, and
> stronger, version originates with the Stoics, who identify virtue with the self
> and believe that self to be sufficient. Consequently all things external to the
> self are lacking in intrinsic value or disvalue and acquire value only in rela-
> tion to an inner disposition or intention. Thus the entire external world for
> the Stoics is a mass of *adiaphora*, which, depending on the circumstances
> "could become either good or evil." The second and more restricted version
> of the doctrine is theological and depends on the distinction between that
> which the Scripture explicitly commands or forbids and that concerning
> which it is silent. (168–69)

2. Conscience here does not simply signify unmediated introspection but
rather "a function of joining introspection with knowledge of universal truths,"
including those of obligation to God and one's sovereign. See Camille Wells
Slights, *The Casuistical Tradition in Shakespeare, Donne, Herbert and Milton*
(Princeton, N.J.: Princeton University Press, 1981), 15–16. On Luther, Melancthon, and their followers in England in relation to the *adiaphora* controversy, see Quentin Skinner, *The Foundations of Modern Political Thought*, 2
vols. (Cambridge: Cambridge University Press, 1978), 2:9, 68–69, 103–104;
C. L. Manschreck, "The Role of Melancthon in the Adiaphora Controversy,"
Archiv für Reformationsgeschichte 47 (1957): 165–82; as well as the works cited
in note 11 below.

3. G. R. Elton, *Reform and Reformation: England, 1509–1558* (Cambridge,
Mass.: Harvard University Press, 1977), 166.

4. See John Calvin, *Institutes of the Christian Religion*, 2 vols., trans. Henry
Beveridge (Grand Rapids, Mich.: Eerdmans, 1983), 2:136: "the use of things
indifferent . . . is . . . perversely interpreted by those who use it as a cloak for their
lusts, and [who think] they may licentiously abuse the good gifts of God. . . . Let
them, therefore, suppress immoderate desire, immoderate profusion, vanity and

arrogance, that they may use the gifts of God with a pure conscience. When their mind is brought to this state of soberness, they will be able to regulate the legitimate use." This accusation was not made only by Protestants; Thomas More criticized Luther's *adiaphorism* as licentious (Verkamp, *The Indifferent Mean*, 115–16). This fear of the licentious use of conscience becomes in the seventeenth-century the fear of antinomianism.

5. *Letters and Papers (Foreign and Domestic) of the Reign of Henry VIII, 1509–47*, ed. J. S. Brewer, James Gairdner, and R. H. Brodie, 21 vols. (London: Longmans, 1862–1910), vol. 14, no. 285. This letter, dated 1540 in *Letters and Papers*, is redated to 1537 by later scholars. See W. Gordon Zeeveld, *Foundations of Tudor Policy* (Cambridge, Mass.: Harvard University Press, 1948), 186 n. 86 and Raab, 49. See also John Wesley Horrocks, "Machiavelli in Tudor Opinion and Discussion," unpublished D. Lit. thesis, University of London, 1908.

6. *Letters and Papers*, vol. 15, no. 721.

7. W. Gordon Zeeveld, "Richard Morison, Official Apologist for Henry VIII," *PMLA* 55 (1940): 407.

8. In "Richard Morison," Zeeveld makes a great deal of these references as evidence of the formative influence of Machiavelli on Henrician policy. I think they are more important as evidence of Morison's knowledge of Machiavelli, since the citations do not have a prominent role in the argument of the treatises.

9. Thomas's letter is published in J. Strype, *Ecclesiastical Memorials* (Oxford: Clarendon Press, 1822), vol. 2, part 1, 157–61. On Thomas, see Raab, 40–48; and Peter S. Donaldson, *Machiavelli and Mystery of State* (Cambridge: Cambridge University Press, 1988), 40–44; as well as E. R. Adair, "William Thomas," in *Tudor Studies Presented to . . . Albert Frederick Pollard*, ed. R. W. Seton-Watson (London: Longmans, 1924), 133–60. Adair notes that in 1552 Thomas published *Il Pellegrino Inglese* (The English pilgrim), which is "an undiluted eulogy of Henry VIII and his actions, especially those concerned with the divorce of Catherine of Aragon and the breach with Rome" (138).

10. Raab, 31, also makes this point.

11. In *Foundations of Tudor Policy*, Zeeveld argues that Starkey was influenced by "Melancthon's *Loci communes theologici*, just dedicated to Henry VIII, in which he identified *adiaphora*, or things indifferent for salvation, with human or positive law under the law of nature. Melancthon's Christian adiaphorism, presented in that work as the philosophical basis for Protestant church unity, became, through Starkey, the direct ideological forbear of the Anglican polity. Starkey was sufficiently perspicacious to see the political implications of the idea; and it was through him that it became anglicized in the form in which it appeared in the Thirty-nine Articles, in Hooker's *Of the Laws of Ecclesiastical Polity*, and in Laud" (129). On page 152, note 69, Zeeveld provides references to support his claim that "after Starkey, adiaphorism became an integral part of the Anglican polity."

For further discussion of the importance of the doctrine of things indifferent in the sixteenth century, see Peter Lake, *Moderate Puritans and the Elizabethan Church* (Cambridge: Cambridge University Press, 1982); Arthur E. Barker, *Milton and the Puritan Dilemma* (Toronto: University of Toronto Press, 1942), 52–59, 95–97; Bernard J. Verkamp, *The Indifferent Mean: Adiaphorism in the En-*

glish Reformation to 1554 (Athens: Ohio University Press; Detroit, Mich.: Wayne State University Press, 1977); and Arthur B. Ferguson, *Clio Unbound: Perception of the Social and Cultural Past in Renaissance England* (Durham, N.C.: Duke University Press, 1979), esp. 171–224. In *The Foundations of Modern Political Thought*, Quentin Skinner argues that Zeeveld places too much emphasis on Starkey as the exclusive conduit of the doctrine of *adiaphorism* in England: "The doctrine had already been put into currency some time before Starkey wrote, in particular in the writings of Frith and Barnes. There is no doubt, however, that Starkey was able to make a fruitful use of the concept at a crucial moment, as a means of steering a *via media* between the position of the radical Lutherans and the traditional Catholics" (2:104).

In the reign of Elizabeth, the controversy regarding the doctrine of things indifferent was replayed in the debate between the Anglican John Whitgift and his opponent, the puritan Thomas Cartwright. In 1572 the Presbyterians among the puritans had attacked the Elizabethan Settlement in *An Admonition to Parliament*. Whitgift defended the Settlement by distinguishing between the Church's spiritual government over things "necessary to everlasting life," and Elizabeth's external government over "things indifferent" which vary according to historical circumstance (see Ferguson, *Clio Unbound*, 195–207; I draw here especially on pages 198–99).

12. On Starkey and Cromwell's propaganda campaign, see, in addition to the works cited in note 11, Franklin Le Van Baumer, *The Early Tudor Theory of Kingship* (New Haven, Conn.: Yale University Press, 1940); Skinner, *The Foundations of Modern Political Thought*, 2:99–105; G. R. Elton, *Policy and Police: The Enforcement of the Reformation in the Age of Thomas Cromwell* (Cambridge: Cambridge University Press, 1972); and his *Reform and Renewal: Thomas Cromwell and the Commonweal* (Cambridge: Cambridge University Press, 1973). I quote from the microfilm of the British Museum copy of *An Exhortation to the people instructynge theym to unitie and obedience*, printed by Thomas Berthelet, the King's printer, in 1536. The treatise is unsigned and this copy has no title page, place of publication, or date.

13. In *Clio Unbound*, Arthur Ferguson remarks that "the adiaphoristic principle proved, of course, especially useful to those apologists for the *via media* who liked to think of themselves as part of a universal Catholic Church, yet had, in the interest of their own national church, to stress the historical necessity of diversity within the broader unity of Christendom" (174).

14. Stephen Gardiner, *Of True Obedience*, in *Obedience in Church and State: Three Political Tracts by Stephen Gardiner*, ed. Pierre Janelle (Cambridge: Cambridge University Press, 1930), 105. This edition includes the Latin text and a sixteenth-century Protestant translation with marginal glosses.

15. In *Reform and Reformation*, G. R. Elton writes: "The Protestant exiles greatly embarrassed Gardiner by publishing in 1553 an English translation of his *De vera obedientia*, and the suspects he interrogated often twitted him with his earlier views" (389 n. 11). And in the notes to *Obedience in Church and State*, Pierre Janelle remarks that the translation often makes Gardiner seem even more Protestant than he was trying to appear. But in the introduction he argues, "Gardiner's attack on the Papacy has little in common with that of Tyndale and other

Protestant controversialists, who consider the Roman See as the main source of doctrinal errors." Rather, *De vera* is closer to "contemporary defenders of the authority of the State, whose opposition to ecclesiastical privileges implied no dislike of the old religion" (lxi). This is not surprising since the purpose of the treatise *was* to defend the authority of the state.

16. Peter Donaldson, *Machiavelli and Mystery of State*, 76–77.

17. Thomas Starkey, *A Dialogue between Cardinal Pole and Thomas Lupset*, ed. J. M. Cowper, in *England in the Reign of King Henry the Eighth*, Part 1: *Starkey's Life and Letters*, ed. Sidney J. Herrtage, Early English Text Society, no. 32 (London: N. Trübner, 1878), 179. The *Dialogue* was written in 1532–33 in Padua. In *Henry VIII* (Berkeley and Los Angeles: University of California Press, 1968), J. J. Scarisbrick argues that both in the statutes concerning royal supremacy and in the pamphlets defending it, there was an "ideological ambiguity" concerning "whether the king enjoyed his Supremacy as a direct, personal divine grant, or whether it was held by the king of Parliament" (393). "This complexity was matched by a similar complexity in the nature of secular sovereignty. English kings were kings *Dei gratia*, by gift from above, as coronation showed, and by descent; but at the same time, the idea of contract, of responsibility, of 'ascending' power was deeply embedded in English thinking. English monarchy was limited by the Aristotelian principle that political power was vested in and sprang from the whole political community, and by the constitutional fact that the highest form of law-making was the statute—which required the consent of the whole nation represented in Parliament" (394). As Scarisbrick suggests (397), the conflict between the ascending and descending views of royal supremacy and sovereignty anticipates conflicts in the later sixteenth and seventeenth centuries.

18. On these rebellions, often referred to as the Pilgrimage of Grace, and their relation to economic, social, and religious grievances, see J. J. Scarisbrick, *Henry VIII*, 339–48.

19. Quoted by Zeeveld, *Foundations of Tudor Policy*, 255. Not every page of the treatise is paginated; I have supplied pagination where missing.

20. See also sig. I: "This arte of subtiltie of princes (otherwise called policie) consisteth chiefly in this, for a man to appeare outwardly that he is not inwardly . . . till convenient tyme maie be had with least daungier, to execute their conceaved mischief." Ponet goes on to argue for the devilish influence of "the doctour of practices," Stephen Gardiner, on the Henrician and Marian "pollicie" of force and especially fraud.

21. Christopher Goodman, *How Superior Powers Ought to be Obeyed*, Facsimile Text Society (Geneva, 1558; New York: Columbia University Press, 1931), preface and 36.

22. If the sphere of indifference is the object of James's Machiavellian absolutism, it also allows Machiavellian considerations of another sort: in *Basilikon Doron*, James treads the fine line between humanist teaching by moral example and Machiavellian "policie" when he recommends that his son use his behavior in things indifferent to manifest his virtue to the public. Such behavior, he implies, is dictated by *virtù* as much or more than by virtue: it "will serve . . . to augment or empaire your fame and authoritie at the handes of your people" (4); it may

even serve to augment the realm by persuading the English to accept the Scottish monarch (51).

23. On the equation (both positive and negative) of reason of state with royal prerogative in seventeenth-century England, see David S. Berkowitz, "Reason of State and the Petition of Right," in *Staatsräson*, ed. Roman Schnur (Berlin: Duncker and Humblot, 1975), 165–212. In *Philosophy and Government, 1572–1651* (Cambridge: Cambridge University Press, 1993), Richard Tuck discusses the widespread use of the language of reason of state in late-sixteenth- and early-seventeeth-century English political debate (104–19, 222–59).

24. See George L. Mosse, *The Holy Pretence: A Study in Christianity and Reason of State from William Perkins to John Winthrop* (Oxford: Blackwell, 1957), 45, 53–60, and passim on *dolus bonus*. See also chapters 3 and 4 above.

25. William Bradshaw, *A Treatise of Things Indifferent* (London, 1605), marginal gloss on 25.

26. See Parker and Goodwin in *Tracts on Liberty in the Puritan Revolution*, 3 vols., ed. William Haller (New York: Columbia University Press, 1934), 2:209–10, 236–37.

27. The association of the appearance of indifference with doing "as we please" is reminiscent of Roger Ascham's definition of Machiavellism as libertinism or as the doctrine of those who "thincke, say and do what soever may best serve for profit and pleasure." See Roger Ascham, *A Report and Discourse . . . of the affaires and state of Germany* (c. 1551), quoted in Raab, 33.

28. On Parker, see *MM*, 368–71; Richard Tuck, *Natural Rights Theories* (Cambridge: Cambridge University Press, 1979), 146–51; Tuck, *Philosophy and Government*, 226–35; and W. K. Jordan, *Men of Substance: A Study of the Thought of Two English Revolutionaries, Henry Parker and Henry Robinson* (Chicago: University of Chicago Press, 1942).

29. Referring to the law of the commonwealth as "the transcendent *archē* of all Politiques," Parker adds, "Neither can the right of conquest be pleaded to acquit Princes of that which is due to the people as the Authors, or ends of all power, for meere force cannot alter the course of nature, or frustrate the tenour of Law" (Haller, 2:169). Parker is alluding to the defense of absolute sovereignty in terms of the de facto political power established by the Norman conquest. I return to the argument from conquest at the end of this chapter.

It is important to note that Parker did not always condemn reason of state as Machiavellian. In his *Contra-Replicant* (1642), he discusses reason of state as the legitimate use of extra-legal means to preserve the state in times where the ordinary workings of the law are not enforced or will not suffice: "Lawes ayme at *Justice*, Reason of state aimes at *Safety*. . . . To deny to Parliament recourse to reason of State in these miserable times of warre and danger [is] to deny them self-defence" (24–25).

30. According to Parker, consent is a source of legitimate political power, which he describes in Machiavellian vocabulary as "a supply of vertue" to the king (Haller, 2:175). In his much later, enormously popular *Advice to a Son* (1656; London: David Nutt, 1896), Francis Osborne still equates the determination of things indifferent with the arbitrary exercise of power on the part

of king and priesthood: "For as the most subtile Wind got into the narrow and delicate Parts of our Body, is able to act the Stone, Gout, and other most acute Diseases, not really present; so doth *Superstition* represent in this changeable and Concave Glass of a suborned *Conscience*, things for Sinful, that are indeed but Natural and Indifferent; and other Pious, that are really Vain and Destructive; the prosecution of which leads readily to Atheism, or an over-biassed Holiness, which prosecutes all that carry the impress of contrary Tenets" (118). Osborne sees the determination of things indifferent as necessary for or contrary to salvation as a theatrical performance designed to aggrandize the power of the church. And, when things indifferent are made a matter of "religious ceremony," then "custom," "unquestioned Ancient Tradition," and "idolatry" are not far behind (119).

31. Thomas Hobbes, *Leviathan*, ed. C. B. Macpherson (Harmondsworth, England: Penguin, 1975), chap. 42, p. 526; and chap. 41, p. 516; cf. chap 42, pp. 525, 551, 557–58 588, 592, and 596.

32. See the treatises by Lord Brooke, Robinson, and Parker, in Haller, *Tracts*; and the excerpts from *Ancient Bounds*, in A.S.P. Woodhouse, ed., *Puritanism and Liberty* (London: Dent, 1938), 247–65. Also see Milton's remarks in *Of Civil Power* quoted below, as well as *Christian Doctrine*, book 1, chap. 15; and chap. 27 in Hughes.

33. Marchamont Nedham, *The Case of the Commonwealth of England, Stated*, ed. Philip A. Knachel (Charlottesville: University of Virginia Press, 1969). I return to Nedham at the end of this chapter.

In a frequently cited passage, Ernst Cassirer once remarked that Hobbes and the puritans were alike in subordinating faith to "an absolute will based on power." In his study of radical puritan ideology, *The Revolution of the Saints* (Cambridge, Mass.: Harvard University Press, 1965), Michael Walzer arrives at the same conclusion, arguing that "For both Hobbes and the Calvinists, the antidote to wickedness and disorder was arbitrary power" (159). And in *Reviving Liberty: Radical Christian Humanism in Milton's Great Poems* (Cambridge, Mass.: Harvard University Press, 1989), Joan S. Bennett, although taking issue with Walzer's unified interpretation of puritanism, makes the same argument about royalists and some puritans in the seventeenth century (7, 24, 222 n. 18). Yet, what is striking about seventeenth-century political and religious debate— whether from the royalist or parliamentary, Anglican, or puritan point of view— is the consistent effort to distinguish legitimate from arbitrary power.

34. James I, *The Trew Law of Free Monarchies*, in *The Political Works of James I*, 67.

35. Sibbes is quoted in William Haller, *The Rise of Puritanism* (New York: Harper and Row, 1938), 160.

36. *The Practical Works of the Rev. Richard Baxter*, 23 vols., ed. William Orme (London: James Duncan, 1830), 17:11.

37. *The Soul's Conflict with Itself*, in *The Works of Richard Sibbs*, 3 vols. (Aberdeen: J. Chalmers, 1809), 2:155. See also Sibbes's preface to volume 1.

38. John Downame, *Christian Warfare* (1609); quoted in Haller, *Rise of Puritanism*, 130.

39. *Free-Grace: or, The Flowings of Christs Blood Freely to Sinners* (London, 1645), epistle dedicatory, and 147; cf. 163.

40. "Right Reformation . . ." (1646), in *Several Sermons of William Dell* (London, 1652), 120, 122.

41. A.S.P. Woodhouse, ed., *Puritanism and Liberty*, 250.

42. Quoted in Arthur Barker, *Milton and the Puritan Dilemma*, 201. See Hughes, 853; cf. 847, 852, as well as *The Tenure of Kings and Magistrates*, in Hughes, 771–72; and *Christian Doctrine*, book 1, chaps. 15 and 27.

43. William Haller cites Preston in *The Rise of Puritanism*, 167. Here and earlier, Haller anticipates Michael Walzer's argument in *The Revolution of the Saints* that puritan rhetoric was particularly well suited to forging revolutionary consciousness. According to Haller, by their emphasis on "an aristocracy of the spirit, chosen by God and destined to inherit heaven and earth. . . . the [puritan] preachers were in effect organizing a discontented minority into an opposition" (168). See also Haller's comments on John Downame's rhetoric of Christian warfare: "The loyalty which Downame sought . . . to instill in spiritual soldiers would presently be accorded to Captain Cromwell as well as to Captain Christ, and King Charles like Satan would discover that he had a fight on his hands" (158).

44. See L. F. Solt, *Saints in Arms: Puritanism and Democracy in Cromwell's Army* (Stanford, Calif.: Stanford University Press, 1959), esp. 73–88; and Gertrude Huehns, *Antinomianism in English History, with special reference to the period 1640–1660* (London: Cresset, 1951), esp. 71–88.

45. Quoted in Woodhouse, *Puritanism and Liberty*, 185.

46. On Saltmarsh's attitude toward "policy," see John Saltmarsh, *The Practice of Policie in a Christian Life* (1639). According to Solt, this work provides Machiavellian maxims and opposing views. "The true practice of policy, Saltmarsh claimed, was an accommodation of one's acts to the model set forth in the Holy Scriptures; such a course would make men capable of philosophy without vanity, oratory without rhetoric, and 'Policy' without cunning" (86). Saltmarsh was later critical of such "policy."

47. See Mario Praz, "Machiavelli and the Elizabethans," *Proceedings of the British Academy* 13 (1928), 49–97; and Napoleone Orsini, " 'Policy' or the Language of Elizabethan Machiavellianism," *Journal of the Warburg and Courtauld Institutes* 9 (1946), 122–34.

48. On Peter, see Haller, *Liberty and Reformation*, 208–209; on Cromwell, see Haller, *Liberty and Reformation*, 319–58; Woodhouse, *Puritanism and Liberty*, 105–106; Christopher Hill, *God's Englishman: Oliver Cromwell and the English Revolution* (New York: Harper and Row, 1970), esp. 217–50.

49. *Writings and Speeches*, 1:365; quoted in Solt, *Saints in Arms*, 77.

50. For a different reading, see Steven Jablonski, " 'Evil Days': Providence and Politics in the Thought of John Milton and His Age," Ph.D. dissertation, Princeton University, 1993. Jablonski argues that Milton tries to have it both ways by emphasizing that success is determined by "justice *and* victory" (chap. 4).

51. In *The Trew Law*, James I is also sensitive to the dangers of arguing from success, specifically the success of revolutionaries: "And the smiling successe, that unlawfull rebellions have oftentimes had against Princes in aages past (such

hath bene the misery, and iniquitie of the time) hath by way of practise stengthened many in their errour: albeit there cannot be a more deceivable argument; then to judge ay the justnesse of the cause by the event thereof" (54); see also 67–68.

52. William Prynne, *The Sword of Christian Magistracy Supported* . . . (London, 1653), 88. Dell is Prynne's chief adversary in this work; see, especially, 88–105 for Prynne's justification of parliament's use of force in religious matters.

53. *The Writings and Speeches*, 4:460. Cromwell's defense of necessity is analogous to contemporary defenses of rhetoric: the abuse of rhetoric should not cast aspersions on its correct use.

54. See Clarendon, *Selections from "The History of the Rebellion" and "The Life by Himself"*, ed. Gertrude Huehns (Oxford: Oxford University Press, 1978), 304–306, quoted as the epigraph to the introduction to this book. Yet, elsewhere Clarendon writes that Cromwell "was not a man of blood, and totally declined Machiavel's method; which prescribes, upon any alteration of government, as a thing absolutely necessary, to cut off the heads of all those, and extirpate their families, who are friends to the old one" (358).

On contemporary discussions of Cromwell as Machiavellian, see Raab, 130–54; Joseph Anthony Mazzeo, "Cromwell as Machiavellian Prince in Marvell's 'Horatian Ode,'" in his *Renaissance and Seventeenth-Century Studies* (New York: Columbia University Press, 1964), 166–82; Christopher Hill, *God's Englishman*, 265–66; Blair Worden, "Andrew Marvell, Oliver Cromwell, and the Horatian Ode," in *Politics of Discourse*, ed. Kevin Sharpe and Steven N. Zwicker (Berkeley and Los Angeles: University of California Press, 1987), 147–80, esp. 162–68. Worden gives references to Nedham's remarks on the Machiavellian Cromwell in *Mercurius Politicus*.

55. On Lilburne's shifting appreciation of Machiavelli, see Perez Zagorin, *A History of Political Thought in the English Revolution* (London: Routledge and Kegan Paul, 1954), 18; and George L. Mosse, *The Holy Pretence*, 29–30. The anonymous *The Levellers (Falsly so called) Vindicated* (n.d., n.p.), reprinted in A. L. Morton, ed., *Freedom in Arms: A Selection of Leveller Writings* (New York: International Publishers, 1975), also describes the behavior of the leaders of the army, presumably including Cromwell, in Machiavellian terms: "All their successes, and advancements over the People, gain'd by their perjury, fraud, equivocations, treacheries and deceipts they ascribe to the immediate approving hand of God" (313). Solt calls our attention to the related criticism by "the anonymous author of *Anti-Machiavell, or Honesty against Policy*" (1647), who "attested to the Machiavellian 'policy' of the New Model Army as 'a mixt body cemented together, with the human mortar of interests' and activated by 'an Independent intelligence or spirit'" (84–85).

56. In the following pages I rely on John Wallace, *Destiny His Choice: The Loyalism of Andrew Marvell* (Cambridge: Cambridge University Press, 1968); Perez Zagorin, *A History of Political Thought in the English Revolution*; a series of articles by Quentin Skinner: "History and Ideology in the English Revolution," *The Historical Journal* 8 (1965): 151–78; "The Ideological Context of Hobbes's Political Thought," *Historical Journal* 98 (1966): 286–317; "The Context of Hobbes' Theory of Political Obligation," in *Hobbes and Rousseau: A Collection*

of Critical Essays, ed. Maurice Cranston and R. S. Peters (New York: Double-day Anchor, 1972), 109–42; "Conquest and Consent: Thomas Hobbes and the Engagement Controversy," in *The Interregnum: The Quest for Settlement,* ed. G. E. Aylmer (New York: Macmillan, 1972), 79–98; J.G.A. Pocock, *The Ancient Constitution and the Feudal Law,* A Reissue with a Retrospect (Cambridge: Cambridge University Press, 1987), 306–34; and Blair Worden, "Providence and Politics in Cromwellian England," *Past and Present* 109 (1985): 55–99.

57. James I, *The Trew Law of Free Monarchies,* 67.

58. John Wallace distinguishes between newer and older arguments in "The Engagement Controversy 1649–52: An Annotated List of Pamphlets," *Bulletin of the New York Public Library* 68 (1964): 388–89.

59. There are some exceptions. In *The Engagement Vindicated* (London, 1650), John Lilburne rejects the argument for government by pure conquest (6). In *The Case of the Engagement* (1650; published 1668), Robert Sanderson also distinguished between legitimate and illegitimate government, at the same time that he argued for the oath of engagement. But the distinction had no practical consequences as long as the government had the power to protect its subjects. See *The Works of Robert Sanderson, D.D.,* ed. William Jacobson, 6 vols. (Oxford: Oxford University Press, 1854), 5:20–36.

60. John Dury, *Considerations Concerning the Present Engagement* (1649; Exeter: The Rota, 1979), 15.

61. Francis Osborne, *A Perswasive to a Mutuall Compliance under the Present Government, together with A Plea for a Free State compared with Monarchy* (London, 1652), 37. The pagination is continuous between the two works.

62. Scholars differ as to whether the parliamentarians among the Engagers simply adopted royalist arguments from the first half of the century to their own purposes or whether their emphasis on force was a significant departure. Wallace, in *Destiny His Choice,* argued for the presence of arguments from conquest in early divine right theory; he then went on to claim that the appeal to power was the royalists' fatal error. Zagorin, in *A History of Political Thought,* also noted the presence of arguments from conquest, but pointed out that the Engagers differed from early royalist arguments by refusing to join the argument of de facto power to other, more conservative arguments for political legitimacy.

63. I have discussed Hobbes's rhetoric in *Rhetoric, Prudence, and Skepticism in the Renaissance* (Ithaca, N.Y.: Cornell University Press, 1985), chap. 6.

64. As Hobbes does in the *Leviathan,* the Engagers displace *virtù* from the individual subject to the absolute sovereign, or Protector, at the same time that they relocate it in the subject as reader.

65. In a work of the same title (n.p., 1650).

66. See, for example, Robert Sanderson, *The Case of the Engagement,* esp. 25.

67. In the last chapter of *The Case of the Commonwealth, Stated,* Nedham draws a parallel between England in 1650 and Machiavelli's account in the *Discourses* of societies that have become so corrupt that they can only be regenerated through the *virtù* of an extraordinary individual or—in the case of the commonwealth—of "a party" of "men of valor and virtue"; see 111–14.

68. For Machiavelli's influence on Nedham, see Zagorin, *History of Political*

Thought, 121–27; Raab, 159–64, who traces Nedham's various uses of Machiavelli within individual tracts and throughout his career; and Knachel's introduction to *The Case of the Commonwealth, Stated*. On Milton's acquaintance with Nedham, see Blair Worden, "Andrew Marvell, Oliver Cromwell and the Horatian Ode," and Worden, "Milton's Republicanism and the Tyranny of Heaven," in *Milton and Republicanism*, ed. Gisela Bock, Quentin Skinner, and Maurizio Viroli (Cambridge: Cambridge University Press, 1990), 227. Anthony Ascham, *Discourse, wherein is examined, what is particularly lawfull during the Confusions and Revolutions of Government* (London, 1648), 71, also refers to Machiavelli on private interest.

69. On Bovey, see chapter 4 above.

70. Although Wallace, in *Destiny His Choice*, does not use the term *rhetorical politics*, he gives a sympathetic portrait of arguments for the Engagement.

71. See also Pocock, *JH*; Slights, *The Casuistical Tradition*; Perez Zagorin, *Ways of Lying: Dissimulation, Persecution, and Conformity in Early Modern Europe* (Cambridge, Mass.: Harvard University Press, 1990).

72. The language of necessity is everywhere in Ascham's treatise. In most cases, it is equivalent to the right of self-preservation (19–20, 30–38, 56, 68). It is also sometimes equated with de facto political power and is a criterion of reason of state (67). Necessity is thus both what leads individuals to obey de facto political power, contrary to their previous oaths; and what justifies that power. According to Ascham, natural laws are not subject to deliberation or interpretation; human laws, reason of state, the realm of politics—and the best response to necessity in any given circumstance—are subject to deliberation (6–7). In this light, necessity may be considered another name for contingency and may be seen as, at least in part, a matter of interpretation. It is precisely this association of necessity with contingency and arbitrary interpretation that reminded contemporaries of Machiavelli.

73. London, 1642; quoted in Wallace, *Destiny His Choice*, 28 n. 1.

74. See Dury, *A Second Parcel*, 37–38: "If I should think, that becaus I suppose such an event will follow, that therefore I must not intend my present dutie . . . then I walk not in simplicitie, but according to the wisdom of this world; and I predetermine in my thoughts, the events which are onely in God's hands."

75. Note also that, in divorcing intention and effect, this argument also gives an ironic twist to the topic of virtue and success: although the subject's civic virtue or obedience to the present government is conditional on the recent success of the government, it is no guarantee of future success.

76. In *Philosophy and Government, 1572–1651*, which appeared when this book was in press, Richard Tuck makes an argument that is complementary to the one I have offered in this chapter. According to Tuck, the republican thinkers of the English civil war were less concerned with constitutional issues than they were with what Tuck calls the "new humanism," that is, with a Tacitean reason of state: "In a European context the English rebellion was justified in extremely *modern* terms. All the key words of the new humanism were present in an astonishingly extensive pamphlet literature—'necessity,' *'salus populi,'* 'reason of state,' and, above all, *interest*" (222–223). Tuck correctly notes that "The English

[civil] war was waged by *humanists*, and its public rhetoric . . . was drawn from history and from Tacitism" (225). As I argue throughout this book, the features that Tuck ascribes to Tacitism were also ascribed in the seventeenth century to Machiavelli.

PART THREE
MILTON

1. Felix Raab summarizes the arguments for and against Milton's knowledge of Machiavelli as a republican theorist, and argues that there is no evidence of such knowledge before the 1651–52 entries in his commonplace book (175–81). On Milton as a classical republican, see also Zera S. Fink, *The Classical Republicans* (Evanston, Ill.: Northwestern University, 1945), 90–122; Joseph Allen Bryant, "A Note on Milton's Use of Machiavelli's *Discorsi*," *Modern Philology* 47 (1950): 217–21; Maurice Kelley, "Milton and Machiavelli's *Discorsi*," *Studies in Bibliography* 4 (1951–52): 123–27; Perez Zagorin, *A History of Political Thought in the English Revolution* (London: Routledge and Kegan Paul, 1954), 106–20; Zagorin, *Milton, Aristocrat and Rebel* (Rochester, N.Y.: D. S. Brewer, 1992); Blair Worden, "Classical Republicanism and the Puritan Revolution," in *History and Imagination: Essays in Honor of H. R. Trevor-Roper*, ed. Hugh Lloyd-Jones, Valerie Pearl, and Blair Worden (New York: Holmes and Meier, 1981), 182–200; Worden, "Milton's Republicanism and the Tyranny of Heaven," in *Machiavelli and Republicanism*, ed. Gisela Bock, Quentin Skinner, and Maurizio Viroli (Cambridge: Cambridge University Press, 1990), 225–46; and Annabel Patterson, "The Good Old Cause," in her *Reading Between the Lines* (Madison: University of Wisconsin Press, 1993), 210–75. In *MM*, Pocock both groups Milton with Harrington and Algernon Sidney (507) as other historians of classical republicanism do, and recognizes that Milton's aim was to set up an "aristocracy of saints" (414). In the usual accounts of Milton's Machiavellism, his references to the stereotypical "Machiavell" are judged to be of little significance, little more than a commonplace term of abuse. See the index to Milton's *Commonplace Book* in *The Complete Prose Works of John Milton*, 8 vols., ed. Don M. Wolfe et al. (New Haven, Conn.: Yale University Press, 1953–82), vol. 1; and Ruth Mohl, *John Milton and His Commonplace Book* (New York: Frederick Ungar, 1969).

2. John Aubrey, *Collections for the Life of Milton*, in Hughes, 1024. In "Milton's Republicanism," Worden usefully summarizes the Machiavellian (classical republican) topics of Milton's prose: "In the references to Machiavelli in the commonplace book for 1651–52, and even in the pamphlets, we can glimpse Milton's interest in Machiavelli's arguments about the evils of hereditary rule; about the greater willingness of republics to honour virtue; about the appropriateness of armed resistance to tyranny; about the role of political and military participation in the fulfillment of citizenship; about the military benefits of frugality, the domestic consequences of military expansion, the benefits of tumults . . . , the advantages of constitutional renewal" (233).

3. Worden also makes this point in "Milton's Republicanism and the Tyranny of Heaven," 230. Yet, by the end of the essay, he once again distinguishes between religious and secular, political vocabulary, claiming, "It is the archfiend's false

application of political vocabulary, not of religious vocabulary that Milton exposes" (243). And he suggests that Milton gives Satan a republican vocabulary not only to express Milton's disappointment with Cromwell but also to register his doubts concerning his own claims for "the language of *secular* politics" (244, my emphasis).

4. I owe much of this formulation to an incisive comment by Joan Bennett on an earlier version of this chapter.

CHAPTER SIX
A RHETORIC OF INDIFFERENCE

1. Thomas Fitzherbert, *The First Part of a Treatise concerning policy and religion* (Douai, 1606), 27.

2. John Milton, *Commonplace Book*, in *The Complete Prose Works of John Milton*, 8 vols., ed. Don M. Wolfe et al. (New Haven, Conn.: Yale University Press, 1953–82), 1:475–77.

3. See *The Complete Prose Works of John Milton*, vol. 2 (1643–48), ed. Ernest Sirluck (New Haven, Conn.: Yale University Press; London: Oxford University Press, 1959). Commenting on *Of Reformation* (1641), Sirluck writes: "Dealing with the objection that the speedy establishment of Presbyterianism might be politically dangerous, he had asked: 'Who should oppose it? The *Papists*? They dare not. The *Protestants* otherwise affected. They were mad. There is nothing will be remoov'd but what to them is profess'dly indifferent.' Again, to the Episcopalian argument that the church was empowered to decide in things indifferent, he had not replied that in such things the individual Christian was at liberty to decide for himself; rather, he had insisted that the things at issue were not matters of indifference but of prescription" (181–82).

4. In *The Indifferent Mean: Adiaphorism in the English Reformation to 1554* (Athens, Ohio: Ohio University Press; Detroit, Mich.: Wayne State University Press, 1977), Bernard J. Verkamp notes that Milton's "opinion that adiaphora are by nature beyond legislation . . . [was] an opinion which few, if any, earlier adiaphorists had shared" (132). For a rhetorical argument related to the one presented here, see Nigel Smith, "*Areopagitica*: Voicing Contexts, 1643–45," in *Politics, Poetics and Hermeneutics in Milton's Prose*, ed. David Loewenstein and James Grantham Turner (Cambridge: Cambridge University Press, 1990), 103–21, who discusses Milton's use of Sarpi and Davanzati contrary to their intentions.

5. Joan S. Bennett, *Reviving Liberty: Radical Christian Humanism in Milton's Great Poems* (Cambridge, Mass.: Harvard University Press, 1989), 86, quoting Milton's *Ready and Easy Way*.

6. In "Driving from the letter: truth and indeterminacy in Milton's *Areopagitica*," in *Re-membering Milton*, ed. Mary Nyquist and Margaret W. Ferguson (New York and London: Methuen, 1987), 234–54. Stanley Fish argues that Milton takes an antinomian position in *Areopagitica* (251). I have been suggesting that this is only one pole of Milton's argument.

7. This seems to be one of the functions of the refusal to extend toleration to Catholics at the end of the treatise. This conclusion functions rhetorically like the end of Machiavelli's *The Prince*: it puts a check on the contingency and indiffer-

ence that have been stressed up to this point by asserting that Truth is the ultimate censor and that Catholicism is simply falsehood.

8. On allegorical personification, see Steven Knapp, *Personification and the Sublime: Milton to Coleridge* (Cambridge, Mass.: Harvard University Press, 1985); Neil Saccamano, "The Sublime Force of Words in Addison's 'Pleasures,'" *ELH* 58 (1991): 98–103; and chapter 8 below.

9. As we have seen in chapter 5, once force is admitted into discussion, the question of fraud inevitably follows. As Henry Robinson remarked in *Liberty of Conscience* (1643) in *Tracts on Liberty in the Puritan Revolution*, 3 vols., ed. William Haller (New York: Columbia University Press, 1934), "We see by daily experience that men are by nothing so much obliged and engaged, as by courtesie and affable proceedings, these both win and keep the heart fast, whilst violence and constraint can at best, but prevail upon the body, the soul even in that instant so much more alienated, as the body and outward man was forced to play the hypocrite and yeeld obedience" (3:130). In Milton's case this seems to apply equally to the force of truth.

10. Thomas Wilson, *The Rule of Reason* (London, 1553), 42.

11. Christ is apostrophied as "thou . . . who didst redeem us from being servants of men," in *The Ready and Easy Way* (Hughes, 898). Hughes comments: "Christ has redeemed us from 'being servants of men' either on the religious level or the political, because 'in Christ we are alike all priests' (*Christian Doctrine* 1, xxviii . . .) and because the whole political meaning of the gospel is that God 'human left from human free' (*PL*, 12.71)" (898n.122).

CHAPTER SEVEN
VIRTUE AND *VIRTÙ* IN *COMUS*

1. Angus Fletcher makes this point in *The Transcendental Masque* (Ithaca, N.Y.: Cornell University Press, 1971), 175.

2. Stephen Orgel, *The Illusion of Power: Political Theater in the English Renaissance* (Berkeley and Los Angeles: University of California Press, 1975), 40.

3. This is now a commonplace of Renaissance studies. See the works cited in the introduction to part 2, nn. 4 and 5.

4. See Daniel Javitch, *Poetry and Courtliness in Renaissance England* (Princeton, N.J.: Princeton University Press, 1978); Frank Whigham, *Ambition and Privilege: The Social Tropes of Elizabethan Courtesy Theory* (Berkeley and Los Angeles: University of California Press, 1984); Louis Montrose, "Of Gentlemen and Shepherds: The Politics of Elizabethan Pastoral Form," *ELH* 50 (1983): 415–59.

5. See Michael Walzer, *The Revolution of the Saints* (Cambridge, Mass.: Harvard University Press, 1965), 251, on the parallels between handbooks on how to become a gentleman and puritan texts on how to achieve a sense of merit or godliness. On English Arminianism, see, among others, Maurice Kelley's introduction to Milton's *Christian Doctrine* in *The Complete Prose Works of John Milton*, 8 vols., ed. Don M. Wolfe et al. (New Haven, Conn.: Yale University Press, 1953–82), 6:74–85; Dennis Danielson, *Milton's Good God* (Cambridge: Cambridge University Press, 1982); Nicholas Tyacke, *Anti-Calvinists: The Rise of English Arminianism c. 1590–1640* (Oxford: Oxford University Press, 1987); Peter Lake, "Calvinism and the English Church, 1570–1635," *Past*

and Present 114 (1987): 32–76; and Steven Jablonski, "'Evil Days': Providence and Politics in the Thought of John Milton," Ph.D. dissertation, Princeton University, 1993.

6. See Stephen Orgel, *The Jonsonian Masque* (1965; New York: Columbia University Press, 1981), 152, 165.

7. Stephen Orgel, *Jonsonian Masque*, 169, 171, 185. It is perhaps worth noting that *Pleasure Reconcil'd to Virtue* failed at court, reportedly because of too little dancing and Inigo Jones's unsatisfactory spectacle (Orgel, *Jonsonian Masque*, 70–71). Perhaps it also failed to please because of its criticism of the court. The masque was subsequently revised as *For the Honour of Wales. Pleasure Reconcil'd to Virtue* is quoted from *Ben Jonson: Selected Masques*, ed. Stephen Orgel (New Haven, Conn.: Yale University Press, 1970); *Coelum Britannicum* from *The Poems of Thomas Carew with His Masque 'Coelum Britannicum'*, ed. Rhodes Dunlap (London: Oxford University Press, 1949).

8. Jennifer Chibnall, "'To that secure fix'd state': The function of the Caroline masque form," in *The Court Masque*, ed. David Lindley (Manchester: Manchester University Press, 1984), 82, quoting Lawrence Stone.

9. On the specific political conditions that contributed to this tension between active and passive virtue, see Raymond A. Anselment, *Loyalist Resolve: Patient Fortitude in the English Civil War* (Newark: University of Delaware Press, 1988), 21–45.

10. See Maryann Cale McGuire, *Milton's Puritan Masque* (Athens: University of Georgia Press, 1983); Leah Marcus, *The Politics of Mirth: Jonson, Herrick, Milton, Marvell and the Defense of Old Holiday Pastimes* (Chicago: University of Chicago Press, 1986); and David Norbrook, *Poetry and Politics in the English Renaissance* (London: Routledge, 1984), 253.

11. S. R. Gardiner, ed., *Constitutional Documents of the Puritan Revolution 1625–1660* (1889; Oxford: Clarendon Press, 1958), 100.

12. Marcus gives the report of the Venetian ambassador in "The Occasion of Ben Jonson's *Pleasure Reconciled to Virtue*," *SEL* 19 (1979): 283. Norbrook, *Poetry and Politics*, 253, discusses the charge of idolatry.

13. Roger Ascham, *The Scholemaster*, ed. R. J. Schoeck (Don Mills, Ontario: Dent, 1966), 62.

14. Robert Greville, Lord Brooke, *A Discourse opening the nature of episcopacy* (1642), in *Tracts on Liberty in the Puritan Revolution, 1638–1647*, 3 vols., ed. William Haller (New York: Columbia University Press, 1934), 2:59.

15. I owe these references to Stephen Kogan, *The Hieroglyphic King: Wisdom and Idolatry in the Seventeenth-Century Masque* (Rutherford, N.J.: Fairleigh Dickinson University Press, 1986), 263–64.

16. See Marcus, *The Politics of Mirth*, 198. I am in substantial agreement with Marcus's analysis of *Comus* as Milton's intervention in the debate concerning the "Declaration of Sports" and the indifference of holiday pastimes. She argues that "the masque turns Anglican ritual against the Anglican establishment, symbolically freeing the church from the powerful influence of Laud" (177). She does not, however, tie the debate concerning things indifferent either to rhetoric or to Machiavellism. See also the work of Maryann Cale McGuire and Norbrook, cited in note 10 above.

17. On the occasion and political significance of the masque, see Michael

Wilding, "Milton's 'A Masque Presented at Ludlow Castle, 1634': Theatre and Politics on the Border," *Milton Quarterly* 21 (1987), 37. See also, in the same issue, Cedric. C. Brown, "Presidential Travels and Instructive Augury in Milton's Ludlow Masque," 1–12; Leah Sinanoglou Marcus, "The Earl of Bridgewater's Legal Life: Notes toward a Political Reading of *Comus*," 13–23; and *The Politics of Mirth* where Marcus notes that the readings for this holiday from the Book of Common Prayer were particularly concerned with the right use of the things of nature (201–202); as well as John Creaser, " 'The Present Aid of This Occasion': The Setting of *Comus*," in *The Court Masque*, ed. David Lindley (Manchester: Manchester University Press, 1984), 111–34; James G. Taaffe, "Michaelmas, the 'Lawless Hour,' and the Occasion of Milton's *Comus*," *English Language Notes* 6 (1969): 257–62; and William B. Hunter, "The Liturgical Context of *Comus*," *English Language Notes* 10 (1972): 11–15.

The Earl's political leanings are subject to debate. The *DNB* entry is inconclusive; Creaser argues that the Earl was a follower of Buckingham; Christopher Hill, *Milton and the English Revolution*, discusses Bridgewater's puritan leanings (43). Marcus, in *The Politics of Mirth*, describes the Earl as a loyal servant of the king but also as anti-Catholic and anti-Arminian (174). In Marcus's persuasive account, the Earl is both a representative of royal authority and a figure of resistance; the Attendant Spirit is not simply addressing Bridgewater as the symbol of royal power and *virtù* but is also encouraging him to resist the arbitrary exercise of power increasingly characteristic of Charles and Archbishop Laud. However we understand the Earl's political allegiances, the Attendant Spirit's initial compliment takes the form of praising the Earl's nobility and power, his virtue and *virtù*.

18. In *The Politics of Mirth*, Marcus compares Comus and Sabrina: "The two figures are comparable, yet utterly unlike. The difference between them is the difference between the power of virtue and the virtue of power" (200). I will argue that it is often difficult to tell—to paraphrase *Pleasure Reconcil'd to Virtue*— which powers are virtue's and which are not.

19. On the puritan critique of *visibilia*, see Maryann Cale McGuire, *Milton's Puritan Masque*.

20. Critics are divided over the interpretation of *Comus*, one group focusing on the allegorical dimension of the masque and on the harmonious vision it presents, the other analyzing the masque's dramatic elements and its corresponding ambivalence or tensions. Among the first group of critics, see Rosamond Tuve, "Image, Form and Theme in *A Mask*," in John S. Diekhoff, *"A Masque at Ludlow": Essays on Milton's "Comus"* (Cleveland, Ohio: Case Western Reserve University Press, 1968), 133; Stephen Orgel, *Jonsonian Masque*; Stanley E. Fish, "Problem-Solving in *Comus*," in *Illustrious Evidence: Approaches to English Literature of the Seventeenth Century*, ed. Earl Miner (Berkeley and Los Angeles: University of California Press, 1975), 115–31. Among the second, see Angus Fletcher, *The Transcendental Masque*; William Kerrigan, *The Sacred Complex: On the Psychogenesis of "Paradise Lost"* (Cambridge, Mass.: Harvard University Press, 1983); John Guillory, *Poetic Authority: Spenser, Milton, and Literary History* (New York: Columbia University Press, 1983). Both groups of readers give an account of the relation of the masque's allegorical plot to its rhetoric. The first group subordinates the masque's shifting, "indifferent" rhetoric to the allegorical

and theological vision of divine grace, arguing that if the masque presents the earth as the arena of things indifferent, the reader learns to interpret according to the Neoplatonic hierarchy of values, according to which mind is superior to body just as heaven is to earth. The end result is that "an ethic of intention is substituted for an ethic of observable effects" (Fish, 129). The second group of critics stresses the conflict between Comus's Shakespearean eloquence and the Lady's Spenserian defense, and sees the masque as resisting its own allegorical plot. Yet, this second reading involves an allegory of its own, according to which the masque stages a contest between Spenser and Shakespeare. In assuming the identity of "moral and stylistic judgments" in the masque (Guillory, 88), according to which Shakespearean eloquence is associated with the evil Comus and Spenserian allegory with the virtuous Lady, this reading allegorizes away the fact of rhetorical indifference noted by the first group of critics. It sees the masque, instead, as opposing Shakespearean song, rhetoric, and magic on the one hand to chastity, reason, and logic on the other. But such a division of rhetorical labor is too simplistic: as I have already suggested in my remarks about the description of Comus, this courtly Machiavel speaks in the language of both Shakespeare and Spenser as, I will argue below, does the Lady.

21. Kerrigan, *Sacred Complex*, proposes a similar reading of the Lady's chastity. A number of other critics have argued that the Lady's chastity registers the tensions between faith and works, obedience and resistance, allegory and irony, that are central to the masque. In "Milton and Sexuality: A Symptomatic Reading of *Comus*," in *Re-membering Milton*, ed. Mary Nyquist and Margaret W. Ferguson (New York: Methuen, 1988), 43–73, Christopher Kendrick suggests that Milton's choice of chastity as the theme of the masque is theologically, as well as politically, motivated. Politically, Milton's chastity involves an obvious criticism of the royal chastity that was "a privileged theme of the court masque" (47). Theologically, chastity was central to Milton's "personal myth, whose main function was evidently to 'manage' the Protestant antinomy between faith and work. The myth did this by providing Milton's faith with a work (namely chastity) more adequately symptomatic of it than was his real work, which was the—slowly encompassed, potentially idolatrous—study of the classics" (48). See also Richard Halpern, "Puritanism and Maenadism in *A Mask*," in *Rewriting the Renaissance*, ed. Margaret W. Ferguson, Maureen Quilligan, and Nancy J. Vickers (Chicago: University of Chicago Press, 1986), 88–105. Halpern argues that the Lady's chastity reproduces the ideological contradictions of women's place in puritanism: virginity is required up to a point, but not within marriage where it would appear as a form of resistance. Finally, in "A womb of his own: male Renaissance poets in the female body," in *Sexuality and Gender in Early Modern Europe*, ed. James Grantham Turner (Cambridge: Cambridge University Press, 1993), 266–88, Katharine Eisaman Maus describes the Lady's chastity as the locus of a conflict between two kinds of reading: one that draws an analogy between the Lady's physical state and her moral state, and one that insists on the lack of correspondence between the material and spiritual realms (277–86). "In the way *A Mask* . . . represents the body as both separable and inseparable from the soul, dispensable and indispensable for the practice of virtue, it resembles much of Milton's early work" (282).

22. Fish, "Problem-Solving in *Comus*," 118–19, also discusses this passage as an illustration of the indifference of the Lady's surroundings, but he does so in order to argue that *Comus* equates virtue with an ethic of intention.

23. On the sense of hearing in the masque, see Donald M. Friedman, "*Comus* and the Truth of the Ear," in *"The Muses Common-Weale": Poetry and Politics in the Seventeenth Century*, ed. Claude J. Summers and Ted-Larry Pebworth (Columbia: University of Missouri Press, 1988), 119–34.

24. See Fletcher, *Transcendental Masque*, 164–65 and 215–19, on the differences between chastity and virginity in relation to time: Virginity "implies absolute stasis. Chastity . . . can permit the freedom of movement and experiential trial" (165).

25. I owe this reference to David Quint, who discusses Milton's allusion in *Paradise Lost* to this biblical passage in *Origin and Originality in Renaissance Literature: Versions of the Source* (New Haven, Conn.: Yale University Press, 1983), 210.

26. Fletcher's remarks, in *Transcendental Masque*, about the masque's resistance to allegory could also serve as a description of this deferral or warding off of divine intervention. Fletcher defines allegory as "the conversion of image into idea, of concrete detail into abstract theme, of symbol into significance" (175). In *Comus*, "on the contrary, transcendence works by the conversion of one medium into another, and the audience never leaves the plane of medial transformations. A given dance does not primarily convert to an allegorical significance derived from the motions of that dance; rather, the dance converts to song, which may convert to a speech, which converts to a scene shift. Each medium 'mediates,' not a transcendent meaning but another medium. This convertibility of means is based finally on the function of masking itself. The mask is the transcendental device that entertains but finally rejects a complete shift into allegory. Behind each mask there is only another mask—a mystery that fascinated the major poets of the Renaissance" (175–76).

See also Guillory, *Poetic Authority*, who comments on the Lady's speech: "The Lady's words anticipate the full epiphany of the 'superior power,' but the poet evidently feels that he is not yet ready to channel that power into his verse. The Lady declines to speak in the voice of the higher power, and the epiphany remains incomplete" (89).

27. See Kerrigan, *Sacred Complex*, 57–58, who also comments on the way Milton revises Spenser's Garden of Adonis; and E.M.W. Tillyard, "The Action of *Comus*," in Diekhoff, *"A Mask at Ludlow": Essays on Milton's "Comus*," 51–54.

28. On fixity and innovation, see Kerrigan, *Sacred Complex*, 67.

29. See William Haller, *The Rise of Puritanism* (New York: Harper and Row, 1938), 319.

CHAPTER EIGHT
MACHIAVELLIAN RHETORIC IN *PARADISE LOST*

1. In thinking about Milton's rhetoric in *Paradise Lost*, I have benefited in general from the work of Stanley Fish on things indifferent, cited in chapters 4–7, and from Leslie Brisman, *Milton's Poetry of Choice and Its Romantic Heirs* (New

Haven, Conn.: Yale University Press, 1973); Patricia Parker, *Inescapable Romance: Studies in the Poetics of a Mode* (Princeton, N.J.: Princeton University Press, 1979), 114–58; William Kerrigan, *The Sacred Complex: On the Psychogenesis of "Paradise Lost"* (Cambridge, Mass.: Harvard University Press, 1983); Sanford Budick, *The Dividing Muse: Images of Sacred Disjunction in Milton's Poetry* (New Haven, Conn.: Yale University Press, 1985); and Joan S. Bennett, *Reviving Liberty: Radical Christian Humanism in Milton's Great Poems* (Cambridge, Mass.: Harvard University Press, 1989). Particular debts will be indicated in the notes below.

2. On Satan's use of republican language and his description of God as a tyrant or absolute monarch, see Stevie Davies, *Images of Kingship in "Paradise Lost"* (Columbia: University of Missouri Press, 1983); Christopher Hill, *Milton and the English Revolution* (Harmondsworth, England: Penguin, 1979), 365–75; Joan S. Bennett, *Reviving Liberty*, 33–58; Blair Worden, "Milton's Republicanism and the Tyranny of Heaven," in *Machiavelli and Republicanism*, ed. Gisela Bock, Quentin Skinner, and Maurizio Viroli (Cambridge: Cambridge University Press, 1990), 225–46. On Milton's self-consciousness about the use of the same vocabulary for opposing political purposes, see Worden, "Milton's Republicanism," 239, and especially Mary Ann Radzinowicz, "The Politics of *Paradise Lost*," in *Politics of Discourse*, ed. Kevin Sharpe and Steven N. Zwicker (Berkeley and Los Angeles: University of California Press, 1987), 216.

3. Worden, "Milton's Republicanism," 240, 243; Hill, *Milton and the English Revolution*, 365–75.

4. Worden, "Milton's Republicanism," 243; Stevie Davies, *Images of Kingship in "Paradise Lost"*; Northrop Frye, *The Return of Eden* (1965; Toronto: University of Toronto Press, 1975), 103–11.

5. Radzinowicz, "The Politics of *Paradise Lost*," 209–11; Bennett, *Reviving Liberty*, 24–26, and chaps. 2 and 3.

6. Radzinowicz, "The Politics of *Paradise Lost*," 217.

7. In his note on this passage, Alastair Fowler suggests this reading. He glosses "lest . . . boast" as "so that men ought not to boast," and refers the reader to Eph. ii, 8f: "by grace are ye saved . . . Not of works, lest any man should boast" (*Paradise Lost*, ed. Alastair Fowler [London: Longman, 1968]).

8. In considering the Sin and Death episode, I have benefited in particular from the following works: Philip J. Gallagher, "'Real or Allegoric': The Ontology of Sin and Death in *Paradise Lost*," *ELR* 6 (1976): 317–35; Kenneth Knoespel, "The Limits of Allegory: Textual Expansion of Narcissus in *Paradise Lost*," *Milton Studies* 22 (1986): 79–99; Stephen M. Fallon, "Milton's Sin and Death: The Ontology of Allegory in *Paradise Lost*," *ELR* 17 (1987): 329–50; John S. Tanner, "'Say First What Cause': Ricoeur and the Etiology of Evil in *Paradise Lost*," *PMLA* 103 (1988): 45–56; Ruth H. Lindeborg, "Imagination, Inspiration and the Problem of Human Agency in *Paradise Lost*," unpublished paper; Steven Knapp, *Personification and the Sublime: Milton to Coleridge* (Cambridge, Mass.: Harvard University Press, 1985). I have also discussed this episode in "Allegory and the Sublime in *Paradise Lost*," in *Milton*, ed. Annabel Patterson (Longman: London, 1992), 185–201.

9. Angus Fletcher, *Allegory: The Theory of a Symbolic Mode* (Ithaca, N.Y.: Cornell University Press, 1964), 68.

10. George Puttenham, *The Arte of English Poesie* (Kent, Ohio: Kent State University Press, 1970), 197.

11. This discussion of Puttenham is indebted to an unpublished paper on book 1 of *The Faerie Queene* by Neil Saccamano.

12. Cited by Debora K. Shuger, *Sacred Rhetoric: The Christian Grand Style in the English Renaissance* (Princeton, N.J.: Princeton University Press, 1988), 160. The quotation is from *Gerardi Joannis Vossi commentariorum rhetoricorum, sive oratorium institutionum libri sex* (1606).

13. See the note to this passage in *Paradise Lost*, ed. Alastair Fowler.

14. On the Hebrew etymology of sin, see Kenneth Knoespel, "The Limits of Allegory," 82. In *Milton's Spenser: The Politics of Reading* (Ithaca, N.Y.: Cornell University Press, 1983), Maureen Quilligan also discusses this passage in terms of etymological wordplay, but does not note the Hebrew meaning of sin. For the association of sin and sign, Merritt Hughes refers us to Dante's "trapassar del segno" in *Paradiso*, 26.115–17 ("Beyond Disobedience," in *Approaches to "Paradise Lost"*, ed. C. A. Patrides [London: Edward Arnold, 1968], 188–89).

15. I was helped to see this point by the unpublished paper of Ruth H. Lindeborg. See also Maureen Quilligan's chapter, "The Sin of Originality," in *Milton's Spenser*.

16. On Sin's birth as a "linguistic event," see Knoespel, "The Limits of Allegory," 82.

17. See Luther's remarks in his *Lectures on Genesis* (*Luther's Works*, ed. Jaroslav Pelikan [Saint Louis: Concordia, 1955], 1:166), on the sins which are so fully ingrained "that they not only cannot be fully removed but are not even recognized as sin."

18. John Freccero, *Dante: The Poetics of Conversion*, ed. Rachel Jacoff (Cambridge, Mass.: Harvard University Press, 1986), 108.

19. James Grantham Turner, *One Flesh: Paradisal Marriage and Sexual Relations in the Age of Milton* (Oxford: Clarendon Press, 1987), 84, 87–88. Turner glances at the Sin and Death episode when he writes in a discussion of the allegorical interpretations of German mysticism and Neoplatonism, "Indeed, the grotesque figure of Sin [in *Paradise Lost*] . . . may parody the excesses of neo-Gnostic myth making" (155).

20. On the identification of Pelagianism and Arminianism by seventeenth-century Calvinists, see, for example, A.S.P. Woodhouse, ed., *Puritanism and Liberty* (London: Dent, 1938), 54.

21. "Introduction to the Epistle of Saint James and Saint Jude" (1545), in *Works of Martin Luther*, 55 vols., ed. Jaroslav Pelikan and Helmut T. Lehmann (Philadelphia: Muhlenberg Press, 1932), 6:478.

22. John S. Tanner, " 'Say First What Cause,' " 48.

23. In " 'Say First What Cause,' " Tanner makes a similar point, though he does not comment on the significance of the allegorical form of Sin and Death in this context: "Milton's myth thus exposes the irrationalism that lies at the core of ostensibly rational free-will explanations. It acknowledges that, at the deepest level, complete self-determination begins to look more like compulsion than free choice" (49).

24. Quoted in *Milton 1732–1801: The Critical Heritage*, ed. John T. Shawcross (London: Routledge and Kegan Paul, 1972), 236.

25. Quoted in Knapp, *Personification and the Sublime*, 8.

26. Martin Luther, *Commentary on Galatians*, in *Martin Luther: Selections from His Writings*, ed. John Dillenberger (Garden City, N.Y.: Anchor Press, 1961), 141. The passage recalls Botero's description of the sublime in his *Aggiunta* on reputation. See chapter 3 above.

27. Annabel Patterson, "The Good Old Cause," in *Reading Between the Lines* (Madison: University of Wisconsin Press, 1993), 256. Patterson discusses the seventeenth-century editions and translations of Longinus, and the political dimension of Longinus's discussion of the sublime, on pages 258–66. The evidence for the direct influence of Longinus on Milton is circumstantial; Patterson notes that John Hall's translation was dedicated to Bulstrode Whitelocke, "one of the most important, though moderate, members of the revolutionary council of state," and a friend and colleague of Milton.

On the republican dimension of Marvell's poem, see also Andrew Eric Shifflett, "Paradox and Politics in English Neostoic Literature," Ph.D. dissertation, Princeton University, 1993. Shifflett demonstrates that Marvell is echoing Ben Jonson's poem to Thomas May ("To My chosen friend, . . . Thomas May"), the translator of Lucan's republican epic, the *Pharsalia*. Shifflett, following Christopher Hill, reads "That Majesty which through thy Work doth Reign" as a joke shared by the republicans Marvell and Milton (161).

28. The political significance of this indifference may be clarified by noting that the battle between Satan and Death is an Oedipal struggle. It was a commonplace of seventeenth-century political theory—most famously articulated by Filmer's *Patriarcha*—not only that the king was a metaphorical father to his people but that his power had its origin in the actual power of the father over his family, a power that descended from father to son. In the conflict between Sin and Death, we have instead a father and son each claiming absolute authority, and neither recognizing the other. In making the Oedipal conflict of Satan and Death into a conflict of de facto political powers, Milton mocks the patriarchal model of political authority.

29. See Thomas Weiskel, *The Romantic Sublime* (Baltimore, Md.: The Johns Hopkins University Press, 1976), 40–41; Neil Hertz, "The Notion of Blockage in the Literature of the Sublime," in *Psychoanalysis and the Question of the Text*, ed. Geoffrey H. Hartman (Baltimore, Md.: The Johns Hopkins University Press, 1978), 71–76; and Steven Knapp, *Personification and the Sublime*, 74ff. On prophecy as exegesis, see John Milton, *Christian Doctrine*, in *The Complete Prose Works of John Milton*, 8 vols., ed. Don M. Wolfe et al. (New Haven, Conn.: Yale University Press, 1973), 6:582 and 584 (book 1, chap. 30). I am grateful to Victoria Silver for calling my attention to this definition of prophecy in the seventeenth century.

30. Donald E. Pease, "Sublime Politics," *boundary 2* 12/13 (1984): 264.

31. Cf. Jonathan Arac, "The Media of Sublimity: Johnson and Lamb on *King Lear*," *Studies in Romanticism* 26 (1987): 209ff., on the sublime as allowing rebellion or reinforcing conformity; and Ronald Paulson, "Burke's Sublime and the Representation of Revolution," in *Culture and Politics: From Puritanism to the Enlightenment*, ed. Perez Zagorin (Berkeley and Los Angeles: University of California Press, 1980), 241–69, esp. 248–52, on the political ambivalence of the sublime.

32. Joseph Addison, *Critical Essays from the Spectator*, ed. Donald F. Bond (New York: Oxford University Press, 1970), nos. 309 and 273, pp. 102, 68; Samuel Johnson, *Lives of the English Poets*, 2 vols. (London: Dent, 1961), 1:110. Steven Knapp discusses eighteenth-century objections to the Sin and Death episode in *Personification and the Sublime*, 51–65.

33. Anne Ferry, *Milton's Epic Voice: The Narrator in "Paradise Lost"* (Cambridge, Mass.: Harvard University Press, 1963), 116–46. See also Maureen Quilligan, *Milton's Spenser: The Politics of Reading* (Ithaca, N.Y.: Cornell University Press, 1983), 95: "Allegory is the genre of the fallen world, for in a prelapsarian world, at one with God, there is no 'other' for language to work back to since there has been no fatal division. No distance, no divorce, no distaste between God and man, who has not yet known the coherence of good and evil in the rind of one apple tasted."

34. For a related argument, see Sanford Budick, *The Dividing Muse*, 48, 73, 79.

35. This is a traditional understanding of the prohibition. See Martin Luther, *Lectures on Genesis*, 154: "It was God's intention that this command should provide man with an opportunity for obedience and outward worship, and that this tree would be a sort of sign by which man would give evidence that he was obeying God." See also the gloss on this passage in the Geneva Bible, and *Paradise Lost*, 3.93–95.

36. William Bradshaw, *A Treatise of Things Indifferent* (London, 1605), marginal gloss on 25.

37. Saint Augustine, *On Christian Doctrine*, trans. D. W. Robertson, Jr. (Indianapolis, Ind.: Bobbs-Merrill, 1958), 34.

38. I borrow the phrase "rhetorical theology" from Charles Trinkaus, *In Our Image and Likeness*, 2 vols. (London: Constable, 1970).

39. Knapp, *Personification and the Sublime*, 3.

40. Weiskel, *Romantic Sublime*, 41.

CODA
RHETORIC AND THE CRITIQUE OF IDEOLOGY

1. See Victoria Kahn, *Rhetoric, Prudence, and Skepticism in the Renaissance* (Ithaca, N.Y.: Cornell University Press, 1985).

2. Joseph Anthony Mazzeo describes Machiavelli as a critic of ideology, when he writes in *Renaissance and Seventeenth-Century Studies* (New York: Columbia University Press; London: Routledge and Kegan Paul, 1964): "In an ironic way Sir Thomas Browne's definition of man can be applied to Machiavelli's ruler. He is a great Amphibium who lives in divided and distinguished worlds. But each world relates to the other. The threat of the beast can help preserve the rule of law and the action of the beast may create the condition for its institution if it does not exist. Behind all forms of legitimation of power lies power itself whether as the naked power of coercion, the ideologically and publicly constituted power of authority or the unscrupulous manipulation by rulers of the ruled" (104). He also describes Machiavelli as a critic of ideology when he attributes to him the following insight: "The system of political and social appearances of any society is a

form of fraud precisely to the extent that those appearances obscure the true nature of decision and status. The claims of the great human institutions are, in a sense, always partly true and partly false. The cause of freedom and reason is always embedded, so to speak, in the struggle for power within the state and also between states. Furthermore, power and forceful leadership are the indispensable prerequisites for freedom and the exercise of reason. This truth leads to the paradox that, although reason and freedom are intrinsically realized by individuals and not by institutions, special collective structures of power are necessary for the exercise of freedom and reason. They therefore exist in a continual dialogue with force and fraud and this is the eternal condition of their existence" (115). In *Machiavelli and the History of Prudence* (Madison: University of Wisconsin Press, 1987), Eugene Garver also explores the relationship between Machiavelli's "rhetorical politics" and the critique of ideology. See especially 24, 39–40, 89, 92, 137–38.

3. I have also discussed the relevance of Machiavelli's critique of humanist rhetoric to modern debates about the critique of ideology in "Habermas, Machiavelli, and the Humanist Critique of Ideology," *PMLA* 105 (1990): 464–76.

4. That is, a dissimulation whose promulgation and reception is not fully governed by intention; see Paul Ricoeur, *Lectures on Ideology and Utopia*, ed. George H. Taylor (New York: Columbia University Press, 1986), 8; "Hermeneutics and the critique of ideology," in *Hermeneutics and the Human Sciences*, ed. and trans. John B. Thompson (Cambridge: Cambridge University Press; Paris: Editions de la Maison des Sciences de l'Homme, 1981), 85–86. All further references will be to *Lectures on Ideology and Utopia*.

5. Ricoeur borrows the term *rhetoric* from Clifford Geertz's "Ideology as a Cultural System," in *The Interpretation of Cultures* (New York: Basic Books, 1973). Geertz, in turn, is drawing on Kenneth Burke's work on the rhetoric of motives and symbolic action.

6. *Lectures on Ideology and Utopia*, 10; cf. 8, and 144–45 on Althusser. As Althusser recognized, ideology does not distort reality; rather, it distorts the representation of our relation to reality.

7. *Truth and Method*, quoted in Paul Ricoeur, "Hermeneutics and the critique of ideology," 72.

8. See Thomas M. Greene, *The Light in Troy: Imitation and Discovery in Renaissance Poetry* (New Haven, Conn.: Yale University Press, 1982).

APPENDIX
A BRIEF NOTE ON RHETORIC AND REPUBLICANISM
IN THE HISTORIOGRAPHY OF THE ITALIAN RENAISSANCE

1. Hans Baron, *The Crisis of the Early Italian Renaissance*, 1 vol., rev. ed. (Princeton, N.J.: Princeton University Press, 1966).

2. Quoted by Jerrold Seigel, "'Civic Humanism' or Ciceronian Rhetoric," *Past and Present* 34 (1966): 4.

3. Eugenio Garin, *Medioevo e Rinascimento* (Bari: Laterza, 1954); on philology, see in the same volume "Interpretazioni del Rinascimento" and "La storia nel pensiero del Rinascimento," esp. 203–208; as well as the introduction to

L'Umanesimo italiano (Rome, Bari: Laterza, 1978), esp. 11, 22; on conversation, see 180ff. See also the still useful article by Delio Cantimori, "Rhetoric and Politics in Italian Humanism," *Journal of the Warburg Institute* 1 (1937–38): 83–102; and Hanna Holborn Gray, "Renaissance Humanism: The Pursuit of Eloquence," *Journal of the History of Ideas* 24 (1963): 497–514.

4. Garin, *Medioevo*, 134–35.

5. Quoted in Garin, *Medioevo*, 135.

6. See J.G.A. Pocock, *The Machiavellian Moment: Florentine Political Thought and the Atlantic Republican Tradition* (Princeton, N.J.: Princeton University Press, 1975); Quentin Skinner, *The Foundations of Modern Political Thought*, 2 vols. (Cambridge: Cambridge University Press, 1978), and *Machiavelli*, Past Masters Series (New York: Hill and Wang, 1981).

7. See Quentin Skinner, "Machiavelli's *Discorsi* and the pre-humanist origins of republican ideas," in *Machiavelli and Republicanism*, ed. Gisela Bock, Quentin Skinner, and Maurizio Viroli (Cambridge: Cambridge University Press, 1990), 121–42.

8. For a related critique of Skinner, see Nathan Tarcov, "Quentin Skinner's Method and Machiavelli's *Prince*," in *Meaning and Context: Quentin Skinner and His Critics*, ed. James Tully (Princeton, N.J.: Princeton University Press, 1988), 194–203.

9. See Quentin Skinner, *Machiavelli*, v; and 50–51, where Skinner lists the similarities between *The Prince* and the *Discourses*. *Pace* Skinner, Machiavelli is not silent about religion in *The Prince*; he just has nothing religious to say about it. See chapter 18.

INDEX